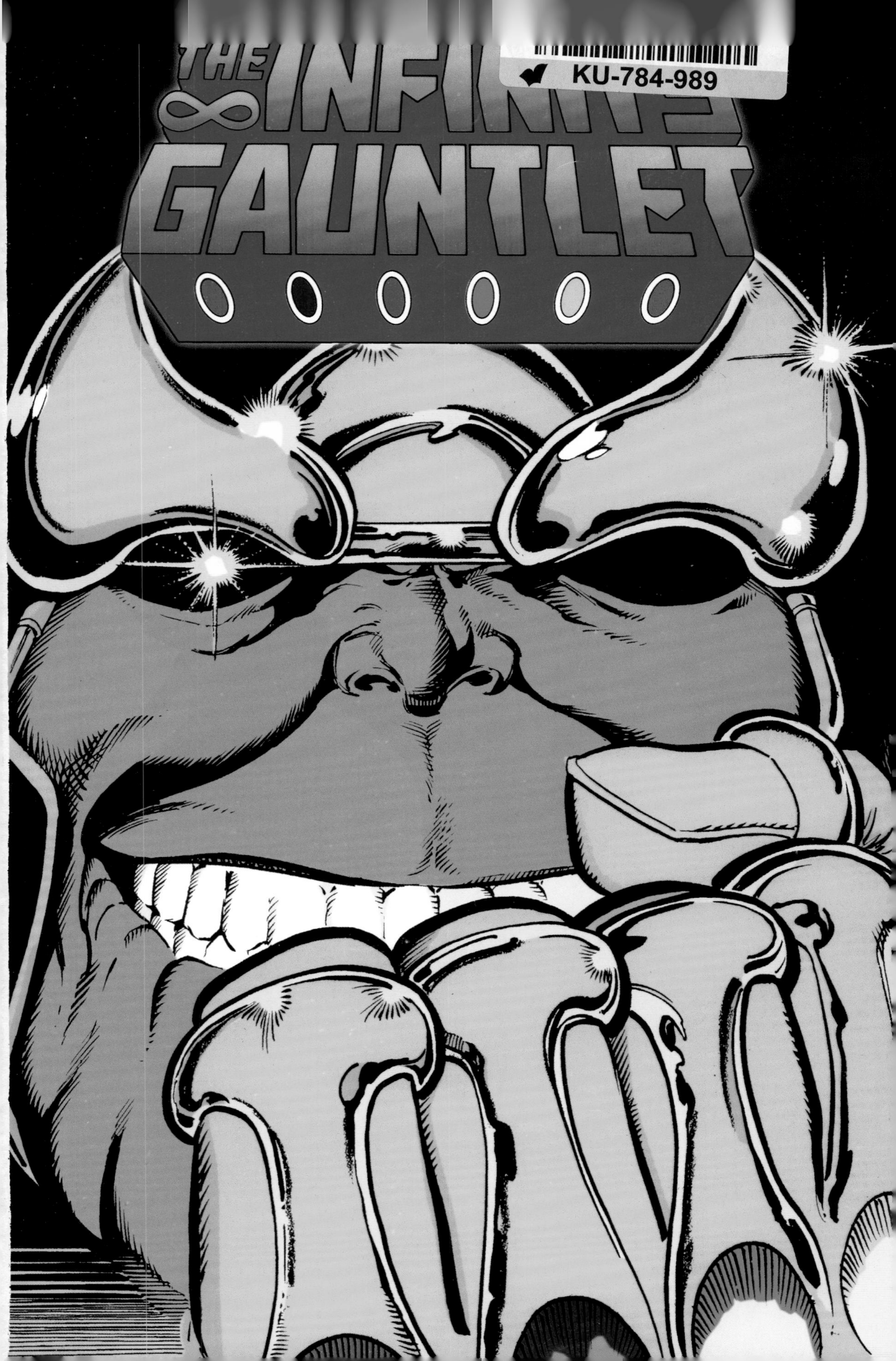
THE
GAUNTLET

THE INFINITY GAUNTLET

WRITER: JIM STARLIN
PENCILLERS: GEORGE PÉREZ (ISSUES #1-4)
& RON LIM (ISSUES #4-6)
INKERS: JOE RUBINSTEIN (ISSUES#1-6)
WITH TOM CHRISTOPHER (ISSUE #1)
& BRUCE SOLOTOFF (ISSUE #4)
COLOURISTS: MAX SCHEELE (ISSUES#1-6)
WITH IAN LAUGHLIN (ISSUES #1 & 3-5)
& EVELYN STEIN (ISSUE #6)
LETTERER: JACK MORELLI

EDITOR: CRAIG ANDERSON

COVER ART: GEORGE PÉREZ

Do you have any comments or queries about The Infinity Gauntlet? Email us at graphicnovels@panini.co.uk
Join us on Facebook at Panini/Marvel Graphic Novels

TM & © 1991 and 2021 Marvel & Subs. Licensed by Marvel Characters B.V. through Panini S.p.A., Italy. All Rights Reserved.
First impression 2018. Fifth impression 2021. Published by Panini Publishing, a division of Panini UK Limited. Mike Riddell,
Managing Director. Alan O'Keefe, Managing Editor. Mark Irvine, Production Manager. Marco M. Lupoi, Publishing
Director Europe. Brady Webb, Reprint Editor. Charlotte Harvey, Designer. Office of publication: Brockbourne House,
77 Mount Ephraim, Tunbridge Wells, Kent TN4 8BS. This publication may not be sold, except by authorised dealers, and
is sold subject to the condition that it shall not be sold or distributed with any part of its cover or markings removed,
nor in a mutilated condition. Printed in the United Kingdom by Zenith Media. ISBN: 978-1-84653-943-5

© 2021 MARVEL

THE STORY SO FAR...

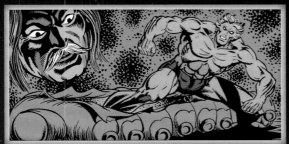

Conceived as the ultimate weapon by a group of rogue scientists, Adam Warlock rebelled against his creators' evil wishes and escaped Earth to travel among the stars.

After encountering a being known as the High Evolutionary, Warlock was sent to a replica of Earth to become the planet's saviour. To help him on his quest, the High Evolutionary gifted Warlock a powerful gem which was embedded in his forehead.

...AND I ASSURE YOU THANOS IS SUCH AN ELEMENT!
I HAD HOPED TO AVOID PERSONAL INVOLVEMENT IN THIS AFFAIR, FOR OTHER, MORE IMPORTANT MATTERS NOW SCREAM FOR MY ATTENTION!
YET, THOSE PLANS DEPEND ON WARLOCK'S CONTINUED WELL-BEING, SO I FIND THAT I AM FORCED TO INTERVENE!
SO THANOS NOW STANDS WITH YOU, ADAM WARLOCK, PREPARED TO FIGHT TO THE

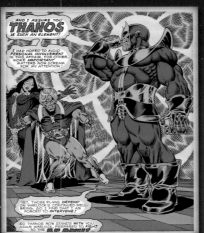

Following his time on Counter-Earth, Warlock next battled the Magus and his tyrannical Church of Universal Truth. During this adventure, Warlock gained new allies in the form of Pip the Troll, Gamora the Assassin, and her evil father — the Mad Titan Thanos.

I AM THE TRUE MAGUS!
MY PLANS REQUIRED A STAND-IN UP TILL NOW! I NEEDED TO KEEP YOU OFF-BALANCE... UNCERTAIN!
OTHERWISE, YOU MIGHT HAVE BEEN ABLE TO ALTER MY PAST-- YOUR FUTURE!
BUT THE DANGER OF THAT HAPPENING HAS PASSED! WE'VE COME TOO FAR DOWN THE PATH OF MY CREATION!
YOU'VE LOST, WARLOCK!
THERE IS ABSOLUTELY NOTHING YOU CAN DO TO CHANGE WHAT'S ABOUT TO OCCUR!
EXT: MADNESS IN THE HOUSE OF THE MAGUS!

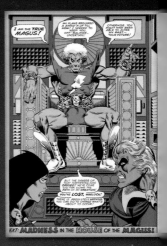

With the Magus defeated, Warlock learned that his gem was one of six special stones of immense power — stones that Thanos greatly desired. Allying himself with Earth's Mightiest Heroes, Warlock was able to stop Thanos, using the power of the stones to turn him into a statue. The heroes who witnessed the battle believed Warlock had been killed. However, his soul had actually been transported into the Soul Gem, where he now lived in a peaceful paradise with Gamora and Pip.

I JUST CAN'T BELIEVE IT!
LESS THAN AN HOUR AGO I WAS DYING FROM WOUNDS SUFFERED AT THANOS' HANDS.
NOW I FIND MYSELF ON THIS PARADISE-LIKE WORLD WITHIN MY SOUL GEM, WITHOUT A CARE OR WORRY TO PLAGUE ME.

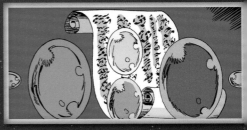

Years later, Thanos was resurrected and sought to possess the six Infinity Gems once more. The Silver Surfer and Drax the Destroyer tried to stop him but failed, only to end up sucked inside the Soul Gem. Within the gem they encountered Adam Warlock and convinced him that they needed his help once more to defeat Thanos.

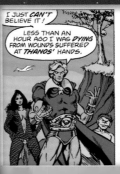

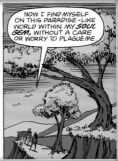

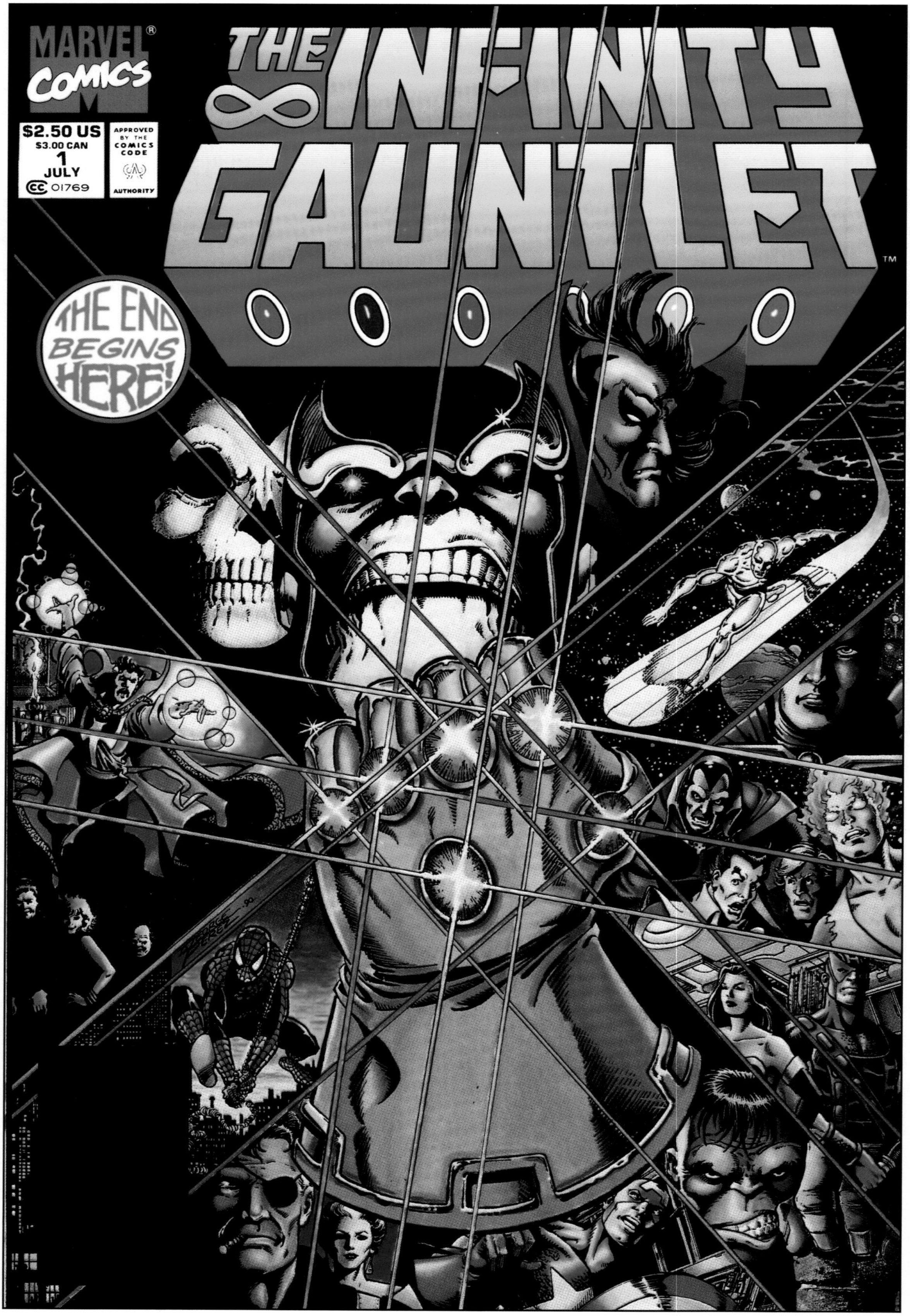
MARVEL® COMICS
THE INFINITY GAUNTLET™
$2.50 US
$3.00 CAN
1
JULY
01769
APPROVED BY THE COMICS CODE AUTHORITY
THE END BEGINS HERE!

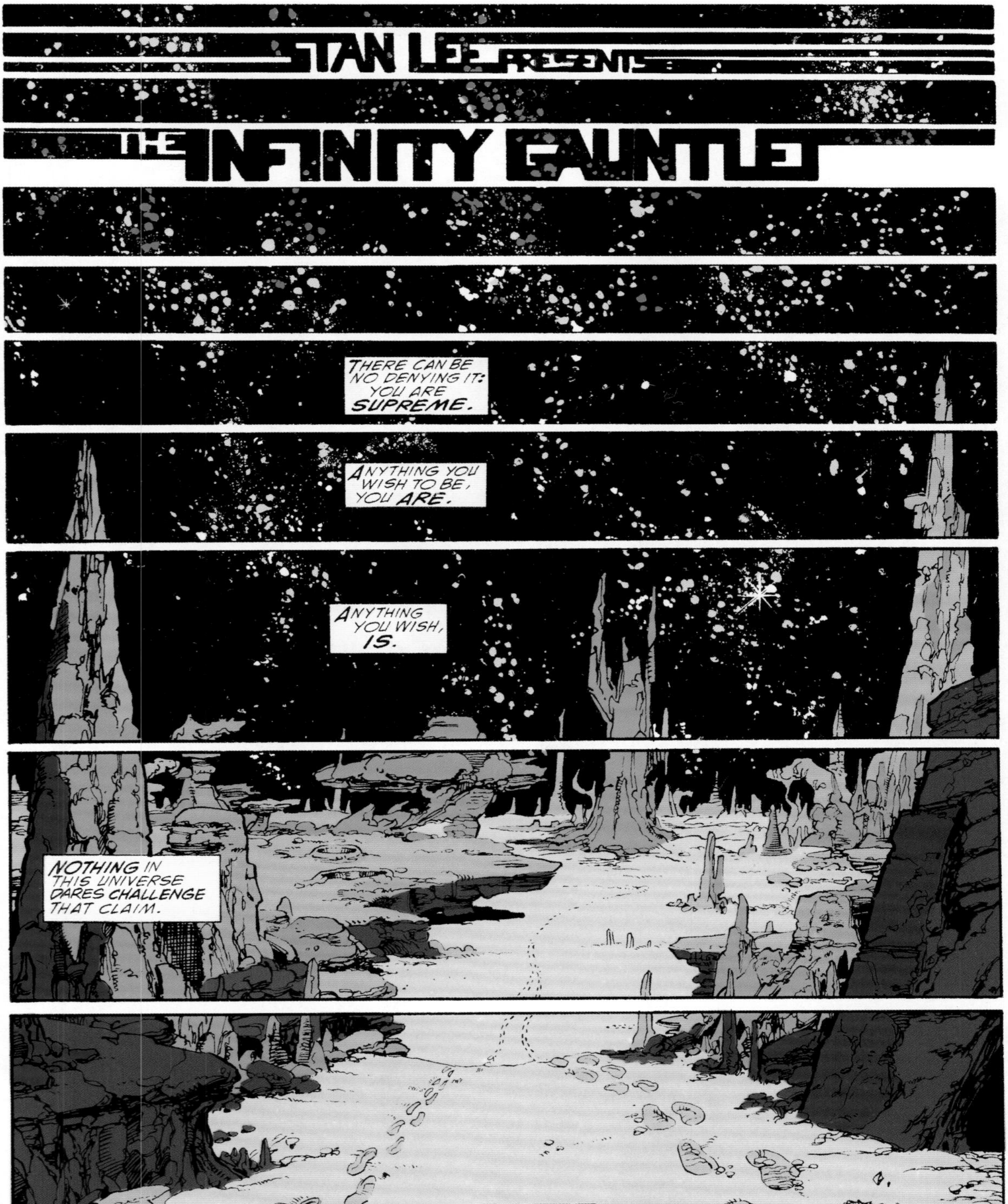
STAN LEE PRESENTS
THE INFINITY GAUNTLET
THERE CAN BE NO DENYING IT: YOU ARE SUPREME.
ANYTHING YOU WISH TO BE, YOU ARE.
ANYTHING YOU WISH, IS.
NOTHING IN THIS UNIVERSE DARES CHALLENGE THAT CLAIM.
THERE BE ONLY ONE WORD TO DESCRIBE YOU...

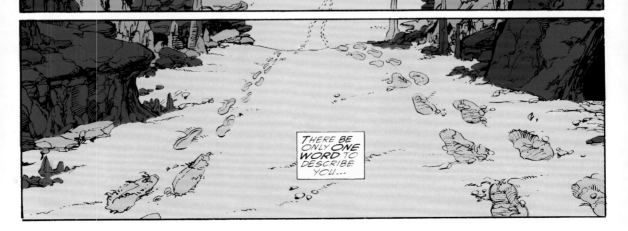

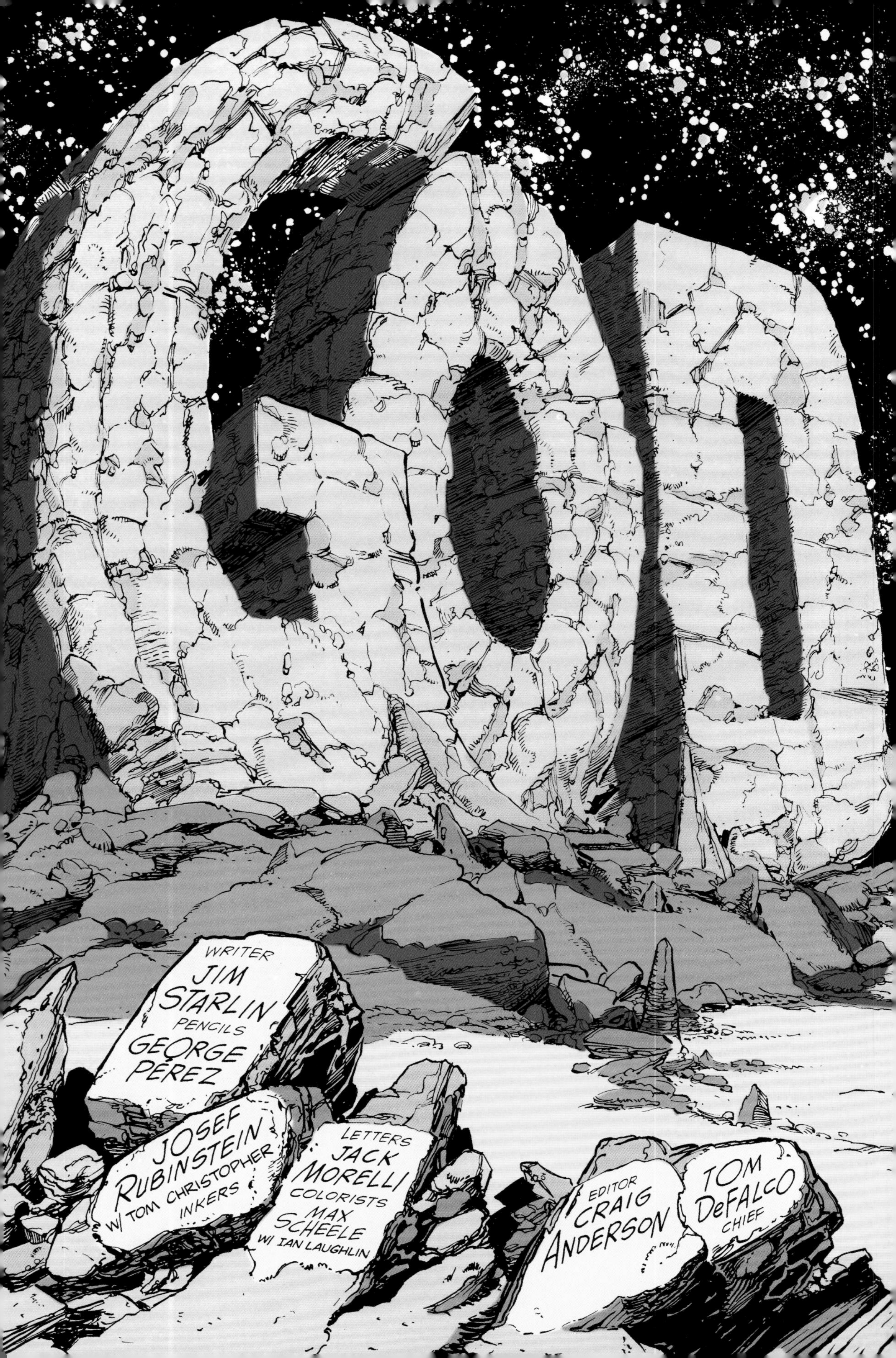
GOD
WRITER
JIM STARLIN
PENCILS
GEORGE PEREZ
JOSEF RUBINSTEIN
W/ TOM CHRISTOPHER
INKERS
LETTERS
JACK MORELLI
COLORISTS
MAX SCHEELE
W/ IAN LAUGHLIN
EDITOR
CRAIG ANDERSON
TOM DeFALCO
CHIEF

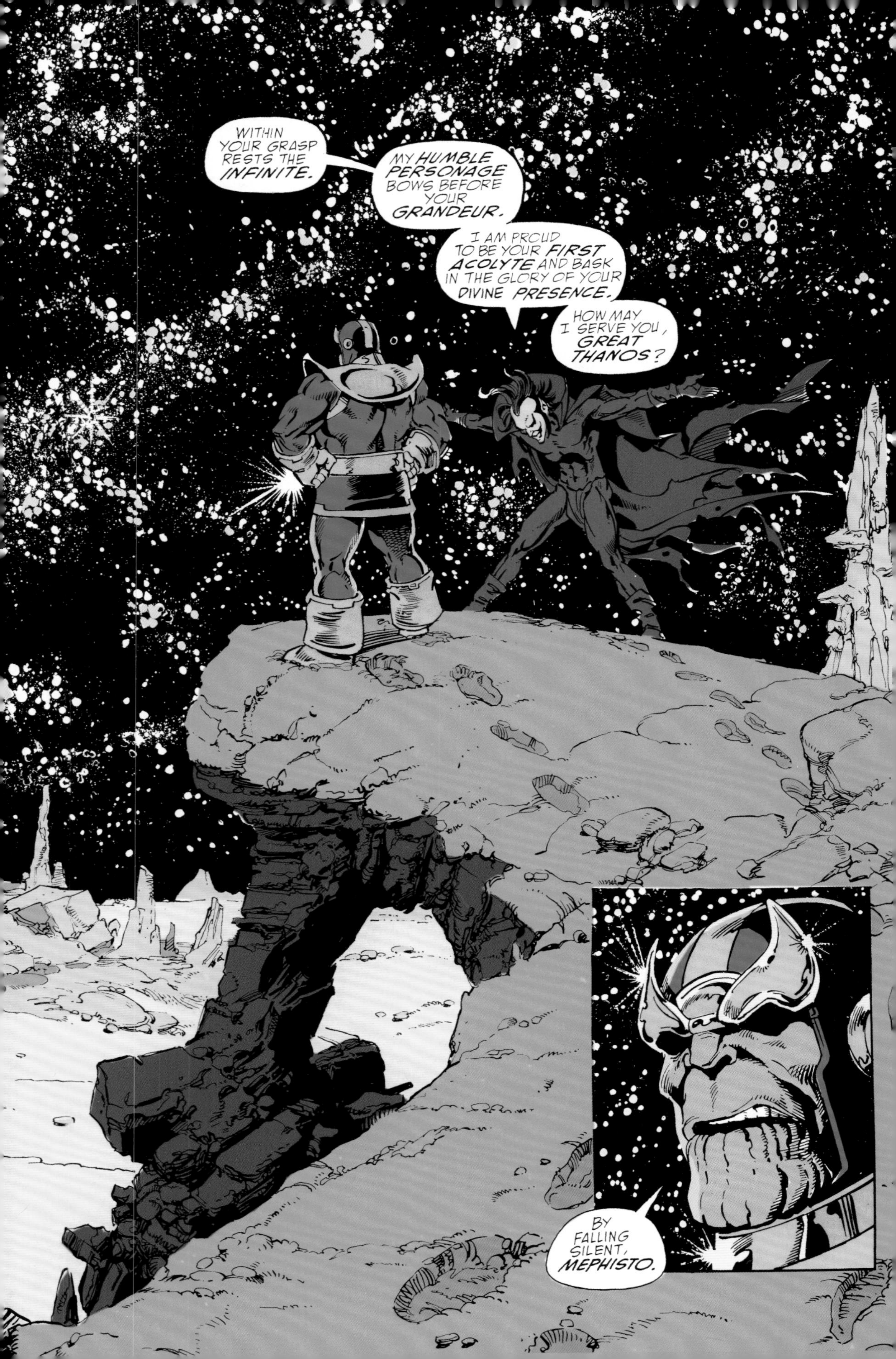
WITHIN YOUR GRASP RESTS THE *INFINITE*.
MY *HUMBLE PERSONAGE* BOWS BEFORE YOUR *GRANDEUR*.
I AM PROUD TO BE YOUR *FIRST ACOLYTE* AND BASK IN THE GLORY OF YOUR DIVINE *PRESENCE*.
HOW MAY I SERVE YOU, *GREAT THANOS?*
BY FALLING SILENT, *MEPHISTO*.

I KNOW, YOU THOUGHT HIM *DEAD.* HE WAS, BUT HE IS *NO LONGER.* HOW COULD ANY OF US KNOW THAT *MISTRESS DEATH* WOULD RESURRECT THIS MONSTER?

APPARENTLY DEATH HAS LONG THOUGHT THE FACT THAT THERE ARE MORE PEOPLE ALIVE TODAY THAN HAVE EVER DIED WAS A TYPE OF COSMIC IMBALANCE.

THIS WAS AN IRREGULAR-ITY SHE SOUGHT TO RIGHT USING THE DARK POWERS AT HER DISPOSAL.

AND SO SHE MADE THE *TRAGIC MISTAKE* OF RETRIEVING *THANOS,* THE *MAD TITAN,* FROM THE *REALM OF THE DEAD.*

THROUGH HIM, DEATH WOULD *MOLD* THE UNIVERSE TO HER *LIKING.*

ALONG WITH RENEWED LIFE, DEATH GAVE HIM GREATLY *AUGMENTED POWER.*

THANOS WOULD NEED THIS MIGHT TO PERFORM THE DARK TASK HIS MISTRESS ASSIGNED HIM.

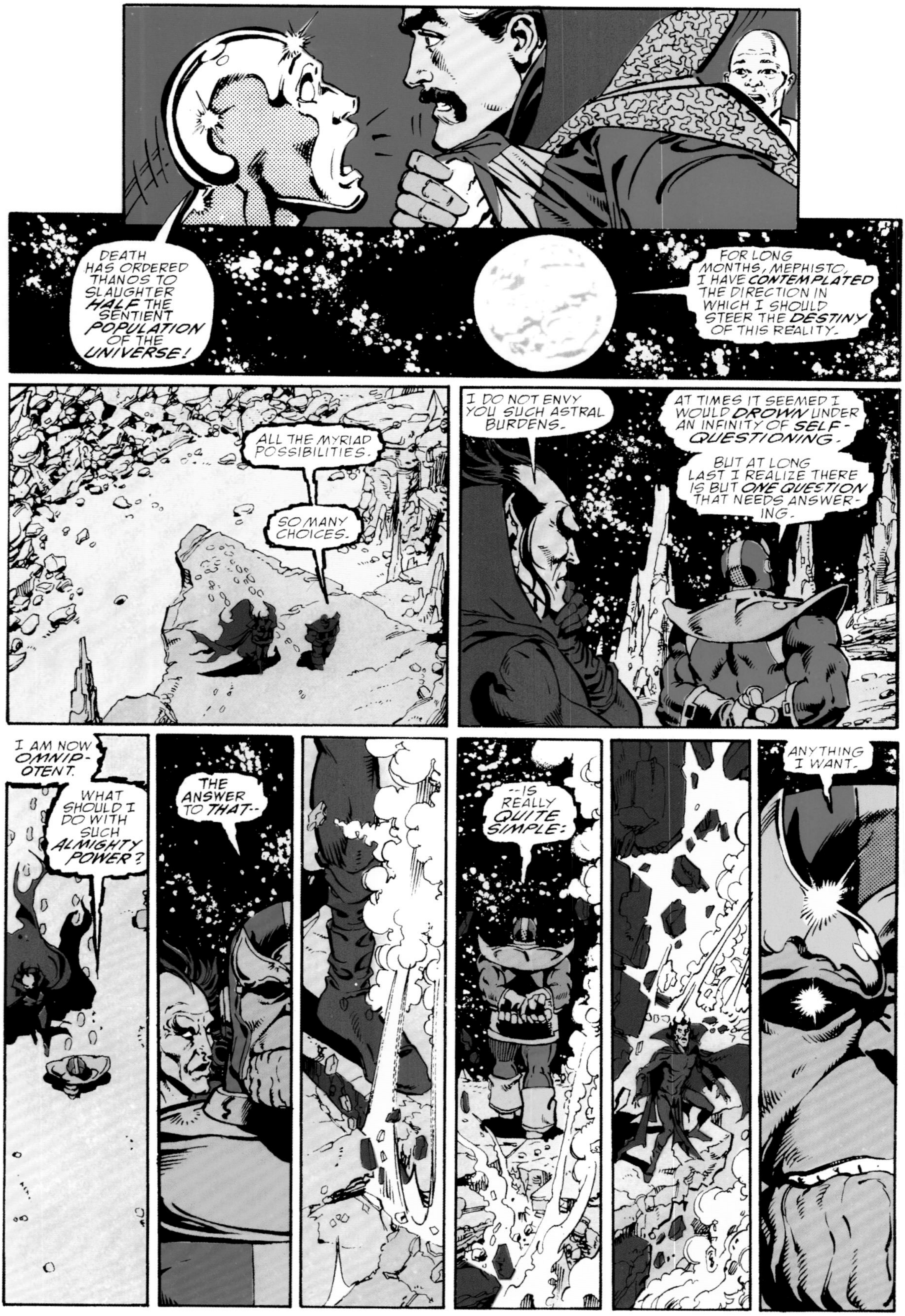
DEATH HAS ORDERED THANOS TO SLAUGHTER HALF THE SENTIENT POPULATION OF THE UNIVERSE!
FOR LONG MONTHS, MEPHISTO, I HAVE CONTEMPLATED THE DIRECTION IN WHICH I SHOULD STEER THE DESTINY OF THIS REALITY.
ALL THE MYRIAD POSSIBILITIES.
SO MANY CHOICES.
I DO NOT ENVY YOU SUCH ASTRAL BURDENS.
AT TIMES IT SEEMED I WOULD DROWN UNDER AN INFINITY OF SELF-QUESTIONING.
BUT AT LONG LAST I REALIZE THERE IS BUT ONE QUESTION THAT NEEDS ANSWERING.
I AM NOW OMNIPOTENT.
WHAT SHOULD I DO WITH SUCH ALMIGHTY POWER?
THE ANSWER TO THAT--
--IS REALLY QUITE SIMPLE:
ANYTHING I WANT.

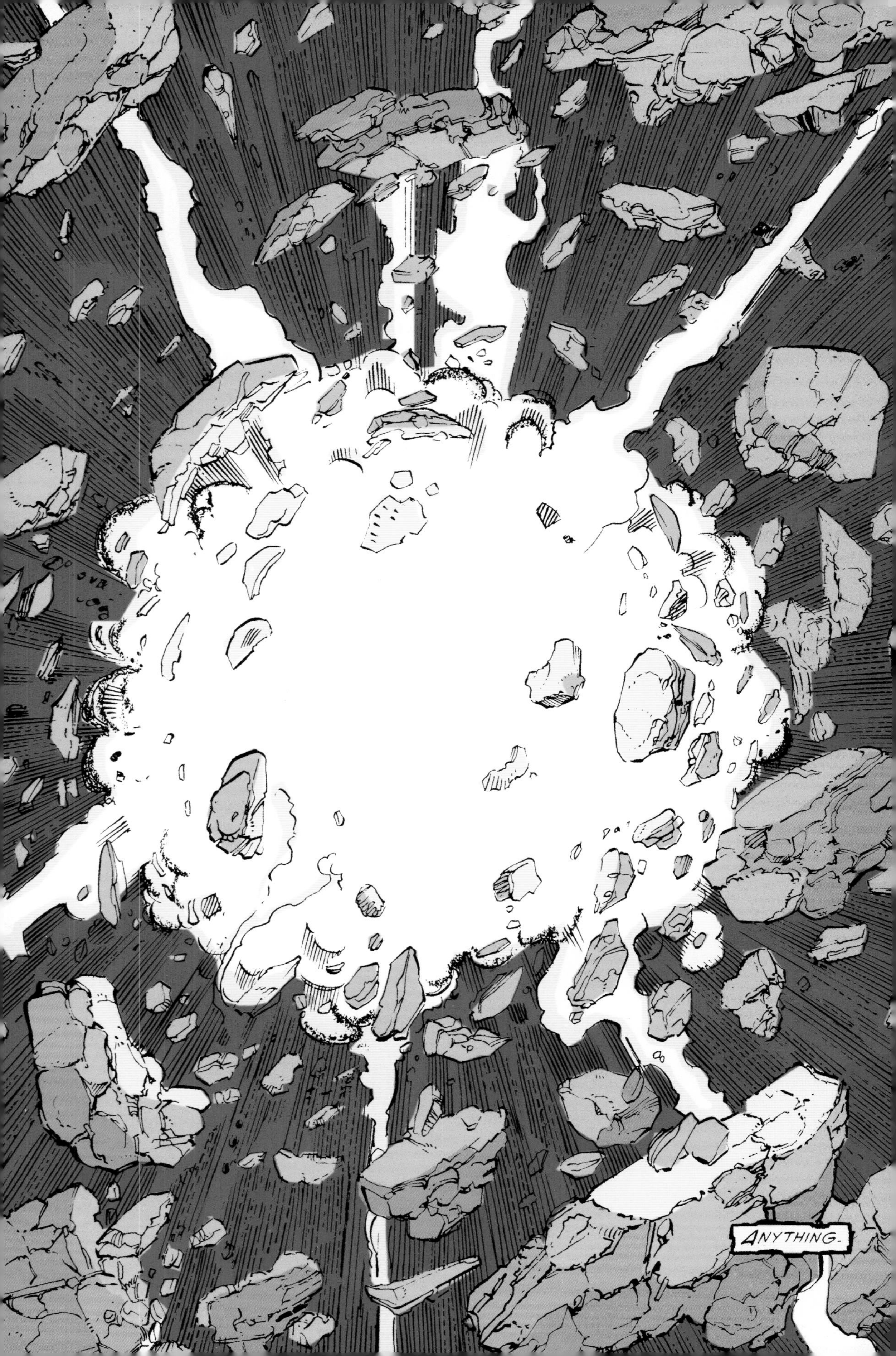
ANYTHING.

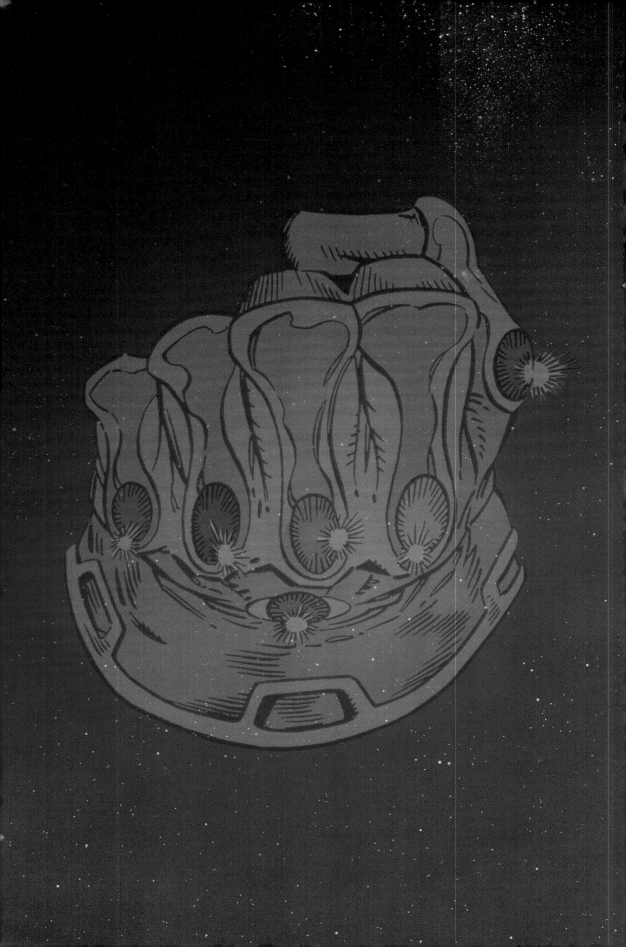

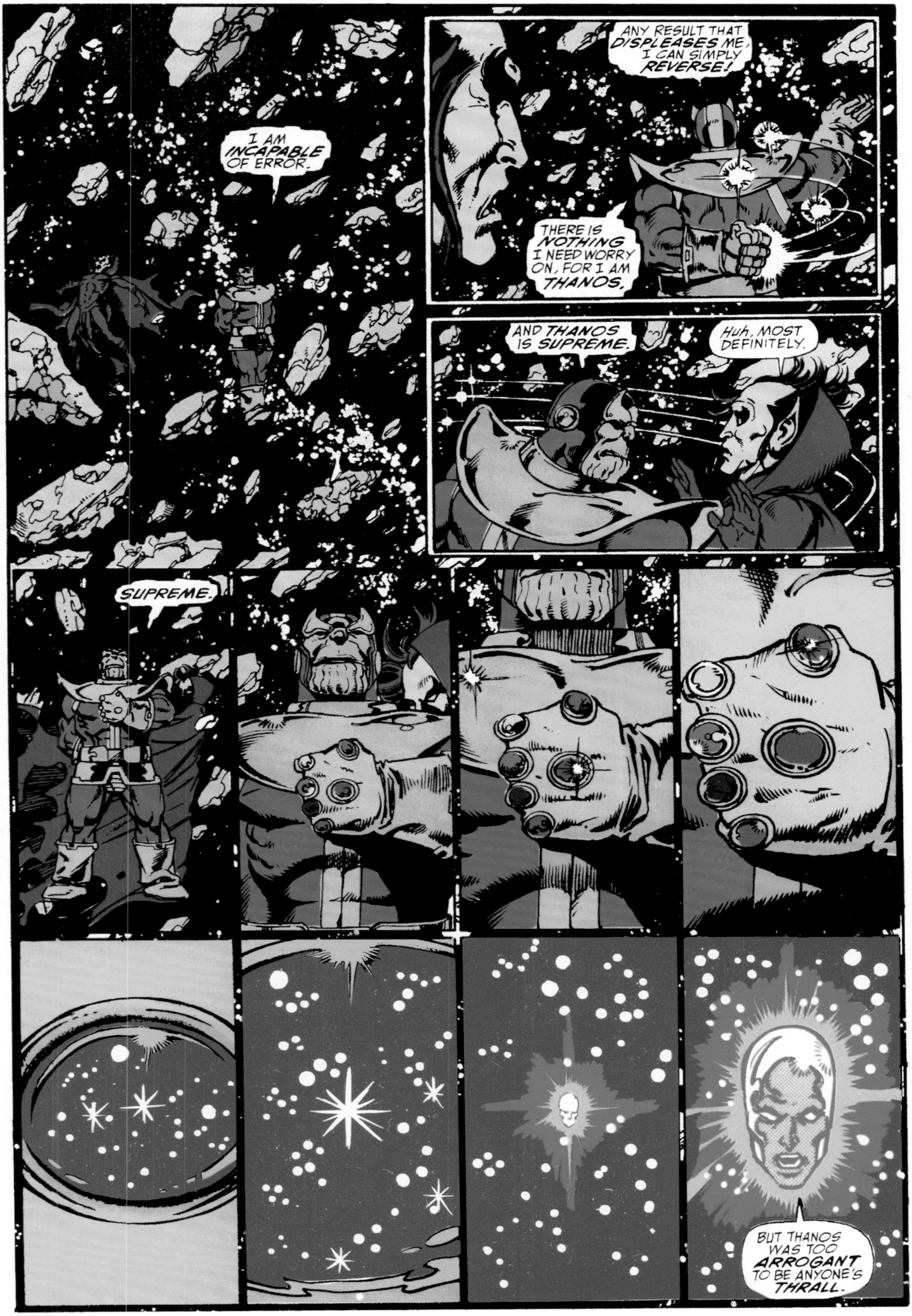
I AM INCAPABLE OF ERROR.
ANY RESULT THAT DISPLEASES ME, I CAN SIMPLY REVERSE!
THERE IS NOTHING I NEED WORRY ON, FOR I AM THANOS.
AND THANOS IS SUPREME.
Huh, MOST DEFINITELY.
SUPREME.
BUT THANOS WAS TOO ARROGANT TO BE ANYONE'S THRALL.

HIS *SINISTER SCHEME* WAS CONCEIVED WHILE GAZING INTO THE DEPTHS OF DEATH'S *INFINITY WELL.*

THERE HE LEARNT OF THE SOUL OR INFINITY GEMS' TRUE POWER AND CONVINCED HIS DARK MISTRESS THAT THE TASK ASSIGNED HIM COULD NOT BE CARRIED TO FRUITION WITHOUT THEM.

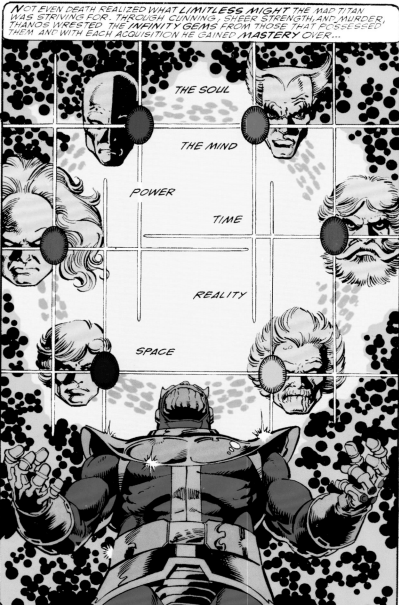

NOT EVEN DEATH REALIZED WHAT **LIMITLESS MIGHT** THE MAD TITAN WAS STRIVING FOR. THROUGH *CUNNING, SHEER STRENGTH,* AND *MURDER,* THANOS WRESTED THE *INFINITY GEMS* FROM THOSE THAT POSSESSED THEM. AND WITH EACH ACQUISITION HE GAINED *MASTERY* OVER...

THE SOUL

THE MIND

POWER

TIME

REALITY

SPACE

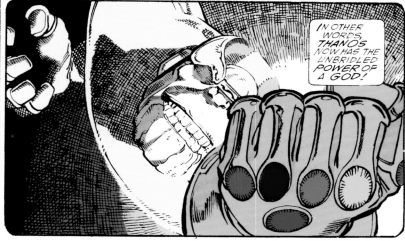

IN OTHER WORDS, THANOS NOW HAS THE UNBRIDLED POWER OF A GOD!

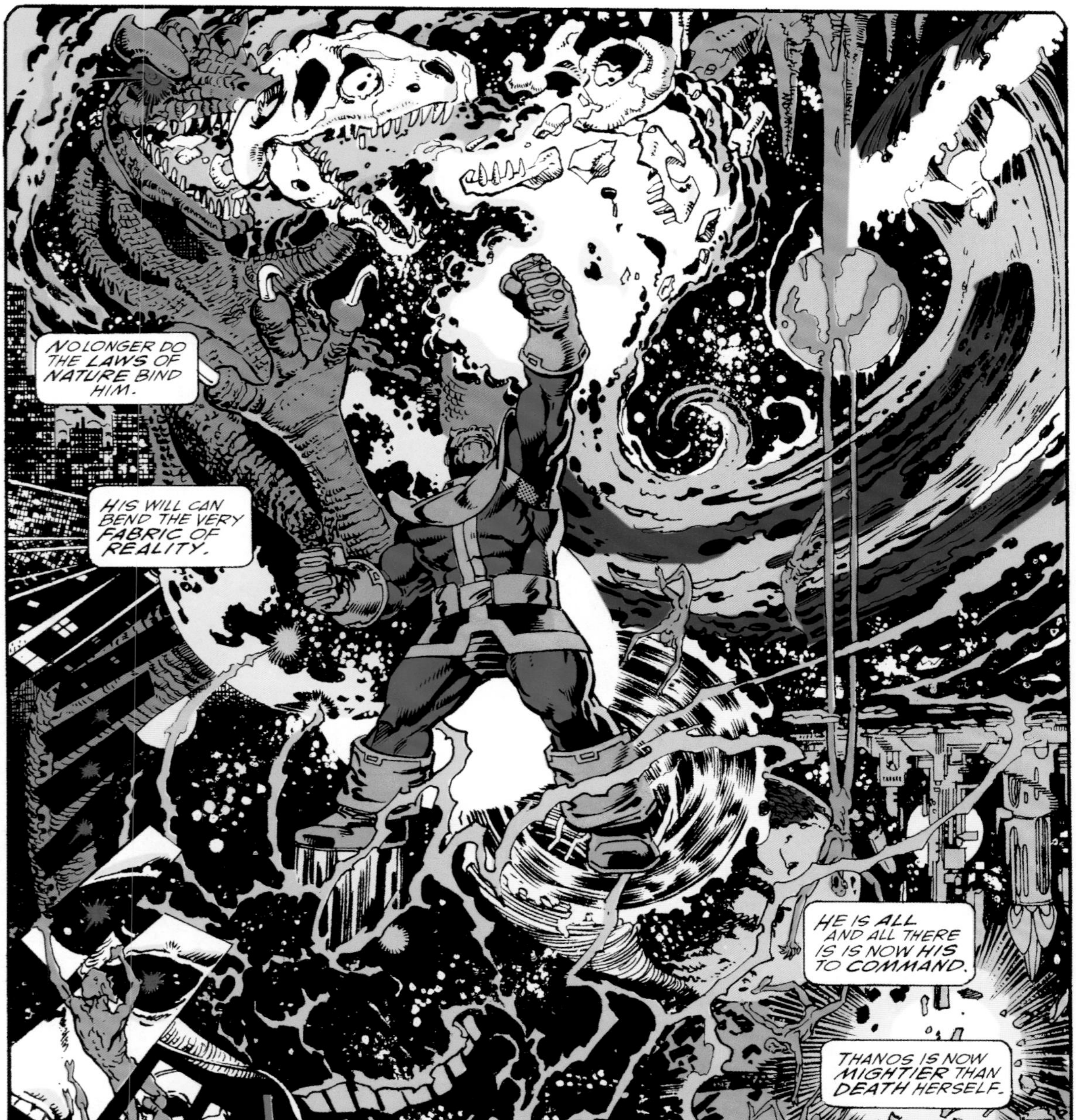
NO LONGER DO THE LAWS OF NATURE BIND HIM.
HIS WILL CAN BEND THE VERY FABRIC OF REALITY.
HE IS ALL AND ALL THERE IS IS NOW HIS TO COMMAND.
THANOS IS NOW MIGHTIER THAN DEATH HERSELF.
MORE POWERFUL THAN ANY FORCE IN THE UNIVERSE.

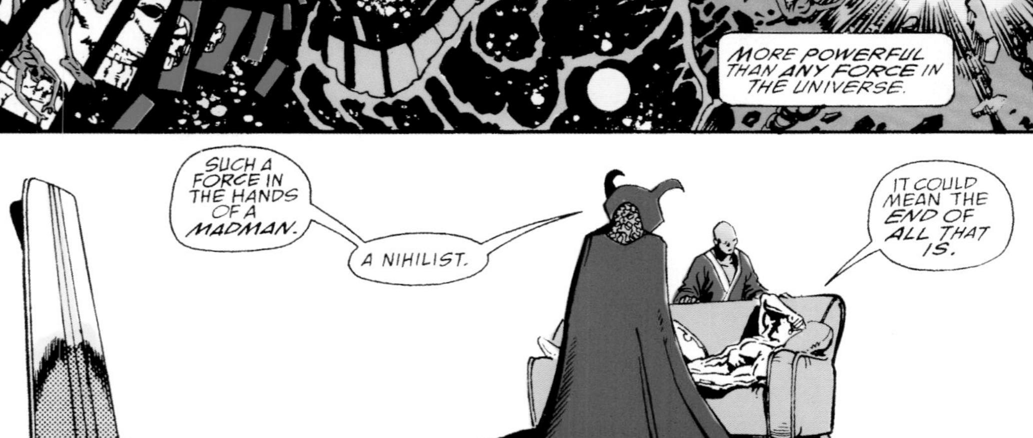
SUCH A FORCE IN THE HANDS OF A MADMAN.
A NIHILIST.
IT COULD MEAN THE END OF ALL THAT IS.

THEY WERE ALL GRADE-A LOSERS.

WE FIRST BECAME AWARE OF THEM AS THEY STEPPED OUT OF A **BAR** IN SOMEPLACE CALLED UPSTATE NEW YORK...

NATURALLY THEY WERE TANKED TO THE GILLS.

WE SHOULDA GOT OUTTA HERE *HOURS* AGO!

WE'RE HOT!

THE RINGLEADER WAS A COLD-EYED BRUTE CALLED JAKE MILLER...

GETTING PRETTY TIRED OF YER ALWAYS *NAGGIN',* FATS.

THE TUB OF LARD WAS *RALPH BUNKER*...

SPECIAL XHIBITION

YA JUST DON'T *KNOCK OFF* A LIQUOR STORE, *WASTE* THE SHOPKEEPER AND SPEND THE REST OF THE DAY IN A *BAR!*

THE BLONDE BIMBO WENT BY THE NAME OF *BAMBI LONG*. CAN YOU BELIEVE IT?

FATS, YA JUST GOTTA LEARN TA *RELAX* AND *ENJOY* LIFE! *Teehee!*

CAN'T YOU TWO GET IT THROUGH YER HEADS WE GOTTA GET *OUTTA* STATE, MAYBE UP TA *CANADA!*

NOW PLAYING: AT THE LOTUS THEATRE BB DIAMOND ABE BROWN HECTOR AYALA KUNG FU

WE ARE.

THE COPS'LL BE LOOKIN' FER US ON THE *THRUWAY.*

THEN WE TAKE THE *BACK ROADS,* NO SWEAT.

I KNOW 'EM LIKE THE *BACK'A* MY *HAND.*

WHAT A JERK THAT JAKE WAS.

GUESS THE BIG LUG *FORGOT* ABOUT ONE *CERTAIN* CURVE ON THE BACK OF HIS HAND.

BECAUSE HE DROVE *OFF* IT DOING BETTER THAN *65* !

NO ONE SURVIVED THE *SUDDEN* STOP AT THE BOTTOM OF THE CLIFF.

WHEN WE AWOKE FROM THE *ORDEAL*, THE DESTROYER AND I FOUND OURSELVES WITHIN THE *METAPHYSICAL WORLD* OF THE *SOUL GEM*.

IT WAS THE MOST *BIZARRE PLACE* I HAVE EVER ENCOUNTERED.

IT WAS THERE THAT I MET A STRANGE AND ENIGMATIC MAN CALLED *ADAM WARLOCK*, APPARENTLY THE SPIRITUAL LEADER OF THE *SOULWORLD*.

ENCOUNTERING HIM WAS AN EXPERIENCE I'LL LONG REMEMBER.

IT WAS THROUGH A *SPELL* CAST BY HIM THAT *THE DESTROYER* AND I WERE ABLE TO RETURN TO THIS *REALITY*.

A *HARROWING ESCAPE.*

BY THE TIME WE REGAINED OUR BODIES, THANOS HAD *DEPARTED* TO AN UNKNOWN DESTINATION TO CONSIDER THE BEST USE HE COULD MAKE OF HIS NEW-FOUND *DIVINITY.*

WE WERE INFORMED OF THIS DE- VELOPMENT BY MY LONGTIME ENEMY *MEPHISTO*, FOR REASONS ALL HIS OWN, AND WARNED THAT WE SHOULD *FORTIFY* OUR UNIVERSE AGAINST THE TITAN'S *INEVITABLE RETURN.*

I IMMEDIATELY SET OUT FOR *EARTH* TO SPREAD THE WORD OF APPROACHING DANGER. BUT, UN- FORTUNATELY, *MANY* AN EVENT KEPT ME FROM REACHING THIS WORLD UNTIL *NOW.*

I PRAY MY WARNING HAS NOT COME *TOO LATE.*

SO DO I!

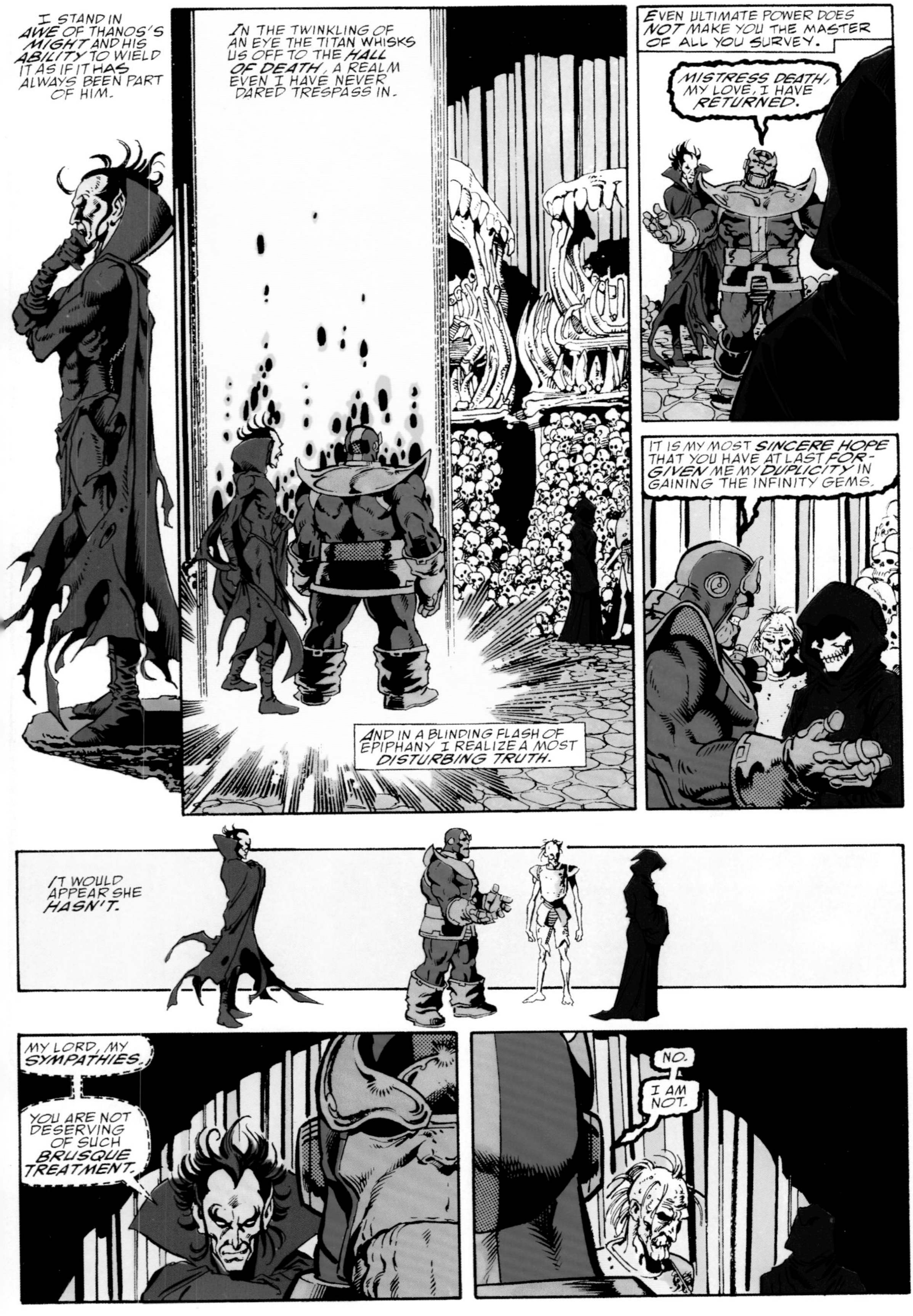
I STAND IN AWE OF THANOS'S MIGHT AND HIS ABILITY TO WIELD IT AS IF IT HAS ALWAYS BEEN PART OF HIM.
IN THE TWINKLING OF AN EYE THE TITAN WHISKS US OFF TO THE HALL OF DEATH, A REALM EVEN I HAVE NEVER DARED TRESPASS IN.
AND IN A BLINDING FLASH OF EPIPHANY I REALIZE A MOST DISTURBING TRUTH.
EVEN ULTIMATE POWER DOES NOT MAKE YOU THE MASTER OF ALL YOU SURVEY.
MISTRESS DEATH, MY LOVE, I HAVE RETURNED.
IT IS MY MOST SINCERE HOPE THAT YOU HAVE AT LAST FOR-GIVEN ME MY DUPLICITY IN GAINING THE INFINITY GEMS.
IT WOULD APPEAR SHE HASN'T.
MY LORD, MY SYMPATHIES.
YOU ARE NOT DESERVING OF SUCH BRUSQUE TREATMENT.
NO. I AM NOT.

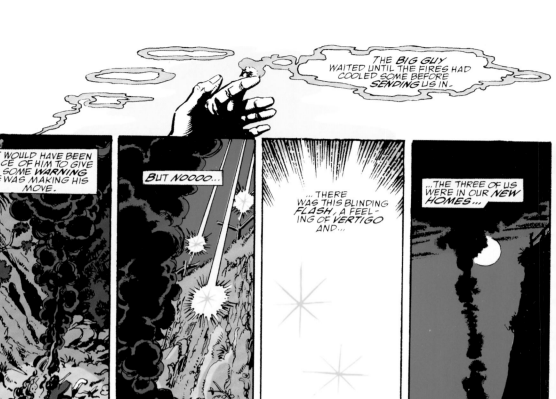

THE *BIG GUY* WAITED UNTIL THE FIRES HAD COOLED SOME BEFORE *SENDING US IN-*

IT WOULD HAVE BEEN NICE OF HIM TO GIVE US SOME *WARNING* HE WAS MAKING HIS MOVE.

BUT *NOOOO...*

*...*THERE WAS THIS BLINDING *FLASH,* A FEELING OF *VERTIGO* AND*...*

*...*THE THREE OF US WERE IN OUR *NEW* HOMES...

..."FOR BETTER...

...OR WORSE.

THIS BODY IS *DEAD!*

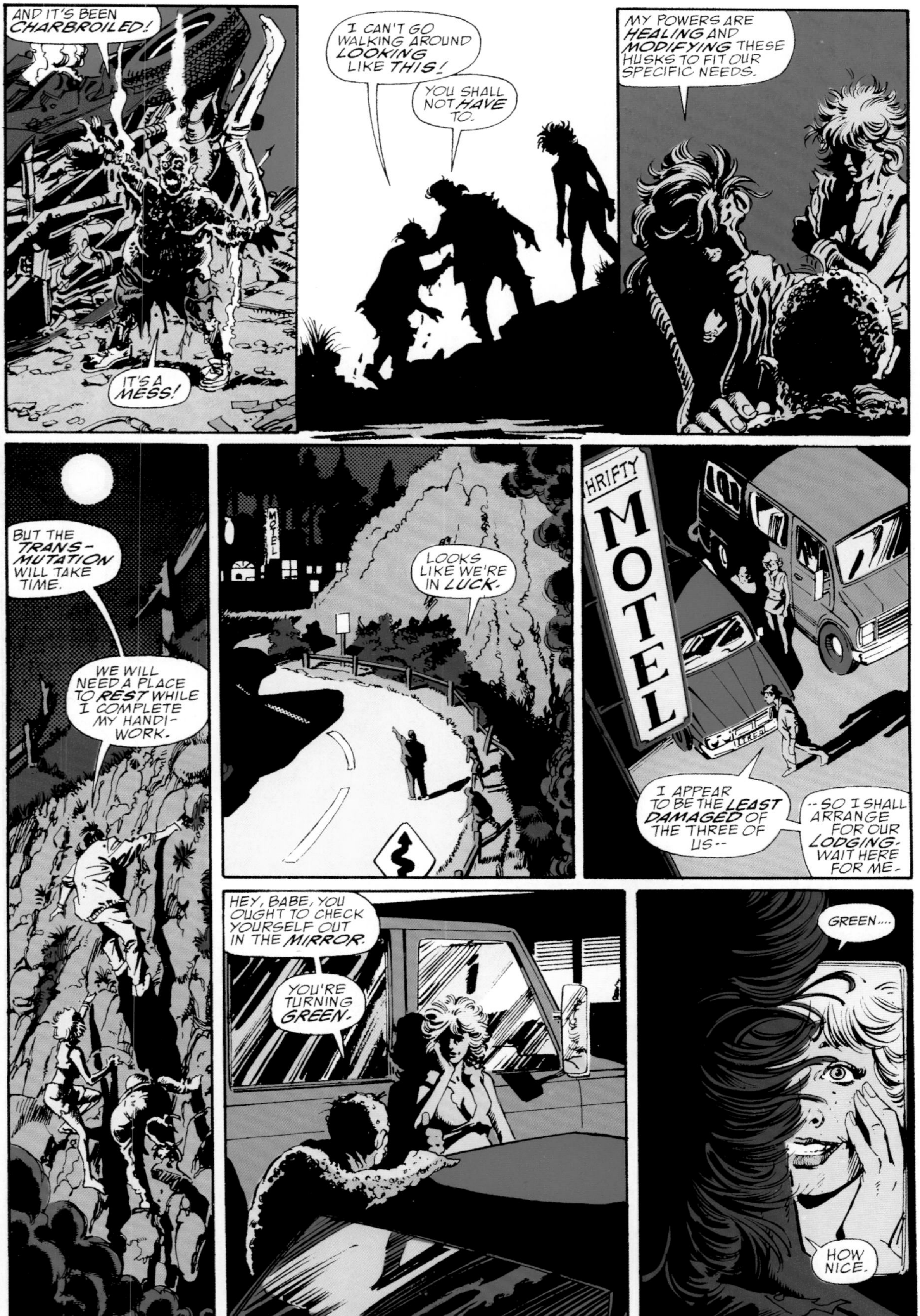
AND IT'S BEEN CHARBROILED!
IT'S A MESS!
I CAN'T GO WALKING AROUND LOOKING LIKE THIS!
YOU SHALL NOT HAVE TO.
MY POWERS ARE HEALING AND MODIFYING THESE HUSKS TO FIT OUR SPECIFIC NEEDS.
BUT THE TRANS-MUTATION WILL TAKE TIME.
WE WILL NEED A PLACE TO REST WHILE I COMPLETE MY HANDI-WORK.
MOTEL
LOOKS LIKE WE'RE IN LUCK.
HRIFTY
MOTEL
I APPEAR TO BE THE LEAST DAMAGED OF THE THREE OF US--
--SO I SHALL ARRANGE FOR OUR LODGING. WAIT HERE FOR ME.
HEY, BABE, YOU OUGHT TO CHECK YOURSELF OUT IN THE MIRROR.
YOU'RE TURNING GREEN.
GREEN....
HOW NICE.

SO MUCH **POWER** IN THE POSSESSION OF ONE WHO HAS BARELY REACHED THE STATUS OF **GODLING**.

THE VERY **THOUGHT** BOGGLES THE MIND.

THANOS COULD DESTROY EVEN **ME** WITH BUT A **THOUGHT**, YET HIS BASIC SOUL REMAINS ON THE EDGE OF **MORTALITY**.

IS HE CAPABLE OF **MANAGING** THE FORCES NOW UNDER HIS COMMAND?

OR WILL HIS **FRAGILE HEART** BE HIS UNDOING?

IT WAS **NEVER** MY INTENTION TO **WRONG** YOU, NOR, DO I BELIEVE, I **HAVE**.

DARLING MISTRESS, YOUR **SCORN** WOUNDS ME **DEEPLY**—

TRUE, I DID USE THE POWERS **YOU** GRANTED ME TO SEEK OUT THE INFINITY GEMS TO BECOME THE **SUPREME BEING** THAT NOW STANDS BEFORE YOU.

BUT I ONLY SOUGHT SUCH **GLORY** IN ORDER TO BE- COME **WORTHY** OF YOUR LOVE.

YOUR HEART DESERVES **BETTER** THAN THE **THRALL** I WAS.

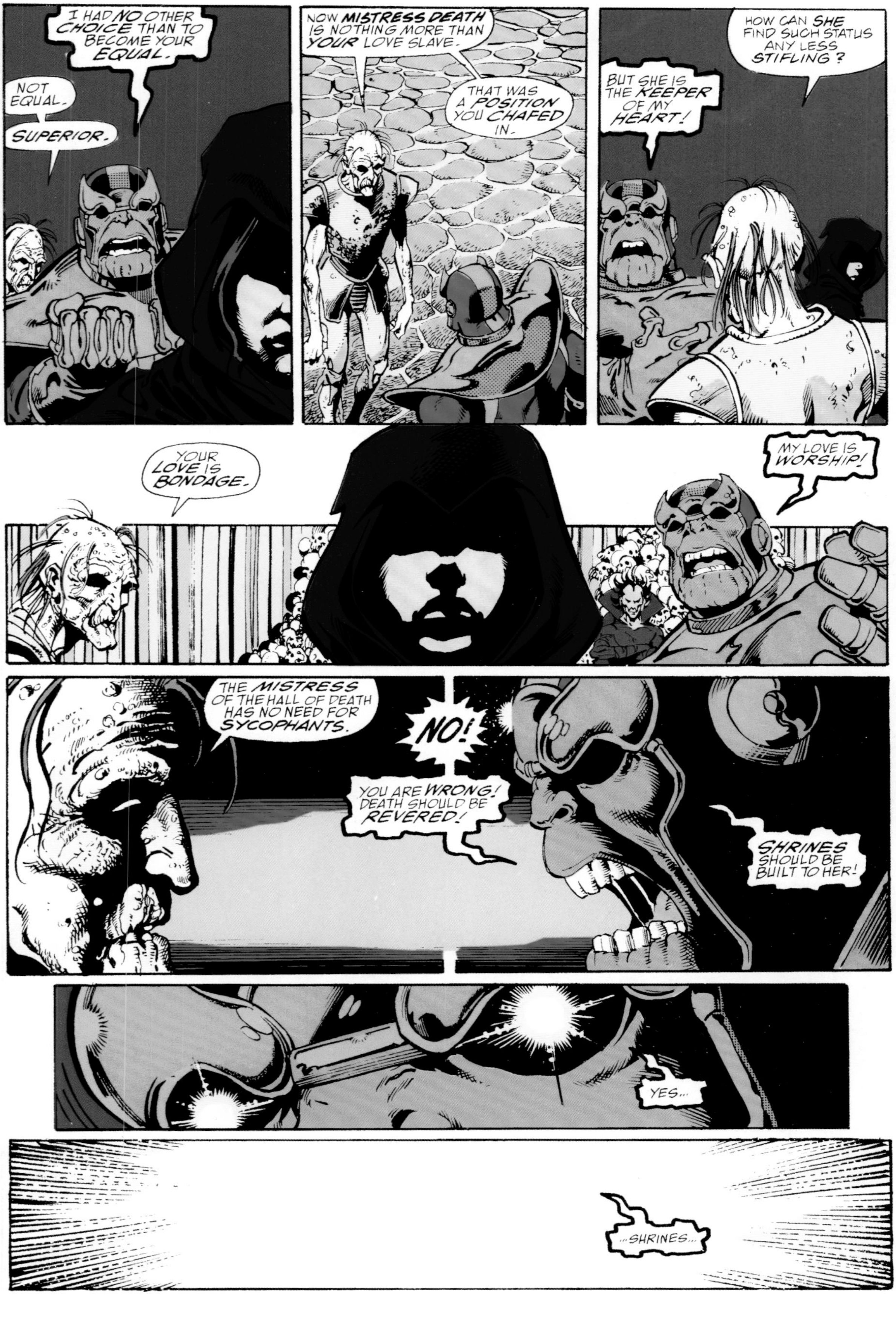
I HAD NO OTHER CHOICE THAN TO BECOME YOUR EQUAL.
NOT EQUAL.
SUPERIOR.
NOW MISTRESS DEATH IS NOTHING MORE THAN YOUR LOVE SLAVE.
THAT WAS A POSITION YOU CHAFED IN.
BUT SHE IS THE KEEPER OF MY HEART!
HOW CAN SHE FIND SUCH STATUS ANY LESS STIFLING?
YOUR LOVE IS BONDAGE.
MY LOVE IS WORSHIP!
THE MISTRESS OF THE HALL OF DEATH HAS NO NEED FOR SYCOPHANTS.
NO!
YOU ARE WRONG! DEATH SHOULD BE REVERED!
SHRINES SHOULD BE BUILT TO HER!
YES...
...SHRINES...

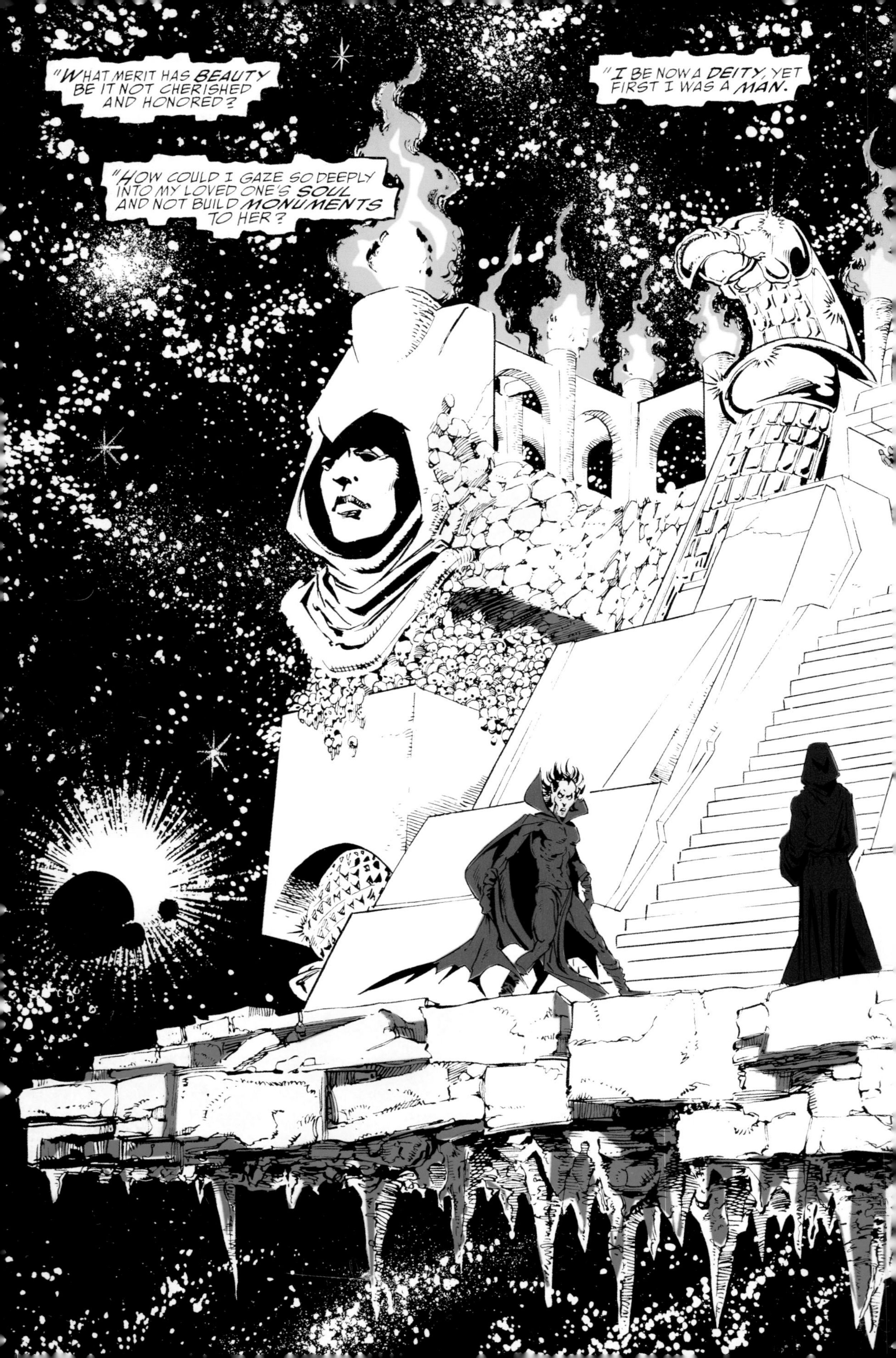
"WHAT MERIT HAS BEAUTY BE IT NOT CHERISHED AND HONORED?
"HOW COULD I GAZE SO DEEPLY INTO MY LOVED ONE'S SOUL AND NOT BUILD MONUMENTS TO HER?
"I BE NOW A DEITY, YET FIRST I WAS A MAN.

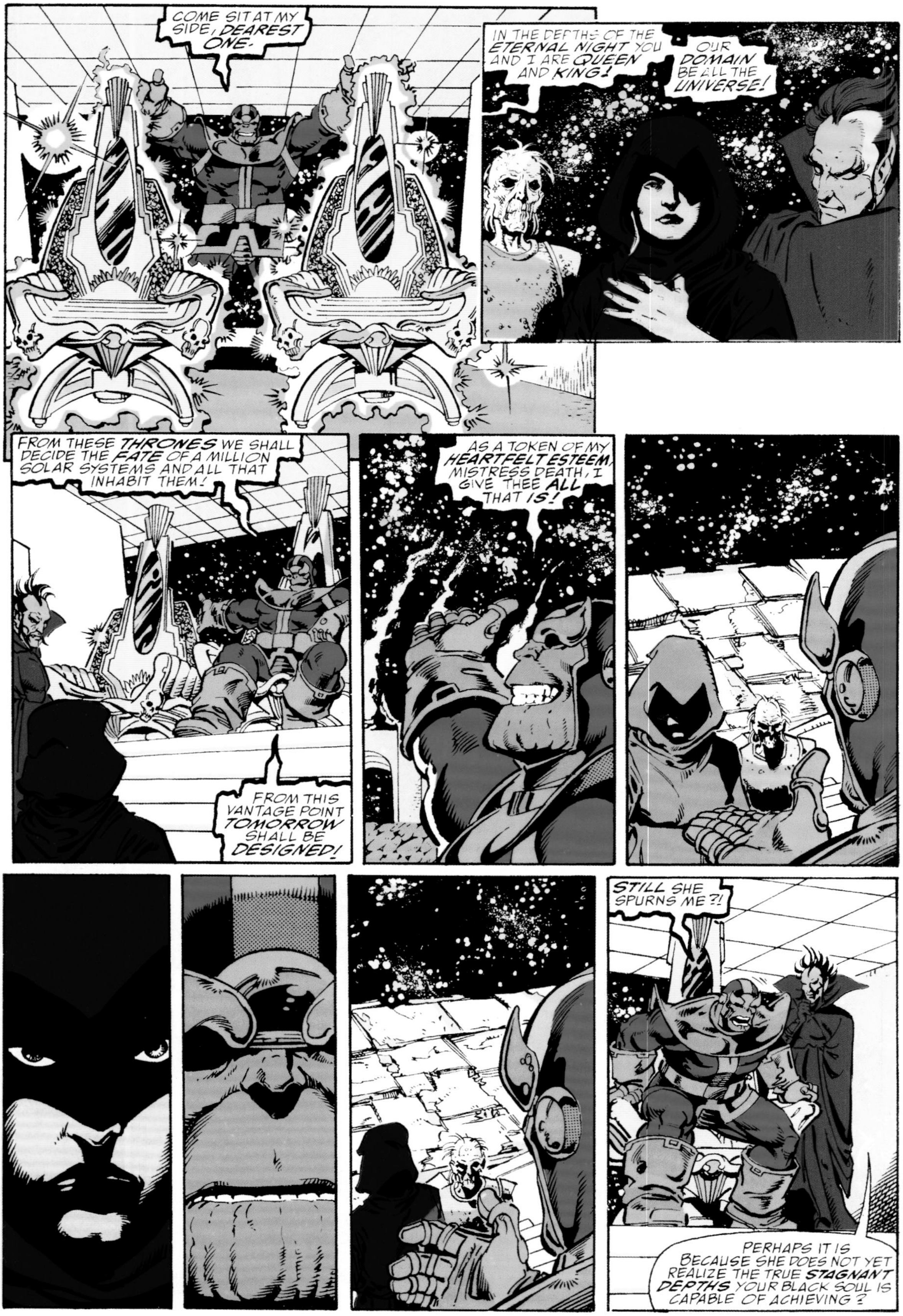
COME SIT AT MY SIDE, DEAREST ONE.
IN THE DEPTHS OF THE ETERNAL NIGHT YOU AND I ARE QUEEN AND KING!
OUR DOMAIN BE ALL THE UNIVERSE!
FROM THESE THRONES WE SHALL DECIDE THE FATE OF A MILLION SOLAR SYSTEMS AND ALL THAT INHABIT THEM!
FROM THIS VANTAGE POINT TOMORROW SHALL BE DESIGNED!
AS A TOKEN OF MY HEARTFELT ESTEEM, MISTRESS DEATH, I GIVE THEE ALL THAT IS!
STILL SHE SPURNS ME?!
PERHAPS IT IS BECAUSE SHE DOES NOT YET REALIZE THE TRUE STAGNANT DEPTHS YOUR BLACK SOUL IS CAPABLE OF ACHIEVING?

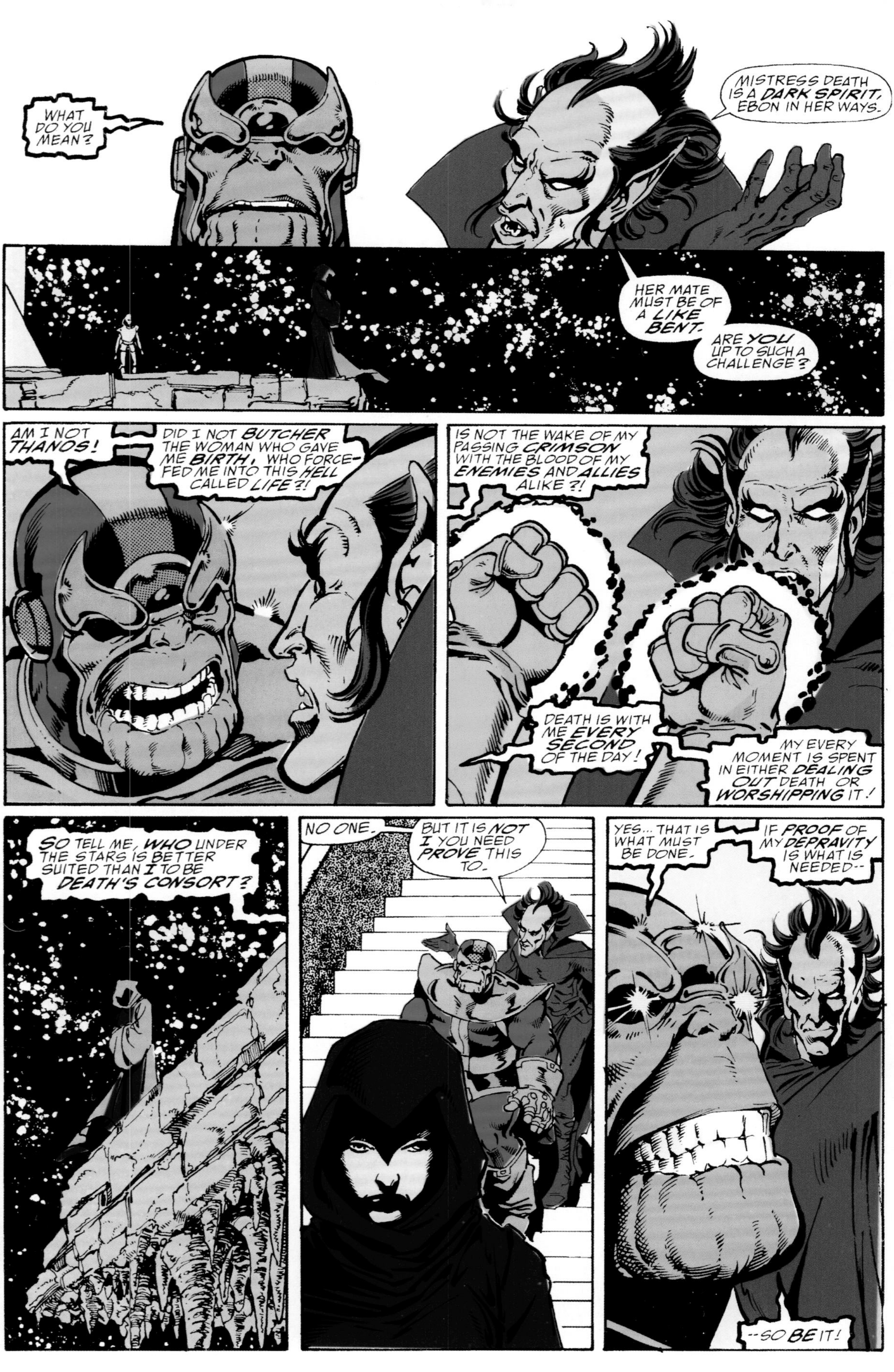

WHAT DO YOU MEAN?
MISTRESS DEATH IS A DARK SPIRIT, EBON IN HER WAYS.
HER MATE MUST BE OF A LIKE BENT.
ARE YOU UP TO SUCH A CHALLENGE?
AM I NOT THANOS!
DID I NOT BUTCHER THE WOMAN WHO GAVE ME BIRTH, WHO FORCE-FED ME INTO THIS HELL CALLED LIFE?!
IS NOT THE WAKE OF MY PASSING CRIMSON WITH THE BLOOD OF MY ENEMIES AND ALLIES ALIKE?!
DEATH IS WITH ME EVERY SECOND OF THE DAY!
MY EVERY MOMENT IS SPENT IN EITHER DEALING OUT DEATH OR WORSHIPPING IT!
SO TELL ME, WHO UNDER THE STARS IS BETTER SUITED THAN I TO BE DEATH'S CONSORT?
NO ONE.
BUT IT IS NOT I YOU NEED PROVE THIS TO.
YES... THAT IS WHAT MUST BE DONE.
IF PROOF OF MY DEPRAVITY IS WHAT IS NEEDED--
--SO BE IT!

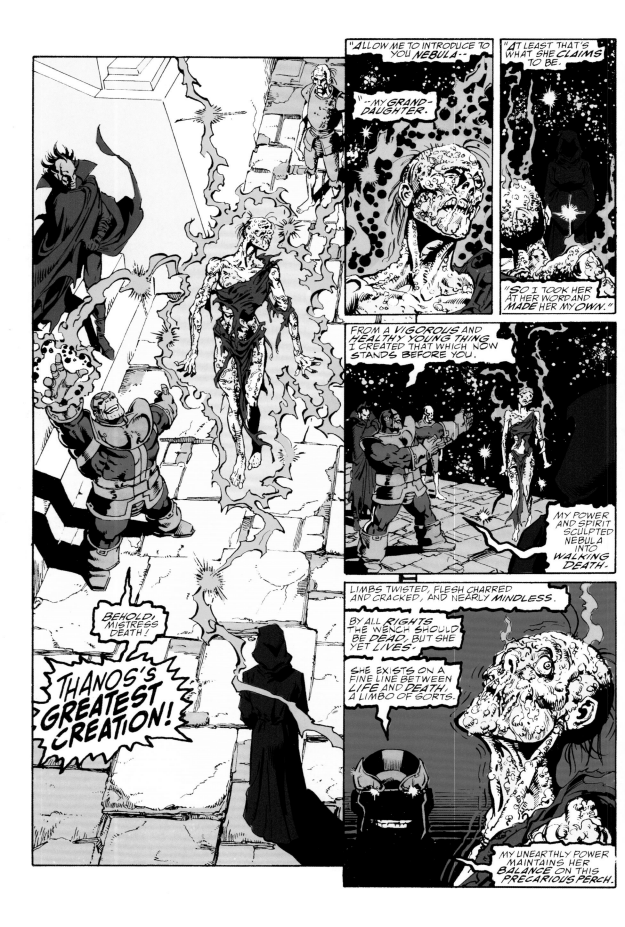

"ALLOW ME TO INTRODUCE TO YOU *NEBULA*--

"--MY *GRAND-DAUGHTER*.

"AT LEAST THAT'S WHAT SHE *CLAIMS* TO BE.

"SO I TOOK HER AT HER WORD AND *MADE HER MY OWN*."

FROM A *VIGOROUS* AND *HEALTHY* YOUNG THING I CREATED THAT WHICH NOW STANDS BEFORE YOU.

MY POWER AND SPIRIT SCULPTED NEBULA INTO *WALKING DEATH*.

BEHOLD, MISTRESS DEATH!

THANOS'S GREATEST CREATION!

LIMBS TWISTED, FLESH CHARRED AND CRACKED, AND NEARLY *MINDLESS*.

BY ALL *RIGHTS* THE WENCH SHOULD BE *DEAD*, BUT SHE YET *LIVES*.

SHE EXISTS ON A FINE LINE BETWEEN *LIFE* AND *DEATH*, A LIMBO OF SORTS.

MY UNEARTHLY POWER MAINTAINS HER *BALANCE* ON THIS *PRECARIOUS PERCH*.

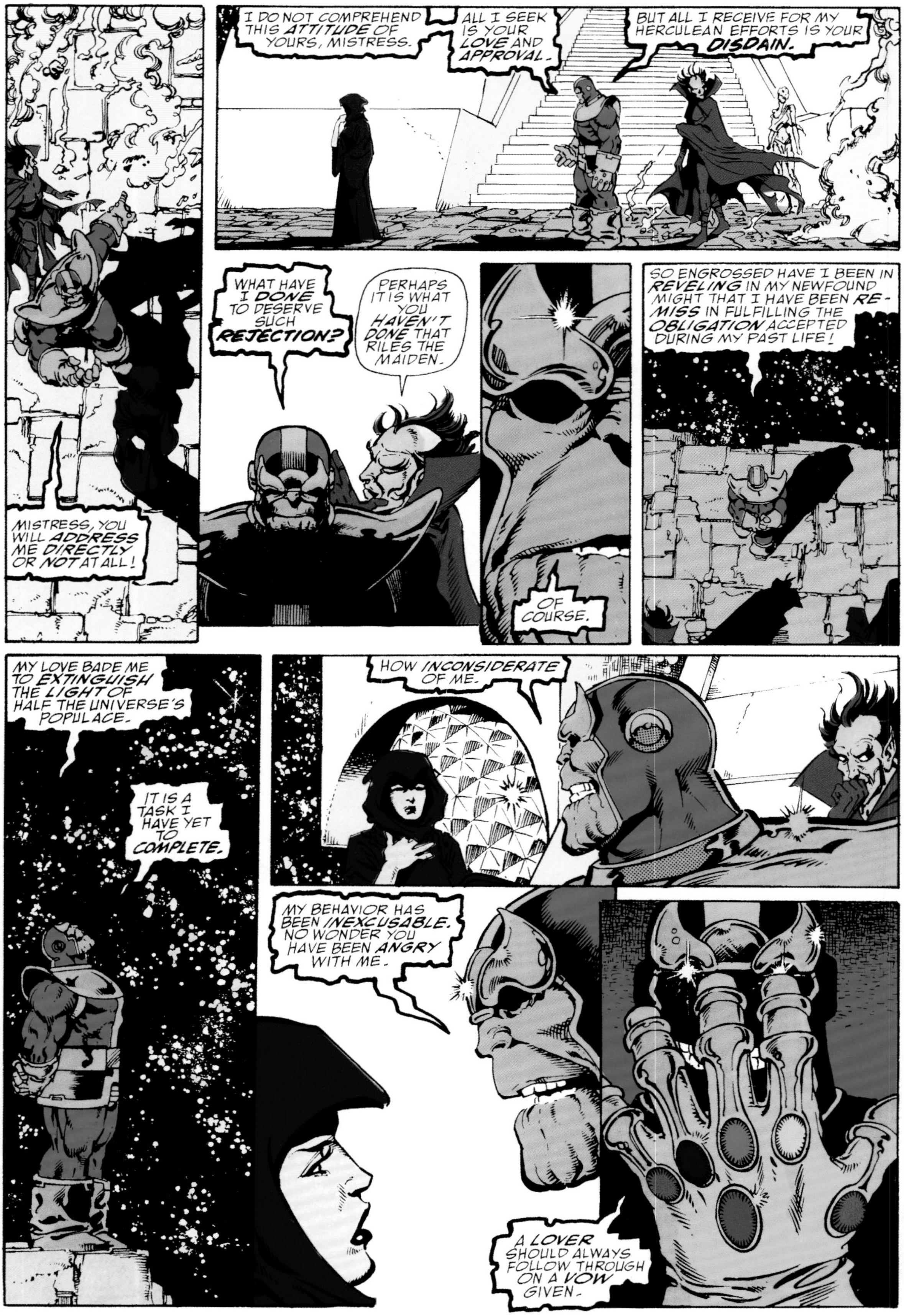

I DO NOT COMPREHEND THIS ATTITUDE OF YOURS, MISTRESS.
ALL I SEEK IS YOUR LOVE AND APPROVAL.
BUT ALL I RECEIVE FOR MY HERCULEAN EFFORTS IS YOUR DISDAIN.
MISTRESS, YOU WILL ADDRESS ME DIRECTLY OR NOT AT ALL!
WHAT HAVE I DONE TO DESERVE SUCH REJECTION?
PERHAPS IT IS WHAT YOU HAVEN'T DONE THAT RILES THE MAIDEN.
OF COURSE.
SO ENGROSSED HAVE I BEEN IN REVELING IN MY NEWFOUND MIGHT THAT I HAVE BEEN RE-MISS IN FULFILLING THE OBLIGATION ACCEPTED DURING MY PAST LIFE!
MY LOVE BADE ME TO EXTINGUISH THE LIGHT OF HALF THE UNIVERSE'S POPULACE.
IT IS A TASK I HAVE YET TO COMPLETE.
HOW INCONSIDERATE OF ME.
MY BEHAVIOR HAS BEEN INEXCUSABLE. NO WONDER YOU HAVE BEEN ANGRY WITH ME.
A LOVER SHOULD ALWAYS FOLLOW THROUGH ON A VOW GIVEN.

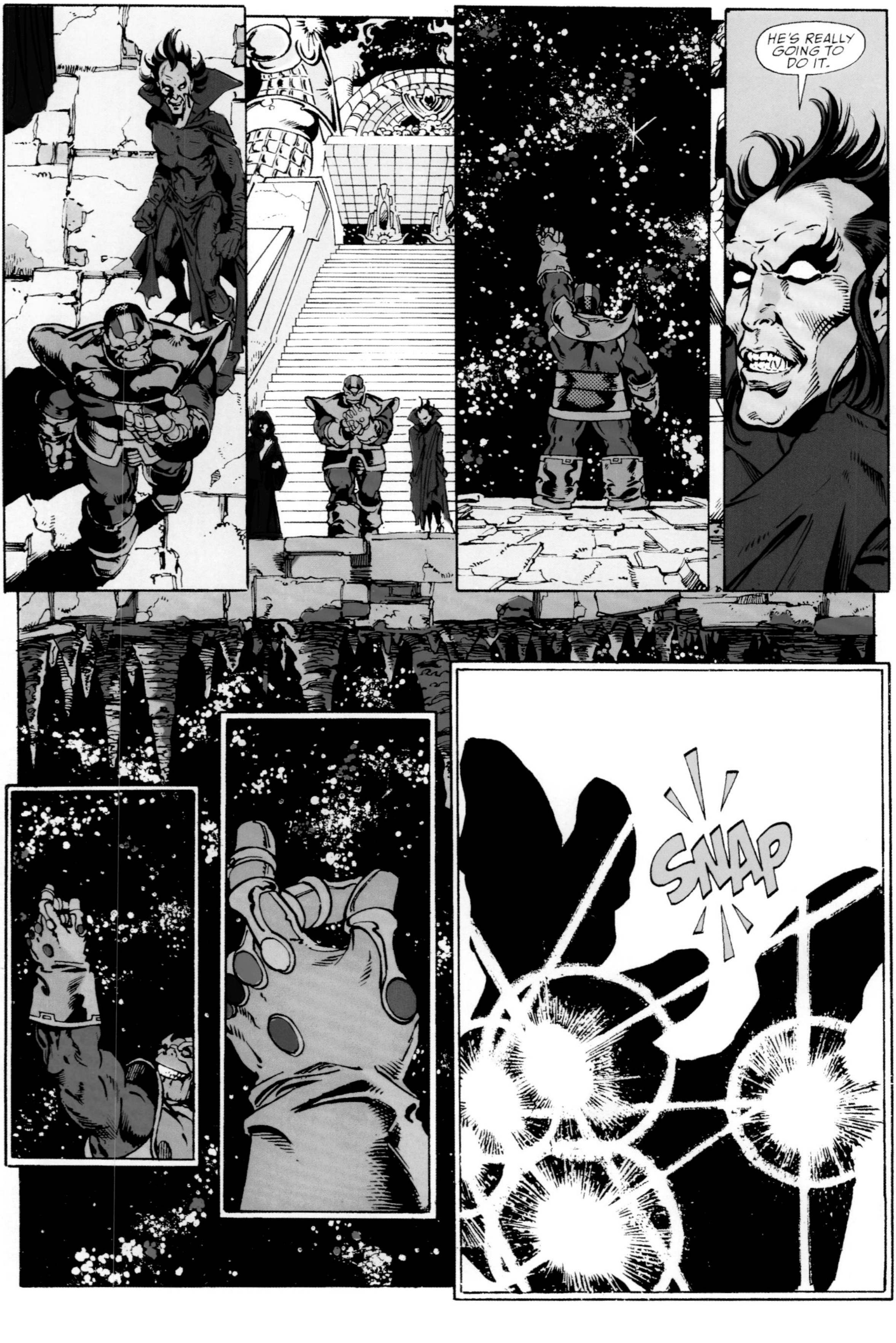
HE'S REALLY GOING TO DO IT.
SNAP

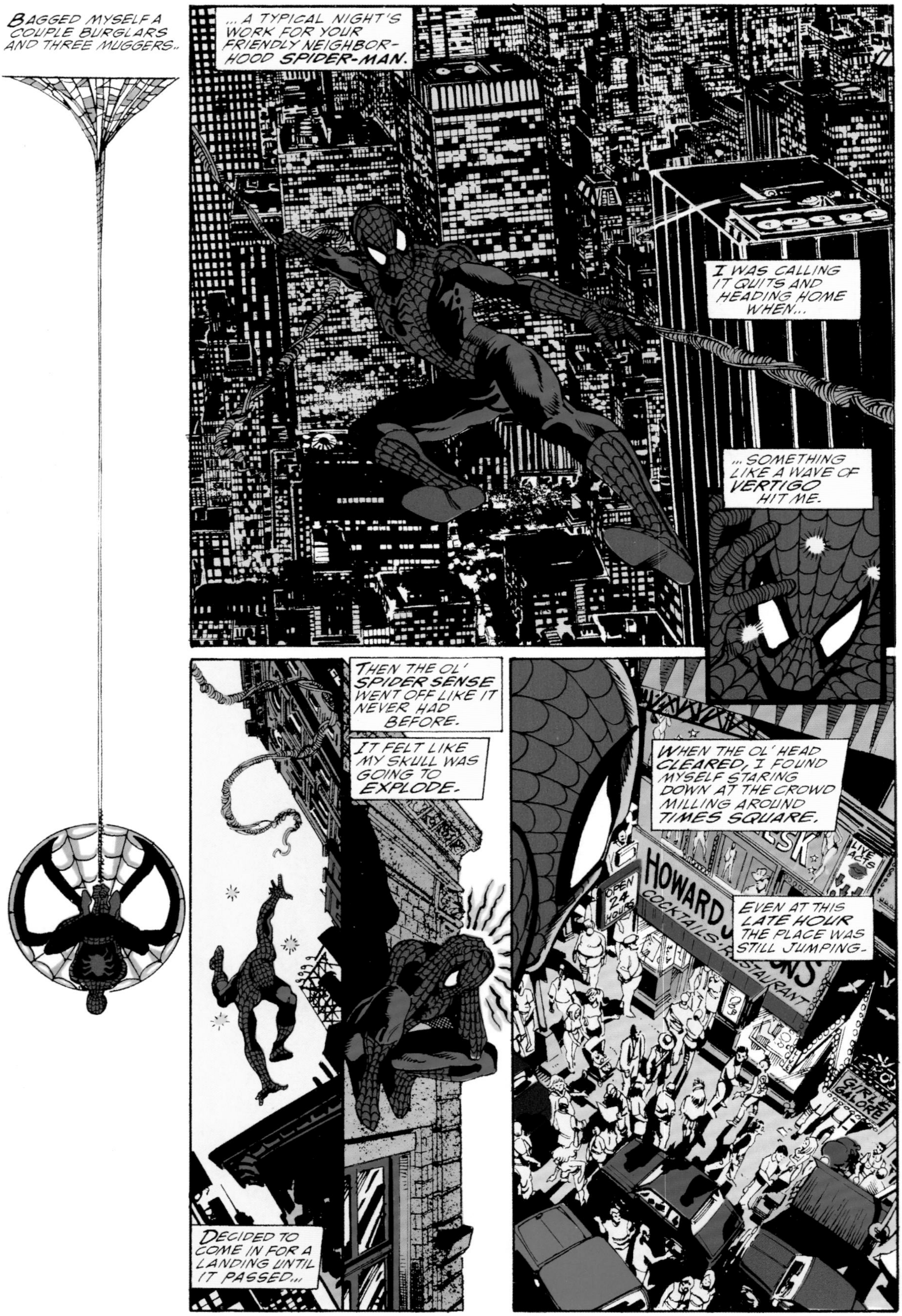
BAGGED MYSELF A COUPLE BURGLARS AND THREE MUGGERS..
...A TYPICAL NIGHT'S WORK FOR YOUR FRIENDLY NEIGHBOR-HOOD SPIDER-MAN.
I WAS CALLING IT QUITS AND HEADING HOME WHEN...
...SOMETHING LIKE A WAVE OF VERTIGO HIT ME.
THEN THE OL' SPIDER SENSE WENT OFF LIKE IT NEVER HAD BEFORE.
IT FELT LIKE MY SKULL WAS GOING TO EXPLODE.
DECIDED TO COME IN FOR A LANDING UNTIL IT PASSED...
WHEN THE OL' HEAD CLEARED, I FOUND MYSELF STARING DOWN AT THE CROWD MILLING AROUND TIMES SQUARE.
LIVE ACTS
HOWARD J
OPEN 24 HOURS
COCKTAILS
EVEN AT THIS LATE HOUR THE PLACE WAS STILL JUMPING-
GIRLS GALORE

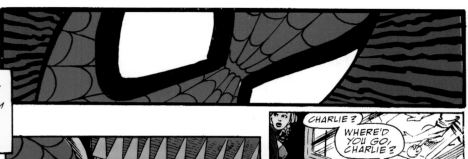

WHY COULDN'T I HAVE KEPT MY EYES SHUT JUST A *FEW SECONDS* LONGER?

BUT I DIDN'T, SO I ENDED UP WITNESSING A *SIGHT* THAT I'M SURE WILL *HAUNT MY DREAMS* FOR YEARS TO COME.

THERE WAS NO *OMINOUS WARNING:* NOT ONE STORM CLOUD, HEAVENLY VOICE NOR ANY OF THE KIND OF THINGS YOU'D THINK WOULD ACCOMPANY SUCH A *CATACLYSMIC EVENT.*

NOTHING.

CHARLIE? WHERE'D YOU GO, CHARLIE?

JUST *HALF* THE PEOPLE DOWN IN THE SQUARE MERELY *VANISHED.*

AT FIRST I THOUGHT I WAS *LOSING MY MIND,* FLIPPING OUT.

MY BABY?!

BUT THEN THE STREET CROWD CONFIRMED THE *REALITY* OF THIS *NIGHTMARE.*

WHO OR WHAT COULD HAVE DONE THIS?

HAD ONLY *TIMES SQUARE* BEEN AFFECTED?

HOWARD ROAST DUCK MMMM

OR WAS THIS HAPPENING ALL OVER THE CITY?

THEN IT HIT ME.

MARY JANE!

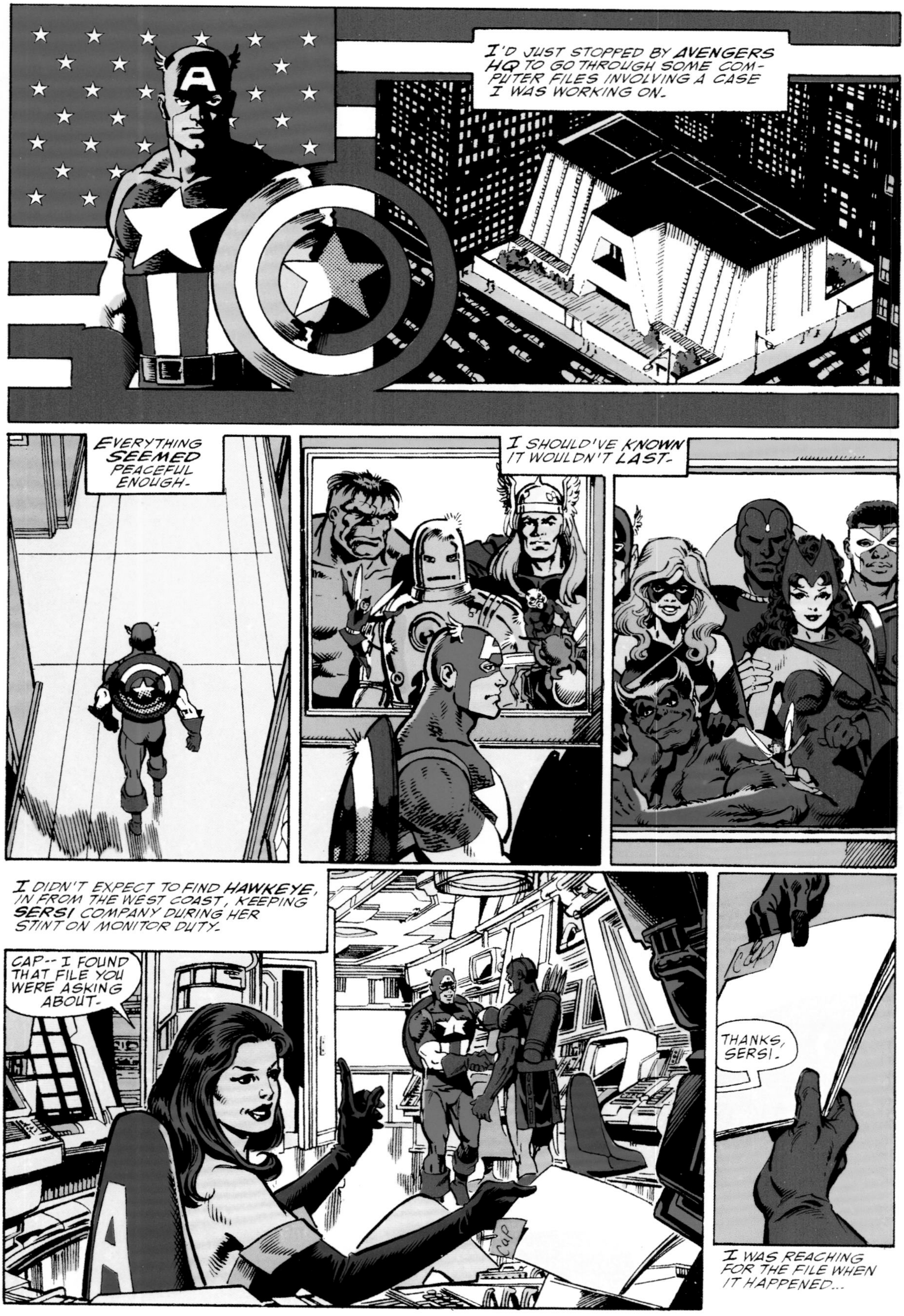
I'D JUST STOPPED BY AVENGERS HQ TO GO THROUGH SOME COMPUTER FILES INVOLVING A CASE I WAS WORKING ON.
EVERYTHING SEEMED PEACEFUL ENOUGH.
I SHOULD'VE KNOWN IT WOULDN'T LAST.
I DIDN'T EXPECT TO FIND HAWKEYE, IN FROM THE WEST COAST, KEEPING SERSI COMPANY DURING HER STINT ON MONITOR DUTY.
CAP-- I FOUND THAT FILE YOU WERE ASKING ABOUT.
CAP
THANKS, SERSI.
CAP
I WAS REACHING FOR THE FILE WHEN IT HAPPENED...

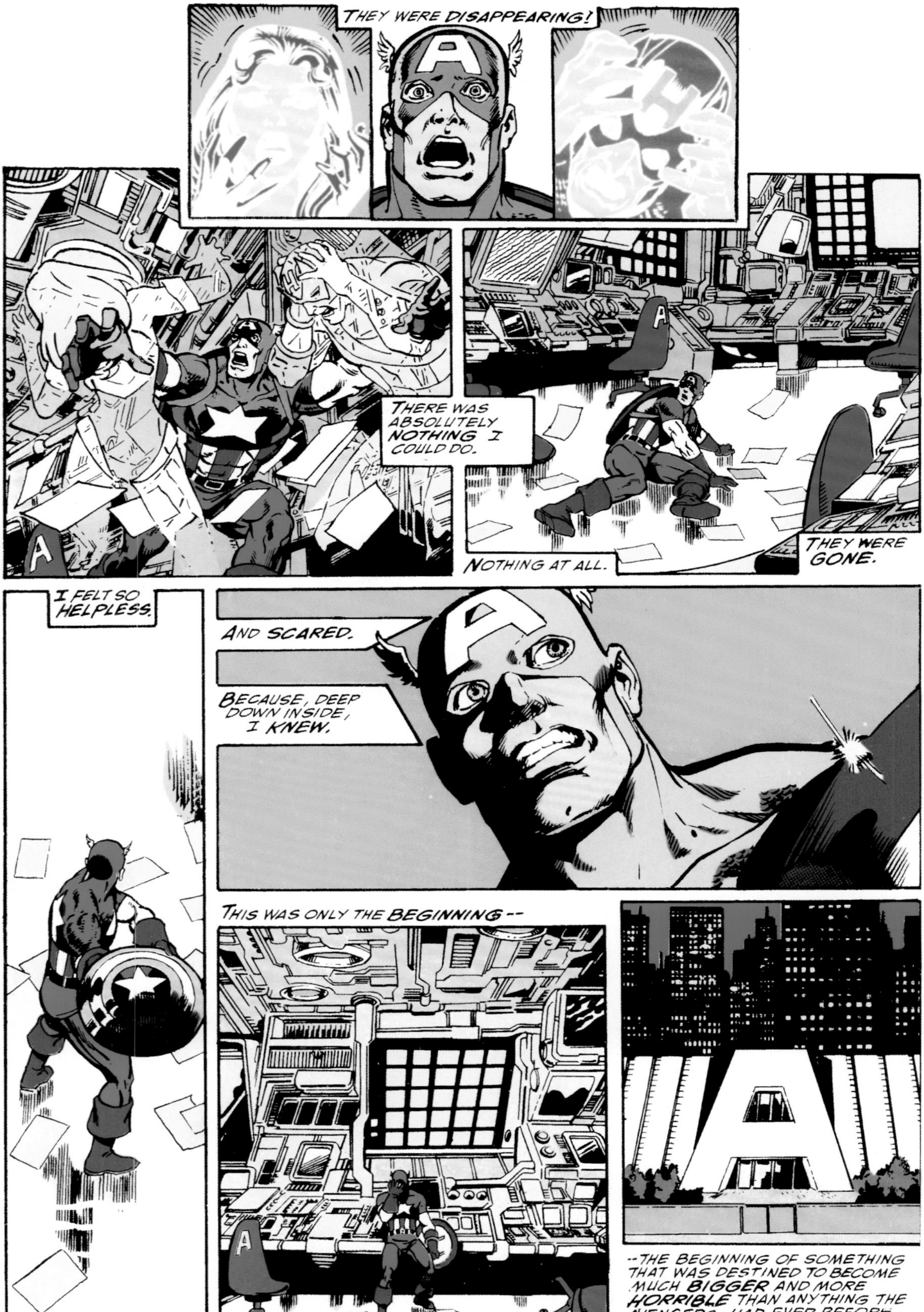
THEY WERE DISAPPEARING!
THERE WAS ABSOLUTELY NOTHING I COULD DO.
NOTHING AT ALL.
THEY WERE GONE.
I FELT SO HELPLESS.
AND SCARED.
BECAUSE, DEEP DOWN INSIDE, I KNEW.
THIS WAS ONLY THE BEGINNING --
--THE BEGINNING OF SOMETHING THAT WAS DESTINED TO BECOME MUCH BIGGER AND MORE HORRIBLE THAN ANYTHING THE AVENGERS HAD EVER BEFORE FACED.

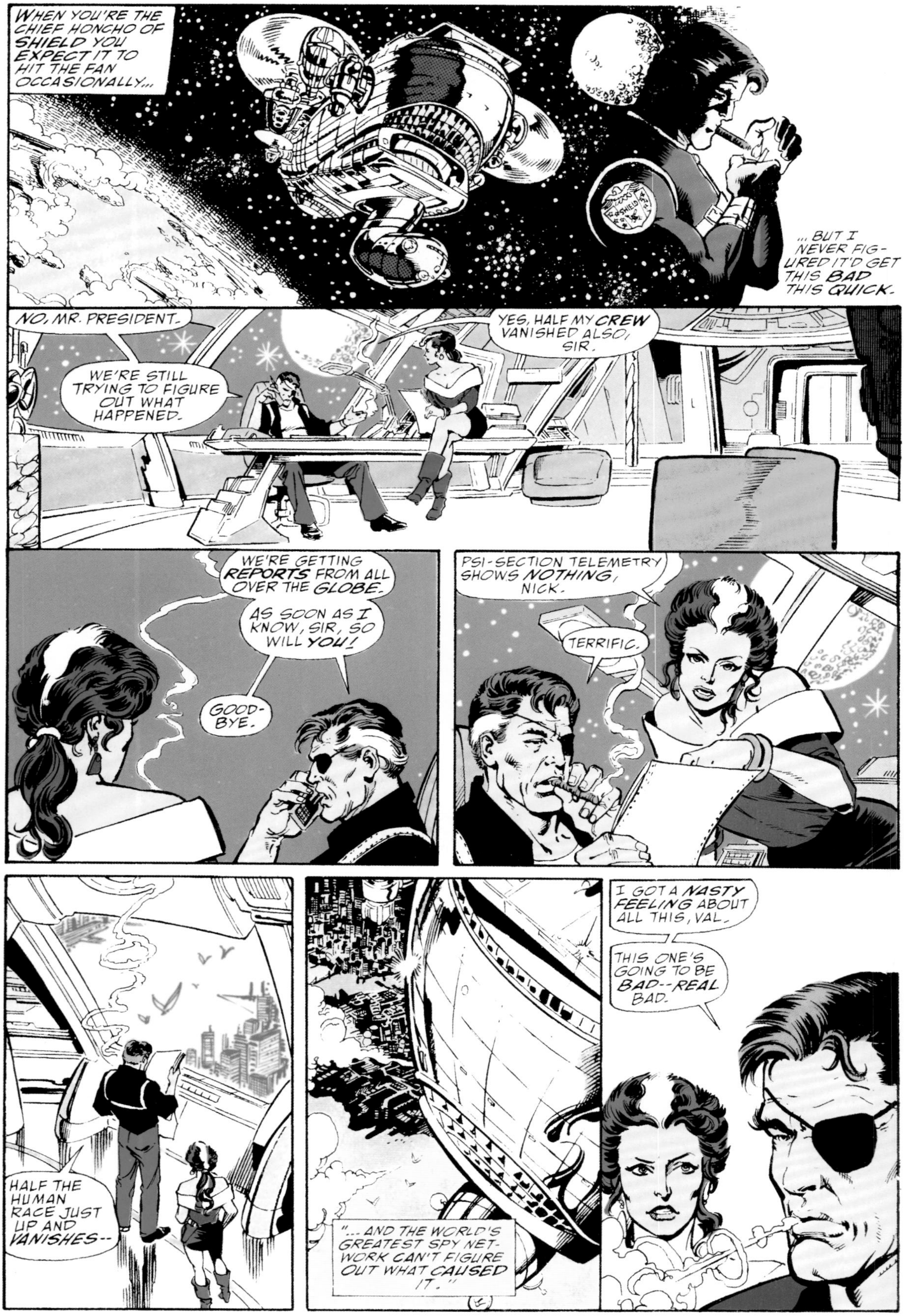
WHEN YOU'RE THE CHIEF HONCHO OF SHIELD YOU EXPECT IT TO HIT THE FAN OCCASIONALLY...
...BUT I NEVER FIGURED IT'D GET THIS BAD THIS QUICK.
NO, MR. PRESIDENT.
WE'RE STILL TRYING TO FIGURE OUT WHAT HAPPENED.
YES, HALF MY CREW VANISHED ALSO, SIR.
WE'RE GETTING REPORTS FROM ALL OVER THE GLOBE.
AS SOON AS I KNOW, SIR, SO WILL YOU!
GOOD-BYE.
PSI-SECTION TELEMETRY SHOWS NOTHING, NICK.
TERRIFIC.
HALF THE HUMAN RACE JUST UP AND VANISHES--
"...AND THE WORLD'S GREATEST SPY NET-WORK CAN'T FIGURE OUT WHAT CAUSED IT."
I GOT A NASTY FEELING ABOUT ALL THIS, VAL.
THIS ONE'S GOING TO BE BAD--REAL BAD.

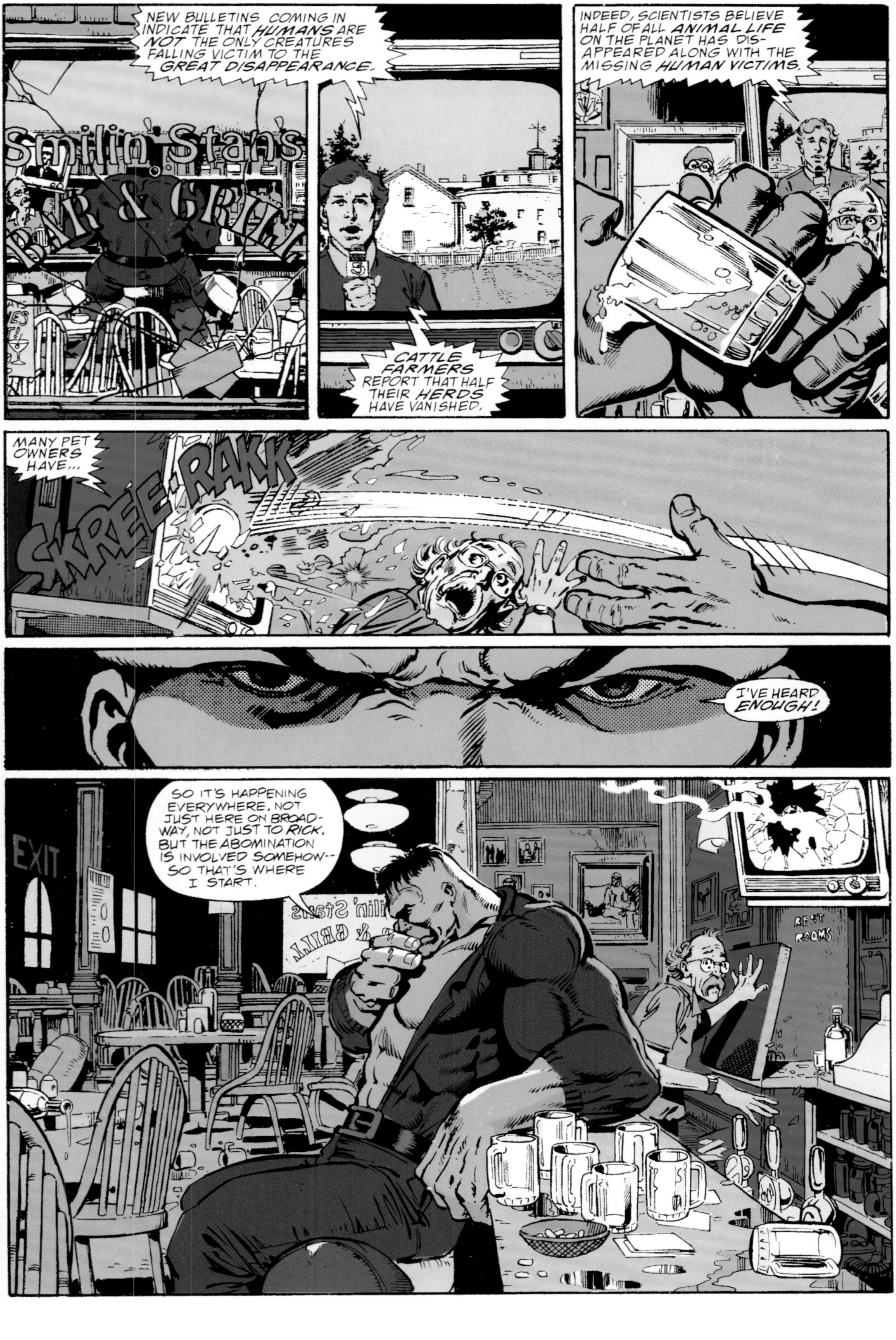
NEW BULLETINS COMING IN INDICATE THAT HUMANS ARE NOT THE ONLY CREATURES FALLING VICTIM TO THE GREAT DISAPPEARANCE.
Smilin' Stans
BAR & GRILL
CATTLE FARMERS REPORT THAT HALF THEIR HERDS HAVE VANISHED.
INDEED, SCIENTISTS BELIEVE HALF OF ALL ANIMAL LIFE ON THE PLANET HAS DISAPPEARED ALONG WITH THE MISSING HUMAN VICTIMS.
MANY PET OWNERS HAVE...
SKREE-RAKK
I'VE HEARD ENOUGH!
SO IT'S HAPPENING EVERYWHERE. NOT JUST HERE ON BROADWAY, NOT JUST TO RICK. BUT THE ABOMINATION IS INVOLVED SOMEHOW-- SO THAT'S WHERE I START.
EXIT
REST ROOMS

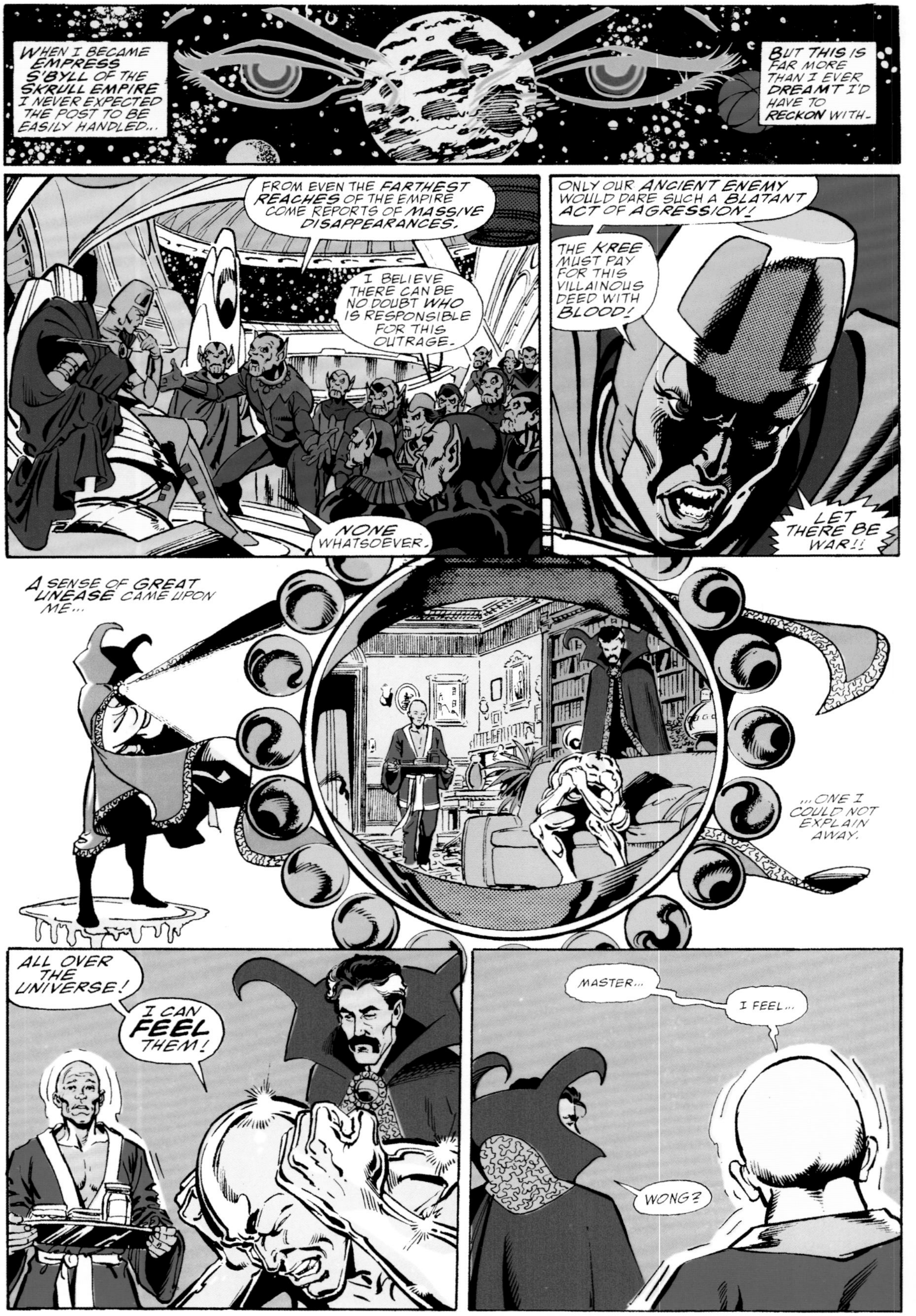

WHEN I BECAME EMPRESS S'BYLL OF THE SKRULL EMPIRE I NEVER EXPECTED THE POST TO BE EASILY HANDLED...
BUT THIS IS FAR MORE THAN I EVER DREAMT I'D HAVE TO RECKON WITH-
FROM EVEN THE FARTHEST REACHES OF THE EMPIRE COME REPORTS OF MASSIVE DISAPPEARANCES.
I BELIEVE THERE CAN BE NO DOUBT WHO IS RESPONSIBLE FOR THIS OUTRAGE.
NONE WHATSOEVER.
ONLY OUR ANCIENT ENEMY WOULD DARE SUCH A BLATANT ACT OF AGRESSION!
THE KREE MUST PAY FOR THIS VILLAINOUS DEED WITH BLOOD!
LET THERE BE WAR!!
A SENSE OF GREAT UNEASE CAME UPON ME...
...ONE I COULD NOT EXPLAIN AWAY.
ALL OVER THE UNIVERSE!
I CAN FEEL THEM!
MASTER...
I FEEL...
WONG?

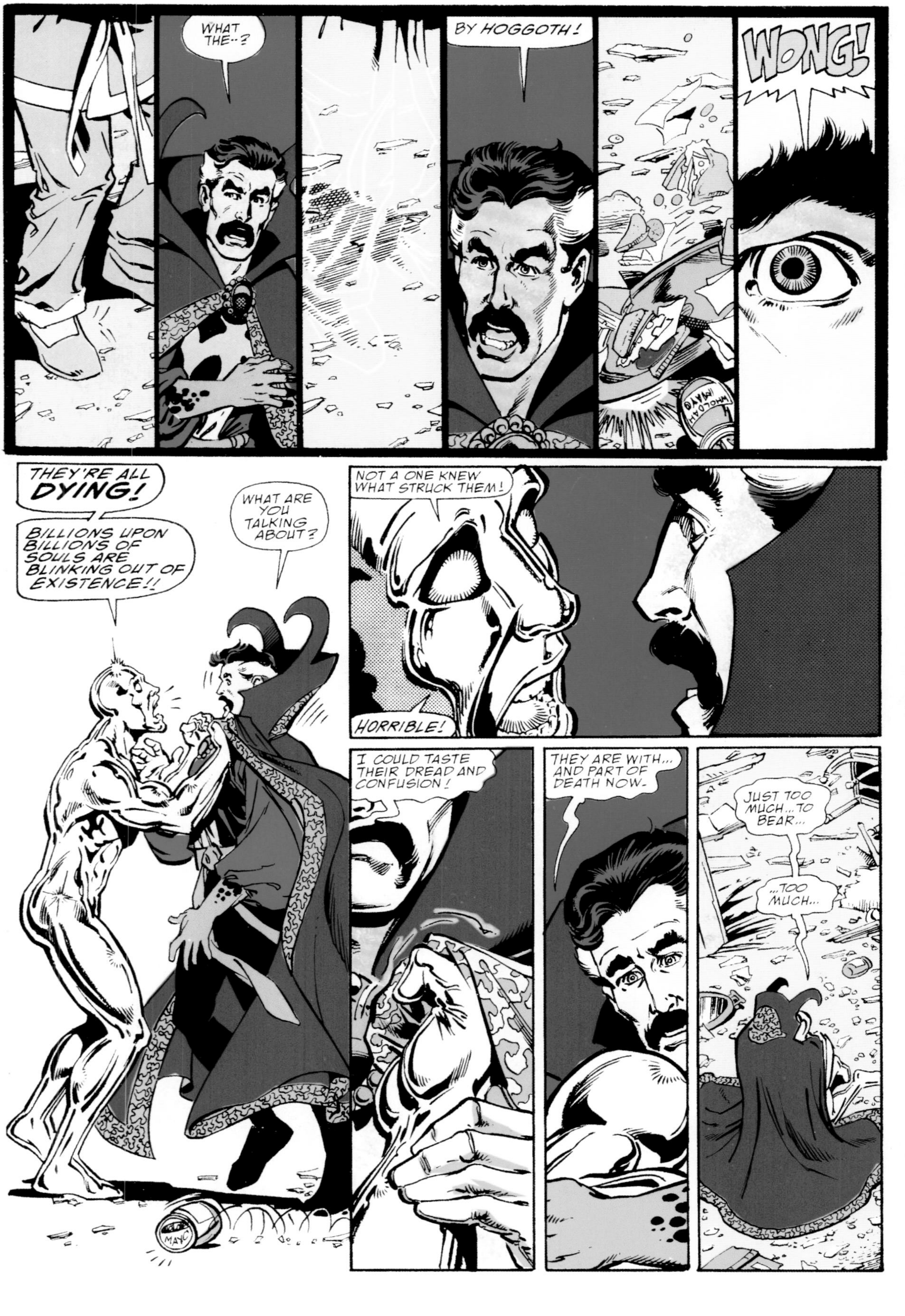
WHAT THE--?
BY HOGGOTH!
WONG!
THEY'RE ALL DYING!
BILLIONS UPON BILLIONS OF SOULS ARE BLINKING OUT OF EXISTENCE!!
WHAT ARE YOU TALKING ABOUT?
NOT A ONE KNEW WHAT STRUCK THEM!
HORRIBLE!
I COULD TASTE THEIR DREAD AND CONFUSION!
THEY ARE WITH... AND PART OF DEATH NOW...
JUST TOO MUCH... TO BEAR...
...TOO MUCH...

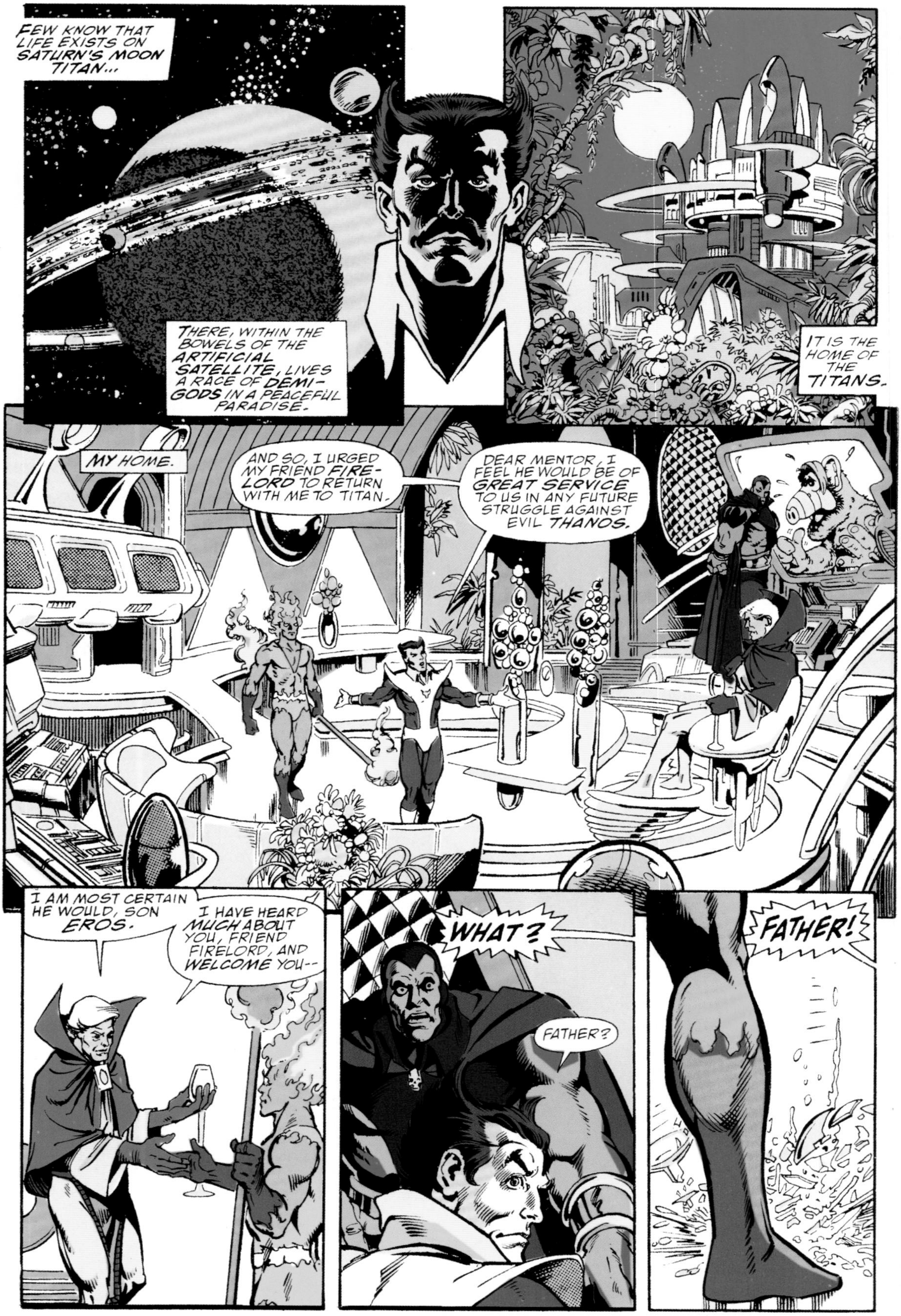

FEW KNOW THAT LIFE EXISTS ON SATURN'S MOON TITAN...
THERE, WITHIN THE BOWELS OF THE ARTIFICIAL SATELLITE, LIVES A RACE OF DEMI-GODS IN A PEACEFUL PARADISE.
IT IS THE HOME OF THE TITANS.
MY HOME.
AND SO, I URGED MY FRIEND FIRE-LORD TO RETURN WITH ME TO TITAN.
DEAR MENTOR, I FEEL HE WOULD BE OF GREAT SERVICE TO US IN ANY FUTURE STRUGGLE AGAINST EVIL THANOS.
I AM MOST CERTAIN HE WOULD, SON EROS.
I HAVE HEARD MUCH ABOUT YOU, FRIEND FIRELORD, AND WELCOME YOU--
WHAT?
FATHER?
FATHER!

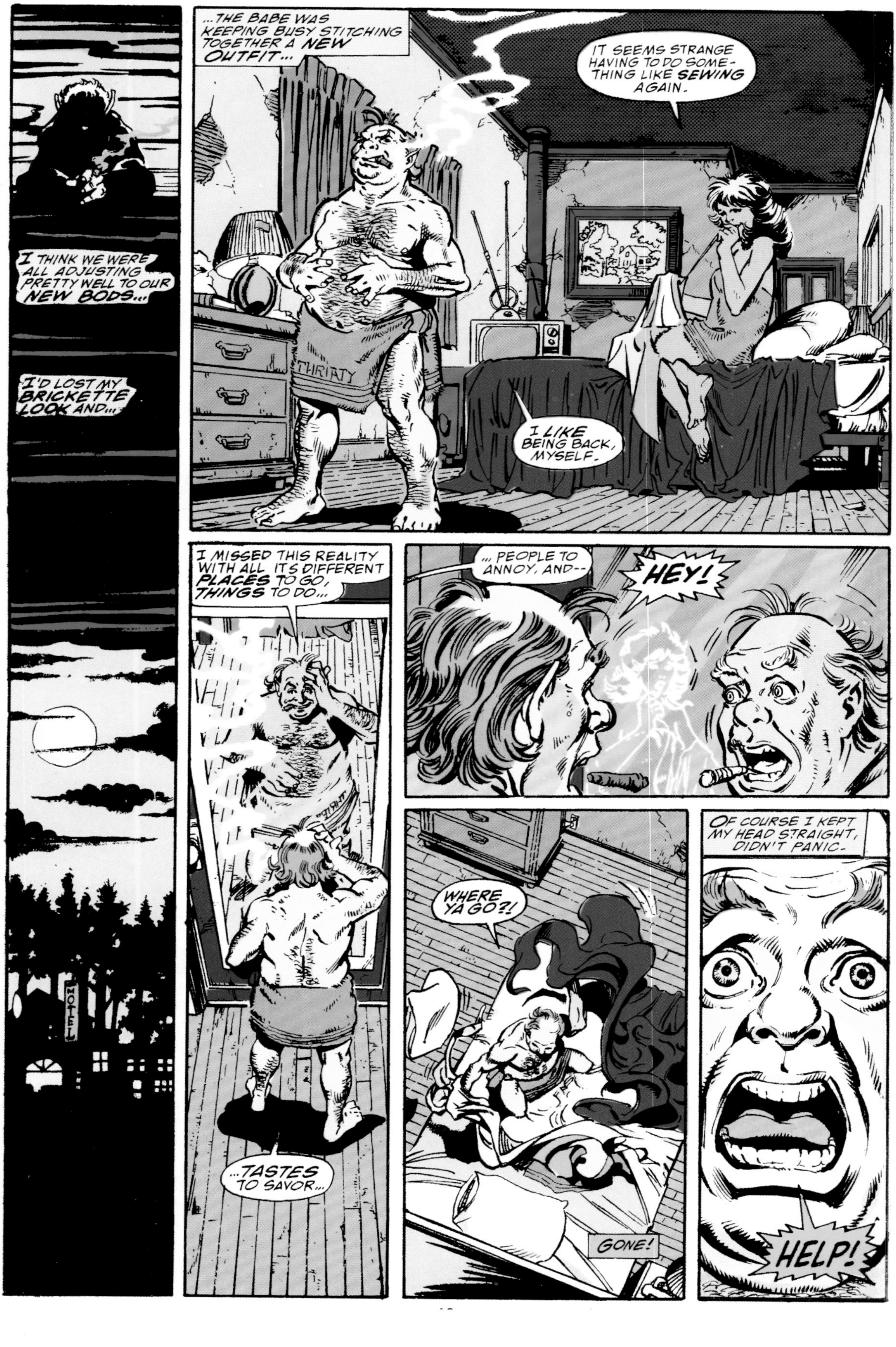
I THINK WE WERE ALL ADJUSTING PRETTY WELL TO OUR NEW BODS...
I'D LOST MY BRICKETTE LOOK AND...
MOTEL
...THE BABE WAS KEEPING BUSY STITCHING TOGETHER A NEW OUTFIT...
IT SEEMS STRANGE HAVING TO DO SOME-THING LIKE SEWING AGAIN.
I LIKE BEING BACK, MYSELF.
I MISSED THIS REALITY WITH ALL ITS DIFFERENT PLACES TO GO, THINGS TO DO...
...TASTES TO SAVOR...
...PEOPLE TO ANNOY, AND--
HEY!
WHERE YA GO?!
GONE!
OF COURSE I KEPT MY HEAD STRAIGHT, DIDN'T PANIC-
HELP!

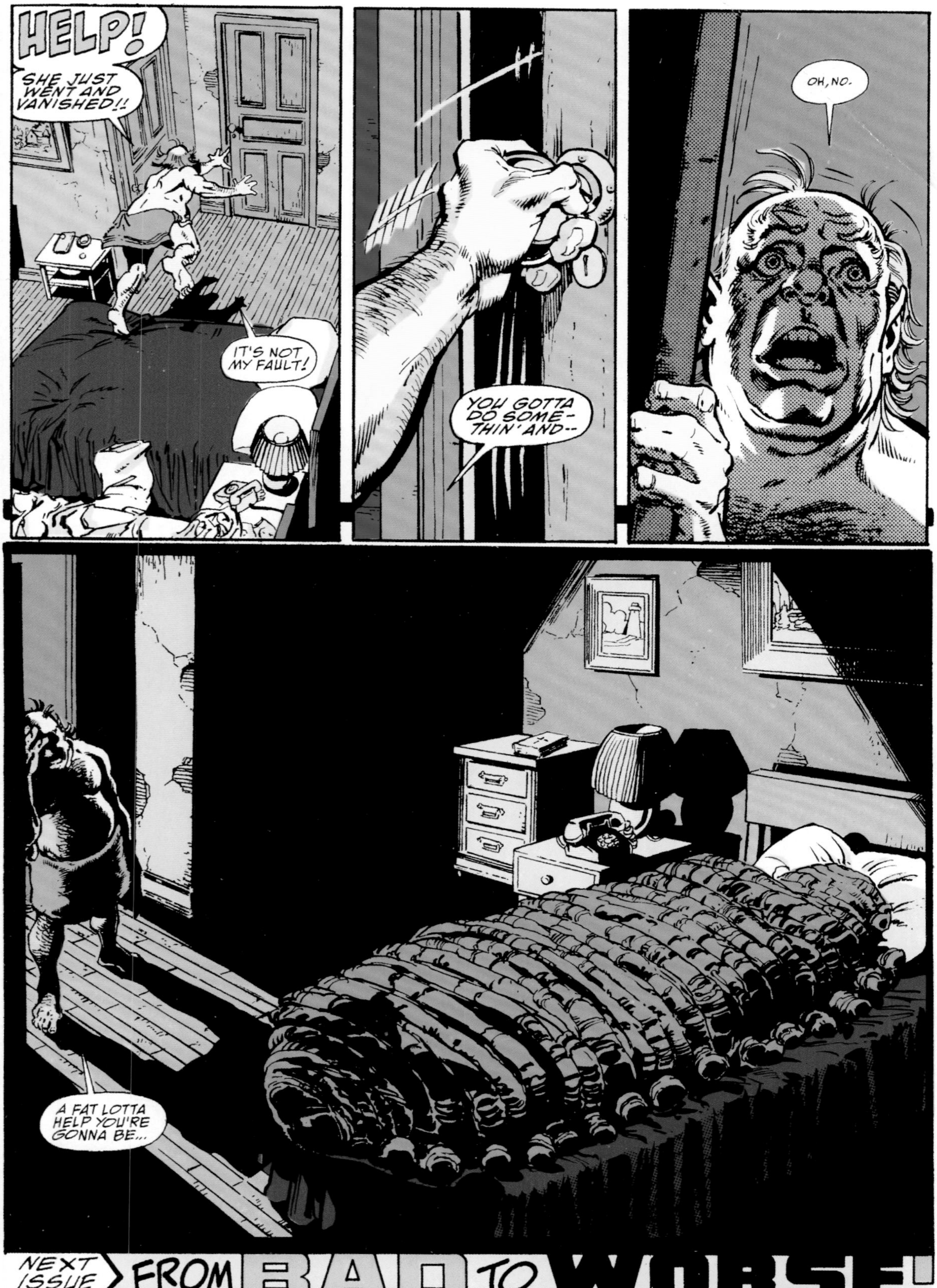
HELP!
SHE JUST WENT AND VANISHED!!
IT'S NOT MY FAULT!
YOU GOTTA DO SOME-THIN' AND--
OH, NO.
A FAT LOTTA HELP YOU'RE GONNA BE...
NEXT ISSUE
FROM BAD TO WORSE!

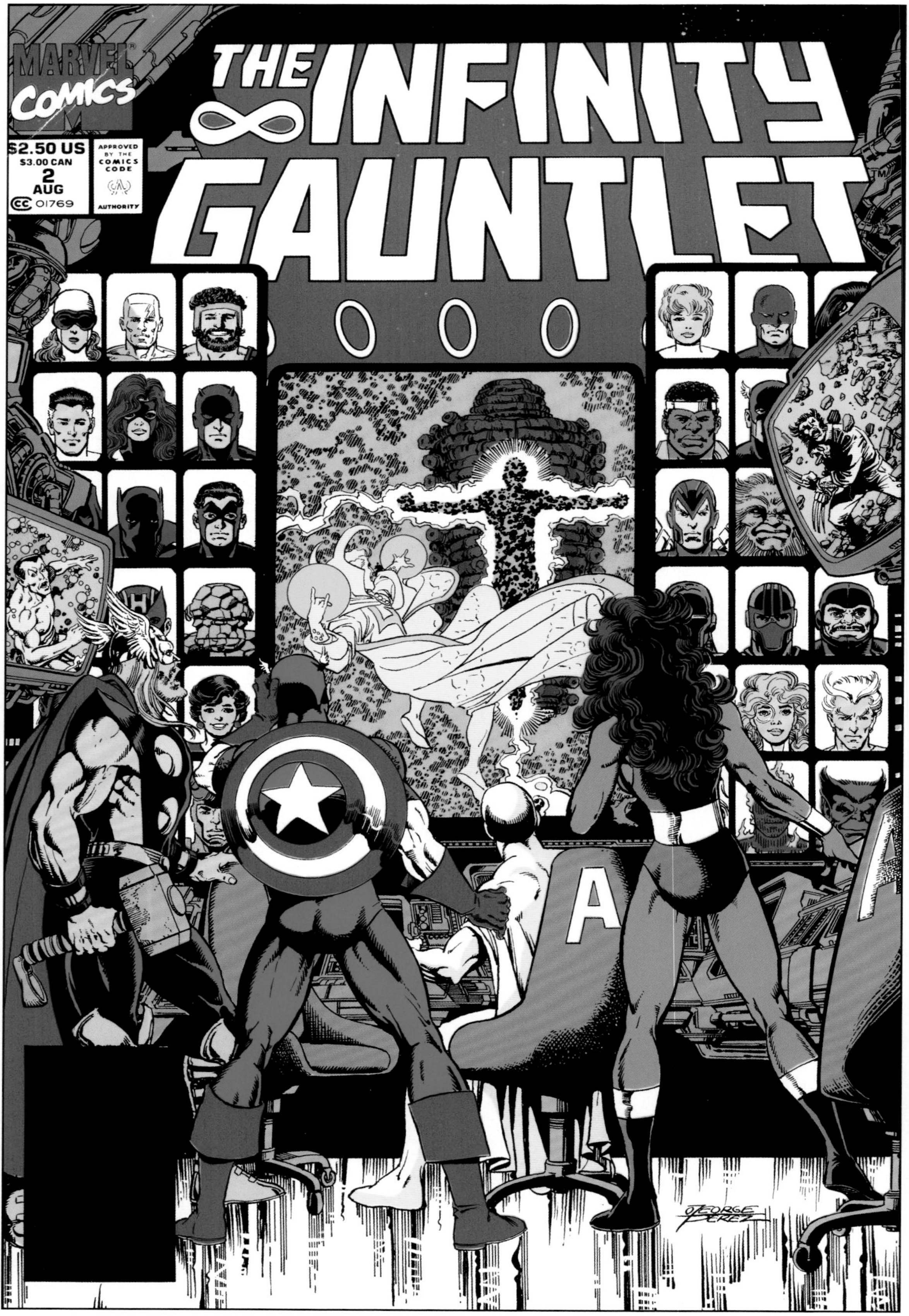
MARVEL COMICS
THE INFINITY GAUNTLET
$2.50 US
$3.00 CAN
2
AUG
CC 01769
APPROVED BY THE COMICS CODE AUTHORITY
A
A
GEORGE PEREZ

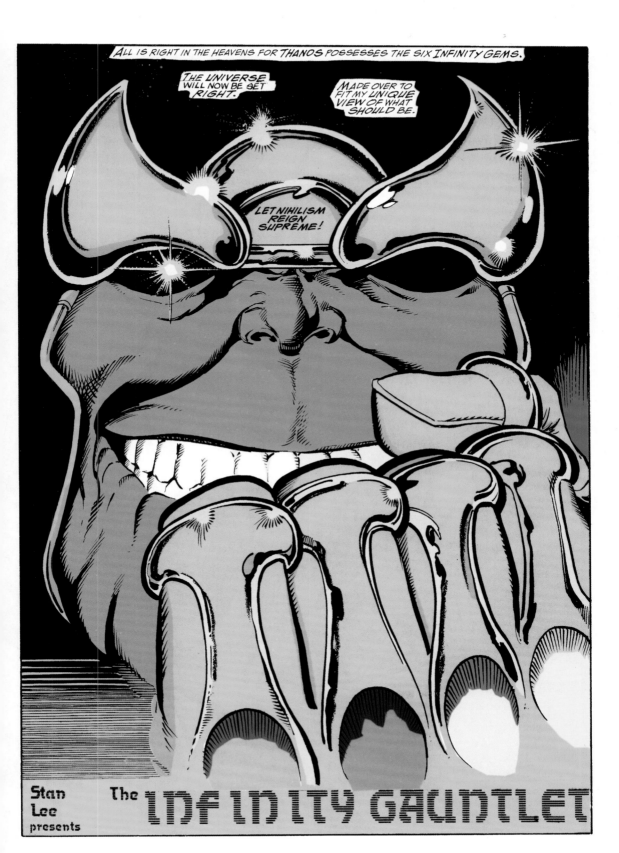

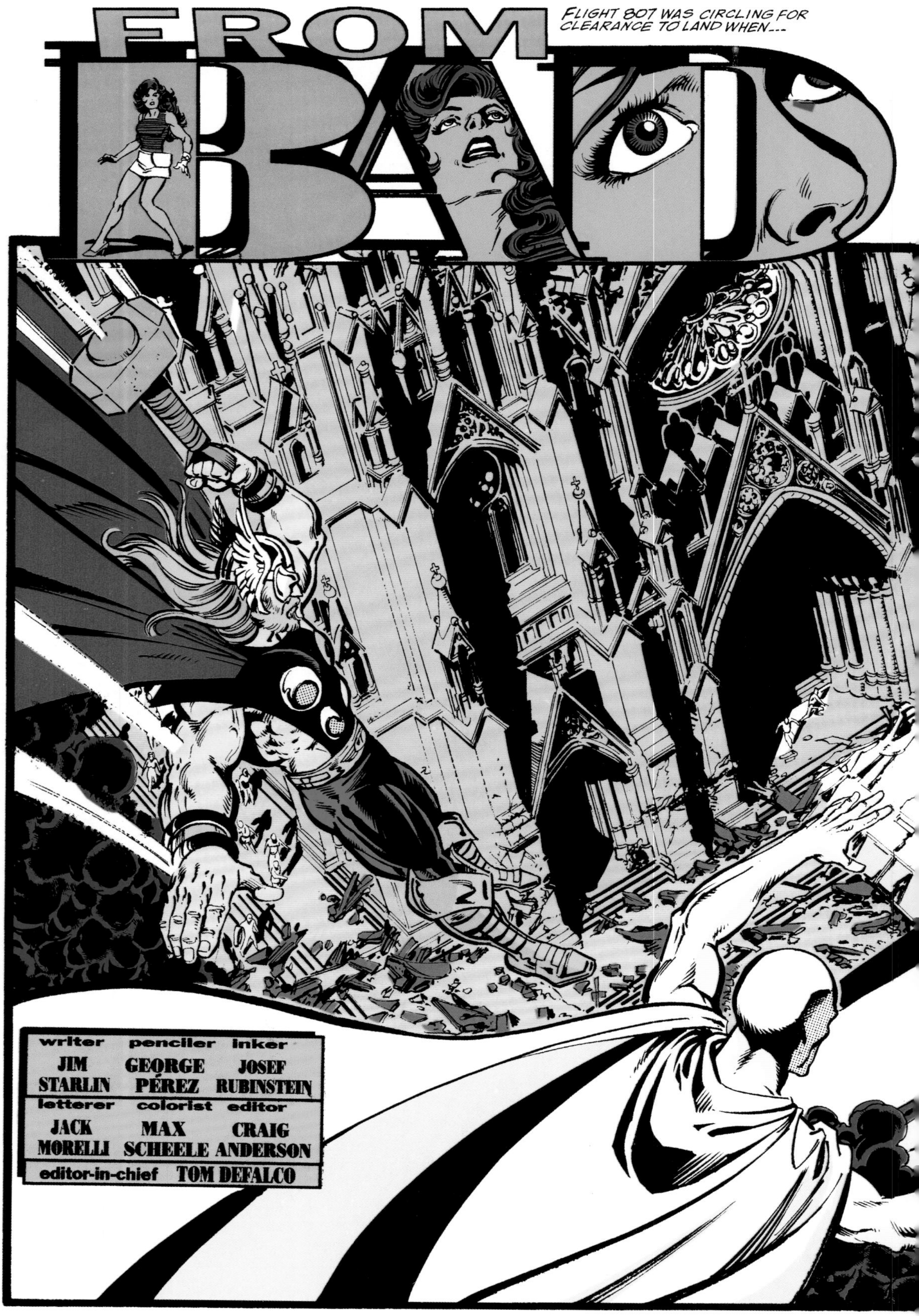
FROM BAD
FLIGHT 807 WAS CIRCLING FOR CLEARANCE TO LAND WHEN---
writer JIM STARLIN
penciler GEORGE PÉREZ
inker JOSEF RUBINSTEIN
letterer JACK MORELLI
colorist MAX SCHEELE
editor CRAIG ANDERSON
editor-in-chief TOM DEFALCO

FIGURE *EPOCH* MIGHT HAVE SOME ANSWERS...

WHEN THE FIRST REPORTS OF THE *GREAT DISAPPEARANCE* COME IN, I'M IN MY OFFICE AT *VAUGHN SECURITY SYSTEMS,* WONDERING WHAT I CAN DO TO HELP.

...BUT BEFORE I CAN ASK HIM...

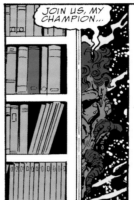

JOIN US, MY CHAMPION...

EPOCH?

WHO'S THAT IN THERE WITH YOU?

ONE WHO HAS MADE CLEAR TO ME JUST HOW *PERILOUS* THIS *UNIVERSE'S* CURRENT SITUATION *IS!*

AND SO...

...THE COSMIC GUARDIAN, **QUASAR,** MUST NOW UNDERTAKE A *NEW* MISSION!

WE'VE AN *ASTRAL* RENDEZVOUS TO ARRANGE...!

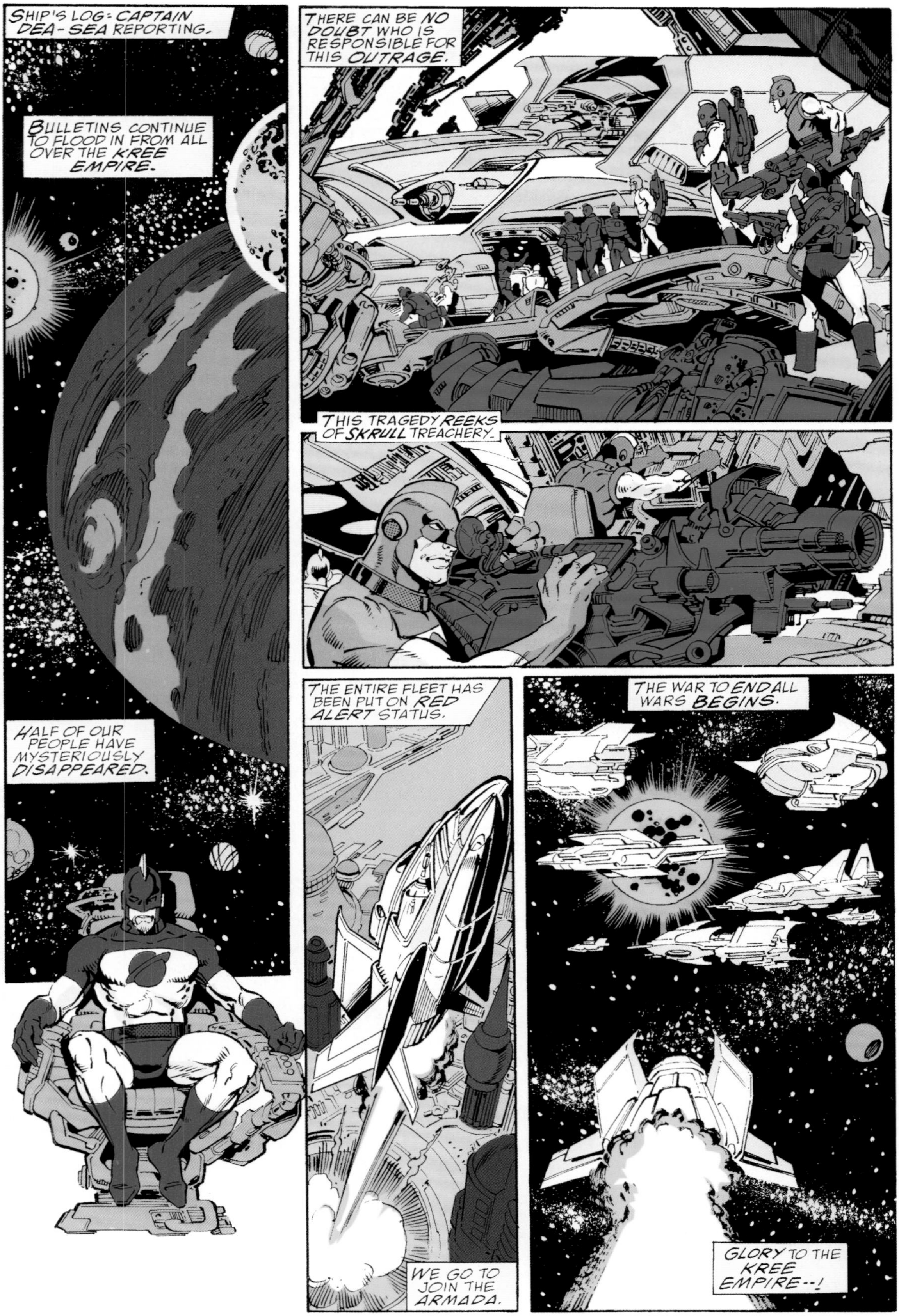
SHIP'S LOG: CAPTAIN DEA-SEA REPORTING.
BULLETINS CONTINUE TO FLOOD IN FROM ALL OVER THE KREE EMPIRE.
HALF OF OUR PEOPLE HAVE MYSTERIOUSLY DISAPPEARED.
THERE CAN BE NO DOUBT WHO IS RESPONSIBLE FOR THIS OUTRAGE.
THIS TRAGEDY REEKS OF SKRULL TREACHERY.
THE ENTIRE FLEET HAS BEEN PUT ON RED ALERT STATUS.
WE GO TO JOIN THE ARMADA.
THE WAR TO END ALL WARS BEGINS.
GLORY TO THE KREE EMPIRE--!

THE CONDITION OF MY UNEXPECTED *HOUSE GUEST* WAS SUCH I THOUGHT IT PRUDENT TO SEEK AN *OUTSIDE CONSULTATION* ON THE MATTER.

FORTUNATELY *DR. HENRY PYM* HAPPENED TO BE IN TOWN.

THE SURFER SEEMS TO BE REGAINING HIS *STRENGTH* JUST BY LYING IN THE *SUN.*

WITH HIS *ALIEN PHYSIOLOGY,* IT WAS THE BEST *REMEDY* I COULD COME UP WITH.

WELL, IT APPEARS TO BE *WORKING.*

I MUST BE GOING NOW, STEPHEN.

I SHOULD BE WITH THE *WEST COAST AVENGERS,* WHAT WITH THIS GREAT DISAPPEARANCE GOING DOWN.

I'LL BRIEF THEM ON WHAT YOU'VE TOLD ME.

YOU'D BEST CONTACT THE *ORIGINAL AVENGERS* DIRECTLY.

OF... OF COURSE.

OF... COURSE...

MASTER?

MASTER--?

IS SOMETHING *WRONG?*

"*SPEAK TO ME!*"

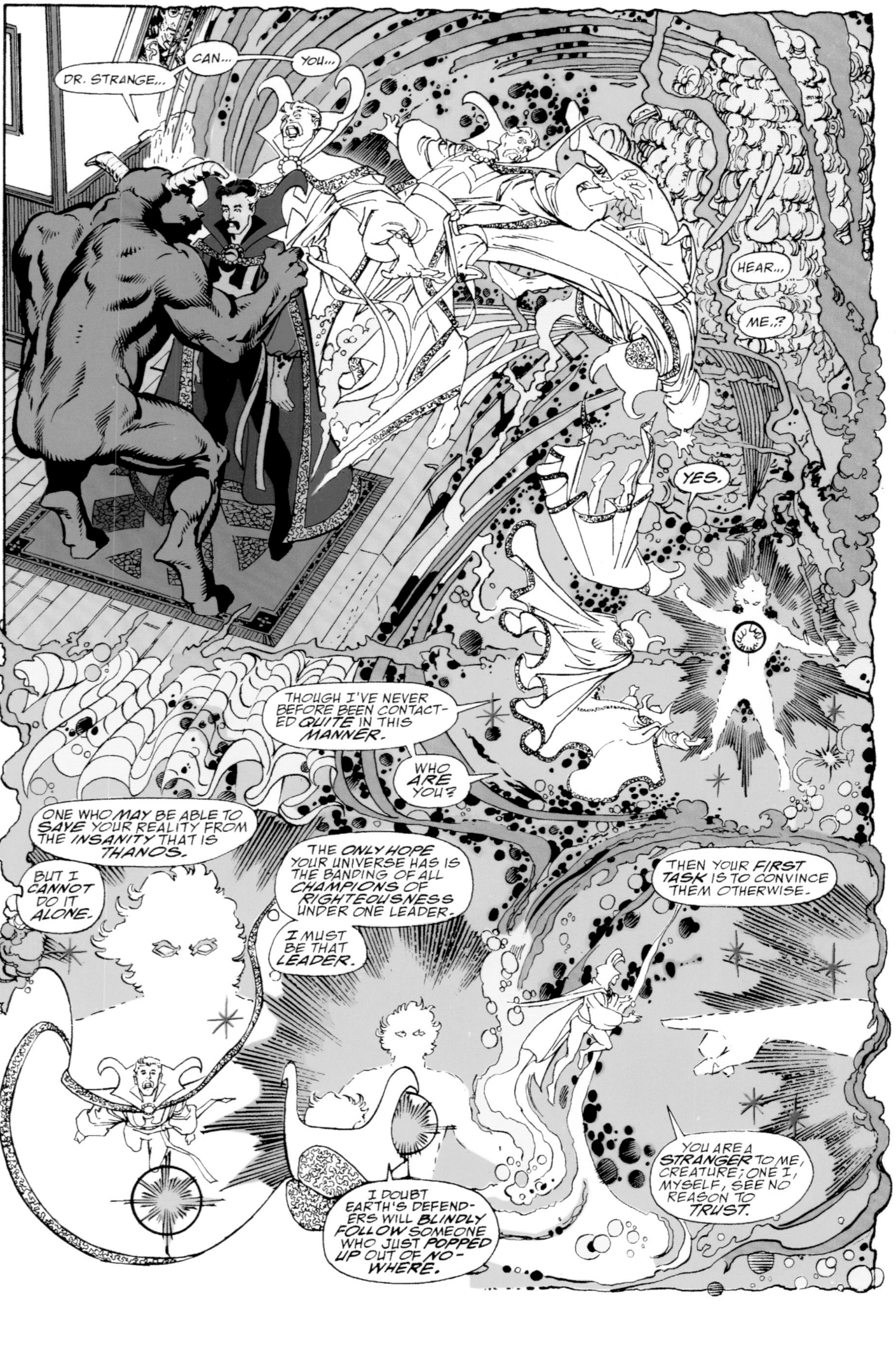
DR. STRANGE...
CAN...
YOU...
HEAR...
ME..?
YES.
THOUGH I'VE NEVER BEFORE BEEN CONTACTED QUITE IN THIS MANNER.
WHO ARE YOU?
ONE WHO MAY BE ABLE TO SAVE YOUR REALITY FROM THE INSANITY THAT IS THANOS.
BUT I CANNOT DO IT ALONE.
THE ONLY HOPE YOUR UNIVERSE HAS IS THE BANDING OF ALL CHAMPIONS OF RIGHTEOUSNESS UNDER ONE LEADER.
I MUST BE THAT LEADER.
I DOUBT EARTH'S DEFENDERS WILL BLINDLY FOLLOW SOMEONE WHO JUST POPPED UP OUT OF NOWHERE.
THEN YOUR FIRST TASK IS TO CONVINCE THEM OTHERWISE.
YOU ARE A STRANGER TO ME, CREATURE; ONE I, MYSELF, SEE NO REASON TO TRUST.

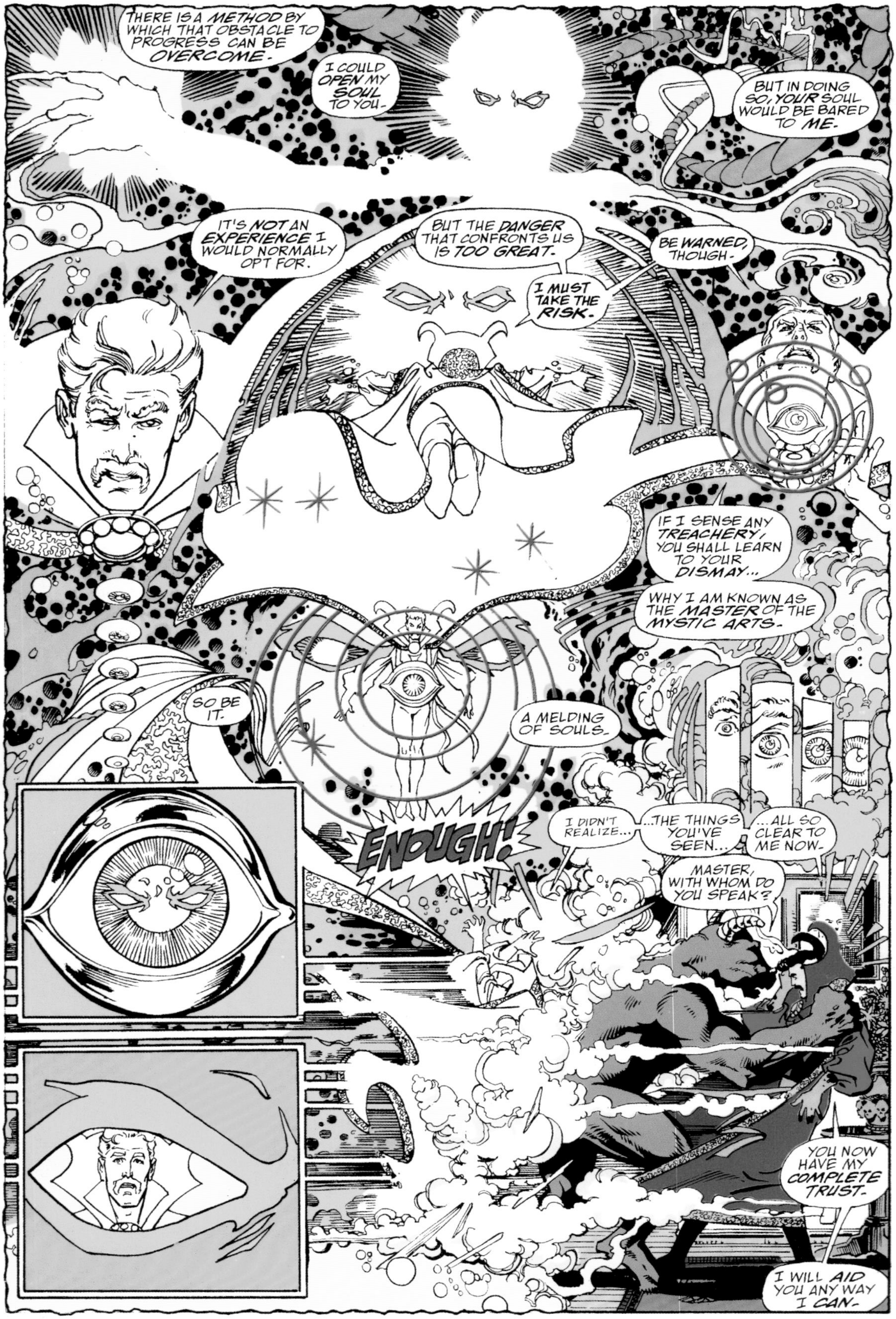
THERE IS A METHOD BY WHICH THAT OBSTACLE TO PROGRESS CAN BE OVERCOME-
I COULD OPEN MY SOUL TO YOU-
BUT IN DOING SO, YOUR SOUL WOULD BE BARED TO ME-
IT'S NOT AN EXPERIENCE I WOULD NORMALLY OPT FOR.
BUT THE DANGER THAT CONFRONTS US IS TOO GREAT-
I MUST TAKE THE RISK-
BE WARNED, THOUGH-
IF I SENSE ANY TREACHERY, YOU SHALL LEARN TO YOUR DISMAY...
WHY I AM KNOWN AS THE MASTER OF THE MYSTIC ARTS-
SO BE IT.
A MELDING OF SOULS-
ENOUGH!
I DIDN'T REALIZE...
...THE THINGS YOU'VE SEEN...
...ALL SO CLEAR TO ME NOW-
MASTER, WITH WHOM DO YOU SPEAK?
YOU NOW HAVE MY COMPLETE TRUST-
I WILL AID YOU ANY WAY I CAN-

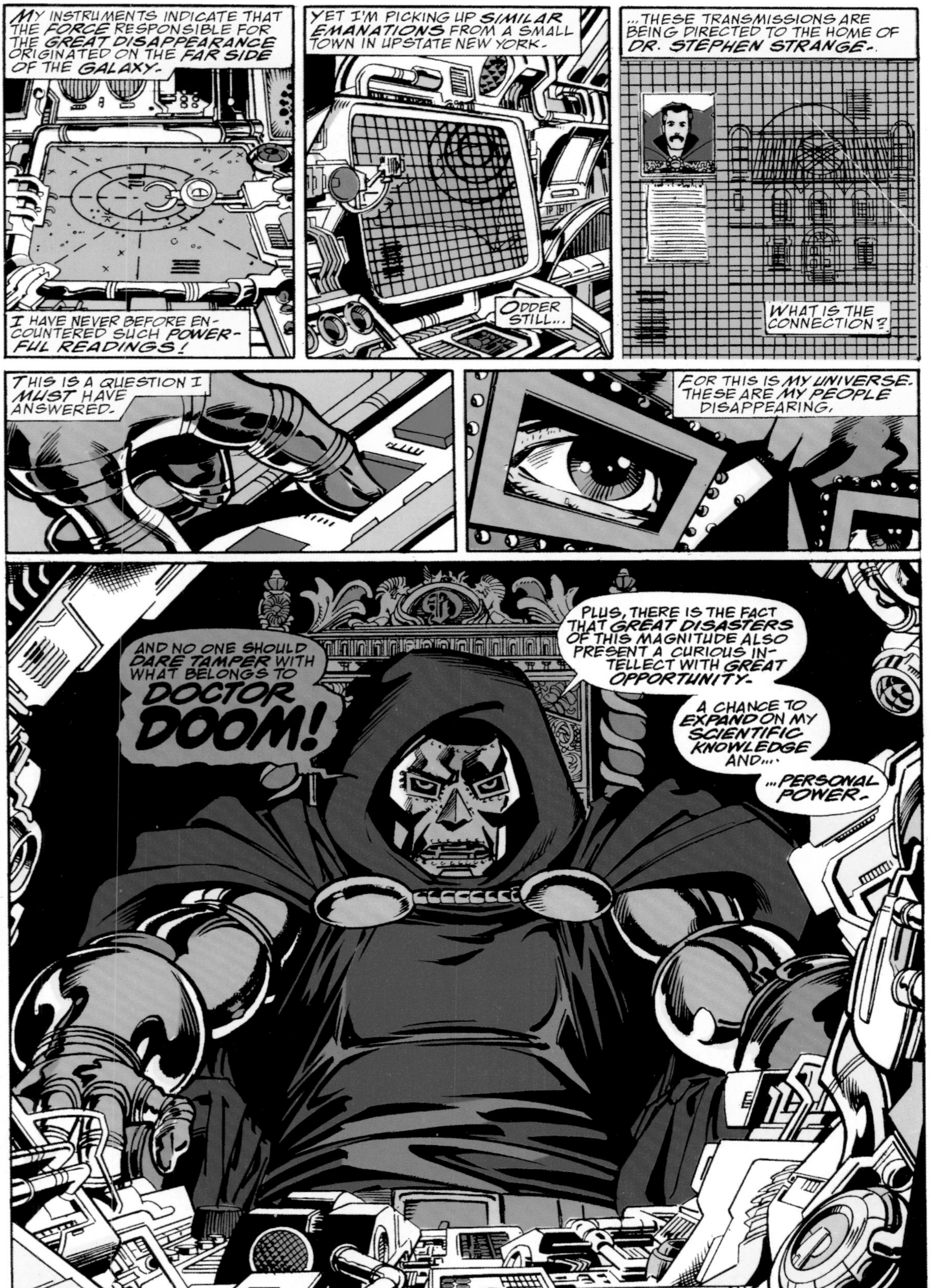
MY INSTRUMENTS INDICATE THAT THE FORCE RESPONSIBLE FOR THE GREAT DISAPPEARANCE ORIGINATED ON THE FAR SIDE OF THE GALAXY.
I HAVE NEVER BEFORE ENCOUNTERED SUCH POWERFUL READINGS!
YET I'M PICKING UP SIMILAR EMANATIONS FROM A SMALL TOWN IN UPSTATE NEW YORK.
ODDER STILL...
...THESE TRANSMISSIONS ARE BEING DIRECTED TO THE HOME OF DR. STEPHEN STRANGE.
WHAT IS THE CONNECTION?
THIS IS A QUESTION I MUST HAVE ANSWERED.
FOR THIS IS MY UNIVERSE. THESE ARE MY PEOPLE DISAPPEARING,
AND NO ONE SHOULD DARE TAMPER WITH WHAT BELONGS TO DOCTOR DOOM!
PLUS, THERE IS THE FACT THAT GREAT DISASTERS OF THIS MAGNITUDE ALSO PRESENT A CURIOUS INTELLECT WITH GREAT OPPORTUNITY.
A CHANCE TO EXPAND ON MY SCIENTIFIC KNOWLEDGE AND...
...PERSONAL POWER.

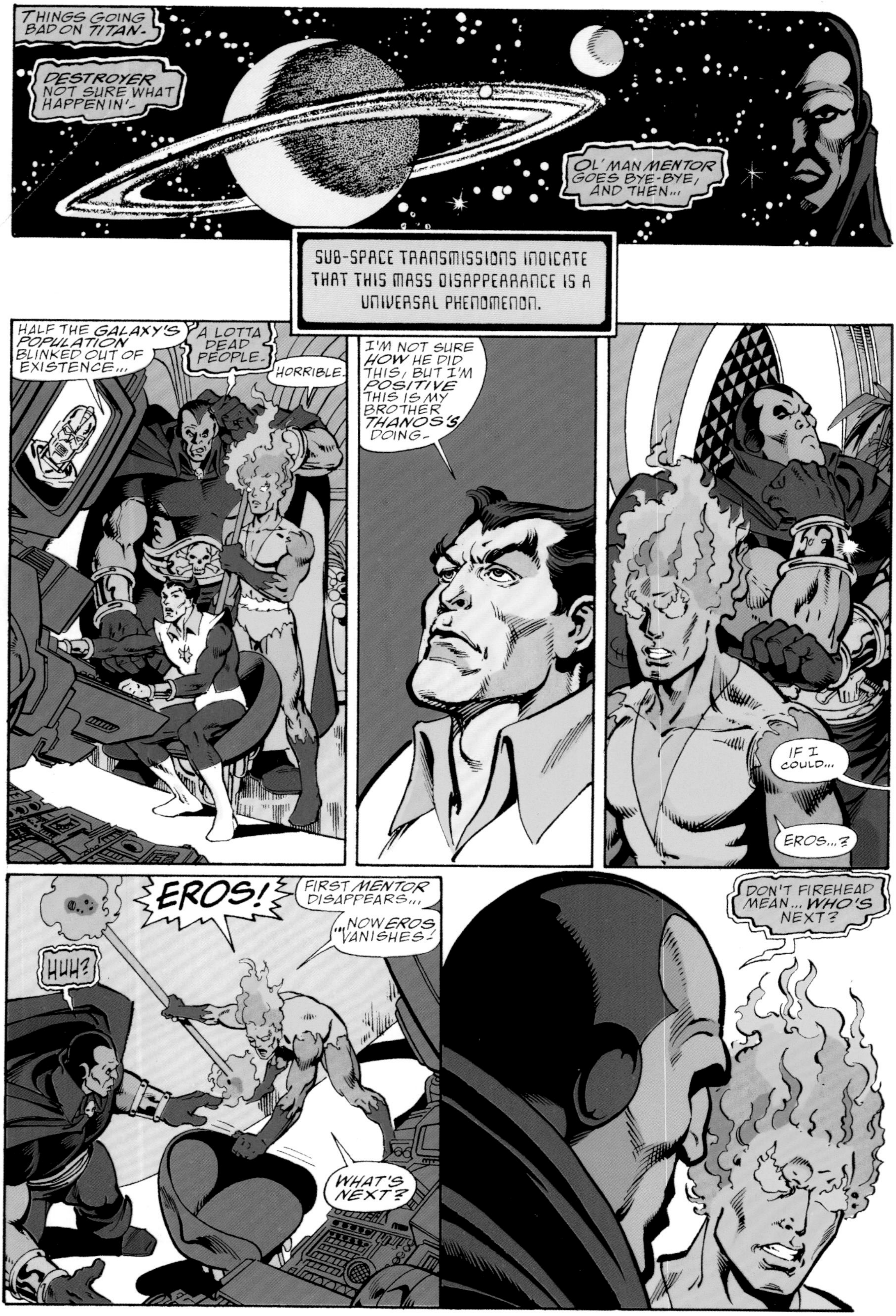
THINGS GOING BAD ON TITAN-
DESTROYER NOT SURE WHAT HAPPENIN'-
OL' MAN MENTOR GOES BYE-BYE, AND THEN...
SUB-SPACE TRANSMISSIONS INDICATE THAT THIS MASS DISAPPEARANCE IS A UNIVERSAL PHENOMENON.
HALF THE GALAXY'S POPULATION BLINKED OUT OF EXISTENCE...
A LOTTA DEAD PEOPLE.
HORRIBLE.
I'M NOT SURE HOW HE DID THIS, BUT I'M POSITIVE THIS IS MY BROTHER THANOS'S DOING.
IF I COULD...
EROS...?
EROS!
FIRST MENTOR DISAPPEARS...
...NOW EROS VANISHES!
HUH?
WHAT'S NEXT?
DON'T FIREHEAD MEAN... WHO'S NEXT?

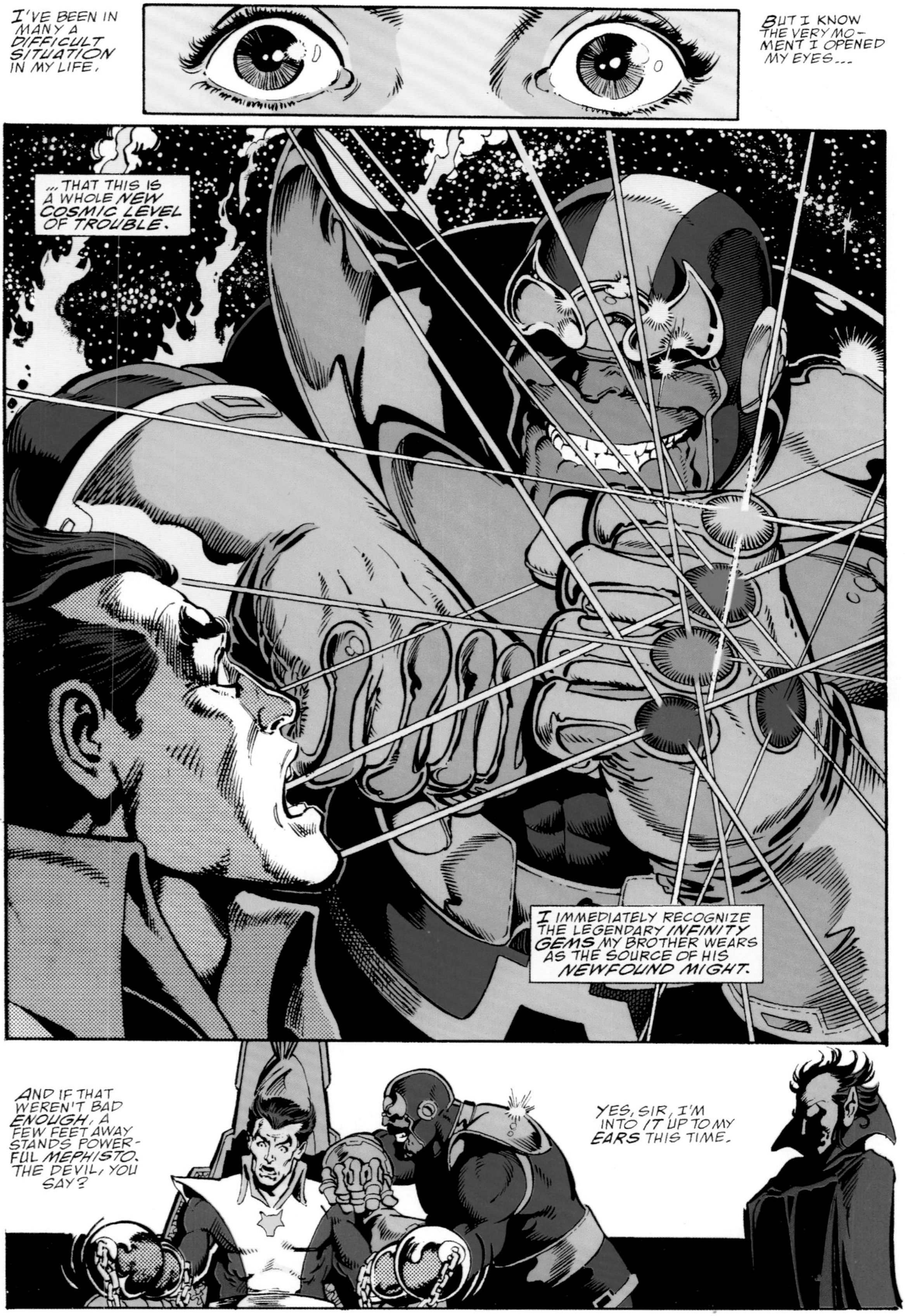
I'VE BEEN IN MANY A DIFFICULT SITUATION IN MY LIFE.
BUT I KNOW THE VERY MOMENT I OPENED MY EYES...
...THAT THIS IS A WHOLE NEW COSMIC LEVEL OF TROUBLE.
I IMMEDIATELY RECOGNIZE THE LEGENDARY INFINITY GEMS MY BROTHER WEARS AS THE SOURCE OF HIS NEWFOUND MIGHT.
AND IF THAT WEREN'T BAD ENOUGH, A FEW FEET AWAY STANDS POWERFUL MEPHISTO. THE DEVIL, YOU SAY?
YES, SIR, I'M INTO IT UP TO MY EARS THIS TIME.

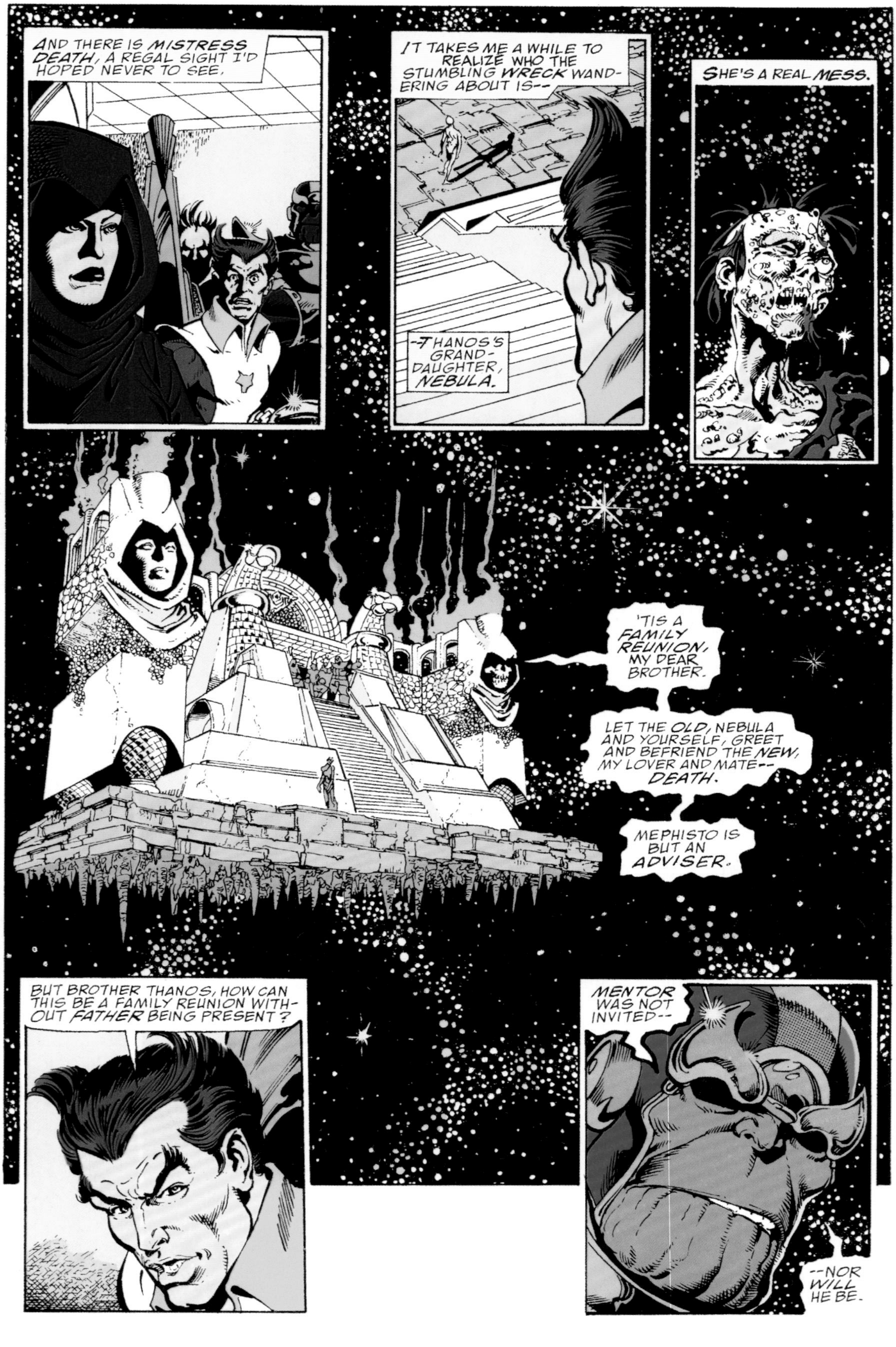
AND THERE IS MISTRESS DEATH, A REGAL SIGHT I'D HOPED NEVER TO SEE.
IT TAKES ME A WHILE TO REALIZE WHO THE STUMBLING WRECK WANDERING ABOUT IS--
--THANOS'S GRAND-DAUGHTER, NEBULA.
SHE'S A REAL MESS.
'TIS A FAMILY REUNION, MY DEAR BROTHER.
LET THE OLD, NEBULA AND YOURSELF, GREET AND BEFRIEND THE NEW, MY LOVER AND MATE--DEATH.
MEPHISTO IS BUT AN ADVISER.
BUT BROTHER THANOS, HOW CAN THIS BE A FAMILY REUNION WITHOUT FATHER BEING PRESENT?
MENTOR WAS NOT INVITED--
--NOR WILL HE BE.

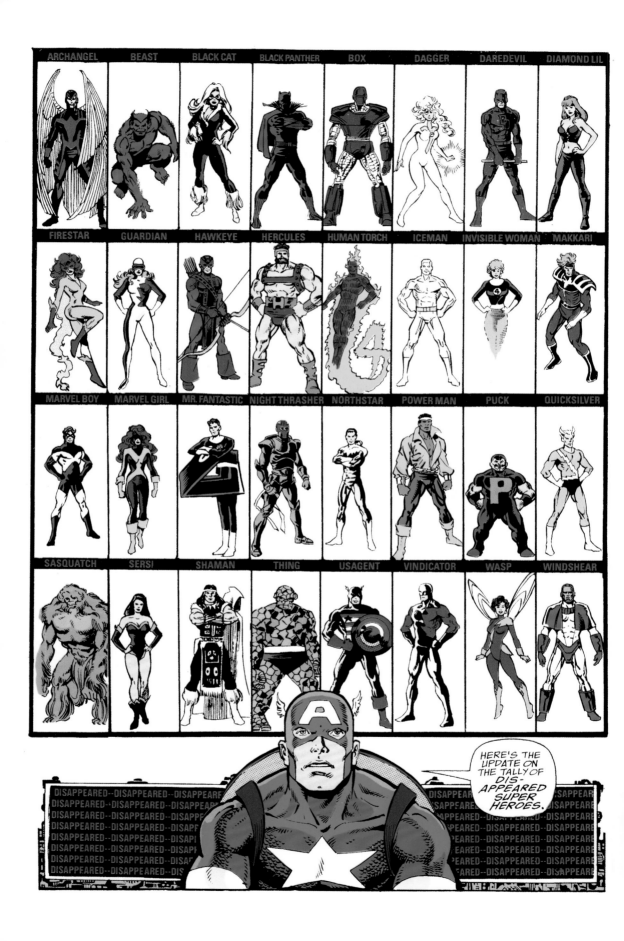

STILL NO WORD ON THE *X-MEN* OR *EXCALIBUR*?

NO. MAYBE THEY'RE OFF THE PLANET.

FEEL CRUMMY DOING THIS, BUT....

...EVEN IN THE MIDST OF THIS CHAOS I'VE GOT TO COVER THAT I'M *NOT* THE ORIGINAL THOR!

I FOUGHT BY THE SIDE OF MANY OF THOSE FALLEN.

THEY SHALT BE MOURNED *DEEPLY.*

THIS IS *BAD.*

REAL BAD.

IT DOESN'T GET *ANY* WORSE.

YOU *SURE* ABOUT THAT CAP...?

NO REPLY

"YOU *ABSOLUTELY* SURE?"

I, GREAT *ODIN,* DIDST WITNESS HALF MY PEOPLE VANISH IN THE TWINKLING OF AN EYE.

THE *CEREMONIAL* EYEPATCH OF SORROW DID I IMMEDIATELY DON.

AND I DID LOOK ABOUT AND SEE THIS *CATASTROPHE* WAS A *UNIVERSAL* PLAGUE.

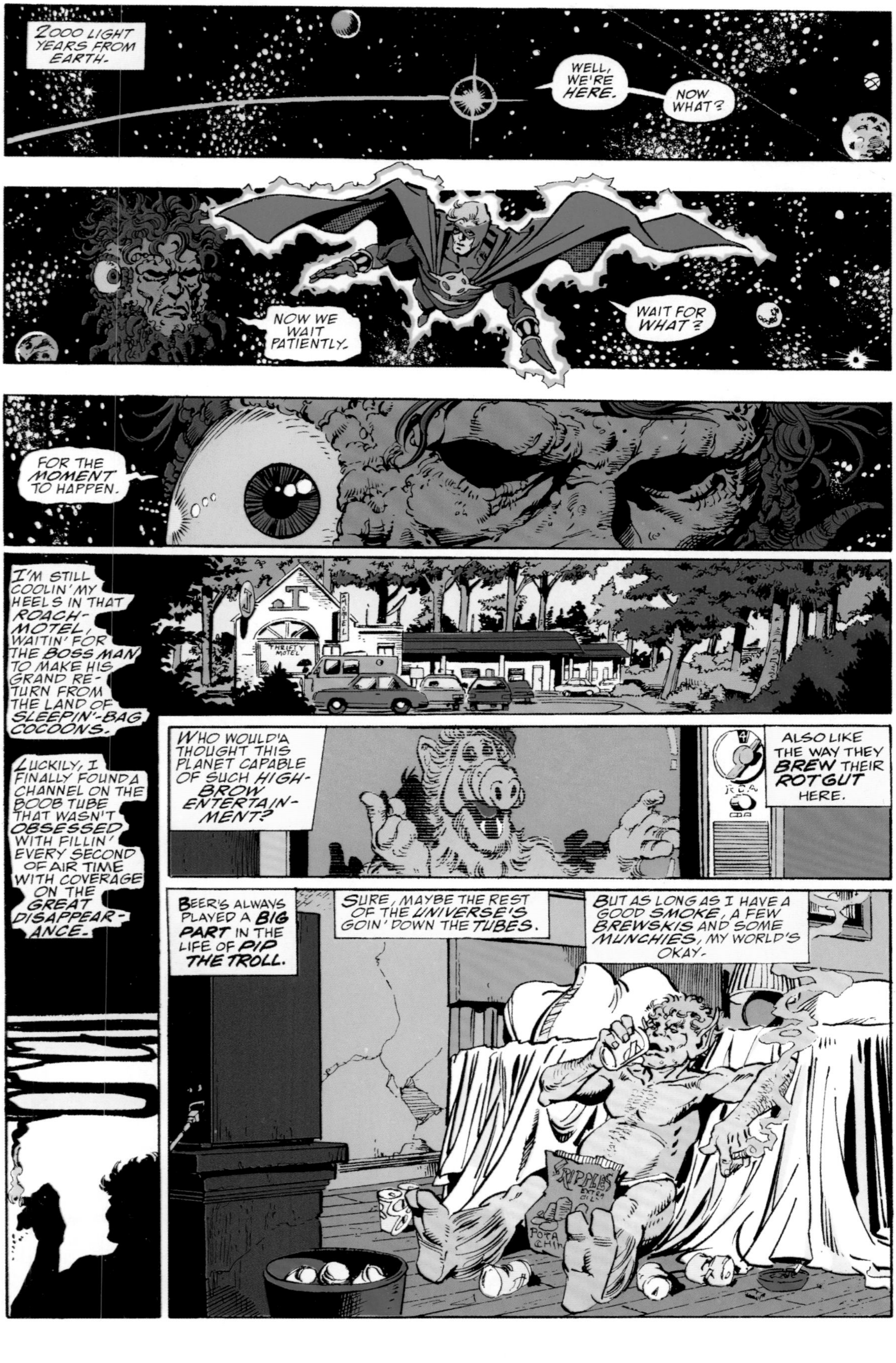

2000 LIGHT YEARS FROM EARTH-
WELL, WE'RE HERE.
NOW WHAT?
NOW WE WAIT PATIENTLY.
WAIT FOR WHAT?
FOR THE MOMENT TO HAPPEN.
I'M STILL COOLIN' MY HEELS IN THAT ROACH-MOTEL, WAITIN' FOR THE BOSS MAN TO MAKE HIS GRAND RETURN FROM THE LAND OF SLEEPIN'-BAG COCOONS.
THRIFTY MOTEL
MOTEL
LUCKILY, I FINALLY FOUND A CHANNEL ON THE BOOB TUBE THAT WASN'T OBSESSED WITH FILLIN' EVERY SECOND OF AIR TIME WITH COVERAGE ON THE GREAT DISAPPEARANCE.
WHO WOULD'A THOUGHT THIS PLANET CAPABLE OF SUCH HIGH-BROW ENTERTAINMENT?
ALSO LIKE THE WAY THEY BREW THEIR ROTGUT HERE.
RCA
BEER'S ALWAYS PLAYED A BIG PART IN THE LIFE OF PIP THE TROLL.
SURE, MAYBE THE REST OF THE UNIVERSE'S GOIN' DOWN THE TUBES.
BUT AS LONG AS I HAVE A GOOD SMOKE, A FEW BREWSKIS AND SOME MUNCHIES, MY WORLD'S OKAY.
SRIPPLES
EXTRA OIL

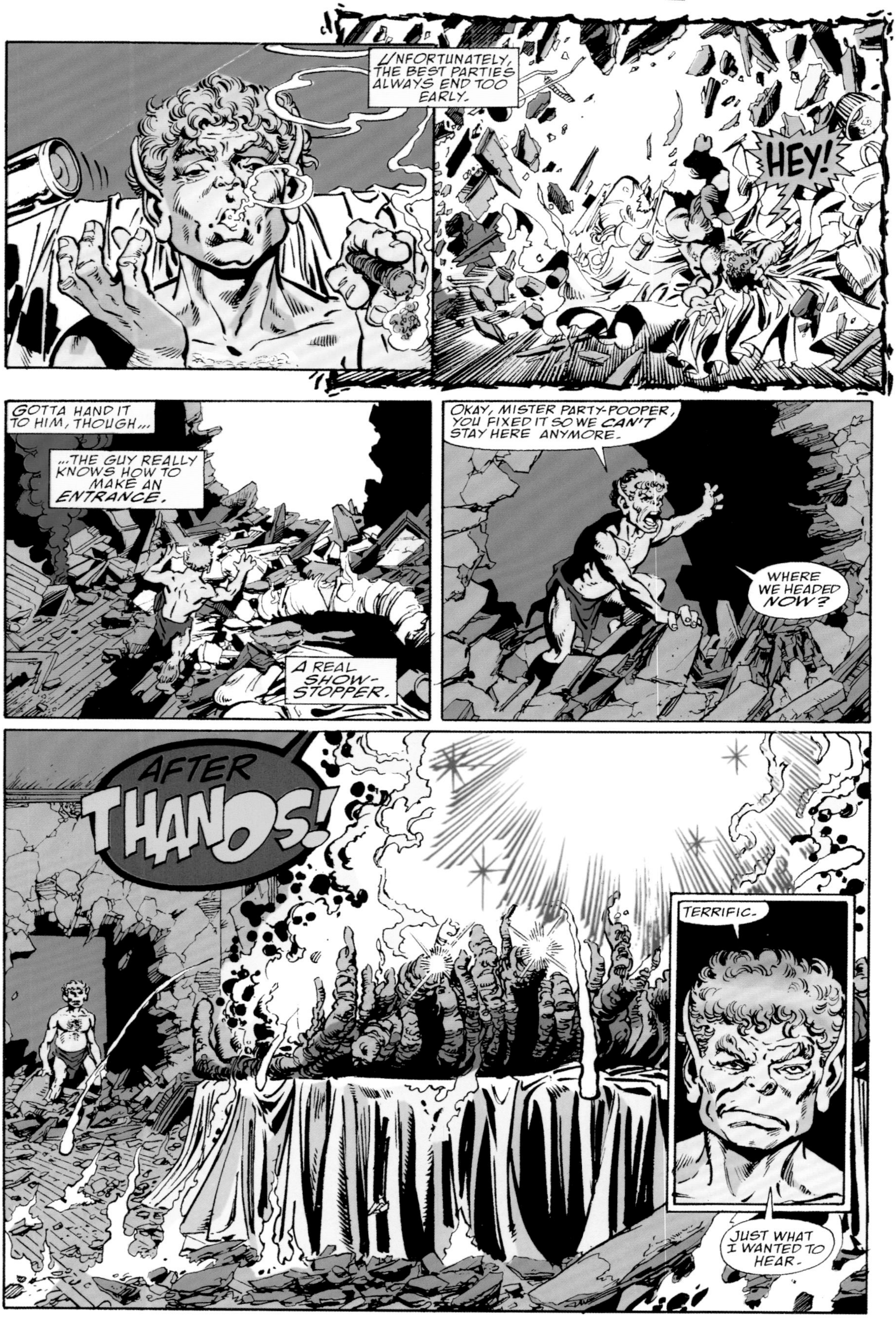
UNFORTUNATELY, THE BEST PARTIES ALWAYS END TOO EARLY.
HEY!
GOTTA HAND IT TO HIM, THOUGH...
...THE GUY REALLY KNOWS HOW TO MAKE AN ENTRANCE.
A REAL SHOW-STOPPER.
OKAY, MISTER PARTY-POOPER, YOU FIXED IT SO WE CAN'T STAY HERE ANYMORE.
WHERE WE HEADED NOW?
AFTER THANOS!
TERRIFIC.
JUST WHAT I WANTED TO HEAR.

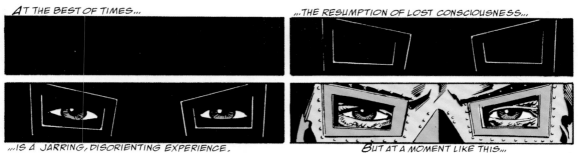

AT THE BEST OF TIMES...

...THE RESUMPTION OF LOST CONSCIOUSNESS...

...IS A JARRING, DISORIENTING EXPERIENCE.

BUT AT A MOMENT LIKE THIS...

WHAT?

...IT CAN BE DEVASTATING.

DR. STRANGE...?

DR. DOOM?

I WARN YOU, DOOM, YOU MEDDLE IN DANGEROUS MATTERS YOU DO NOT FULLY UNDERSTAND!

THEN YOU SHALL ENLIGHTEN ME OR SUFFER FURTHER DISCOMFORT AT MY SERVANTS HANDS.

DOOM! UNHAND MY COMRADE!!

OR I SHALL--

FALL VICTIM TO A SUPERIOR INTELLECT AND POWER AS YOU DID IN OUR LAST ENCOUNTER!

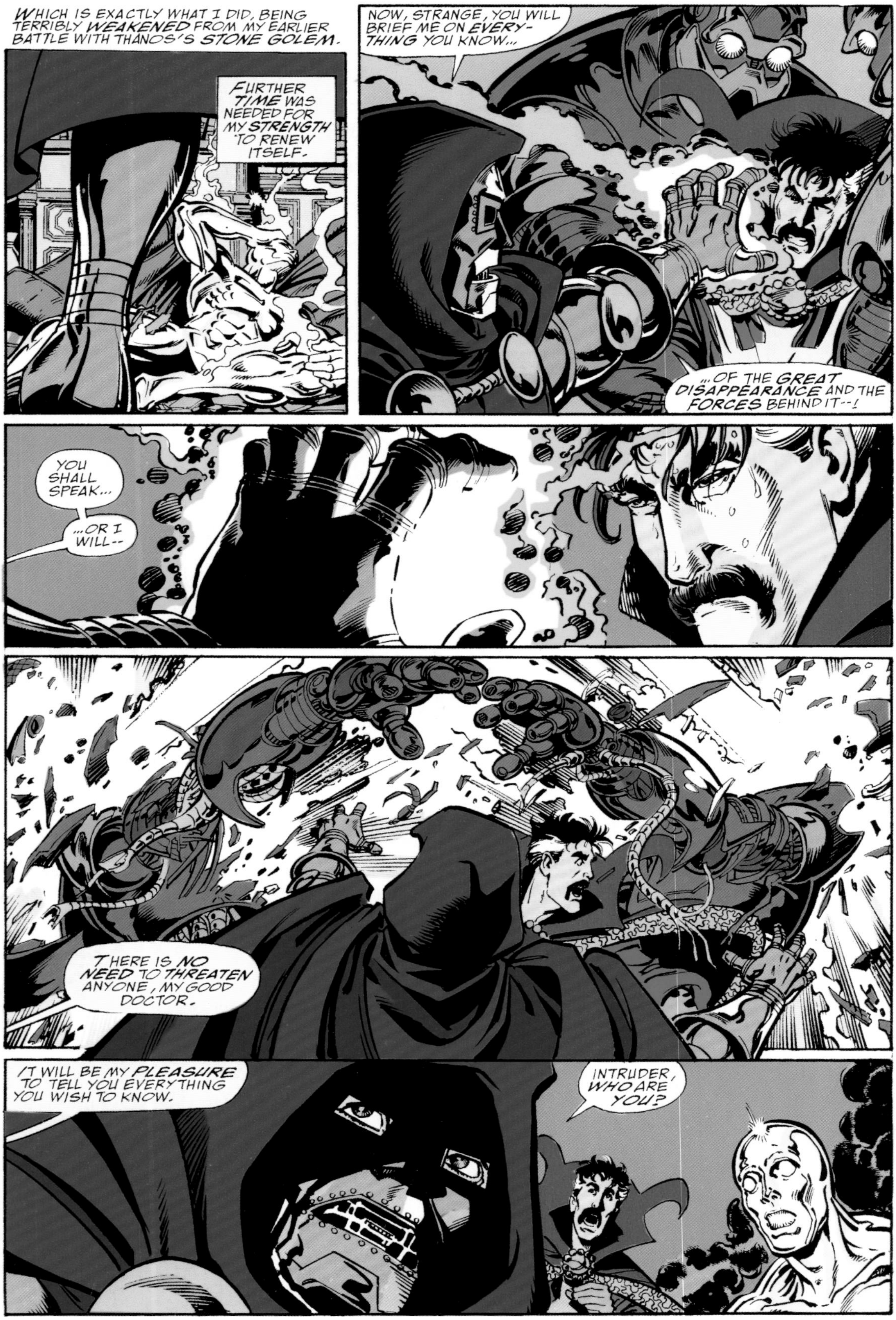
WHICH IS EXACTLY WHAT I DID, BEING TERRIBLY WEAKENED FROM MY EARLIER BATTLE WITH THANOS'S STONE GOLEM.
FURTHER TIME WAS NEEDED FOR MY STRENGTH TO RENEW ITSELF.
NOW, STRANGE, YOU WILL BRIEF ME ON EVERYTHING YOU KNOW...
...OF THE GREAT DISAPPEARANCE AND THE FORCES BEHIND IT--!
YOU SHALL SPEAK...
...OR I WILL--
THERE IS NO NEED TO THREATEN ANYONE, MY GOOD DOCTOR.
IT WILL BE MY PLEASURE TO TELL YOU EVERYTHING YOU WISH TO KNOW.
INTRUDER, WHO ARE YOU?

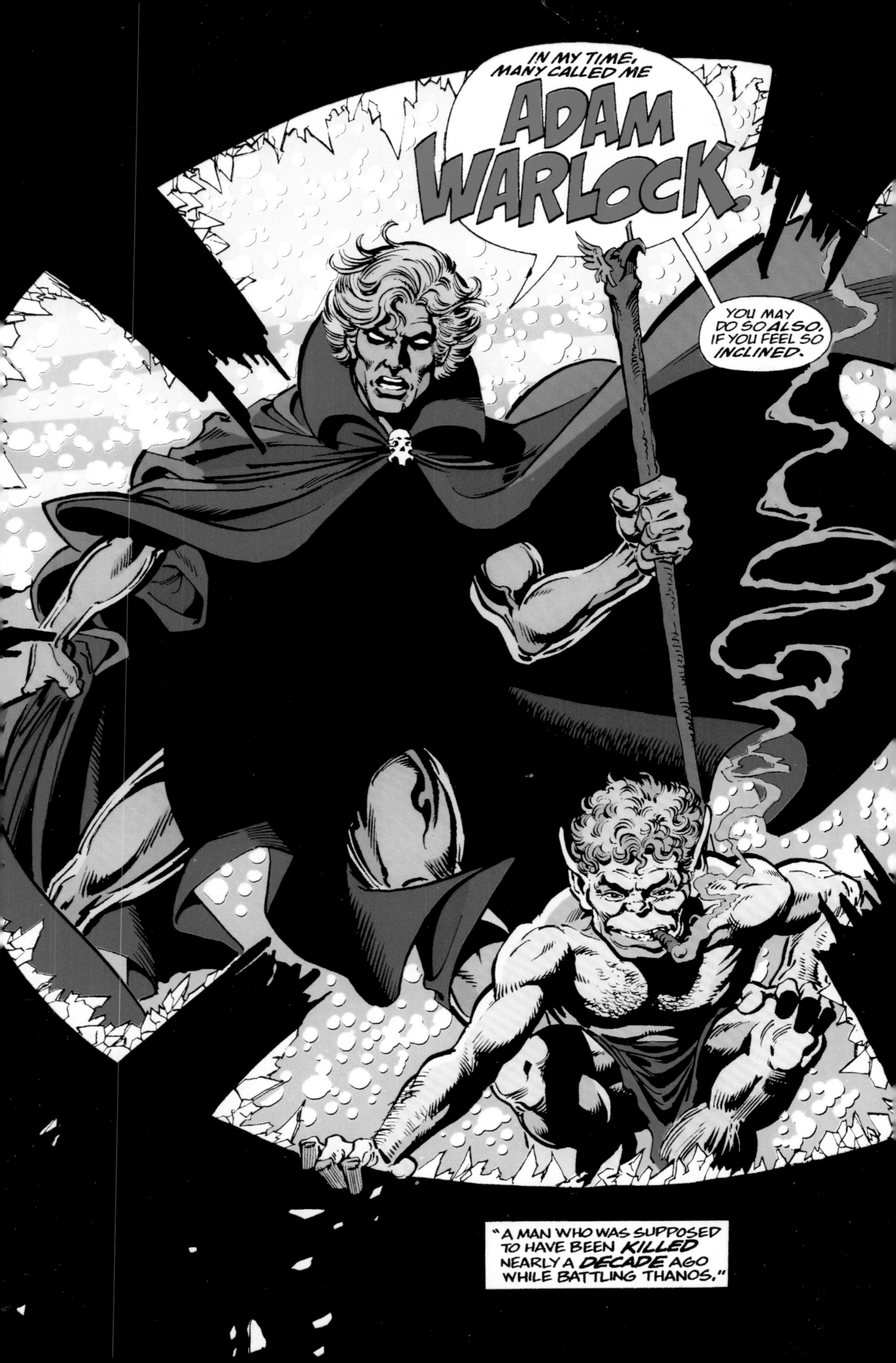
IN MY TIME, MANY CALLED ME ADAM WARLOCK.
YOU MAY DO SO ALSO, IF YOU FEEL SO INCLINED.
"A MAN WHO WAS SUPPOSED TO HAVE BEEN KILLED NEARLY A DECADE AGO WHILE BATTLING THANOS."

NOW DO YOU UNDERSTAND, MY DEAR...

...THE PLEASURES OF HAVING *FAMILY* VISIT?

AMUSING, AREN'T THEY?

MISTRESS DEATH DOESN'T APPEAR TO THINK SO.

EH?

WELL, THAT SITUATION CAN BE EASILY *REMEDIED.*

"NEW ENTERTAINMENT CAN BE DEVISED."

BY THE HEAVENS!

THANOS'S NEWLY ACQUIRED *POWER* HAS OBVIOUSLY *DERANGED* HIM!

HE'S GONE *COMPLETELY INSANE!*

IN HIS CURRENT STATE OF MIND, *ANY-THING* IS POSSIBLE.

HE MIGHT, ON A WHIM, EVEN *DESTROY* THE *UNIVERSE!*

...AND THAT IS HOW THANOS GAINED HIS VAST POWER AND I CAME TO AID IN THE THWARTING OF HIS MAD SCHEMES.

THEN YOU ARE THE ENTITY I COMMUNICATED WITH EARLIER!

AN AMAZING STORY AND A PERIL THAT RIVALS THE COMING OF THE BEYONDER!

IT IS A CHALLENGE WE MUST MEET AND TRIUMPH OVER.

THERE IS BUT ONE WAY THIS CAN BE ACCOMPLISHED.

I MUST LEAD THE FORCES OF SANITY AGAINST THE MAD TITAN.

BY WHAT RIGHT DO YOU CLAIM THE MANTLE OF LEADERSHIP?!

A MAN WHO WAS SUPPOSED TO HAVE BEEN KILLED NEARLY A DECADE AGO-- WHILE BATTLING THANOS!

PERHAPS, BUT I ALONE AM FAMILIAR WITH THE SECRET WORKINGS OF THE INFINITY GEMS.

THAT KNOWLEDGE IS THIS UNIVERSE'S ONLY HOPE.

A BANNER I WILL GLADLY STAND BEHIND.

TIS BETTER THAN FOLLOWING DOOM.

WHAT SAY YOU, SURFER?

THEN RAISE YOUR ARMY AND WE SHALL SEE WHAT COMES OF IT.

BUT IS WARLOCK TRULY THE BEST CHOICE?

HE SEEMS MARKEDLY DIFFERENT FROM THE MAN I MET ON SOUL-WORLD.

THERE'S SO LITTLE ANYONE REALLY KNOWS ABOUT HIM-

HOW CAN WE BE CERTAIN?

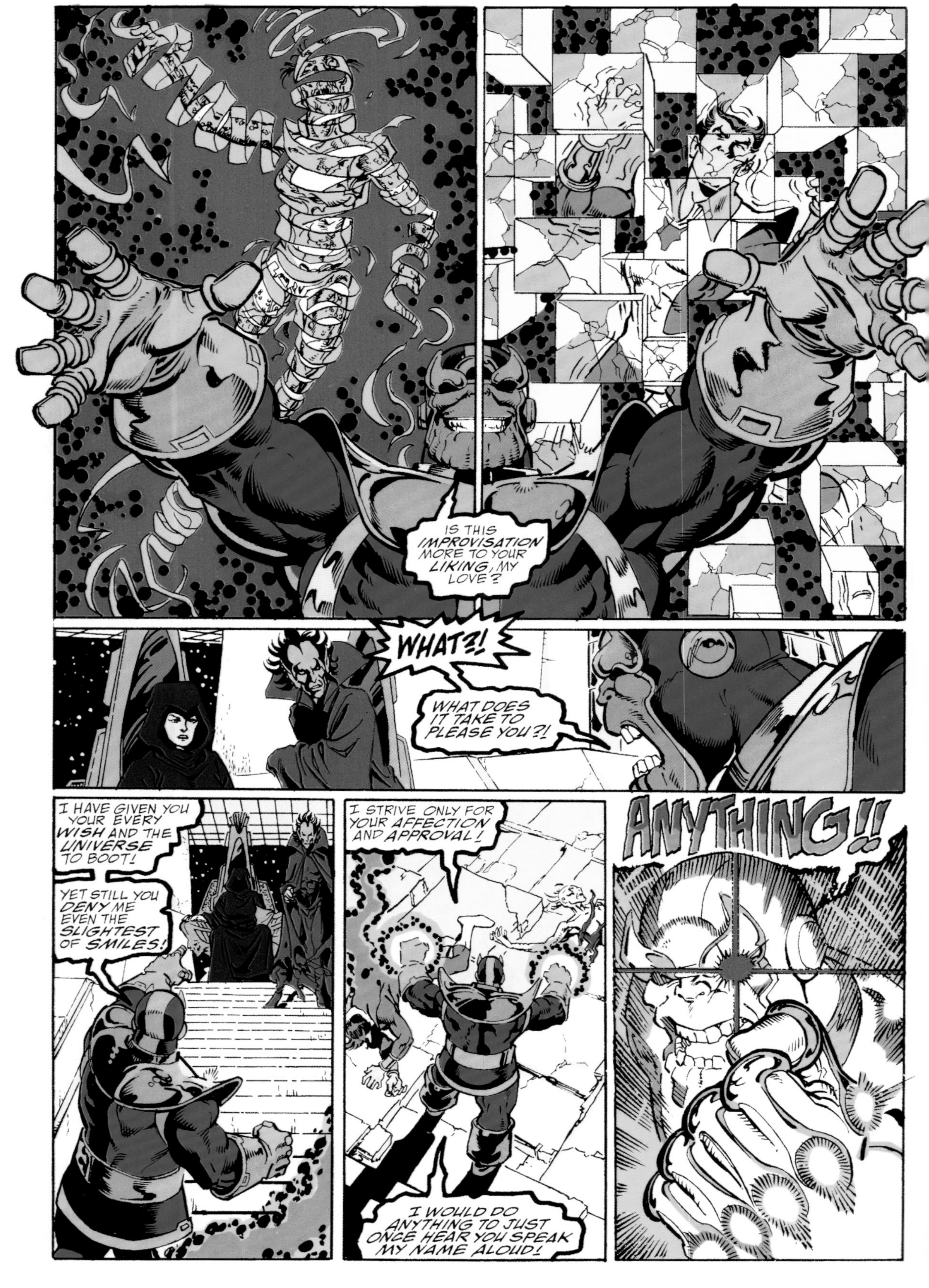

IS THIS IMPROVISATION MORE TO YOUR LIKING, MY LOVE?
WHAT?!
WHAT DOES IT TAKE TO PLEASE YOU?!
I HAVE GIVEN YOU YOUR EVERY WISH AND THE UNIVERSE TO BOOT!
YET STILL YOU DENY ME EVEN THE SLIGHTEST OF SMILES!
I STRIVE ONLY FOR YOUR AFFECTION AND APPROVAL!
I WOULD DO ANYTHING TO JUST ONCE HEAR YOU SPEAK MY NAME ALOUD!
ANYTHING!!

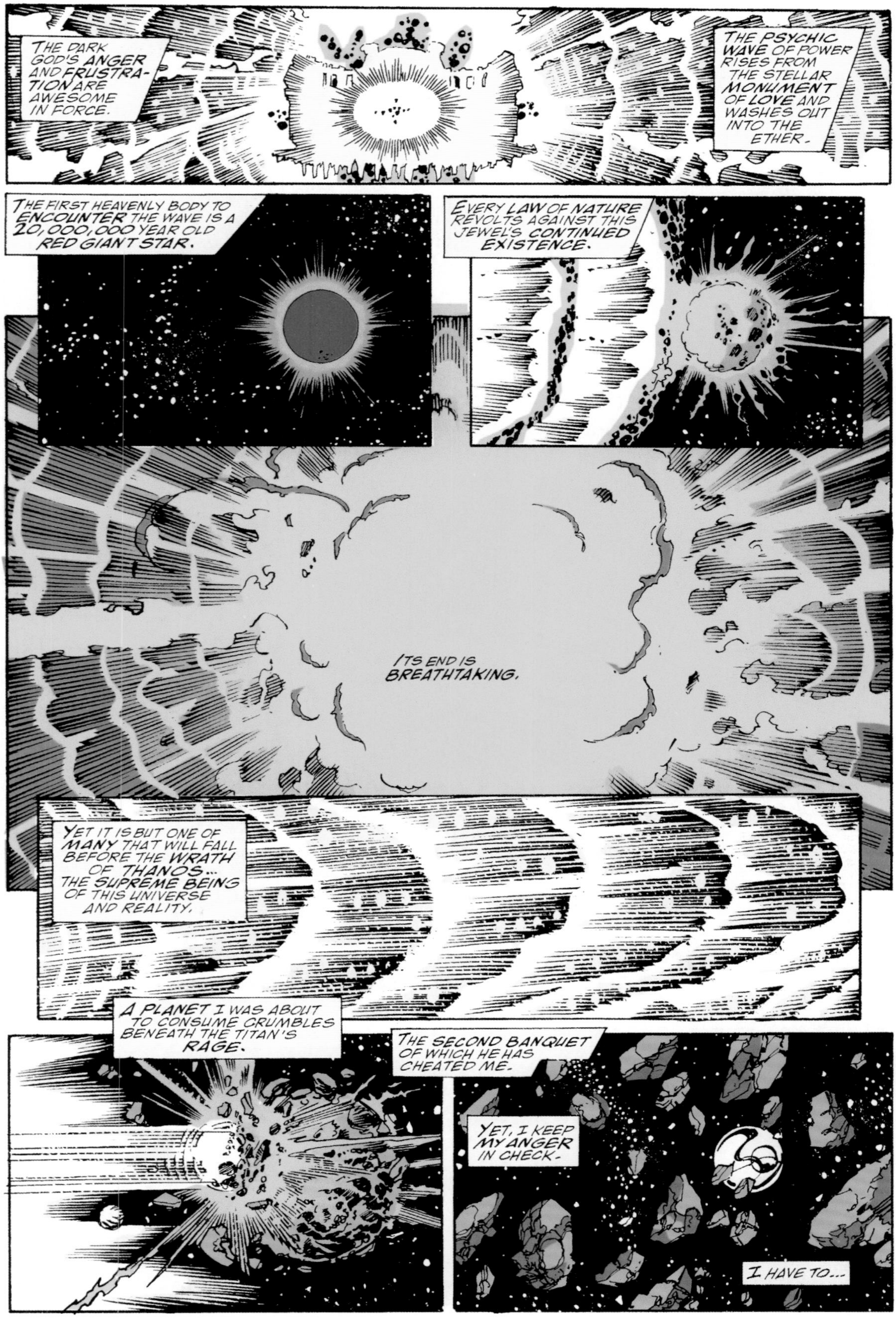
THE DARK GOD'S ANGER AND FRUSTRATION ARE AWESOME IN FORCE.
THE PSYCHIC WAVE OF POWER RISES FROM THE STELLAR MONUMENT OF LOVE AND WASHES OUT INTO THE ETHER.
THE FIRST HEAVENLY BODY TO ENCOUNTER THE WAVE IS A 20,000,000 YEAR OLD RED GIANT STAR.
EVERY LAW OF NATURE REVOLTS AGAINST THIS JEWEL'S CONTINUED EXISTENCE.
ITS END IS BREATHTAKING.
YET IT IS BUT ONE OF MANY THAT WILL FALL BEFORE THE WRATH OF THANOS... THE SUPREME BEING OF THIS UNIVERSE AND REALITY.
A PLANET I WAS ABOUT TO CONSUME CRUMBLES BENEATH THE TITAN'S RAGE.
THE SECOND BANQUET OF WHICH HE HAS CHEATED ME.
YET, I KEEP MY ANGER IN CHECK.
I HAVE TO...

FOR I REALIZE THAT EVEN MY *STAGGERING* MIGHT IS *NOTHING* COMPARED TO THE NEAR INFINITE POWER *THANOS* NOW WIELDS.

BUT THINK NOT THAT *GALACTUS* PLANS TO TURN TAIL AND RUN FROM THIS UPSTART *DEMI-GOD.*

GALACTUS IS A BEING OF POWER AND *INTELLECT.*

PLANS MUST BE CONCEIVED AND ALLIANCES FORMED.

ONLY THEN MAY I SAVOR THE *COLD FEAST* OF *VENGEANCE.*

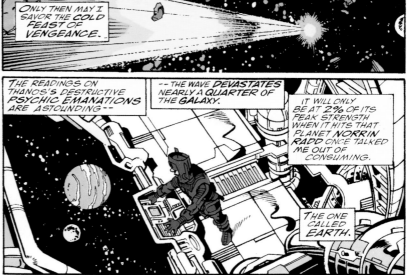

THE READINGS ON THANOS'S DESTRUCTIVE *PSYCHIC EMANATIONS* ARE ASTOUNDING --

-- THE WAVE *DEVASTATES* NEARLY A *QUARTER* OF THE GALAXY.

IT WILL ONLY BE AT 2% OF ITS PEAK STRENGTH WHEN IT HITS THAT PLANET *NORRIN RADD* ONCE TALKED ME OUT OF CONSUMING.

THE ONE CALLED *EARTH.*

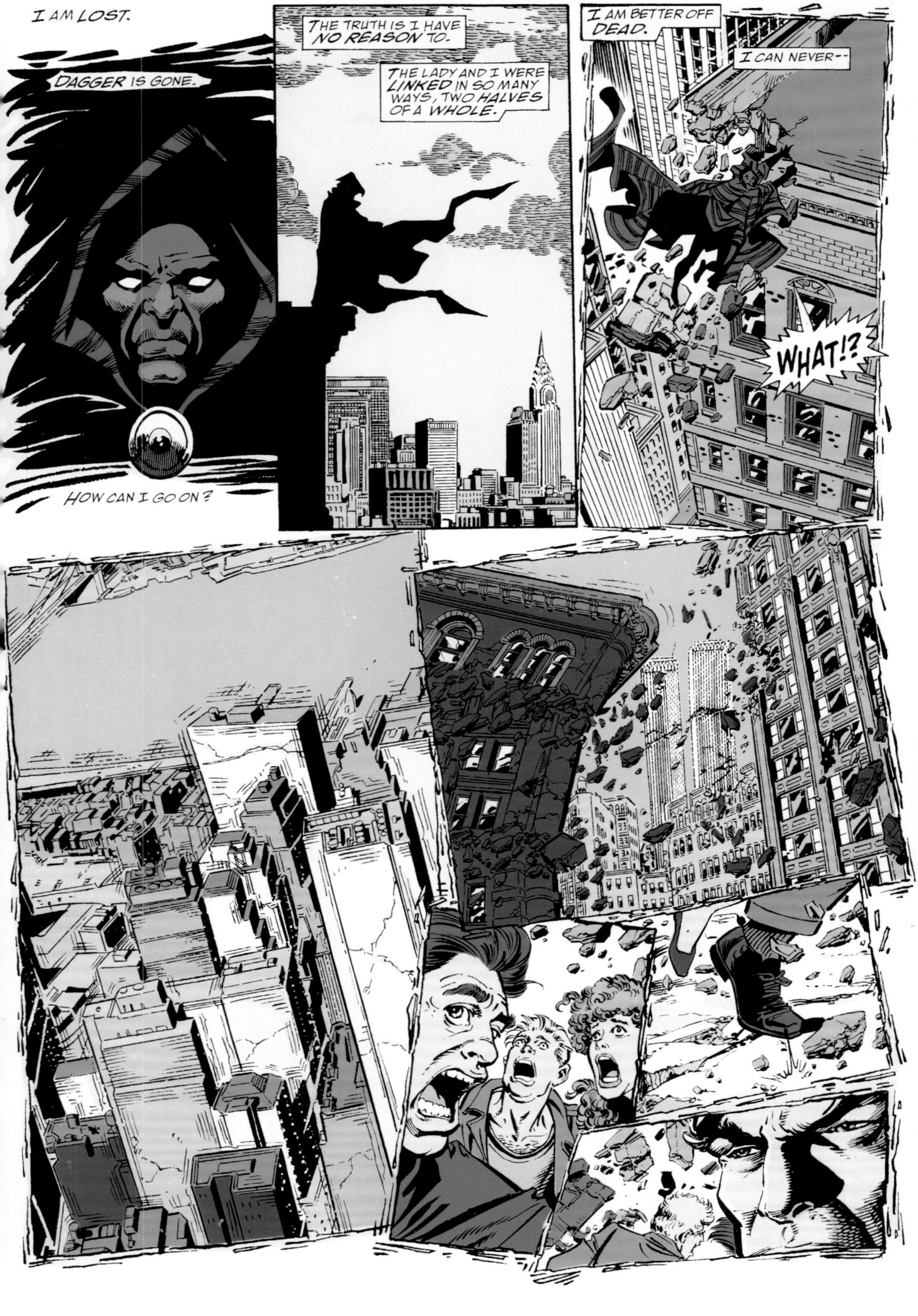
I AM LOST.
DAGGER IS GONE.
HOW CAN I GO ON?
THE TRUTH IS I HAVE NO REASON TO.
THE LADY AND I WERE LINKED IN SO MANY WAYS, TWO HALVES OF A WHOLE.
I AM BETTER OFF DEAD.
I CAN NEVER--
WHAT!?

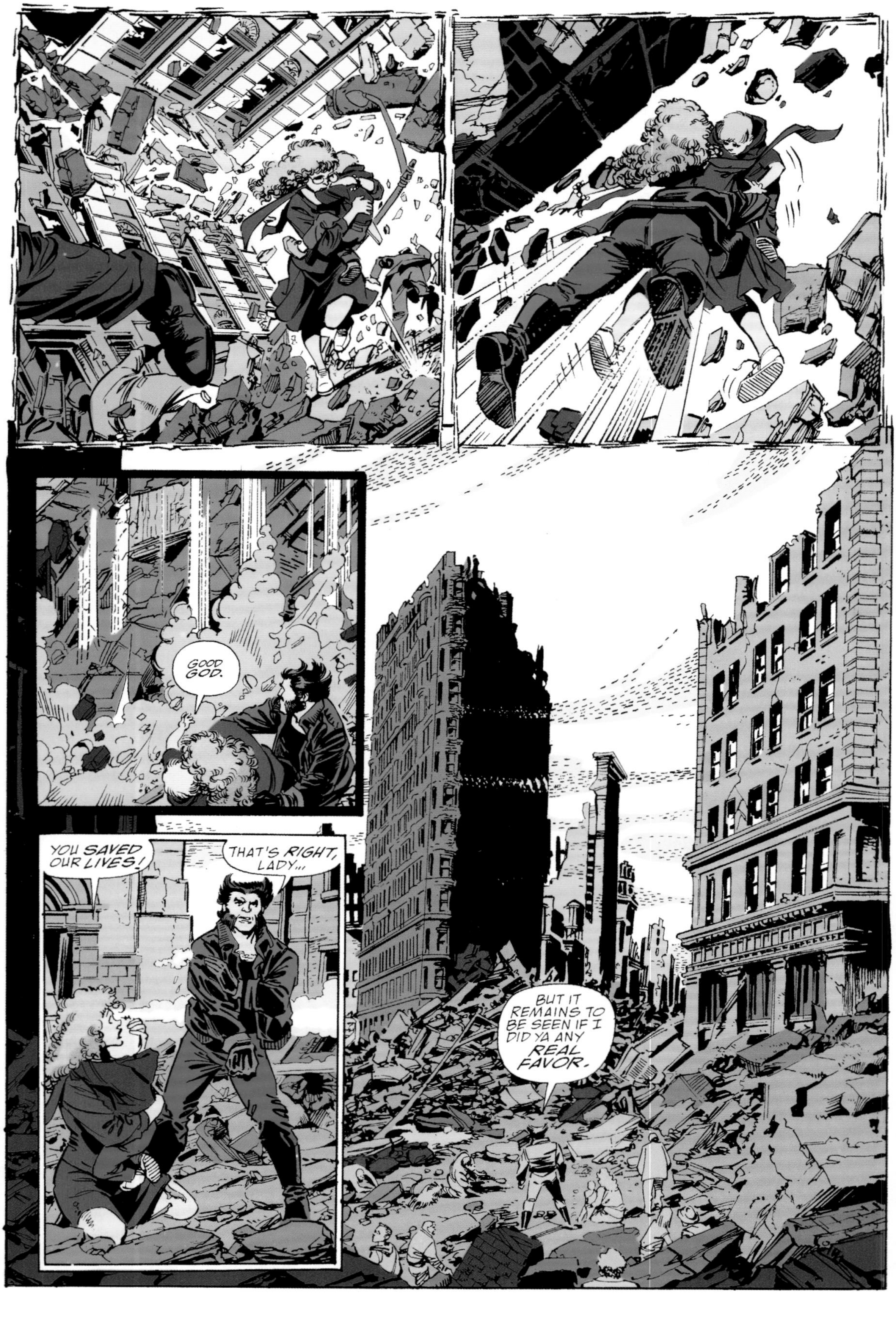

GOOD GOD.
YOU SAVED OUR LIVES!
THAT'S RIGHT, LADY...
BUT IT REMAINS TO BE SEEN IF I DID YA ANY REAL FAVOR.

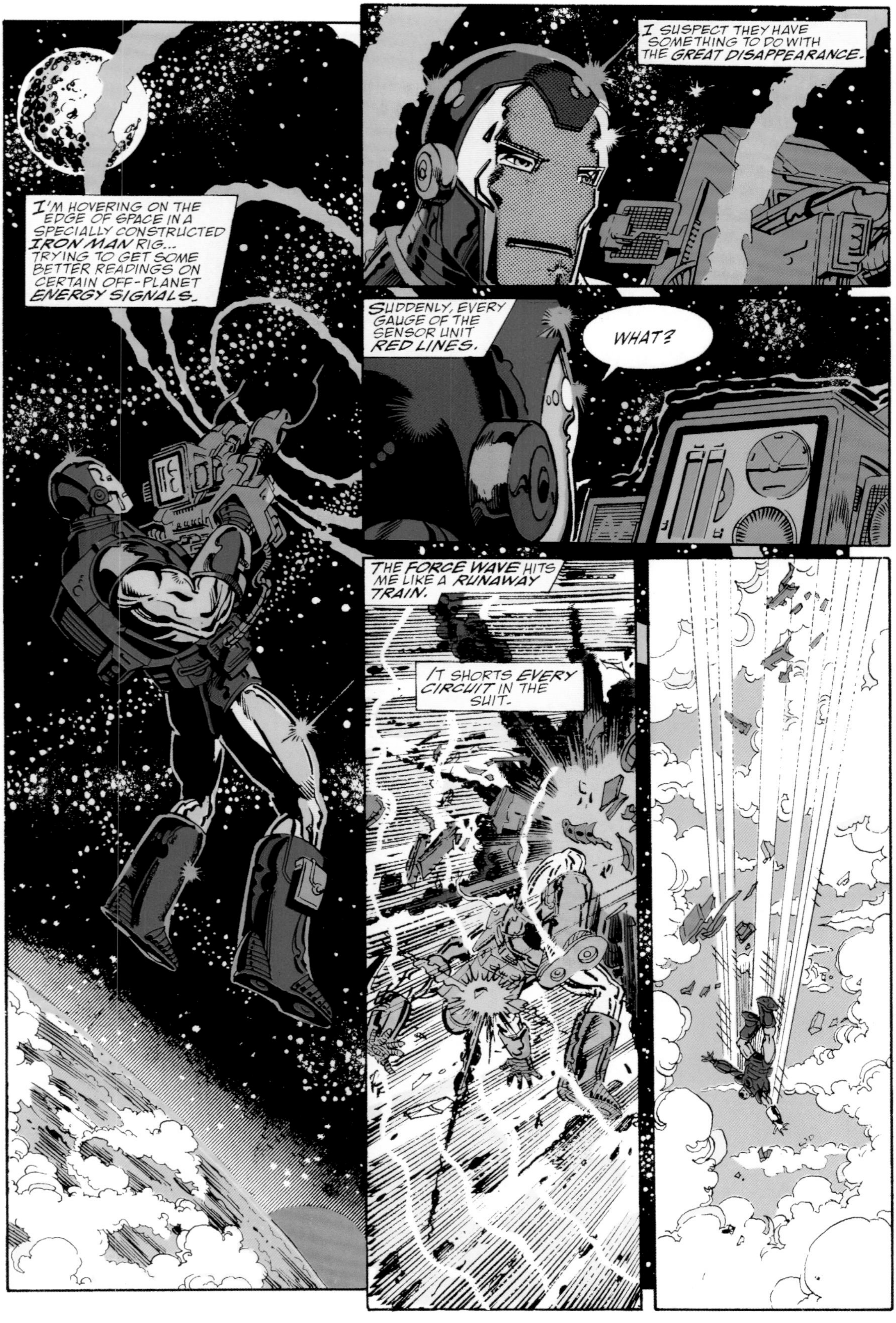
I'M HOVERING ON THE EDGE OF SPACE IN A SPECIALLY CONSTRUCTED IRON MAN RIG... TRYING TO GET SOME BETTER READINGS ON CERTAIN OFF-PLANET ENERGY SIGNALS.
I SUSPECT THEY HAVE SOMETHING TO DO WITH THE GREAT DISAPPEARANCE.
SUDDENLY, EVERY GAUGE OF THE SENSOR UNIT RED LINES.
WHAT?
THE FORCE WAVE HITS ME LIKE A RUNAWAY TRAIN.
IT SHORTS EVERY CIRCUIT IN THE SUIT.

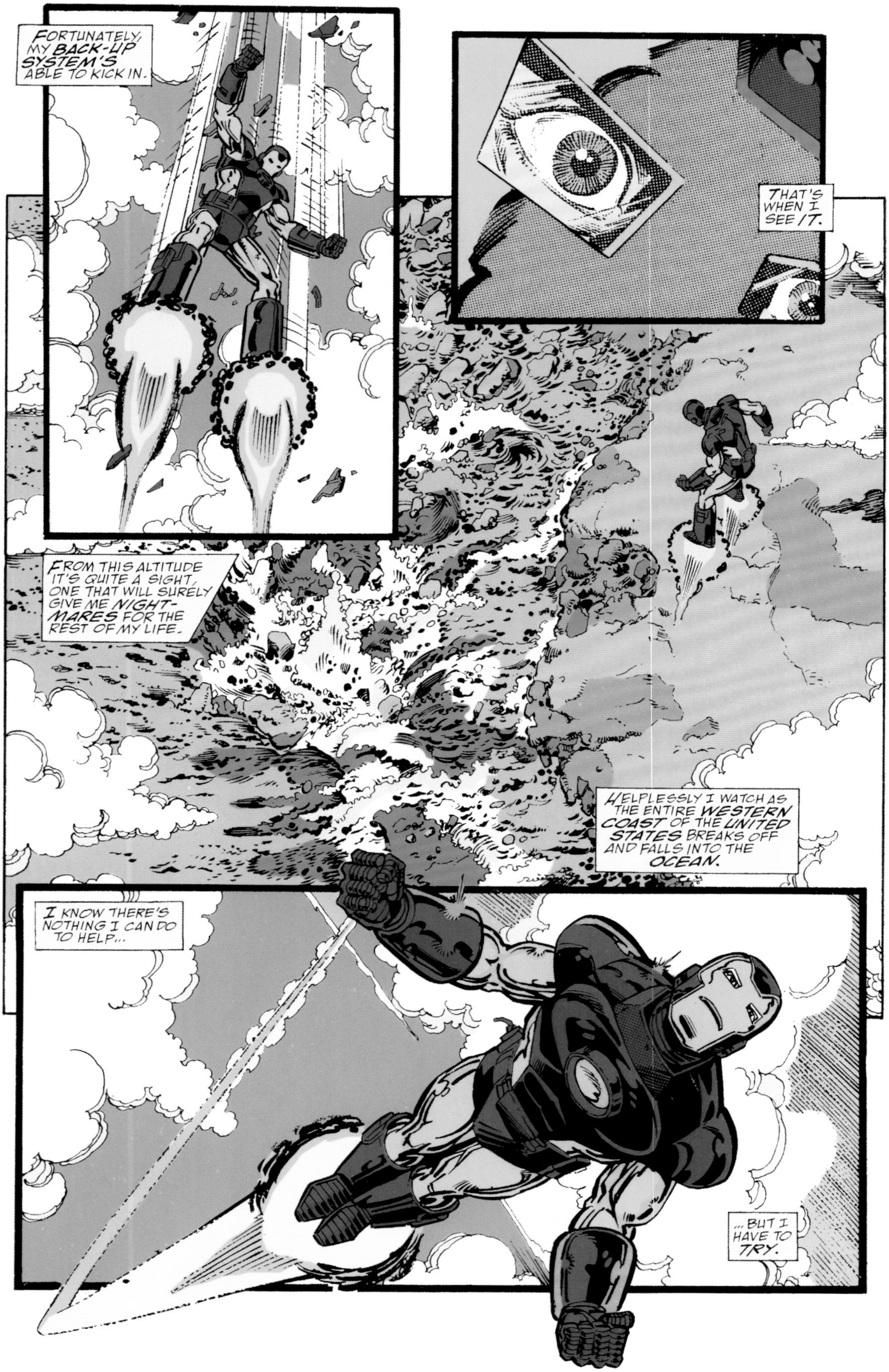
FORTUNATELY, MY BACK-UP SYSTEM'S ABLE TO KICK IN.
THAT'S WHEN I SEE IT.
FROM THIS ALTITUDE IT'S QUITE A SIGHT, ONE THAT WILL SURELY GIVE ME NIGHT-MARES FOR THE REST OF MY LIFE.
HELPLESSLY I WATCH AS THE ENTIRE WESTERN COAST OF THE UNITED STATES BREAKS OFF AND FALLS INTO THE OCEAN.
I KNOW THERE'S NOTHING I CAN DO TO HELP...
...BUT I HAVE TO TRY.

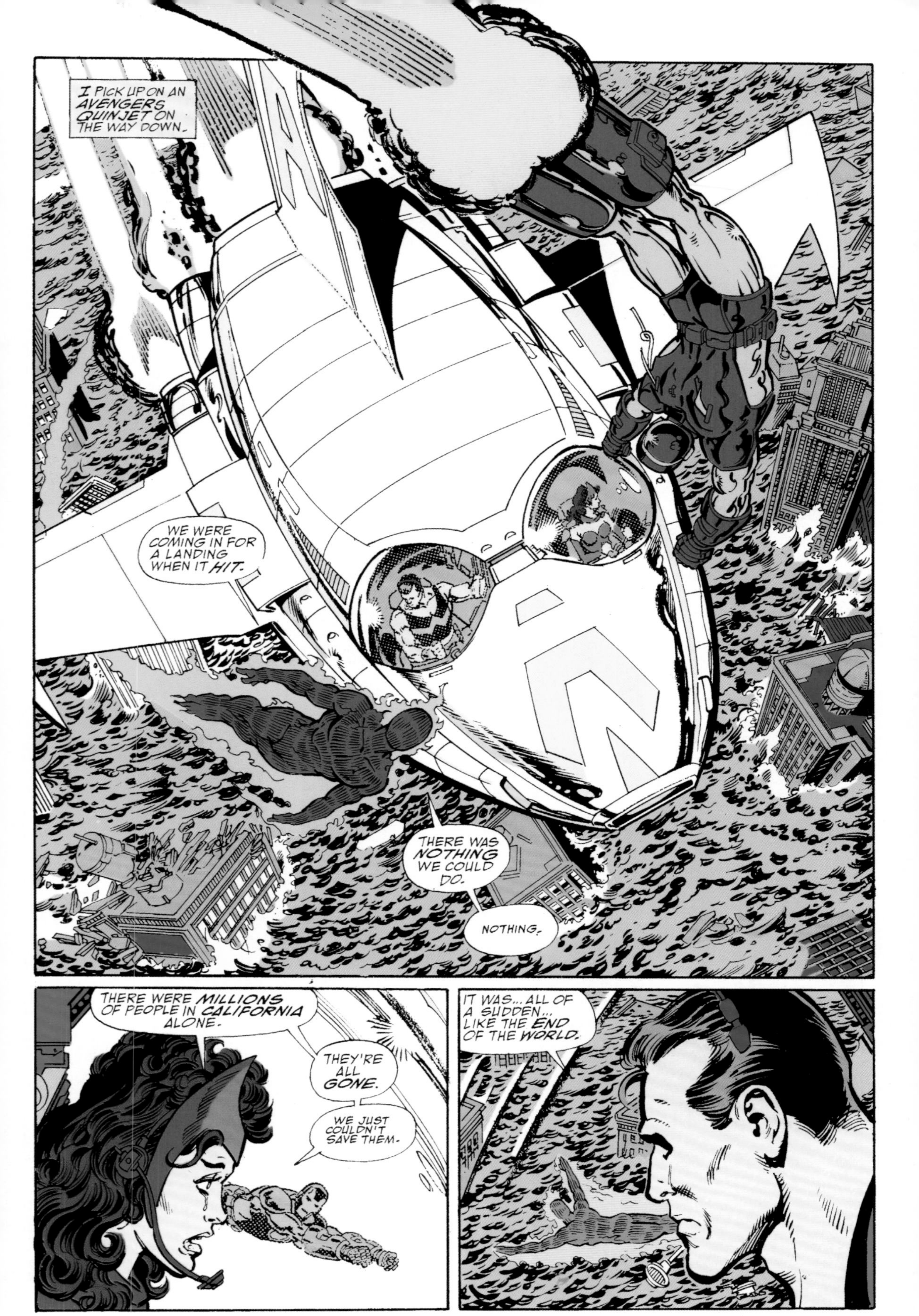

I PICK UP ON AN AVENGERS QUINJET ON THE WAY DOWN.
WE WERE COMING IN FOR A LANDING WHEN IT HIT.
THERE WAS NOTHING WE COULD DO.
NOTHING.
THERE WERE MILLIONS OF PEOPLE IN CALIFORNIA ALONE.
THEY'RE ALL GONE.
WE JUST COULDN'T SAVE THEM.
IT WAS... ALL OF A SUDDEN... LIKE THE END OF THE WORLD.

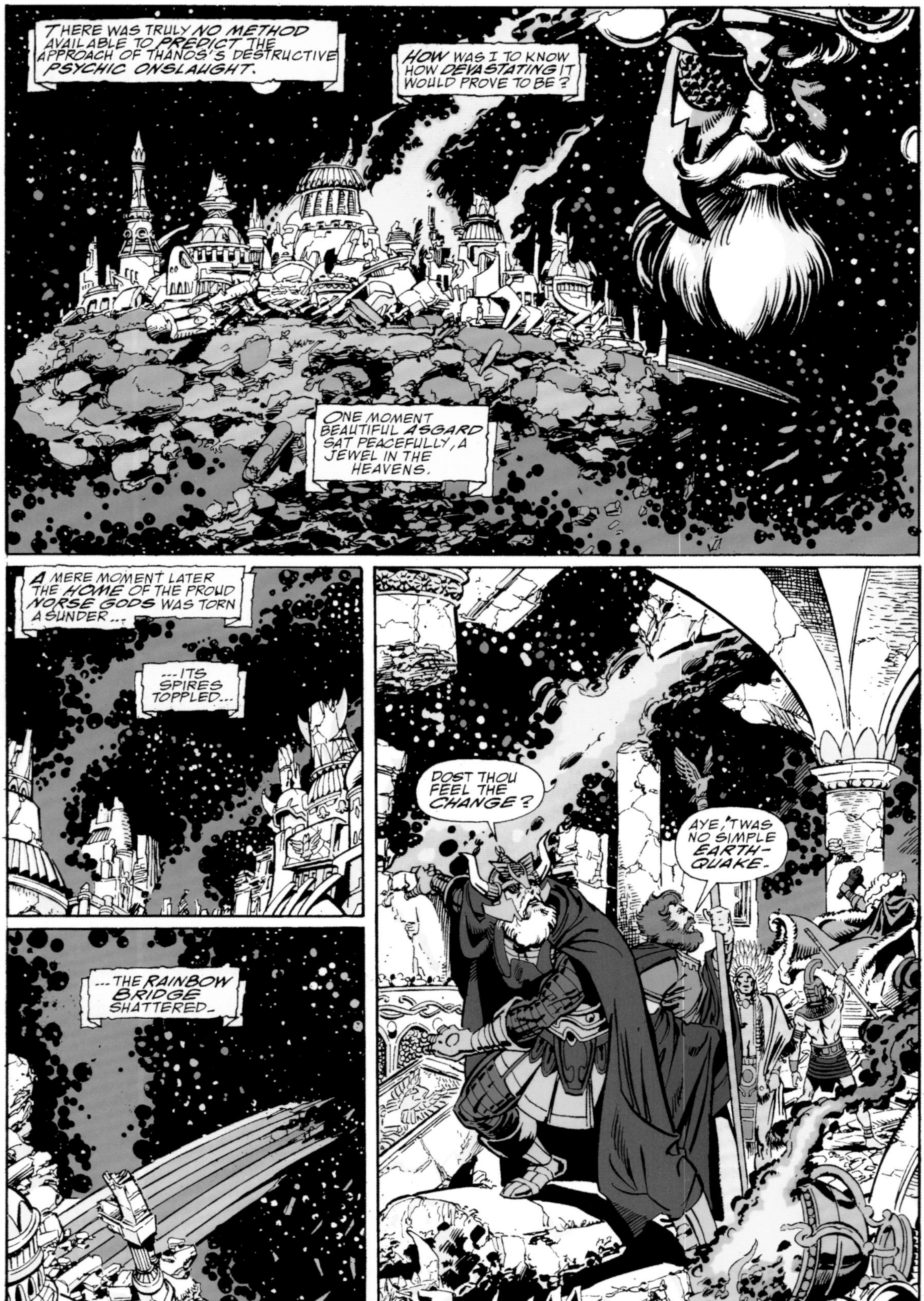
THERE WAS TRULY NO METHOD AVAILABLE TO PREDICT THE APPROACH OF THANOS'S DESTRUCTIVE PSYCHIC ONSLAUGHT.
HOW WAS I TO KNOW HOW DEVASTATING IT WOULD PROVE TO BE?
ONE MOMENT BEAUTIFUL ASGARD SAT PEACEFULLY, A JEWEL IN THE HEAVENS.
A MERE MOMENT LATER THE HOME OF THE PROUD NORSE GODS WAS TORN ASUNDER...
--ITS SPIRES TOPPLED--
--THE RAINBOW BRIDGE SHATTERED--
DOST THOU FEEL THE CHANGE?
AYE, 'TWAS NO SIMPLE EARTH-QUAKE--

THE TURMOIL HAS WROUGHT *INTER-DIMENSIONAL* CHANGES!

THE *SPACE/TIME CON-TINUUM* HAS *SHIFTED!*

WE HATH BEEN *CUT OFF* FROM *MIDGARD* AND ITS *REALITY!*

WE ARE *TRAPPED* ON *ASGARD!*

UNABLE TO *RETURN* AND *PROTECT* OUR *HOMES!*

BLAME *NOT* YOURSELF, MY *BROTHER.*

THERE WAS NO *WAY* YOU COULD HAVE *KNOWN.*

AYE, I REALIZE THIS...

YET...

...STILL MY *HEART* AND *SOUL* DAMN ME FOR A *FOOL.*

I FELT THE *TREMORS* AND TRACED THEM ACROSS THE *ATLANTIC OCEAN FLOOR* TO THEIR *SOURCE.*

WHAT I DISCOVERED WAS THE *INCREDIBLE.*

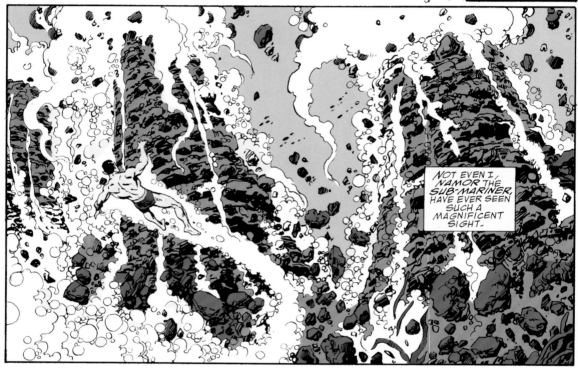

NOT EVEN I, *NAMOR THE SUB-MARINER,* HAVE EVER SEEN SUCH A *MAGNIFICENT SIGHT.*

BUT THEN *MY AWE* IS TEMPERED BY THE *REALIZATION* THAT THE CREATION OF THESE ISLES WILL HAVE *CATA-CLYSMIC RESULTS.*

THERE WILL BE *TIDAL WAVES,* PROBABLY EVEN NOW HEADING TOWARD THE EASTERN COAST OF THE *UNITED STATES.*

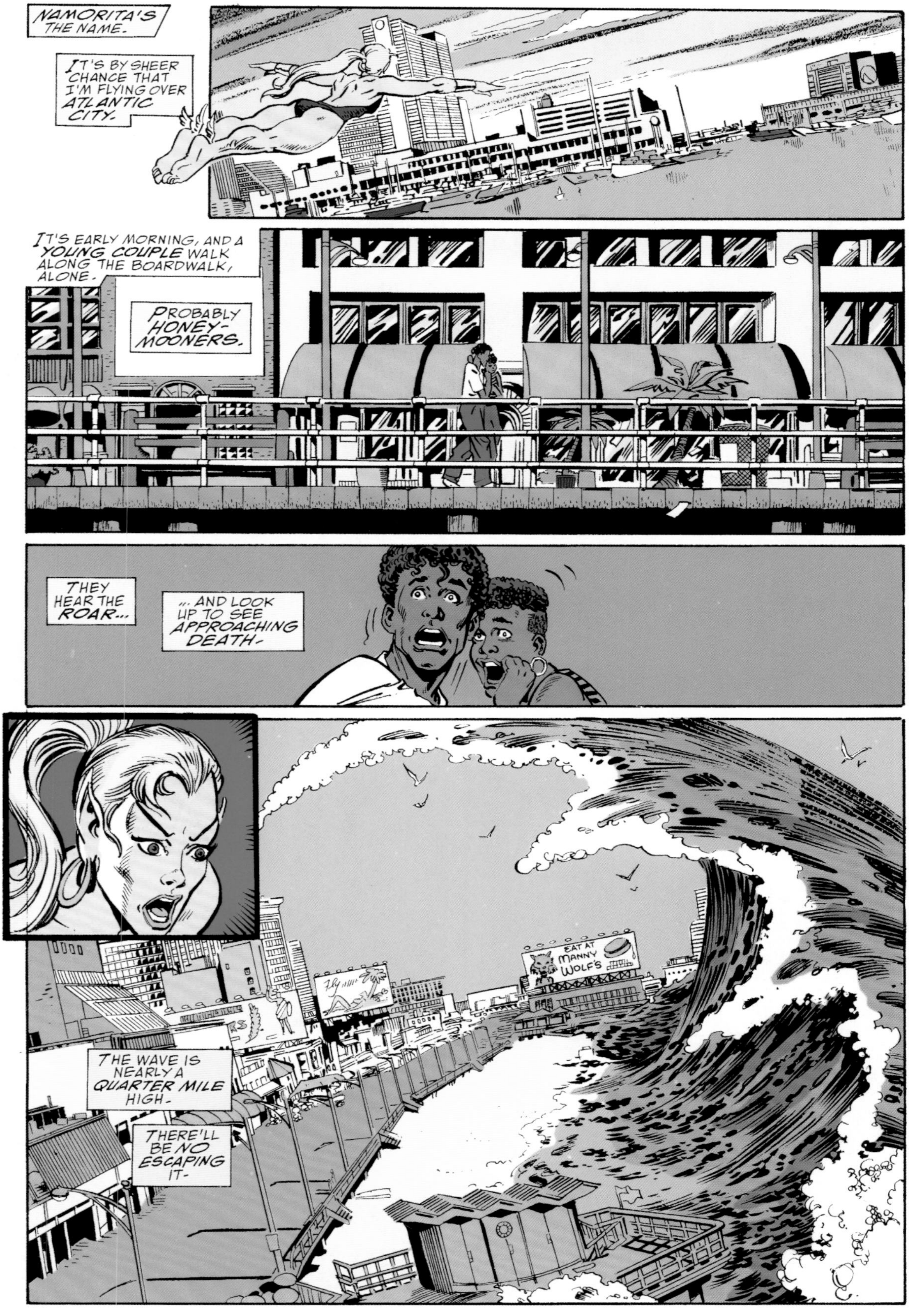
NAMORITA'S THE NAME.
IT'S BY SHEER CHANCE THAT I'M FLYING OVER ATLANTIC CITY.
IT'S EARLY MORNING, AND A YOUNG COUPLE WALK ALONG THE BOARDWALK, ALONE.
PROBABLY HONEY-MOONERS.
THEY HEAR THE ROAR...
...AND LOOK UP TO SEE APPROACHING DEATH-
EAT AT MANNY WOLF'S
THE WAVE IS NEARLY A QUARTER MILE HIGH.
THERE'LL BE NO ESCAPING IT-

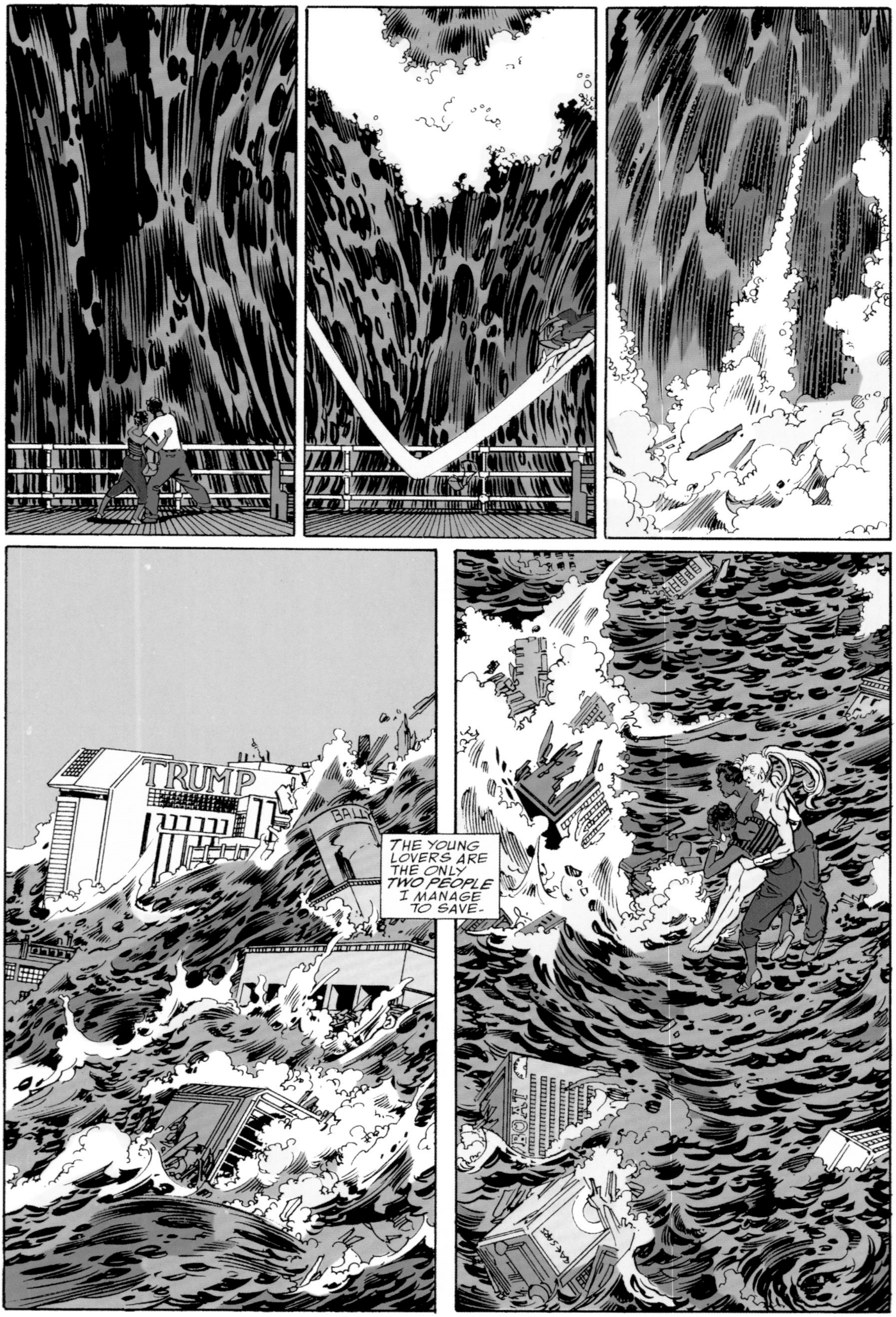
TRUMP
THE YOUNG LOVERS ARE THE ONLY TWO PEOPLE I MANAGE TO SAVE.

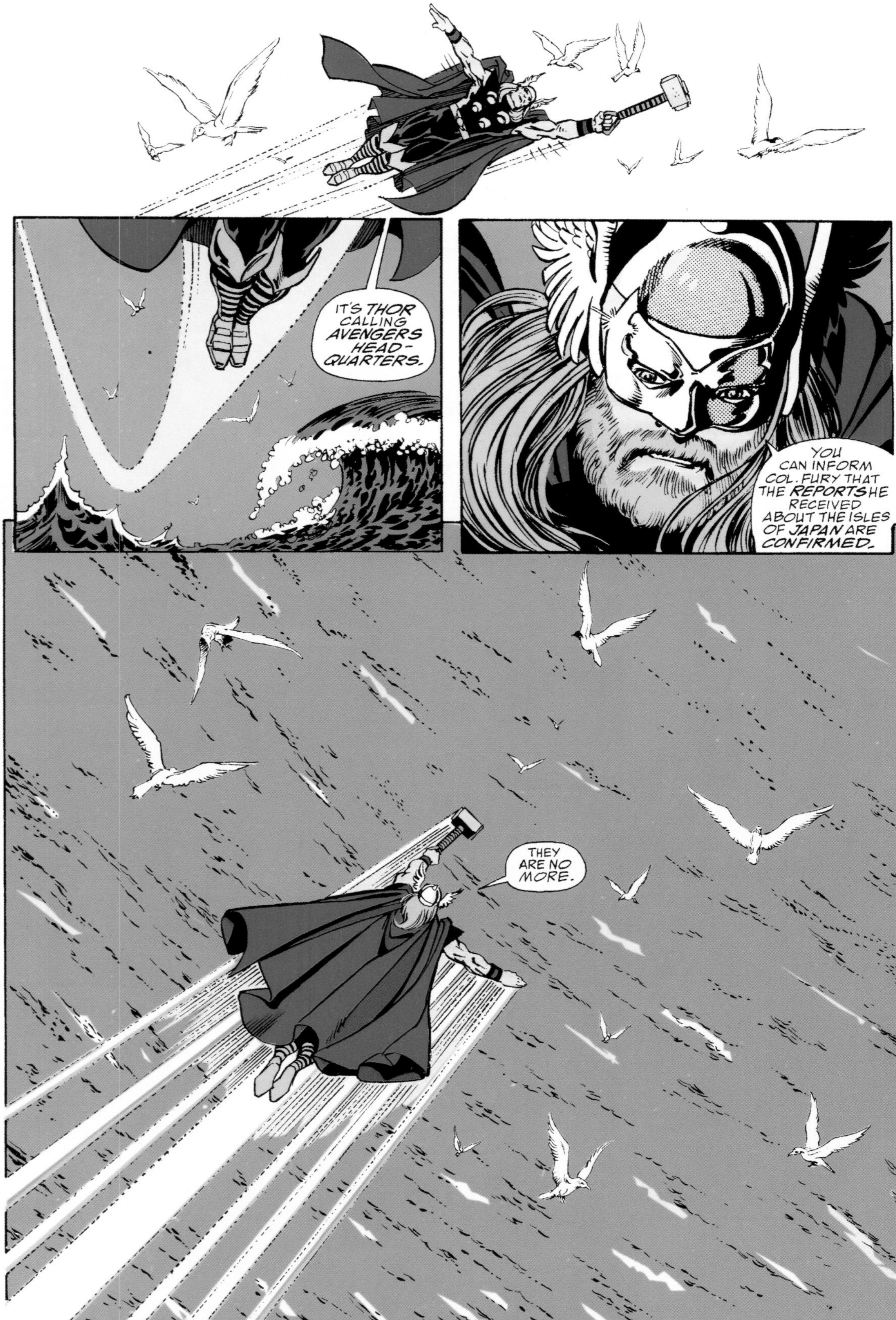
IT'S THOR CALLING AVENGERS HEAD-QUARTERS.
YOU CAN INFORM COL. FURY THAT THE REPORTS HE RECEIVED ABOUT THE ISLES OF JAPAN ARE CONFIRMED.
THEY ARE NO MORE.

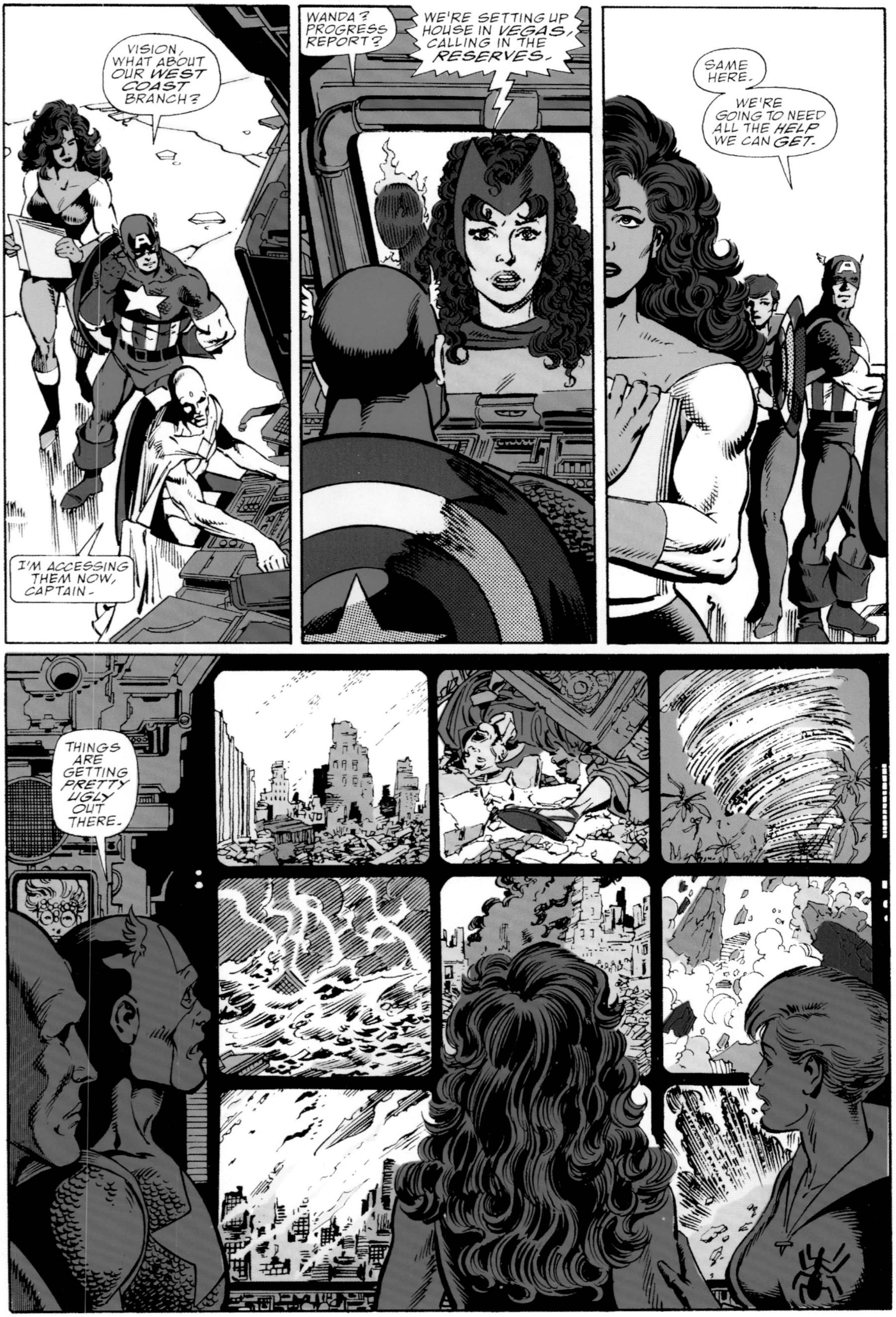
VISION, WHAT ABOUT OUR WEST COAST BRANCH?
I'M ACCESSING THEM NOW, CAPTAIN.
WANDA? PROGRESS REPORT?
WE'RE SETTING UP HOUSE IN VEGAS, CALLING IN THE RESERVES.
SAME HERE.
WE'RE GOING TO NEED ALL THE HELP WE CAN GET.
THINGS ARE GETTING PRETTY UGLY OUT THERE.

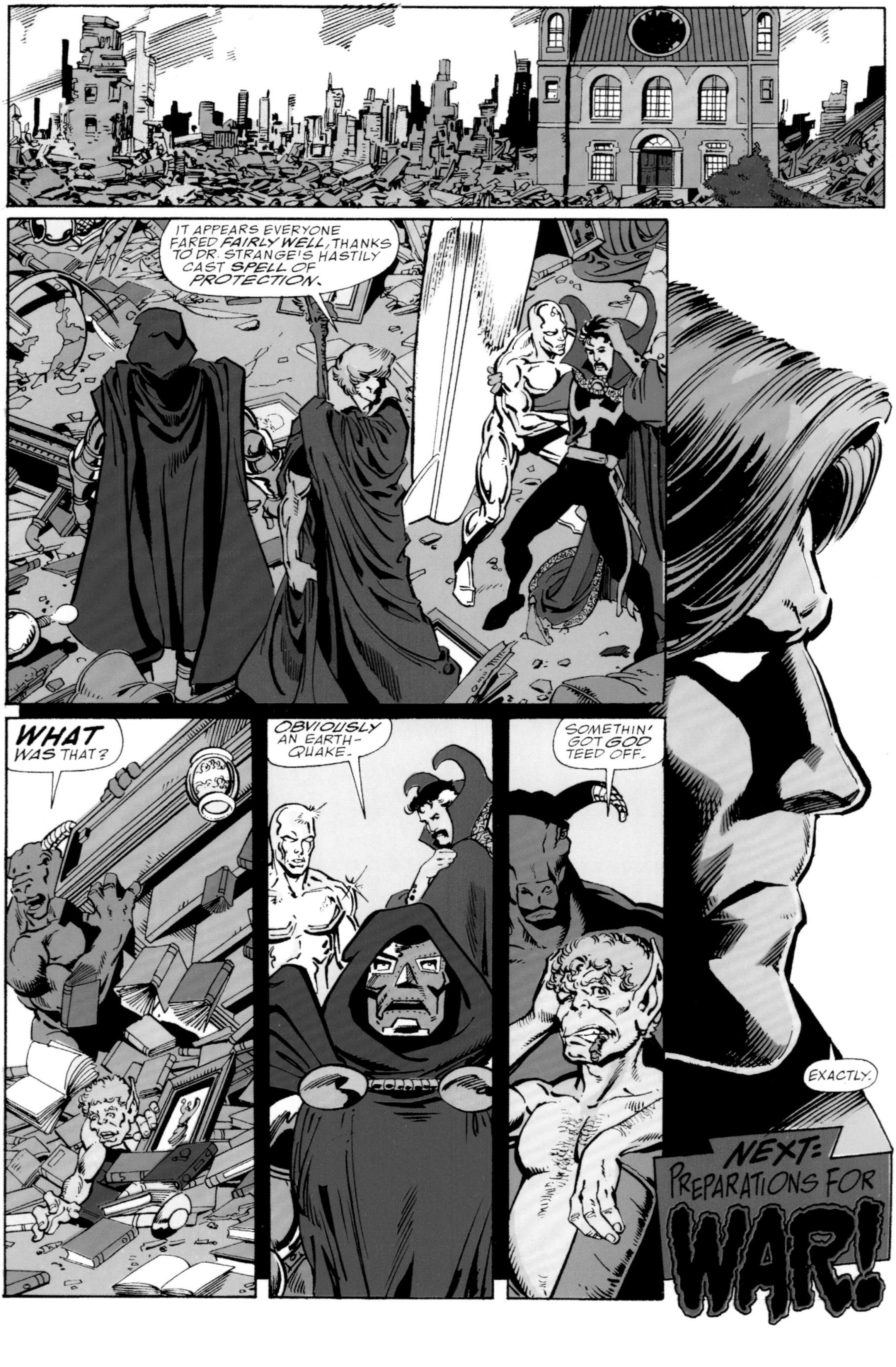
IT APPEARS EVERYONE FARED FAIRLY WELL, THANKS TO DR. STRANGE'S HASTILY CAST SPELL OF PROTECTION.
WHAT WAS THAT?
OBVIOUSLY AN EARTH-QUAKE.
SOMETHIN' GOT GOD TEED OFF.
EXACTLY.
NEXT: PREPARATIONS FOR WAR!

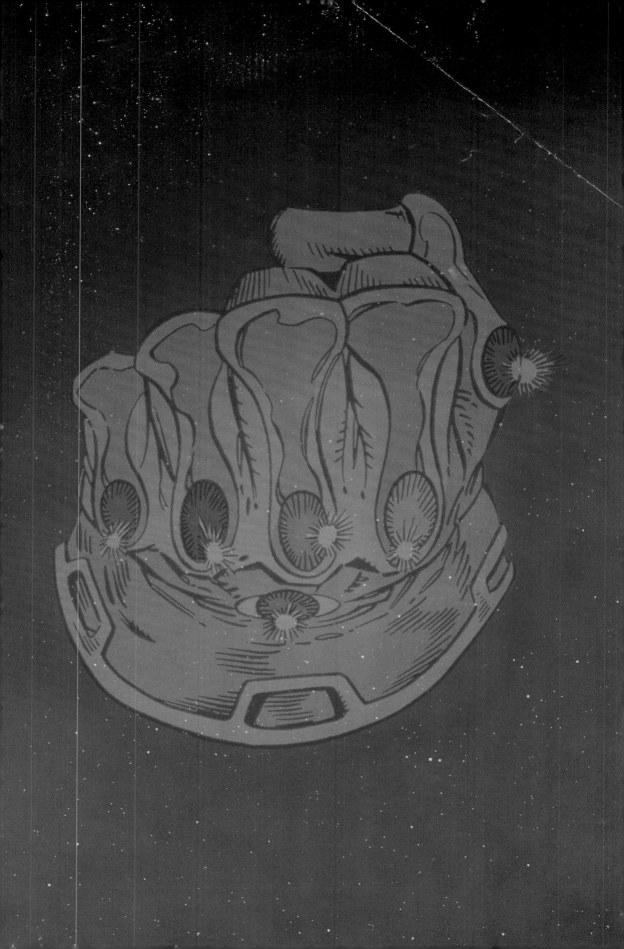

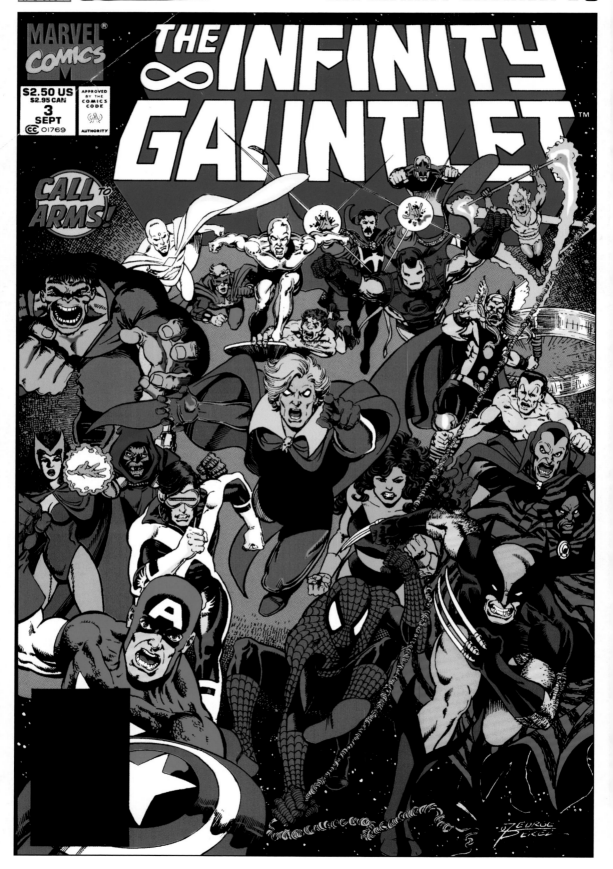

MARVEL COMICS®

$2.50 US
$2.95 CAN
3
SEPT
CC 01769
APPROVED BY THE COMICS CODE AUTHORITY

THE ∞ INFINITY GAUNTLET ™

CALL TO ARMS!

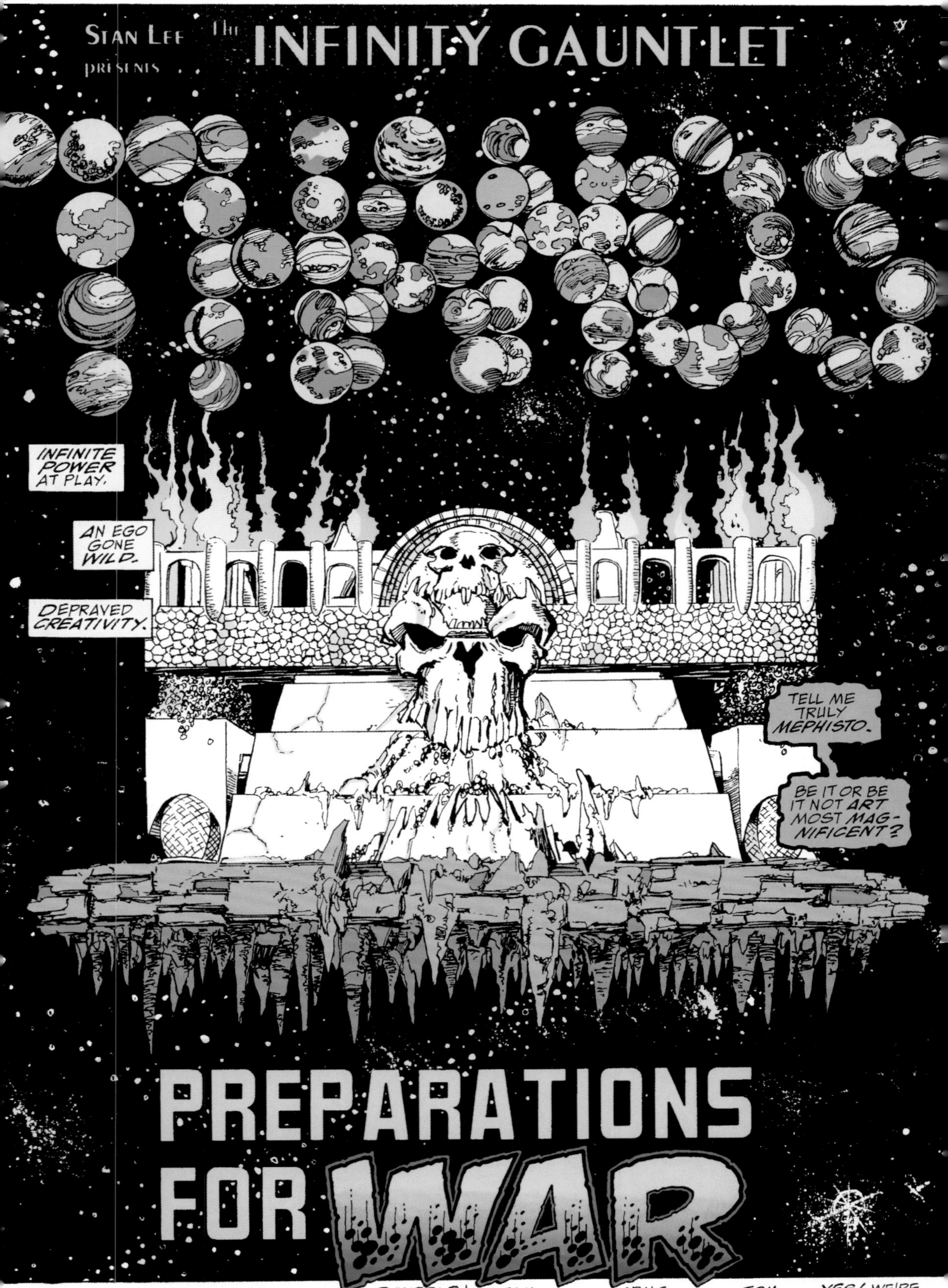
STAN LEE PRESENTS
The INFINITY GAUNTLET
INFINITE POWER AT PLAY.
AN EGO GONE WILD.
DEPRAVED CREATIVITY.
TELL ME TRULY MEPHISTO.
BE IT OR BE IT NOT ART MOST MAG-NIFICENT?
PREPARATIONS FOR WAR

JIM STARLIN WRITER
GEORGE PEREZ PENCILS
JOE RUBINSTEIN INKS
SCHEELE & LAUGHLIN COLORS
JACK MORELLI LETTERS
CRAIG ANDERSON EDITOR
TOM DeFALCO CHIEF
YES! WE'RE ALL STILL HERE!!

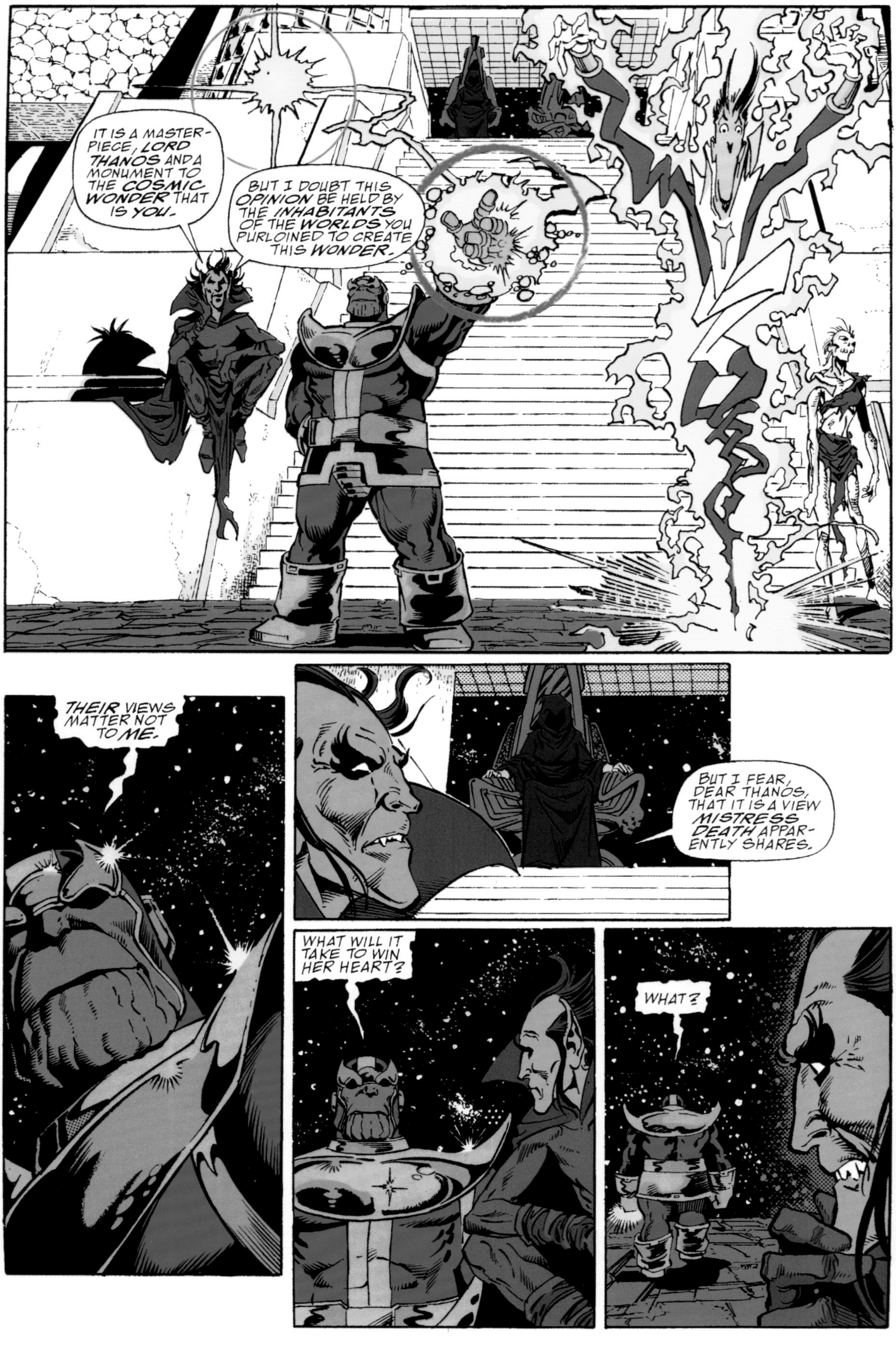
IT IS A MASTERPIECE, LORD THANOS AND A MONUMENT TO THE COSMIC WONDER THAT IS YOU.
BUT I DOUBT THIS OPINION BE HELD BY THE INHABITANTS OF THE WORLDS YOU PURLOINED TO CREATE THIS WONDER.
THEIR VIEWS MATTER NOT TO ME.
BUT I FEAR, DEAR THANOS, THAT IT IS A VIEW MISTRESS DEATH APPARENTLY SHARES.
WHAT WILL IT TAKE TO WIN HER HEART?
WHAT?

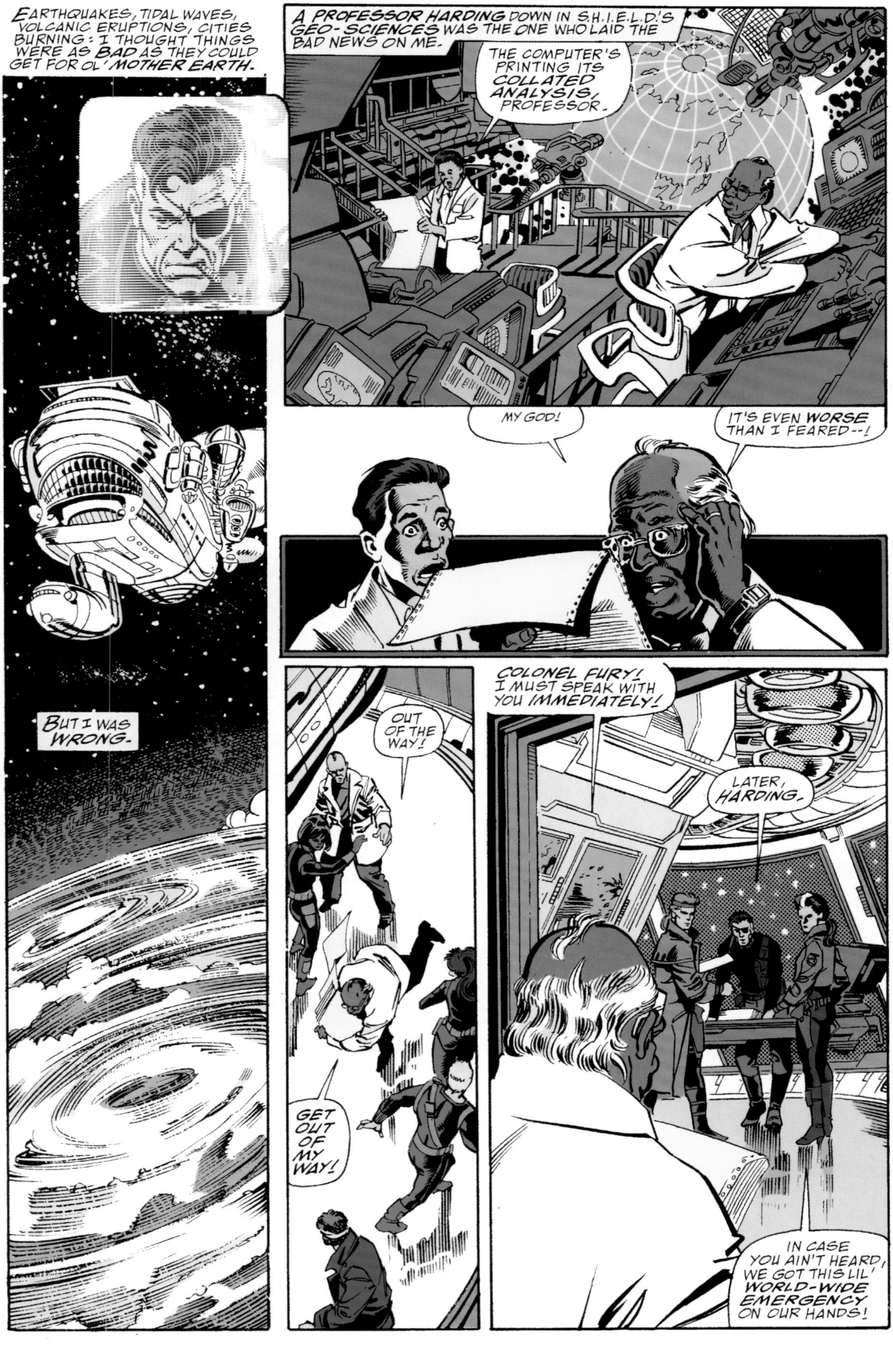
EARTHQUAKES, TIDAL WAVES, VOLCANIC ERUPTIONS, CITIES BURNING: I THOUGHT THINGS WERE AS BAD AS THEY COULD GET FOR OL' MOTHER EARTH.
BUT I WAS WRONG.
A PROFESSOR HARDING DOWN IN S.H.I.E.L.D.'S GEO-SCIENCES WAS THE ONE WHO LAID THE BAD NEWS ON ME.
THE COMPUTER'S PRINTING ITS COLLATED ANALYSIS, PROFESSOR.
MY GOD!
IT'S EVEN WORSE THAN I FEARED--!
OUT OF THE WAY!
GET OUT OF MY WAY!
COLONEL FURY! I MUST SPEAK WITH YOU IMMEDIATELY!
LATER, HARDING.
IN CASE YOU AIN'T HEARD, WE GOT THIS LIL' WORLD-WIDE EMERGENCY ON OUR HANDS!

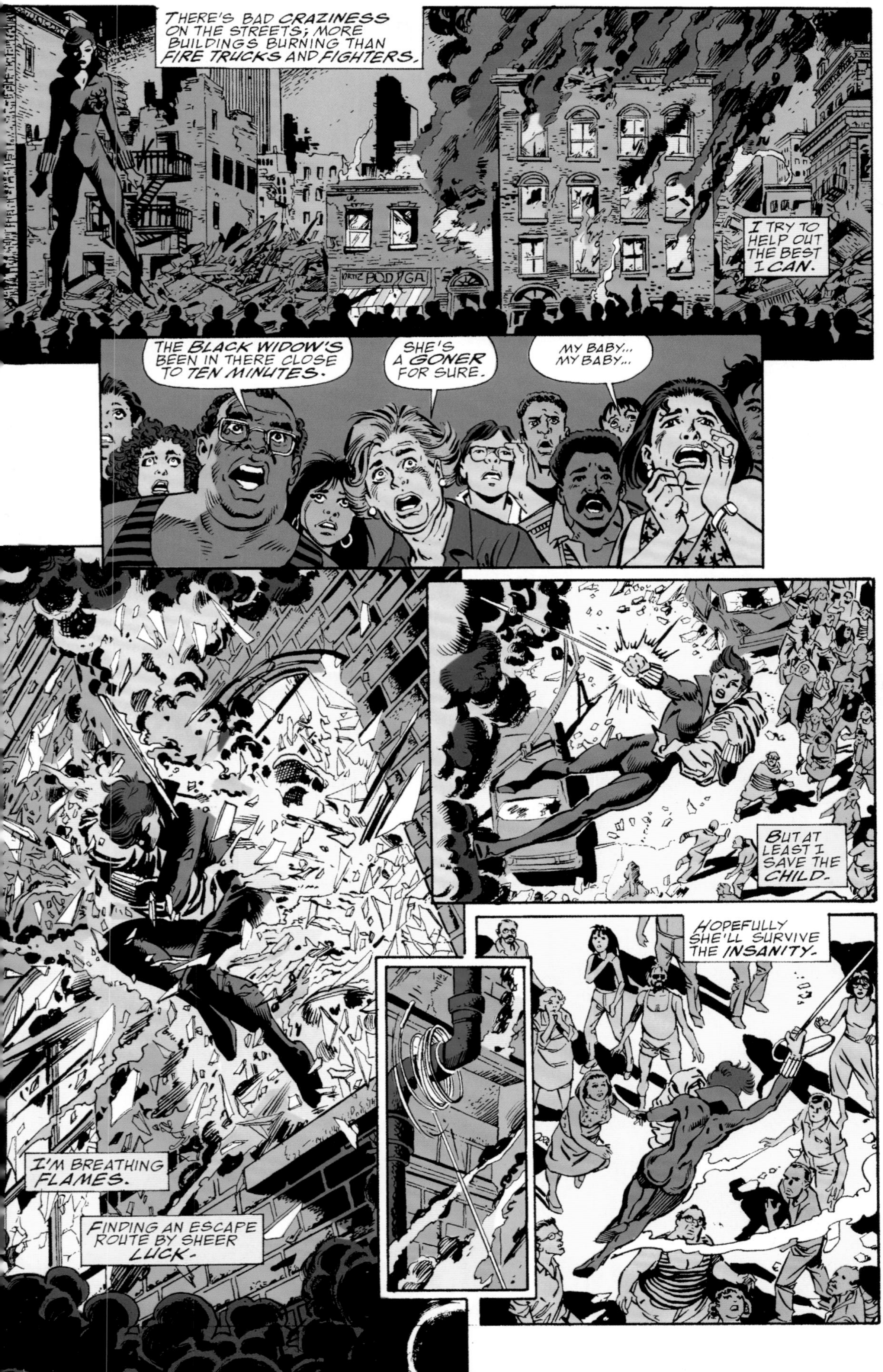
THERE'S BAD CRAZINESS ON THE STREETS; MORE BUILDINGS BURNING THAN FIRE TRUCKS AND FIGHTERS.
BODEGA
I TRY TO HELP OUT THE BEST I CAN.
THE BLACK WIDOW'S BEEN IN THERE CLOSE TO TEN MINUTES.
SHE'S A GONER FOR SURE.
MY BABY... MY BABY...
I'M BREATHING FLAMES.
FINDING AN ESCAPE ROUTE BY SHEER LUCK.
BUT AT LEAST I SAVE THE CHILD.
HOPEFULLY SHE'LL SURVIVE THE INSANITY.

MORE THAN ENOUGH HAVE DIED ALREADY.

LOOK! ON THE FIFTH FLOOR!

HELP ME!

FOR GOD'S SAKE-- SOMEBODY HELP ME!!

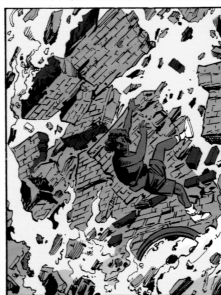

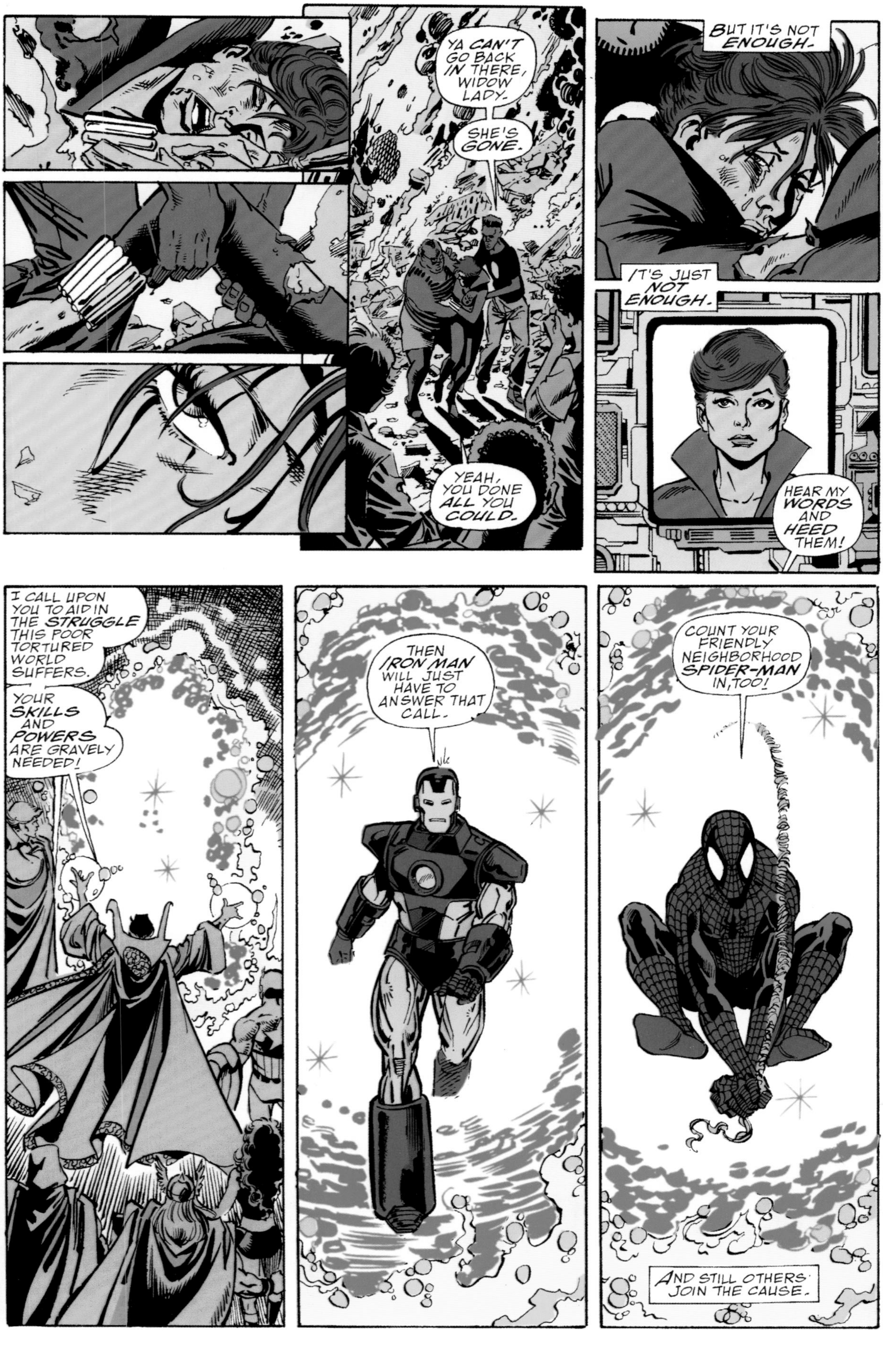
YA CAN'T GO BACK IN THERE, WIDOW LADY.
SHE'S GONE.
YEAH, YOU DONE ALL YOU COULD.
BUT IT'S NOT ENOUGH.
IT'S JUST NOT ENOUGH.
HEAR MY WORDS AND HEED THEM!
I CALL UPON YOU TO AID IN THE STRUGGLE THIS POOR TORTURED WORLD SUFFERS.
YOUR SKILLS AND POWERS ARE GRAVELY NEEDED!
THEN IRON MAN WILL JUST HAVE TO ANSWER THAT CALL.
COUNT YOUR FRIENDLY NEIGHBORHOOD SPIDER-MAN IN, TOO!
AND STILL OTHERS JOIN THE CAUSE.

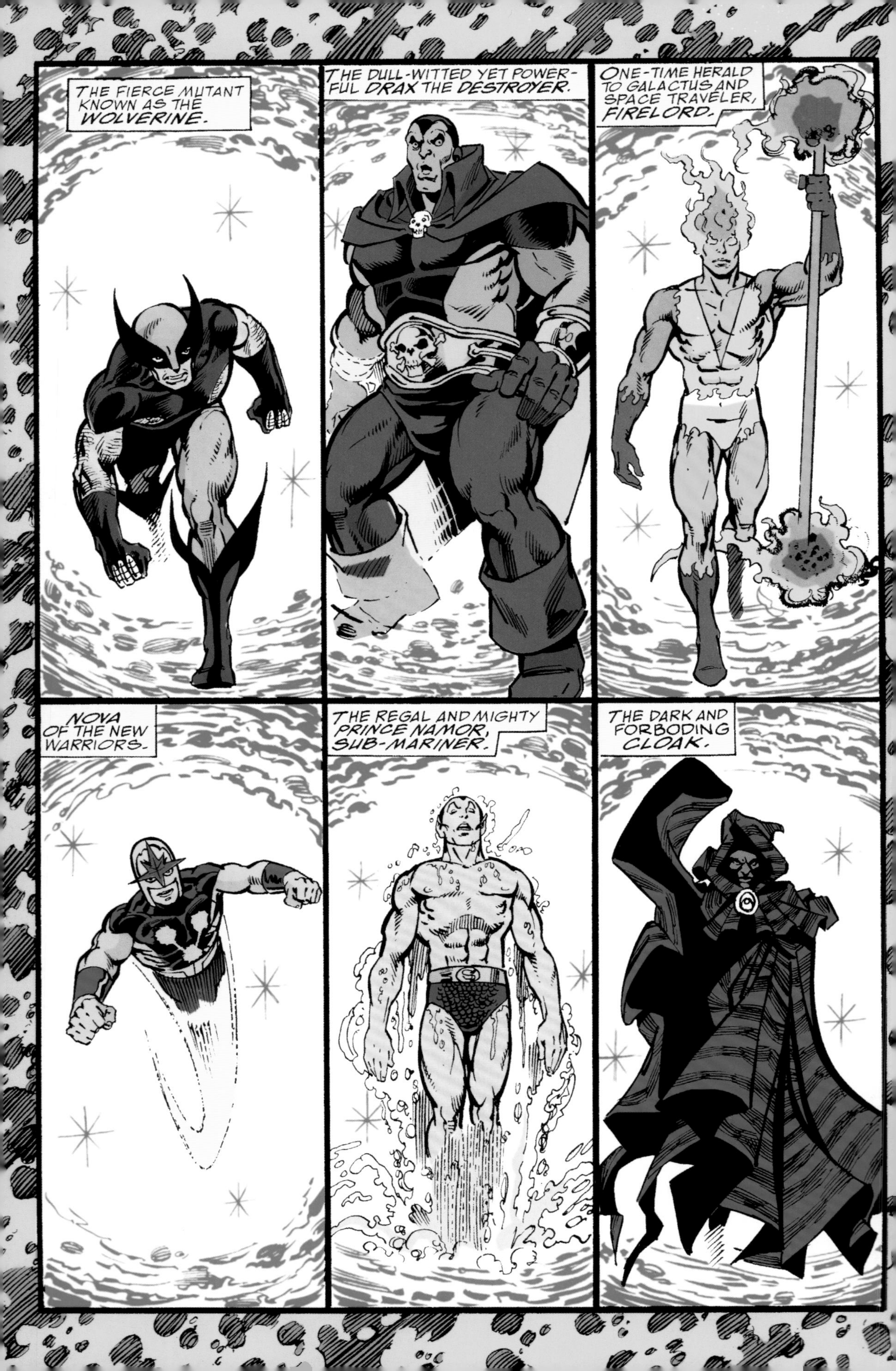
THE FIERCE MUTANT KNOWN AS THE WOLVERINE.
THE DULL-WITTED YET POWERFUL DRAX THE DESTROYER.
ONE-TIME HERALD TO GALACTUS AND SPACE TRAVELER, FIRELORD.
NOVA OF THE NEW WARRIORS.
THE REGAL AND MIGHTY PRINCE NAMOR, SUB-MARINER.
THE DARK AND FORBODING CLOAK.

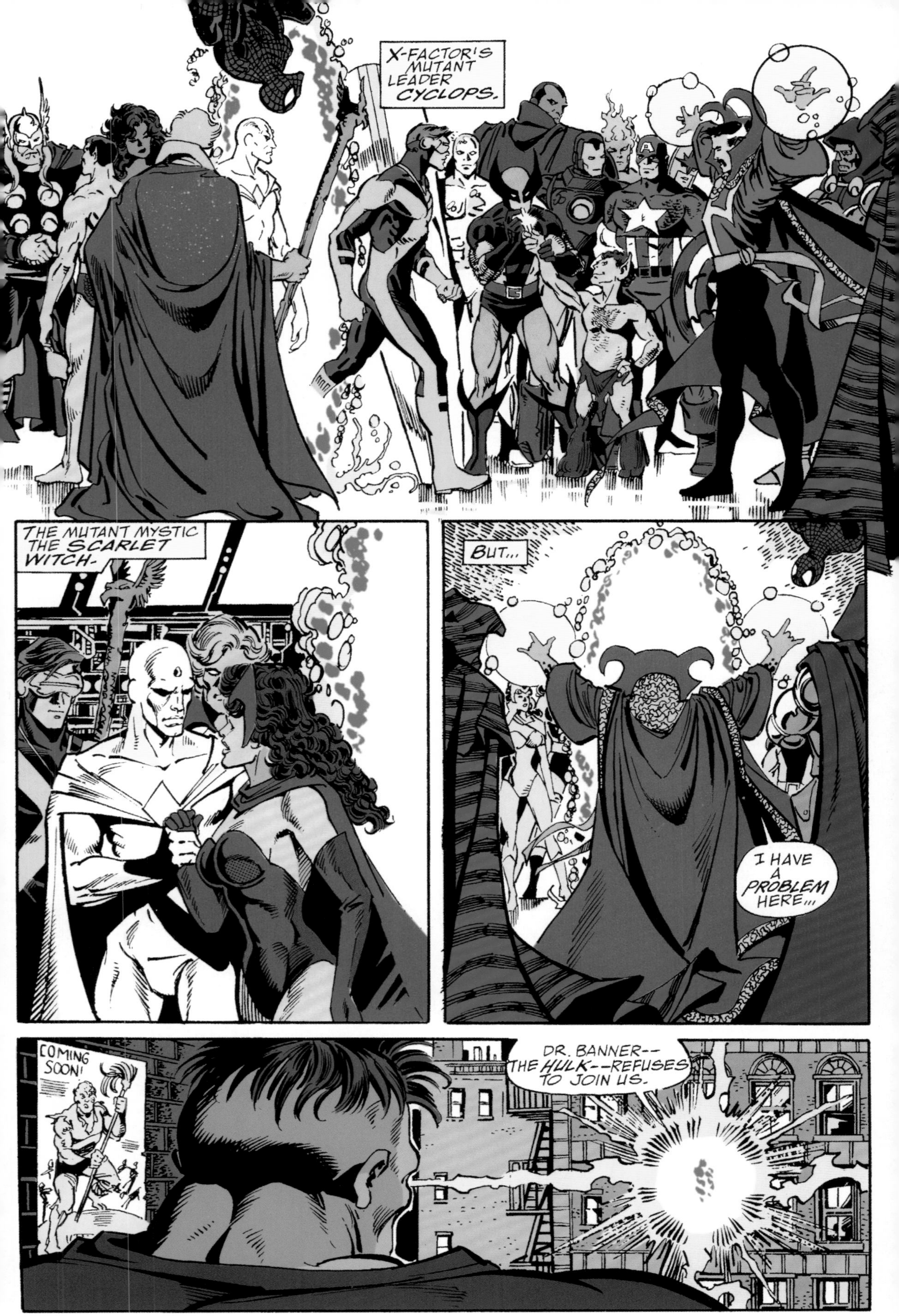

X-FACTOR'S MUTANT LEADER CYCLOPS.
THE MUTANT MYSTIC THE SCARLET WITCH-
BUT...
I HAVE A PROBLEM HERE...
COMING SOON!
DR. BANNER-- THE HULK--REFUSES TO JOIN US.

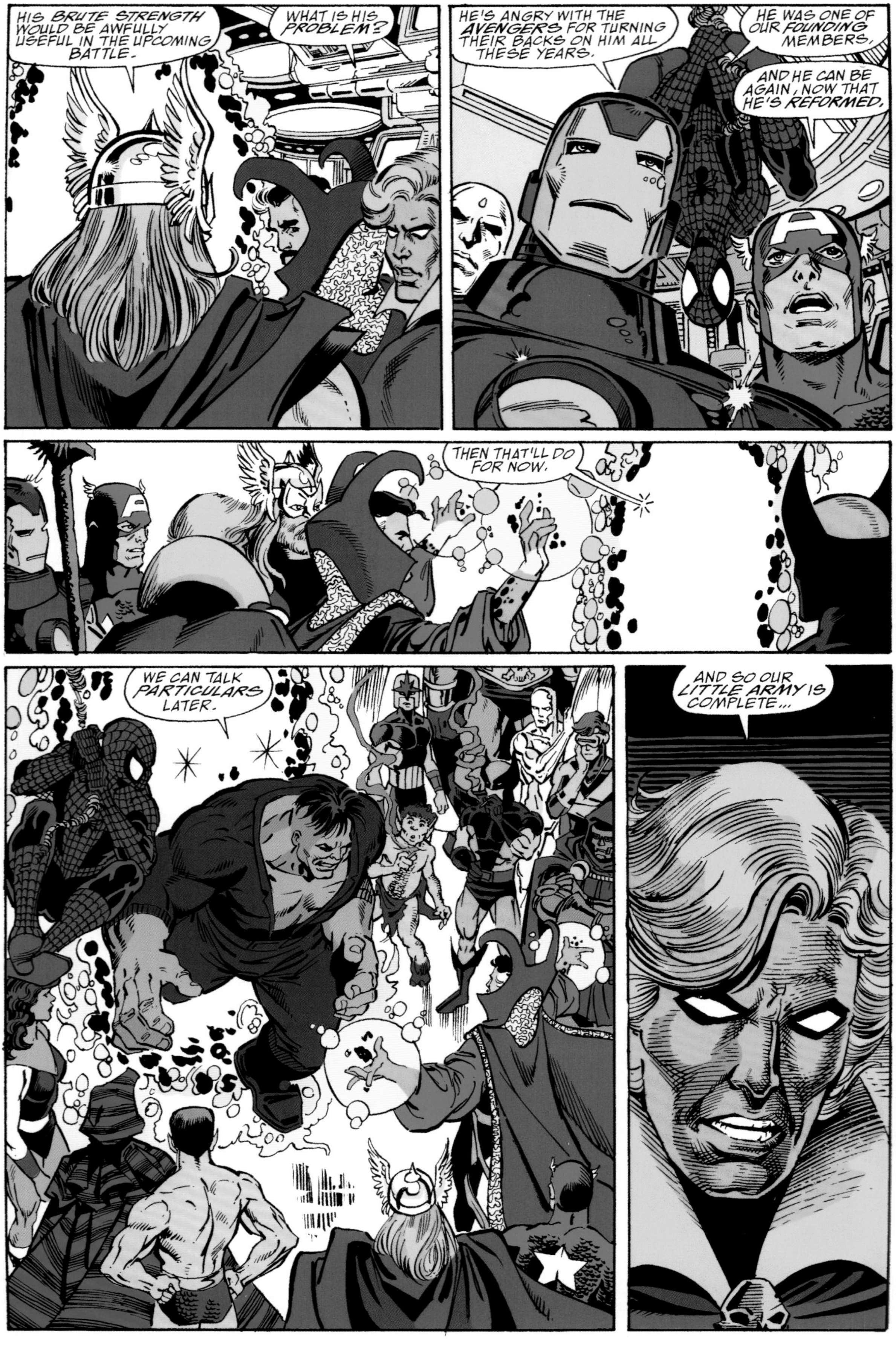
HIS BRUTE STRENGTH WOULD BE AWFULLY USEFUL IN THE UPCOMING BATTLE.
WHAT IS HIS PROBLEM?
HE'S ANGRY WITH THE AVENGERS FOR TURNING THEIR BACKS ON HIM ALL THESE YEARS.
HE WAS ONE OF OUR FOUNDING MEMBERS.
AND HE CAN BE AGAIN, NOW THAT HE'S REFORMED.
THEN THAT'LL DO FOR NOW.
WE CAN TALK PARTICULARS LATER.
AND SO OUR LITTLE ARMY IS COMPLETE...

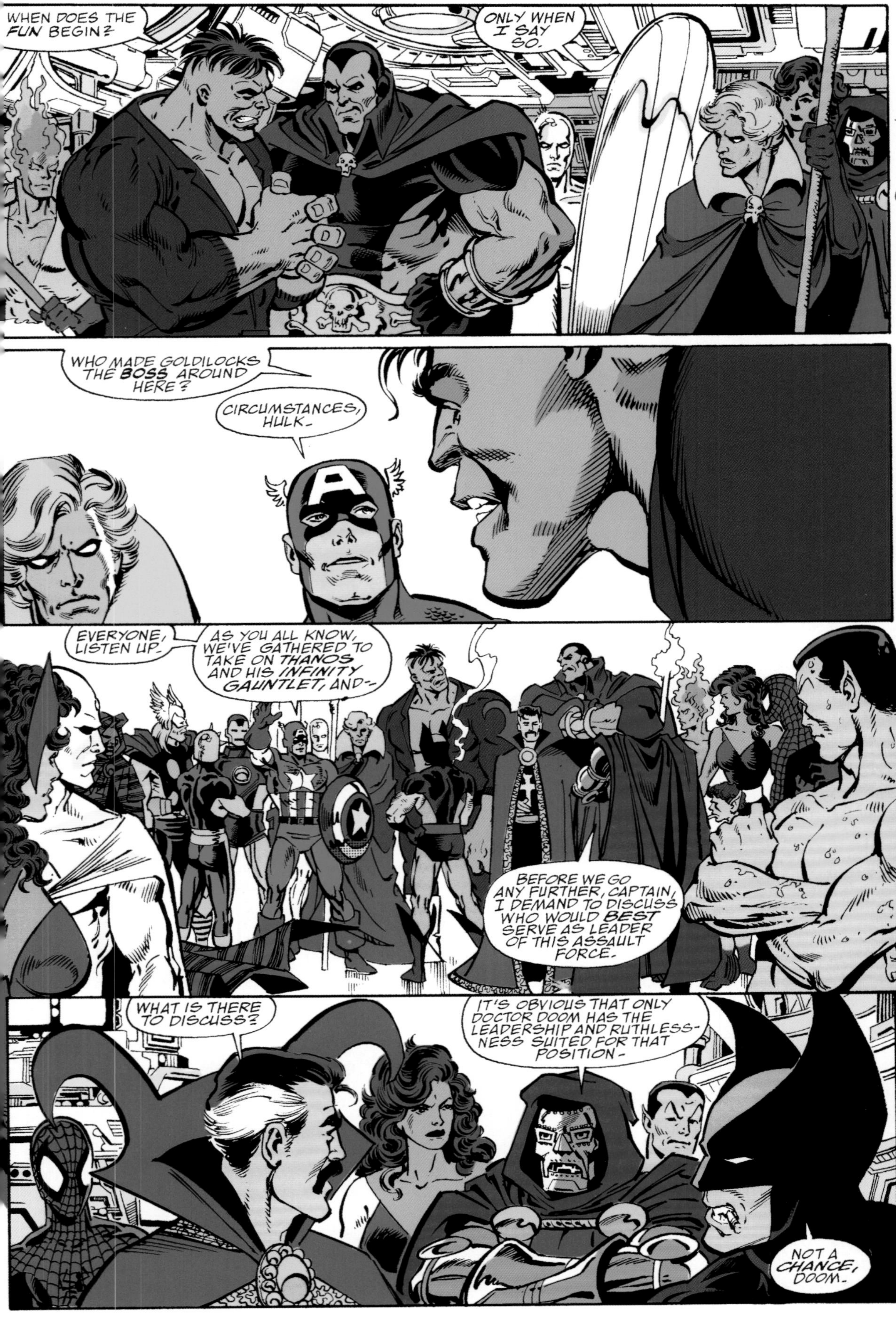

WHEN DOES THE FUN BEGIN?
ONLY WHEN I SAY SO.
WHO MADE GOLDILOCKS THE BOSS AROUND HERE?
CIRCUMSTANCES, HULK.
EVERYONE, LISTEN UP.
AS YOU ALL KNOW, WE'VE GATHERED TO TAKE ON THANOS AND HIS INFINITY GAUNTLET, AND--
BEFORE WE GO ANY FURTHER, CAPTAIN, I DEMAND TO DISCUSS WHO WOULD BEST SERVE AS LEADER OF THIS ASSAULT FORCE.
WHAT IS THERE TO DISCUSS?
IT'S OBVIOUS THAT ONLY DOCTOR DOOM HAS THE LEADERSHIP AND RUTHLESS-NESS SUITED FOR THAT POSITION--
NOT A CHANCE, DOOM.

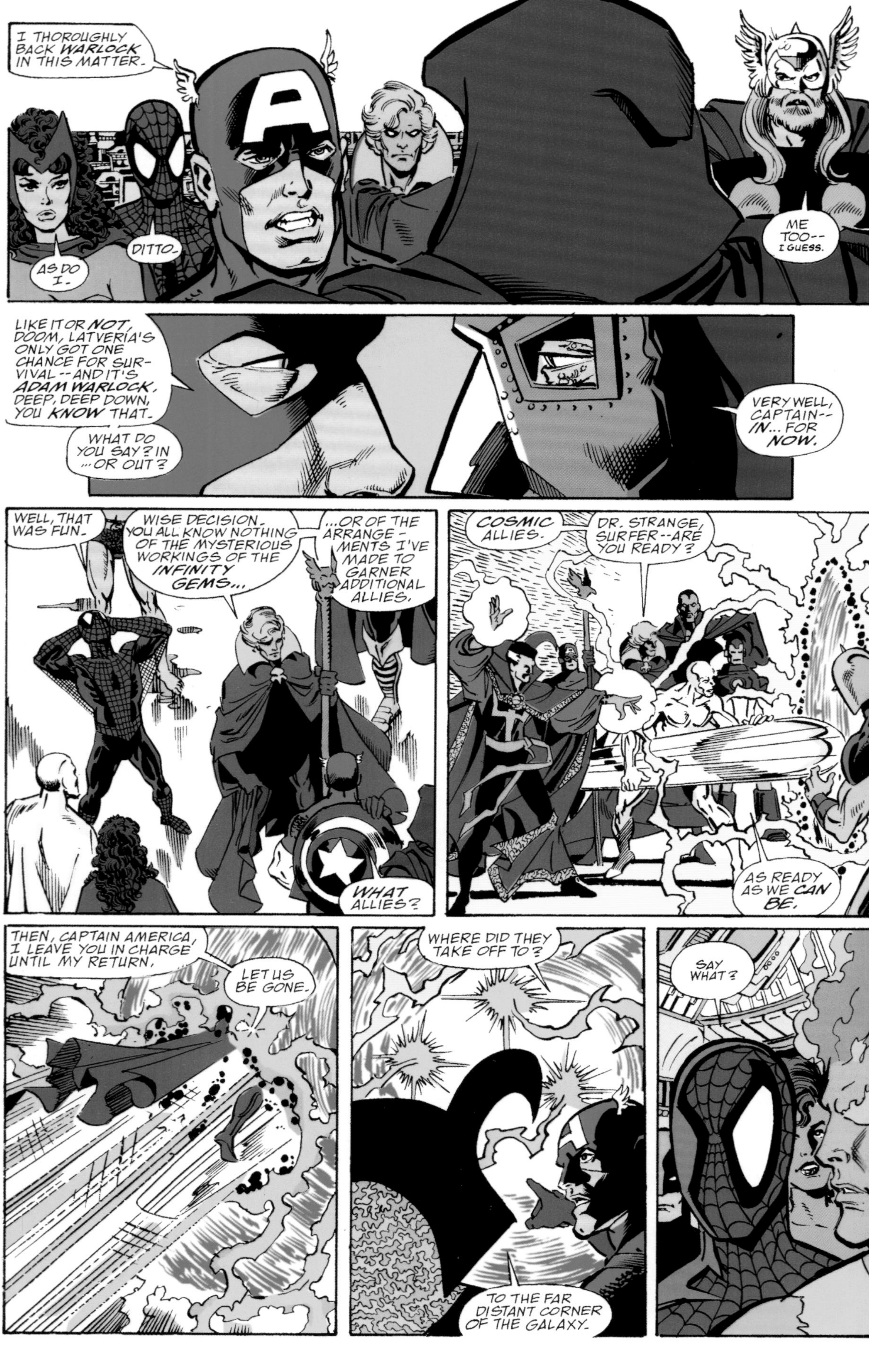
I THOROUGHLY BACK WARLOCK IN THIS MATTER.
DITTO.
AS DO I.
ME TOO-- I GUESS.
LIKE IT OR NOT, DOOM, LATVERIA'S ONLY GOT ONE CHANCE FOR SURVIVAL -- AND IT'S ADAM WARLOCK. DEEP, DEEP DOWN, YOU KNOW THAT.
WHAT DO YOU SAY? IN ...OR OUT?
VERY WELL, CAPTAIN-- IN... FOR NOW.
WELL, THAT WAS FUN.
WISE DECISION. YOU ALL KNOW NOTHING OF THE MYSTERIOUS WORKINGS OF THE INFINITY GEMS...
...OR OF THE ARRANGEMENTS I'VE MADE TO GARNER ADDITIONAL ALLIES.
WHAT ALLIES?
COSMIC ALLIES.
DR. STRANGE, SURFER--ARE YOU READY?
AS READY AS WE CAN BE.
THEN, CAPTAIN AMERICA, I LEAVE YOU IN CHARGE UNTIL MY RETURN.
LET US BE GONE.
WHERE DID THEY TAKE OFF TO?
TO THE FAR DISTANT CORNER OF THE GALAXY.
SAY WHAT?

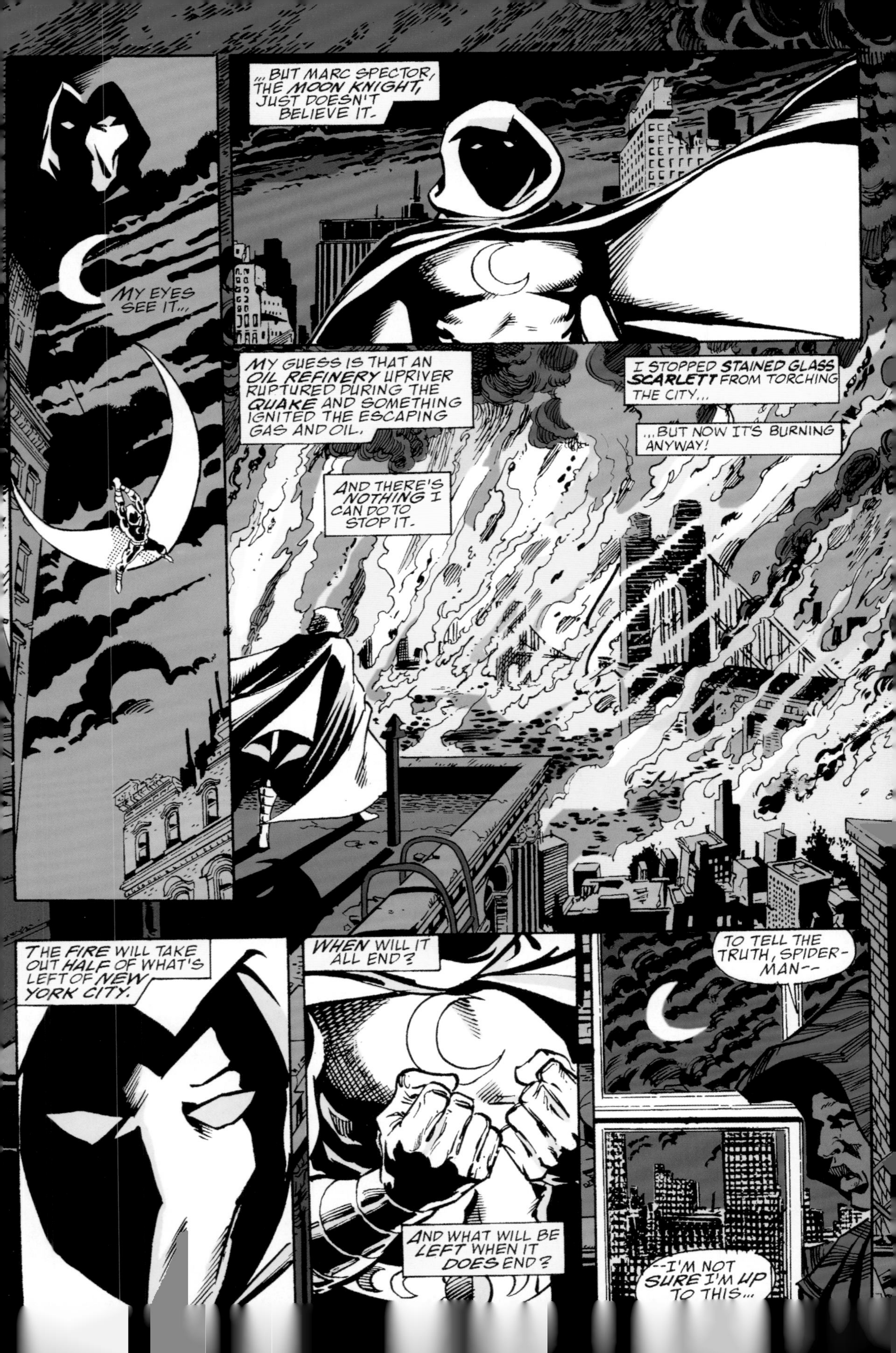

MY EYES SEE IT...
...BUT MARC SPECTOR, THE MOON KNIGHT, JUST DOESN'T BELIEVE IT.
MY GUESS IS THAT AN OIL REFINERY UPRIVER RUPTURED DURING THE QUAKE AND SOMETHING IGNITED THE ESCAPING GAS AND OIL.
AND THERE'S NOTHING I CAN DO TO STOP IT.
I STOPPED STAINED GLASS SCARLETT FROM TORCHING THE CITY...
...BUT NOW IT'S BURNING ANYWAY!
THE FIRE WILL TAKE OUT HALF OF WHAT'S LEFT OF NEW YORK CITY.
WHEN WILL IT ALL END?
AND WHAT WILL BE LEFT WHEN IT DOES END?
TO TELL THE TRUTH, SPIDER-MAN--
--I'M NOT SURE I'M UP TO THIS...

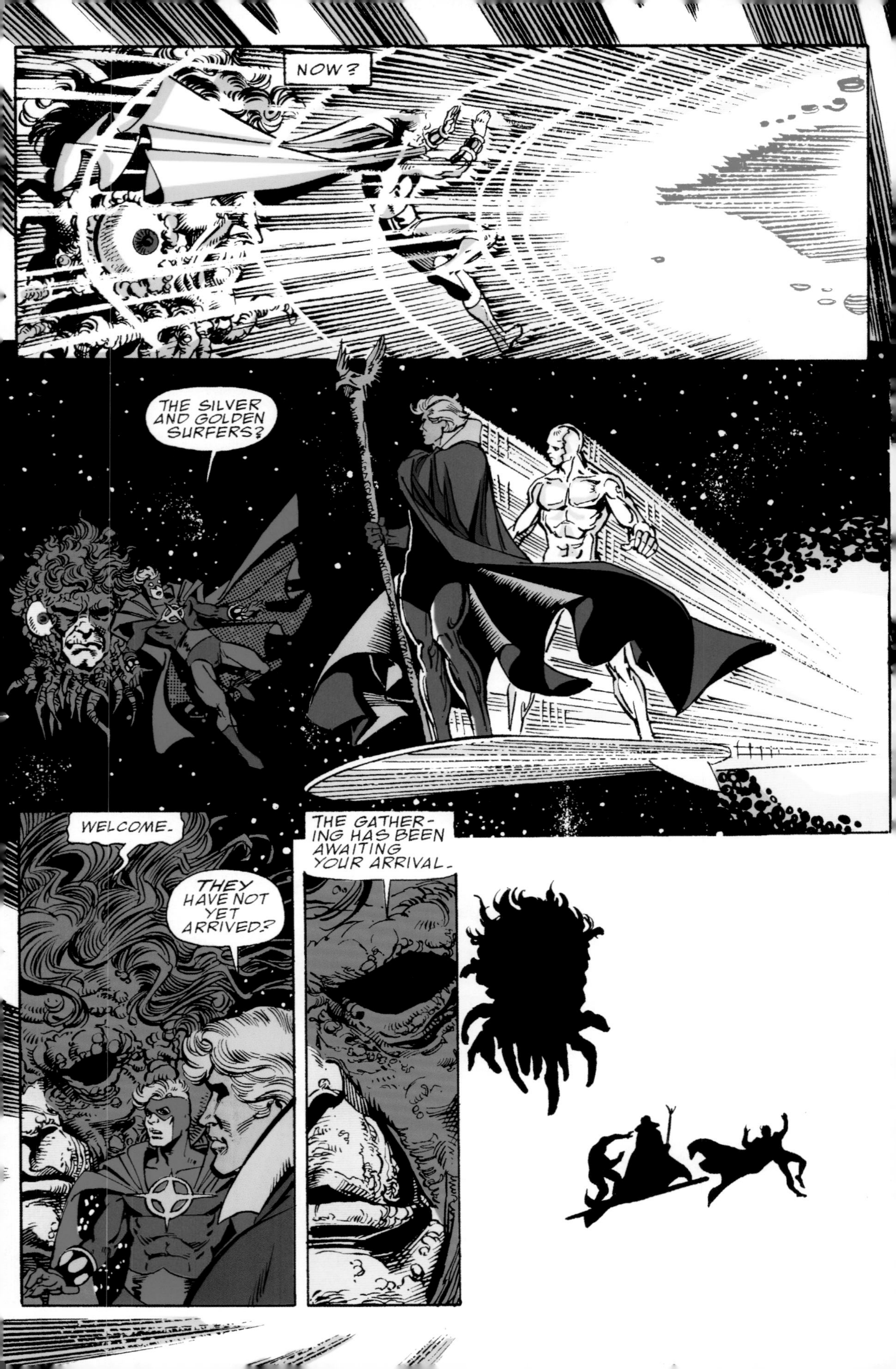
NOW?
THE SILVER AND GOLDEN SURFERS?
WELCOME.
THEY HAVE NOT YET ARRIVED?
THE GATHERING HAS BEEN AWAITING YOUR ARRIVAL.

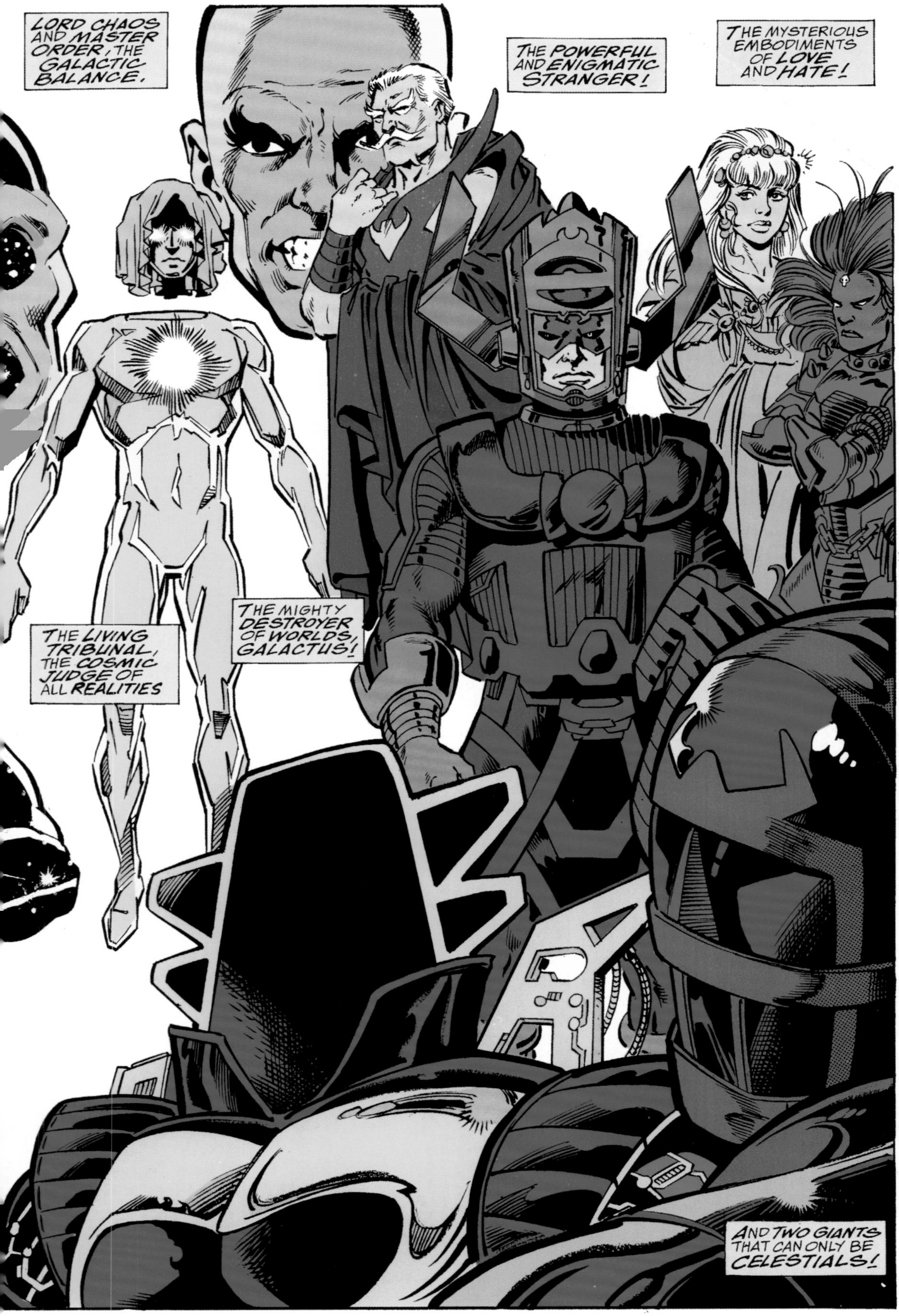
LORD CHAOS AND MASTER ORDER, THE GALACTIC BALANCE.
THE POWERFUL AND ENIGMATIC STRANGER!
THE MYSTERIOUS EMBODIMENTS OF LOVE AND HATE!
THE LIVING TRIBUNAL, THE COSMIC JUDGE OF ALL REALITIES
THE MIGHTY DESTROYER OF WORLDS, GALACTUS!
AND TWO GIANTS THAT CAN ONLY BE CELESTIALS!

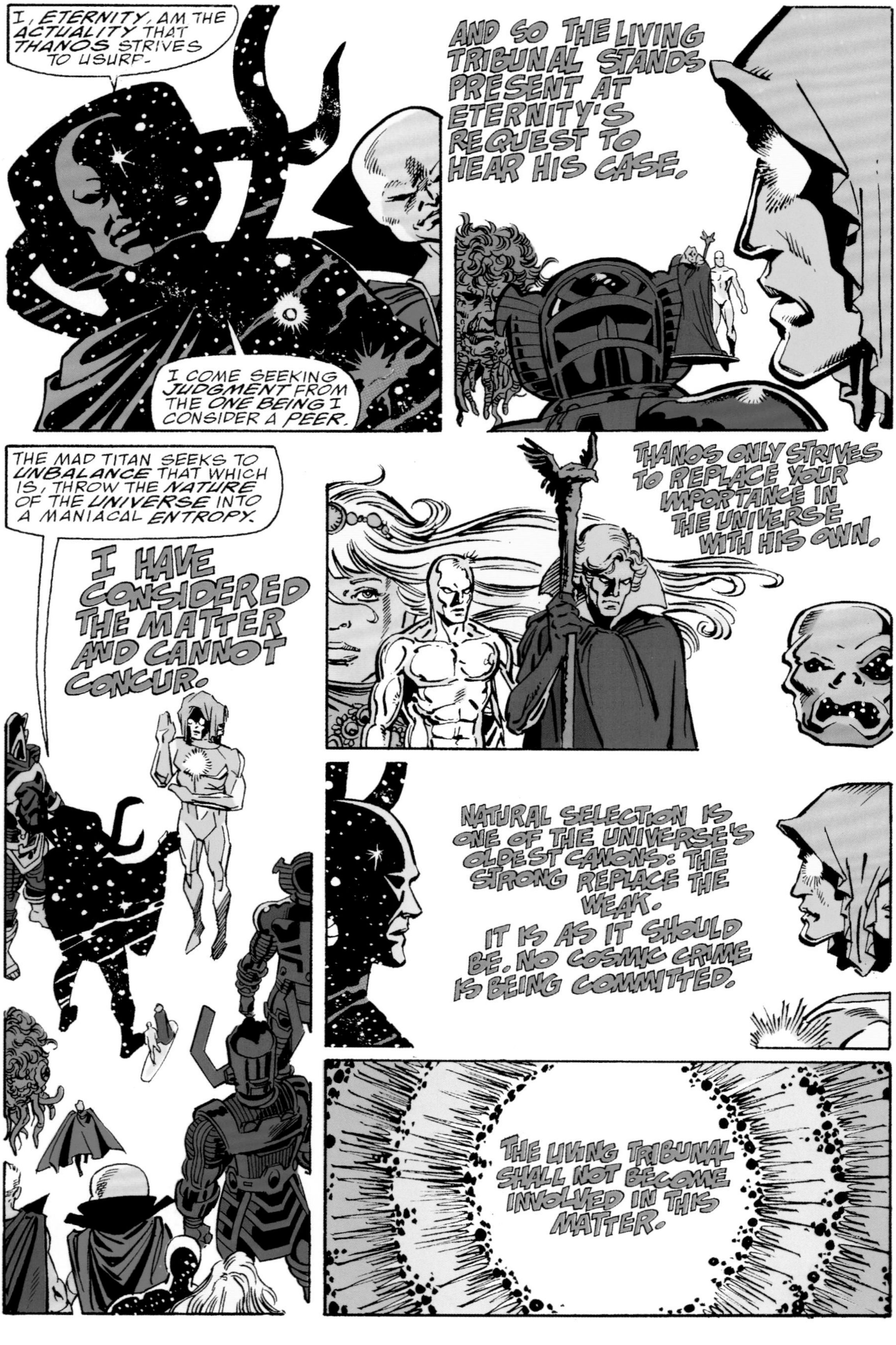

I, ETERNITY, AM THE ACTUALITY THAT THANOS STRIVES TO USURP--
I COME SEEKING JUDGMENT FROM THE ONE BEING I CONSIDER A PEER.
AND SO THE LIVING TRIBUNAL STANDS PRESENT AT ETERNITY'S REQUEST TO HEAR HIS CASE.
THE MAD TITAN SEEKS TO UNBALANCE THAT WHICH IS, THROW THE NATURE OF THE UNIVERSE INTO A MANIACAL ENTROPY.
I HAVE CONSIDERED THE MATTER AND CANNOT CONCUR.
THANOS ONLY STRIVES TO REPLACE YOUR IMPORTANCE IN THE UNIVERSE WITH HIS OWN.
NATURAL SELECTION IS ONE OF THE UNIVERSE'S OLDEST CANONS: THE STRONG REPLACE THE WEAK.
IT IS AS IT SHOULD BE. NO COSMIC CRIME IS BEING COMMITTED.
THE LIVING TRIBUNAL SHALL NOT BECOME INVOLVED IN THIS MATTER.

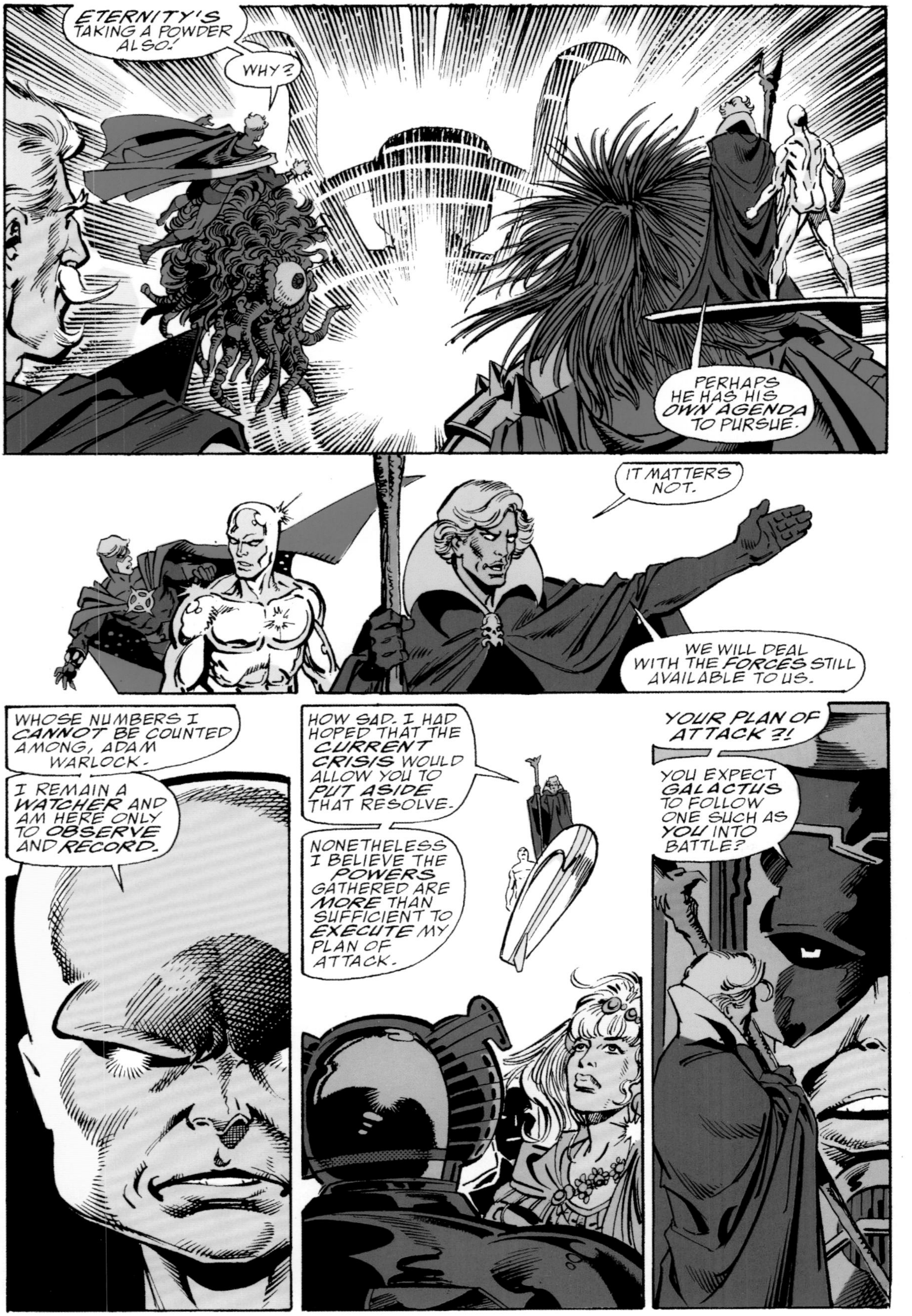
ETERNITY'S TAKING A POWDER ALSO!
WHY?
PERHAPS HE HAS HIS OWN AGENDA TO PURSUE.
IT MATTERS NOT.
WE WILL DEAL WITH THE FORCES STILL AVAILABLE TO US.
WHOSE NUMBERS I CANNOT BE COUNTED AMONG, ADAM WARLOCK.
I REMAIN A WATCHER AND AM HERE ONLY TO OBSERVE AND RECORD.
HOW SAD. I HAD HOPED THAT THE CURRENT CRISIS WOULD ALLOW YOU TO PUT ASIDE THAT RESOLVE.
NONETHELESS I BELIEVE THE POWERS GATHERED ARE MORE THAN SUFFICIENT TO EXECUTE MY PLAN OF ATTACK.
YOUR PLAN OF ATTACK?!
YOU EXPECT GALACTUS TO FOLLOW ONE SUCH AS YOU INTO BATTLE?

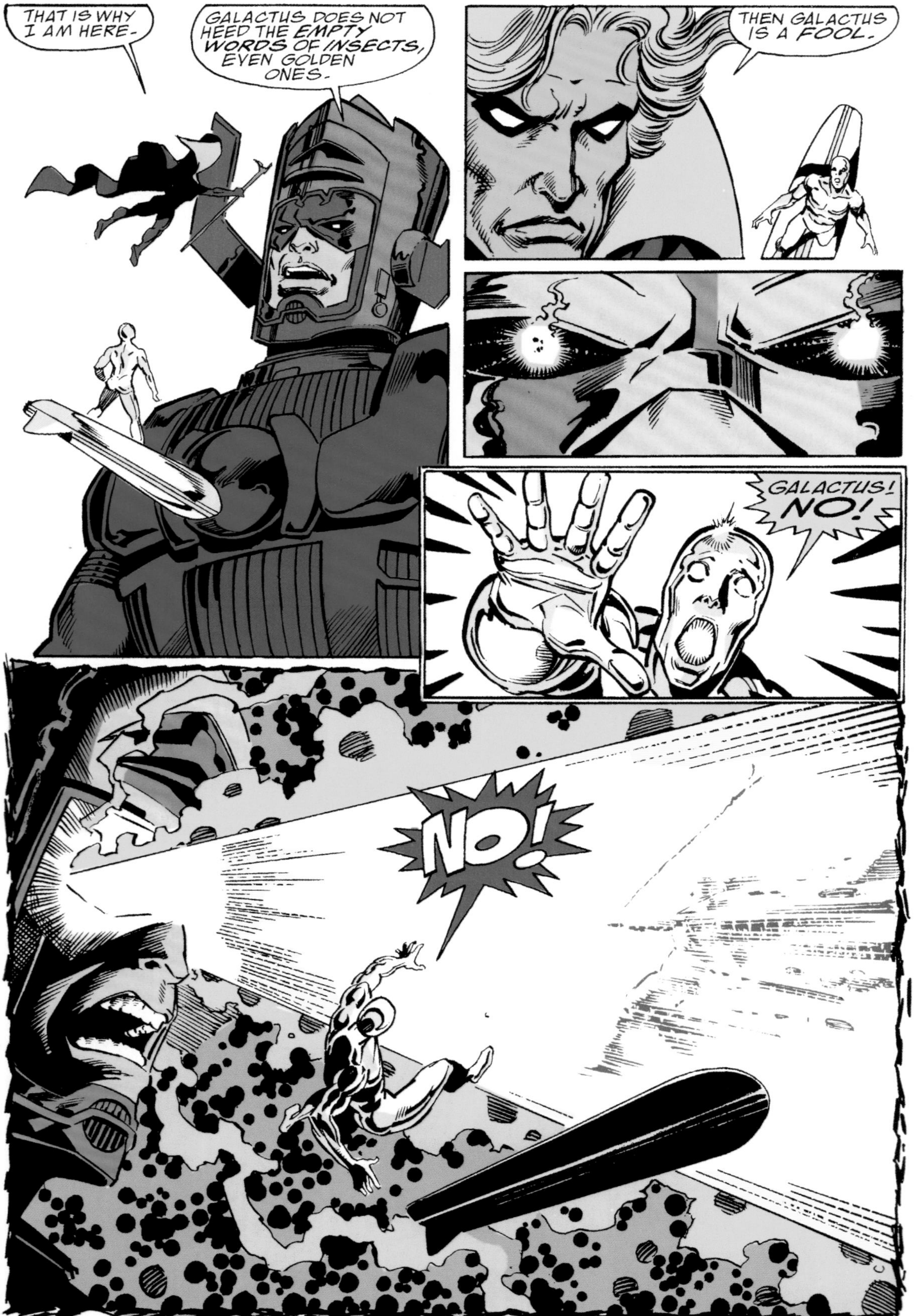
THAT IS WHY I AM HERE.
GALACTUS DOES NOT HEED THE EMPTY WORDS OF INSECTS, EVEN GOLDEN ONES.
THEN GALACTUS IS A FOOL.
GALACTUS! NO!
NO!

WE FACE A *DIRE PERIL* MY FELLOW *TITANS.*

OUR *DEFENSE* WILL BE MORE EASILY PLANNED WITHOUT *YAMMERING MORTALS* TO DIS-TRACT US.

DOES GALACTUS ALWAYS LET HIS *ANGER* SO BADLY CLOUD HIS *JUDGEMENT*?

WHO?

JUST A *YAMMERING MORTAL* WHO KNOWS THAT *NAKED POWER* IS SELDOM THE *ANSWER* TO ANY *PROB-LEM.*

SURELY YOU MUST REALIZE THAT EVEN THIS GROUP'S *COMBINED MIGHT* IS *NOTHING* COMPARED TO THE FORCE THANOS WIELDS.

ONLY A RICHLY *COMPLEX* AND *SKILLFULLY EXECUTED STRATEGY* WILL INSURE YOUR SURVIVAL.

TIME IS *SHORT* AND I *HAVE* SUCH A PLAN.

GALACTUS, *WE* KNOW THIS ADAM WARLOCK.

HE IS ONE OUTSIDE THE *LOOP OF DES-TINY* AND CAPABLE OF *WONDROUS DEEDS.*

MASTER *ORDER* AND LORD *CHAOS* HAVE WEIGHED THE *OPTIONS*...

...AND CHOSE TO *JOIN* FORCES WITH *ADAM WARLOCK.*

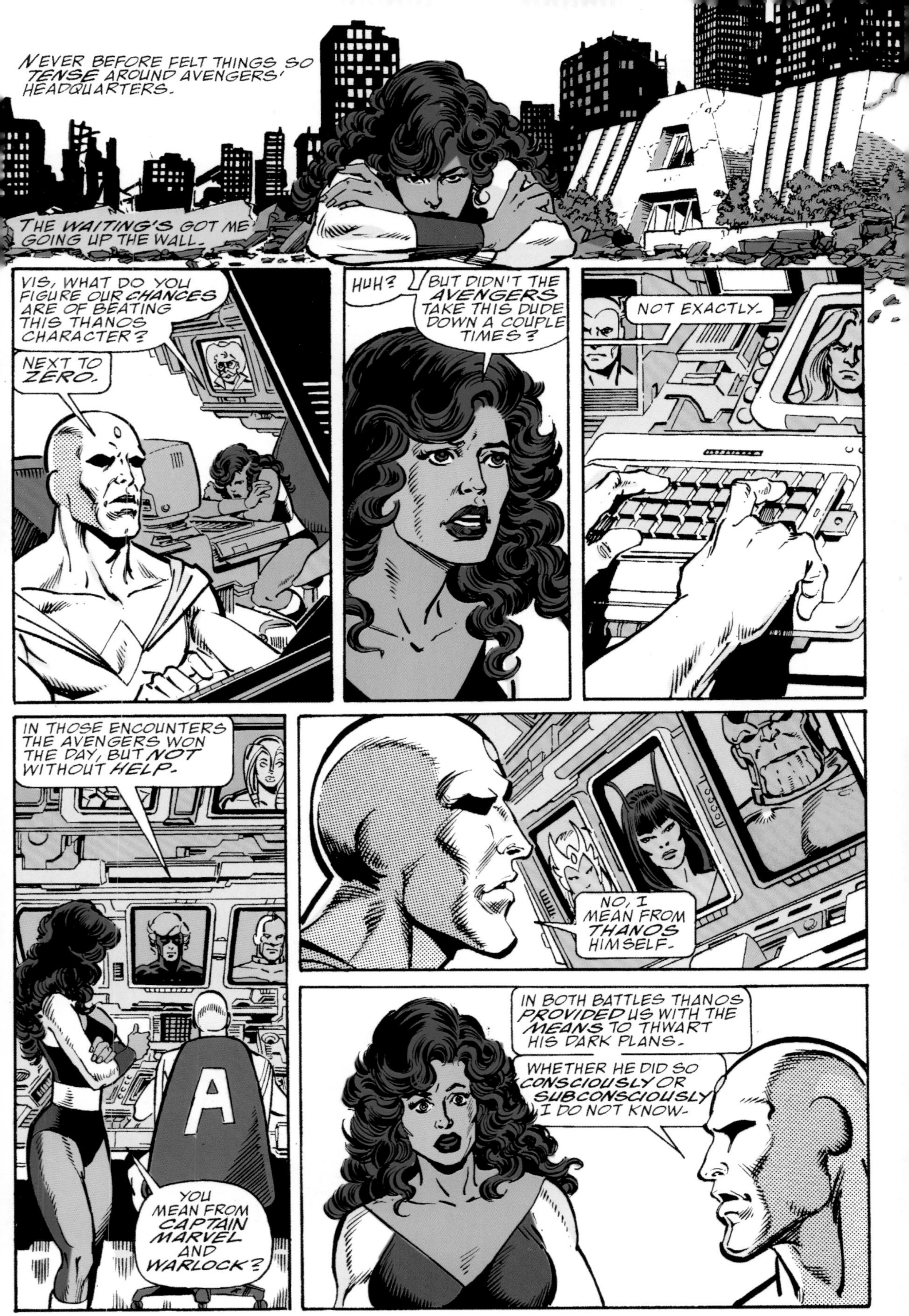
NEVER BEFORE FELT THINGS SO TENSE AROUND AVENGERS' HEADQUARTERS.
THE WAITING'S GOT ME GOING UP THE WALL.
VIS, WHAT DO YOU FIGURE OUR CHANCES ARE OF BEATING THIS THANOS CHARACTER?
NEXT TO ZERO.
HUH?
BUT DIDN'T THE AVENGERS TAKE THIS DUDE DOWN A COUPLE TIMES?
NOT EXACTLY.
IN THOSE ENCOUNTERS THE AVENGERS WON THE DAY, BUT NOT WITHOUT HELP.
YOU MEAN FROM CAPTAIN MARVEL AND WARLOCK?
NO, I MEAN FROM THANOS HIMSELF.
IN BOTH BATTLES THANOS PROVIDED US WITH THE MEANS TO THWART HIS DARK PLANS.
WHETHER HE DID SO CONSCIOUSLY OR SUBCONSCIOUSLY I DO NOT KNOW.

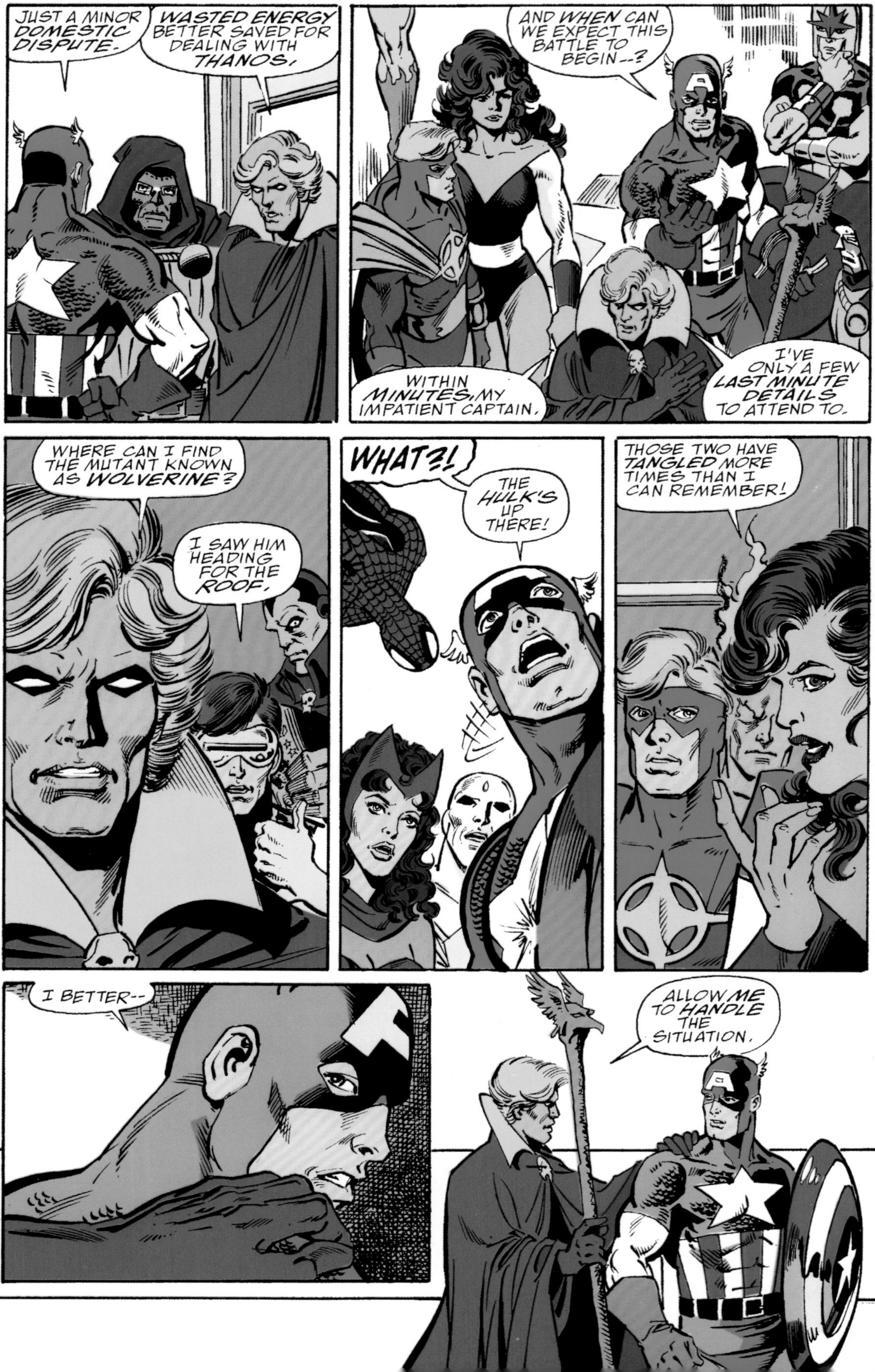
JUST A MINOR DOMESTIC DISPUTE.
WASTED ENERGY BETTER SAVED FOR DEALING WITH THANOS.
AND WHEN CAN WE EXPECT THIS BATTLE TO BEGIN--?
WITHIN MINUTES, MY IMPATIENT CAPTAIN.
I'VE ONLY A FEW LAST MINUTE DETAILS TO ATTEND TO.
WHERE CAN I FIND THE MUTANT KNOWN AS WOLVERINE?
I SAW HIM HEADING FOR THE ROOF.
WHAT?!
THE HULK'S UP THERE!
THOSE TWO HAVE TANGLED MORE TIMES THAN I CAN REMEMBER!
I BETTER--
ALLOW ME TO HANDLE THE SITUATION.

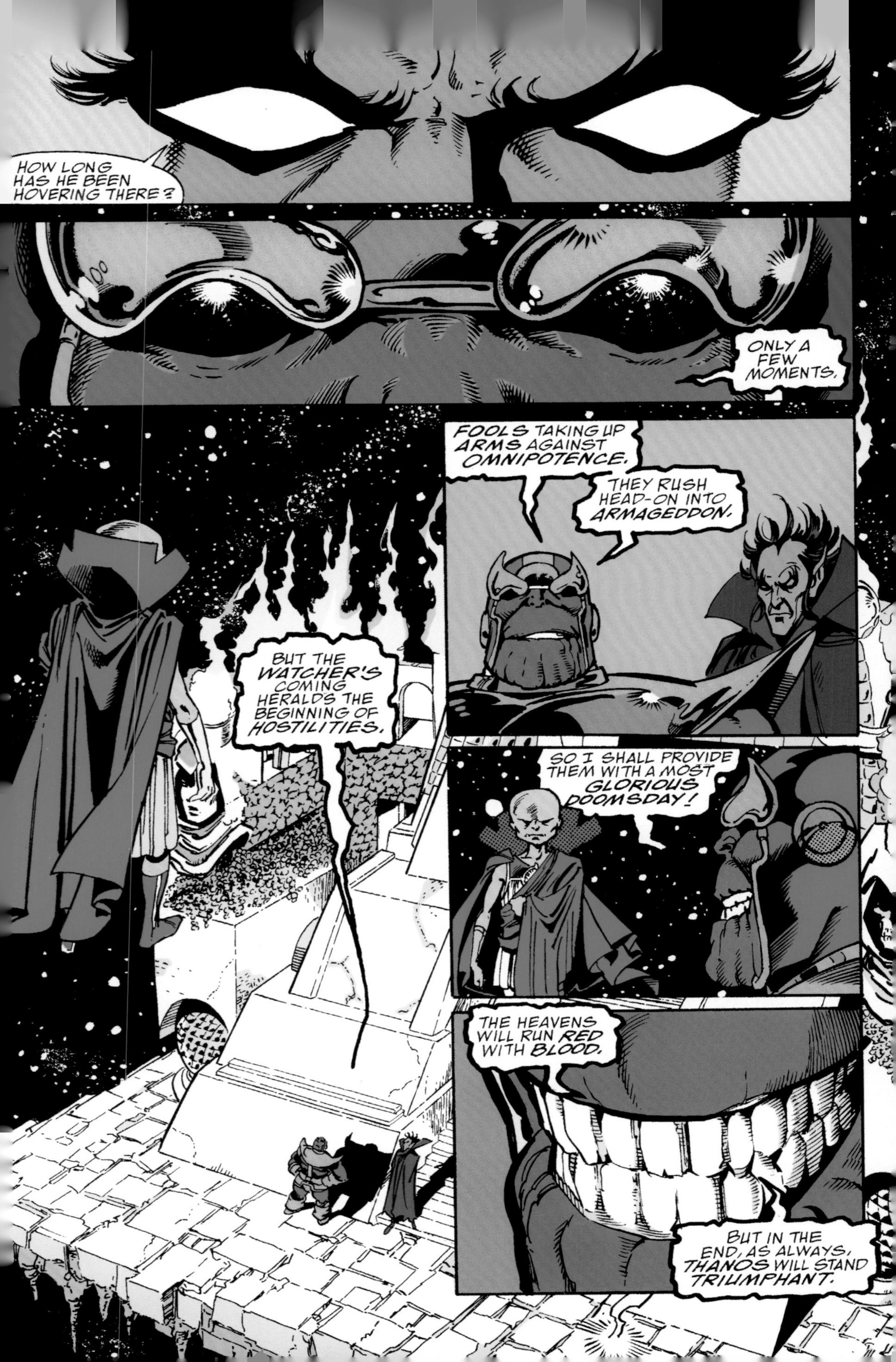
HOW LONG HAS HE BEEN HOVERING THERE?
ONLY A FEW MOMENTS.
BUT THE WATCHER'S COMING HERALDS THE BEGINNING OF HOSTILITIES.
FOOLS TAKING UP ARMS AGAINST OMNIPOTENCE.
THEY RUSH HEAD-ON INTO ARMAGEDDON.
SO I SHALL PROVIDE THEM WITH A MOST GLORIOUS DOOMSDAY!
THE HEAVENS WILL RUN RED WITH BLOOD.
BUT IN THE END, AS ALWAYS, THANOS WILL STAND TRIUMPHANT.

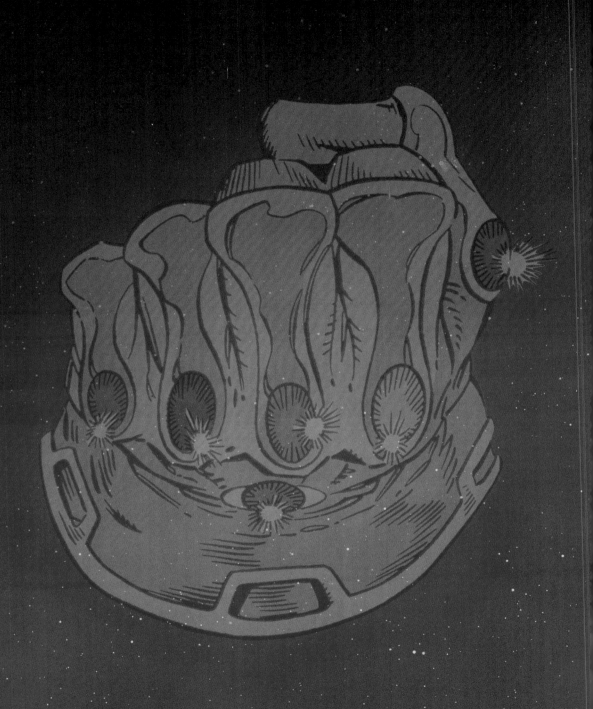

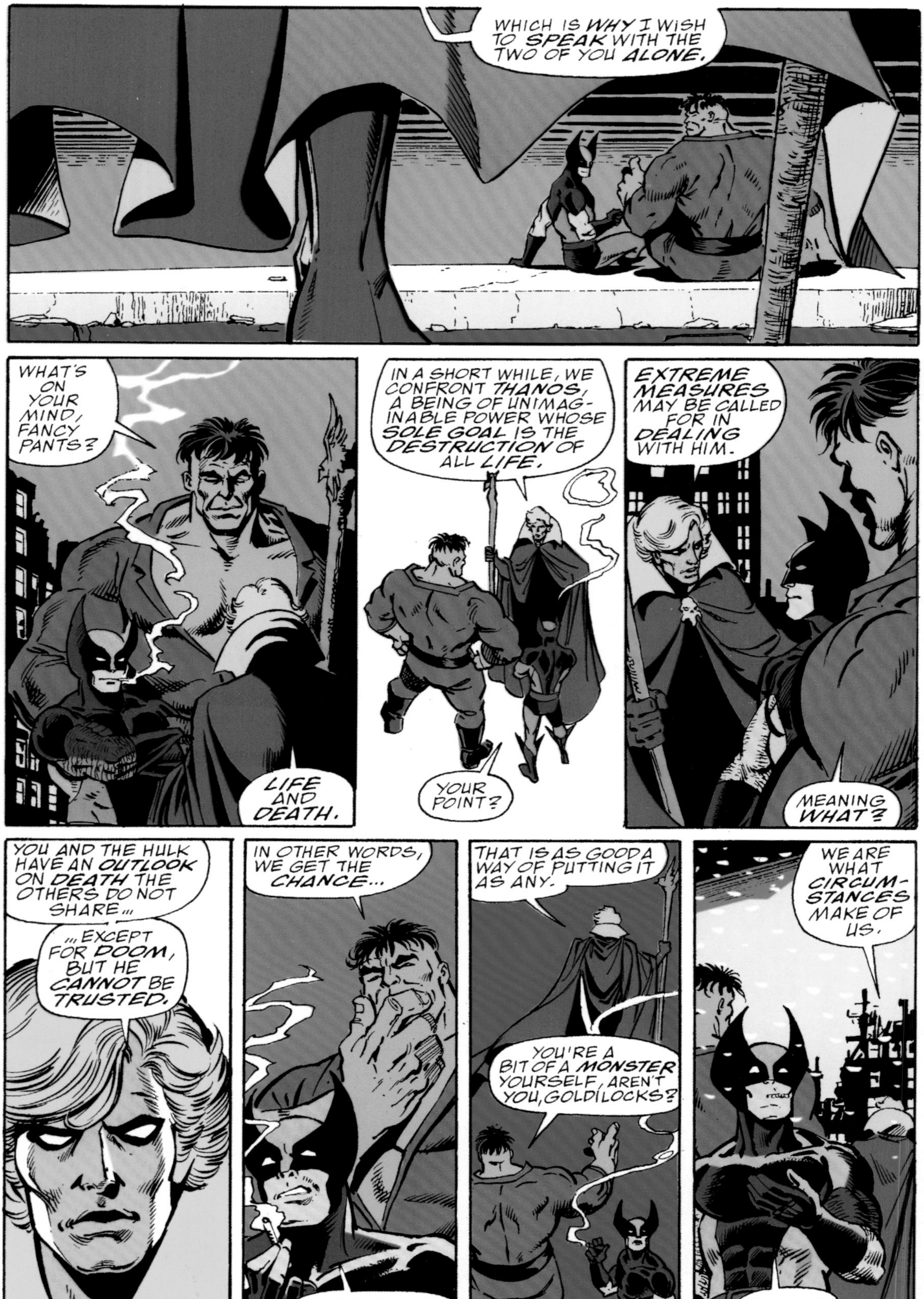
WHICH IS WHY I WISH TO SPEAK WITH THE TWO OF YOU ALONE.
WHAT'S ON YOUR MIND, FANCY PANTS?
LIFE AND DEATH.
IN A SHORT WHILE, WE CONFRONT THANOS, A BEING OF UNIMAGINABLE POWER WHOSE SOLE GOAL IS THE DESTRUCTION OF ALL LIFE.
YOUR POINT?
EXTREME MEASURES MAY BE CALLED FOR IN DEALING WITH HIM.
MEANING WHAT?
YOU AND THE HULK HAVE AN OUTLOOK ON DEATH THE OTHERS DO NOT SHARE...
...EXCEPT FOR DOOM, BUT HE CANNOT BE TRUSTED.
IN OTHER WORDS, WE GET THE CHANCE...
...YOU WANT US TO SANCTION THANOS.
THAT IS AS GOOD A WAY OF PUTTING IT AS ANY.
YOU'RE A BIT OF A MONSTER YOURSELF, AREN'T YOU, GOLDILOCKS?
WE ARE WHAT CIRCUMSTANCES MAKE OF US.
SNOW?
IN MAY?

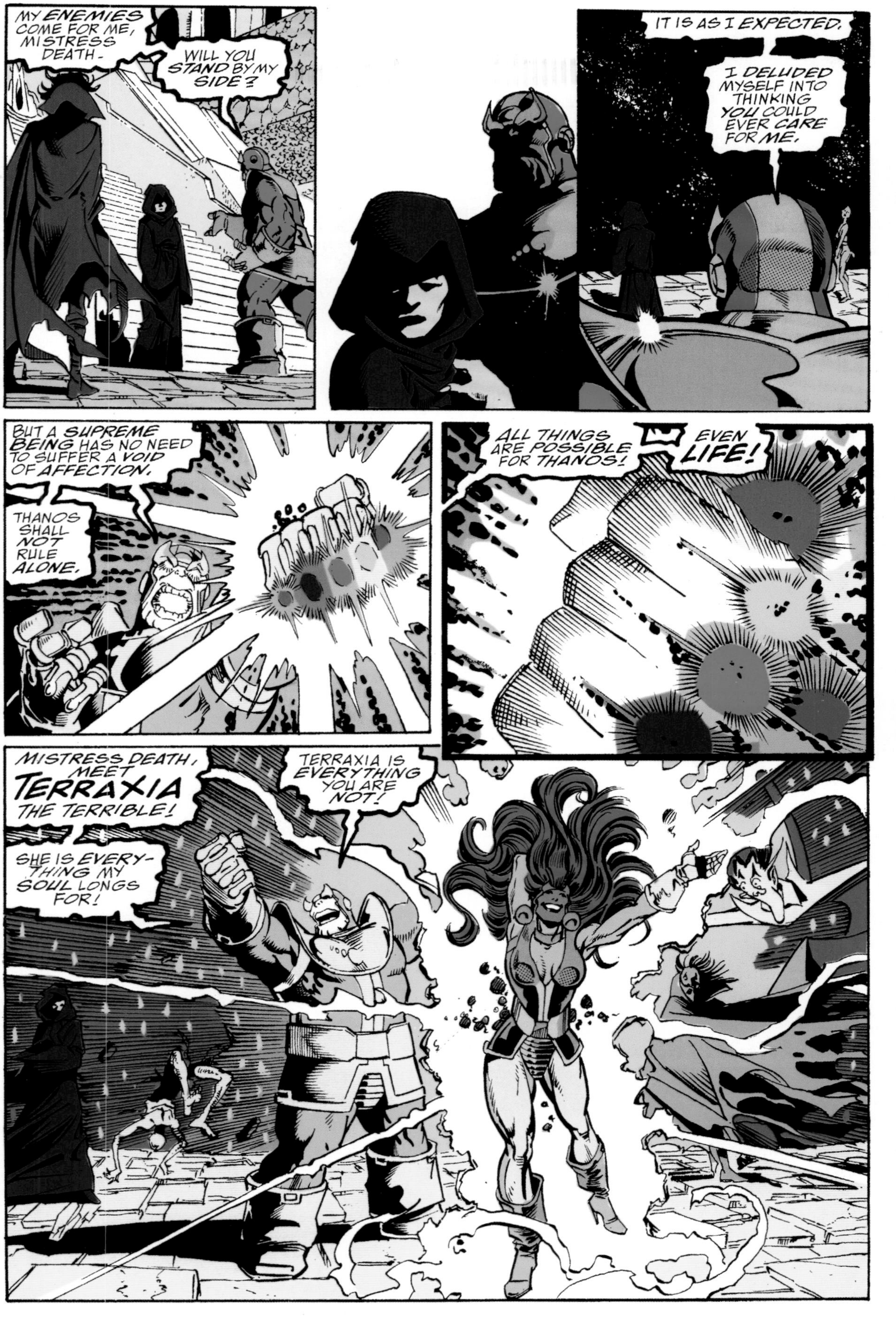
MY ENEMIES COME FOR ME, MISTRESS DEATH -
WILL YOU STAND BY MY SIDE?
IT IS AS I EXPECTED.
I DELUDED MYSELF INTO THINKING YOU COULD EVER CARE FOR ME.
BUT A SUPREME BEING HAS NO NEED TO SUFFER A VOID OF AFFECTION.
THANOS SHALL NOT RULE ALONE.
ALL THINGS ARE POSSIBLE FOR THANOS!
EVEN LIFE!
MISTRESS DEATH, MEET TERRAXIA THE TERRIBLE!
SHE IS EVERY-THING MY SOUL LONGS FOR!
TERRAXIA IS EVERYTHING YOU ARE NOT!

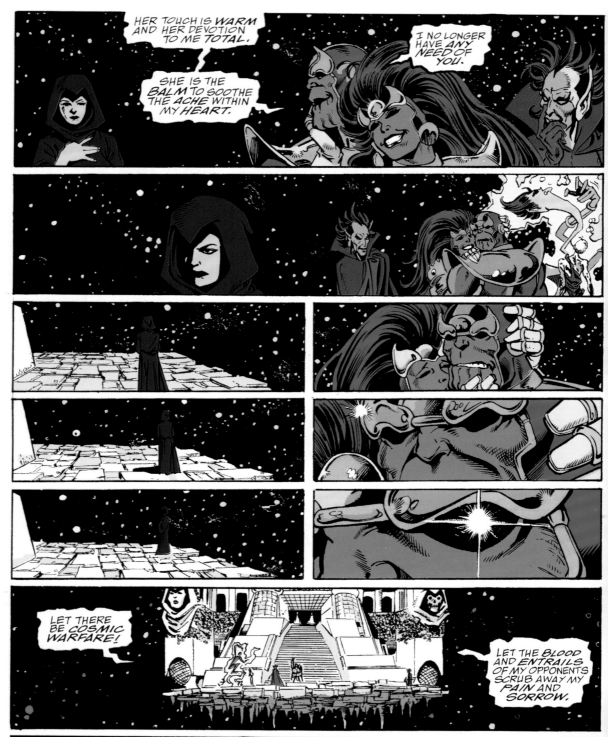

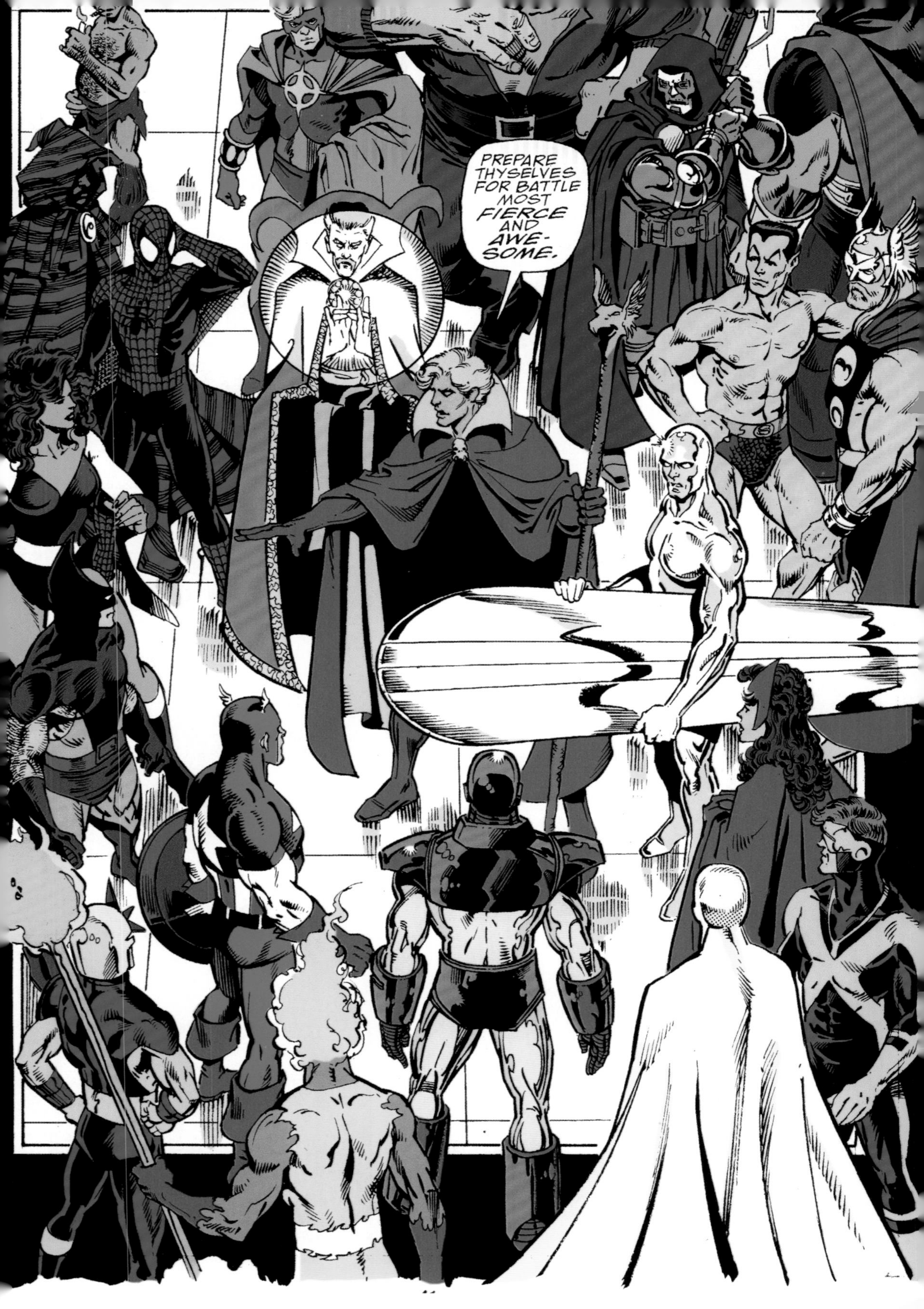
PREPARE THYSELVES FOR BATTLE MOST FIERCE AND AWE-SOME.

DR. STRANGE HAS CONJURED *MYSTIC CONDUITS* WHICH WILL TRANSPORT YOU TO THE *PRECISE LOCATION* YOU MUST BE ONCE THE BATTLE COMMENCES.

EACH OF YOU HAS BEEN *BRIEFED* ON THE *LINE* OF *ATTACK* YOU SHOULD INSTITUTE.

THE LIVES OF YOUR *FELLOW COMBATANTS* AND THE *UNIVERSE* DEPEND ON YOUR FOLLOWING THIS *PLAN.*

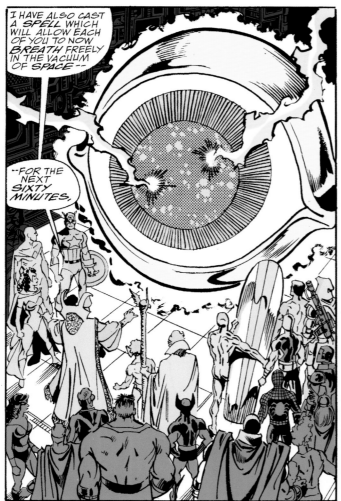

I HAVE ALSO CAST A *SPELL* WHICH WILL ALLOW EACH OF YOU TO NOW *BREATH* FREELY IN THE VACUUM OF *SPACE* --

--FOR THE NEXT *SIXTY MINUTES,*

DR. STRANGE WILL REMAIN BEHIND TO *MONITOR* AND TELEPATHICALLY *APPRISE* ME OF THE SITUATION FROM EACH OF YOUR *POINTS* OF *VIEW.*

HE WILL ALSO FACILITATE THE *EVACUATION* OF ANY COMBATANT TOO *INJURED* TO CONTINUE THE STRUGGLE.

I WISH... WISH EACH OF YOU... THE BEST OF LUCK...

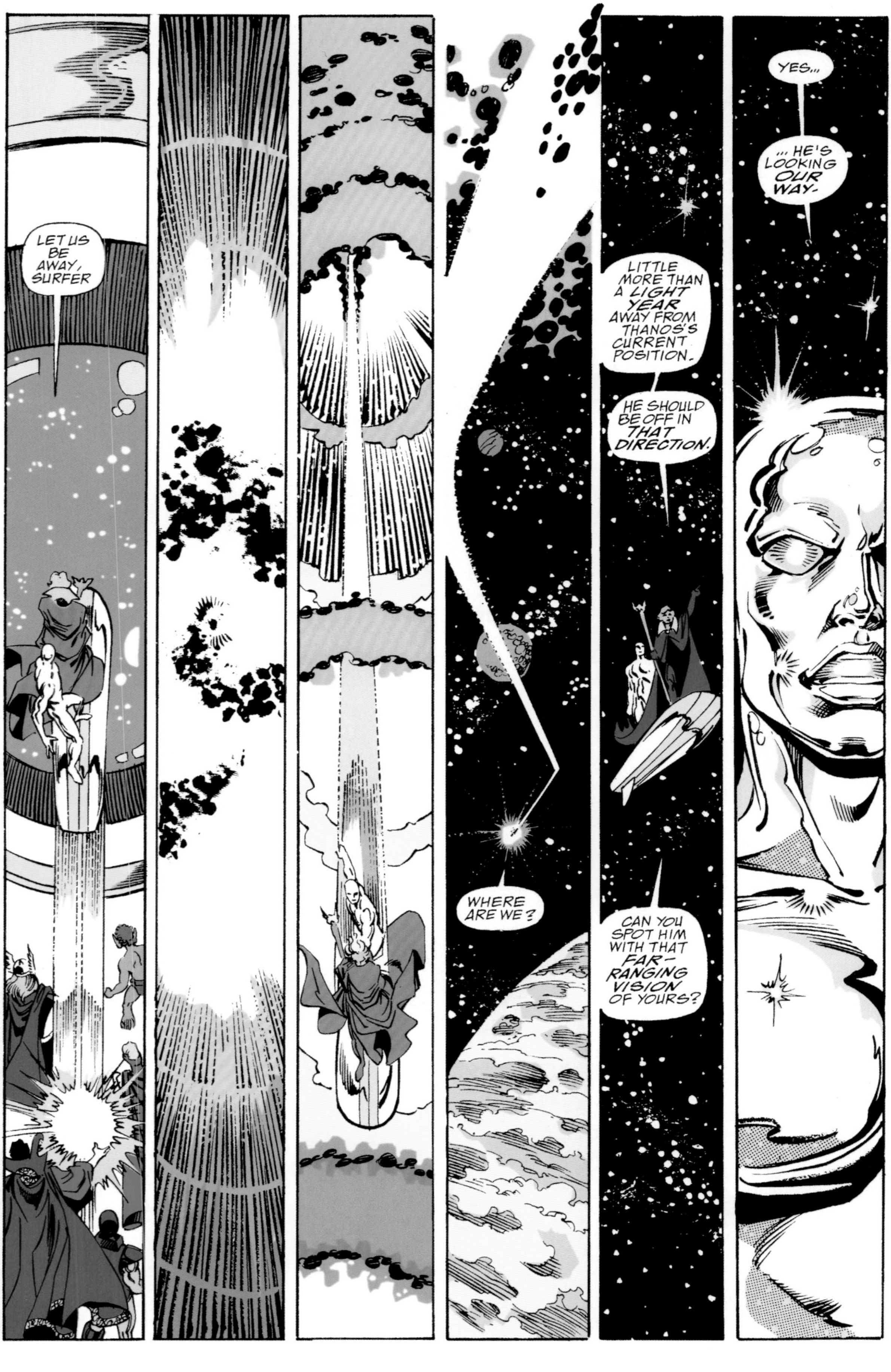
LET US BE AWAY, SURFER
WHERE ARE WE?
LITTLE MORE THAN A LIGHT YEAR AWAY FROM THANOS'S CURRENT POSITION.
HE SHOULD BE OFF IN THAT DIRECTION.
CAN YOU SPOT HIM WITH THAT FAR-RANGING VISION OF YOURS?
YES...
...HE'S LOOKING OUR WAY-

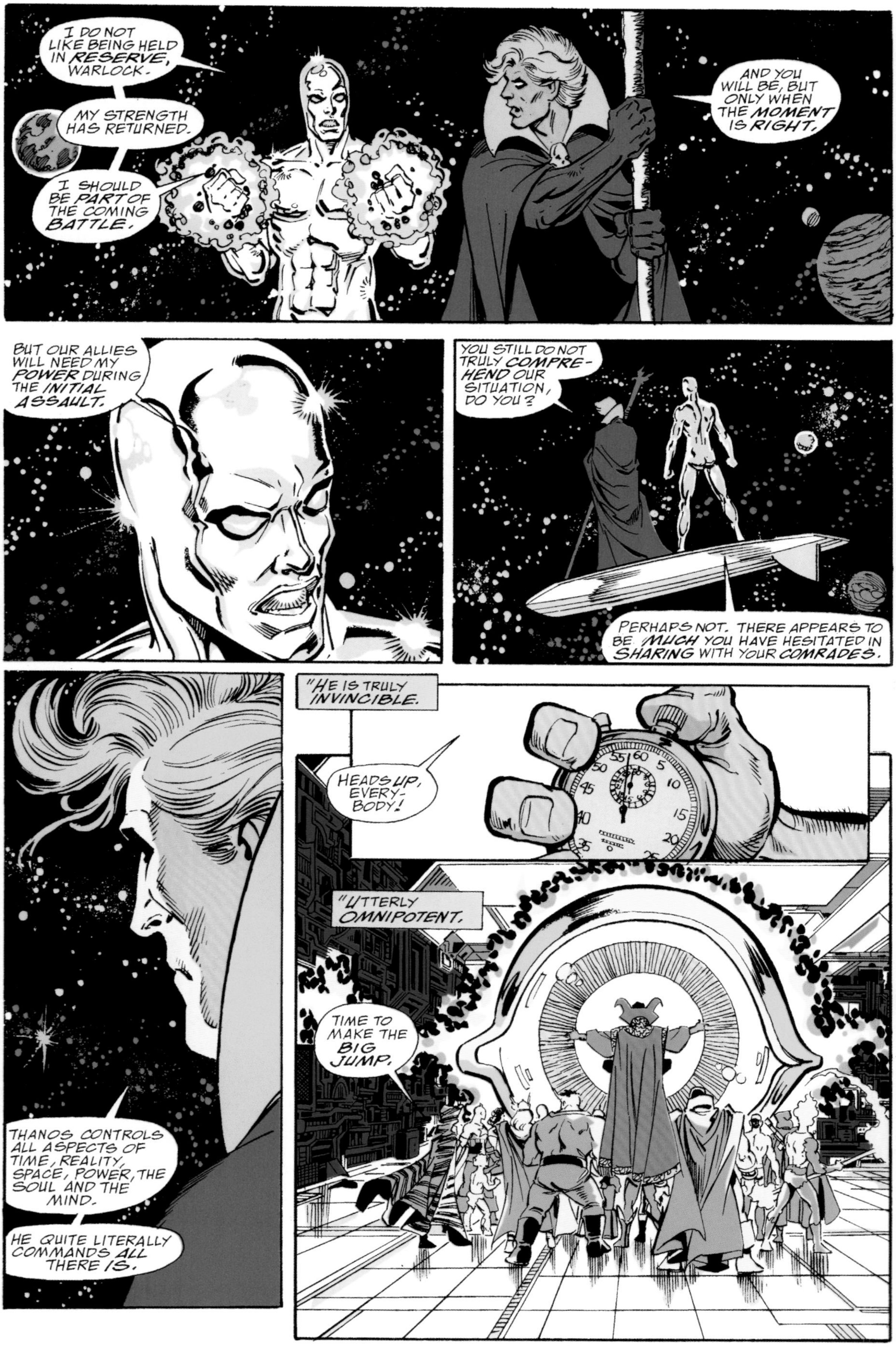
I DO NOT LIKE BEING HELD IN *RESERVE*, WARLOCK.
MY STRENGTH HAS RETURNED.
I SHOULD BE *PART* OF THE COMING *BATTLE*.
AND YOU WILL BE, BUT ONLY WHEN THE *MOMENT* IS *RIGHT*.
BUT OUR ALLIES WILL NEED MY *POWER* DURING THE *INITIAL ASSAULT*.
YOU STILL DO NOT TRULY *COMPRE-HEND* OUR SITUATION, DO YOU?
PERHAPS NOT. THERE APPEARS TO BE *MUCH* YOU HAVE HESITATED IN *SHARING* WITH YOUR *COMRADES*.
THANOS CONTROLS ALL ASPECTS OF TIME, REALITY, SPACE, POWER, THE SOUL AND THE MIND.
HE QUITE LITERALLY COMMANDS *ALL* THERE *IS*.
"HE IS TRULY *INVINCIBLE*.
HEADS *UP*, EVERY-BODY!
"UTTERLY *OMNIPOTENT*.
TIME TO MAKE THE *BIG JUMP*.

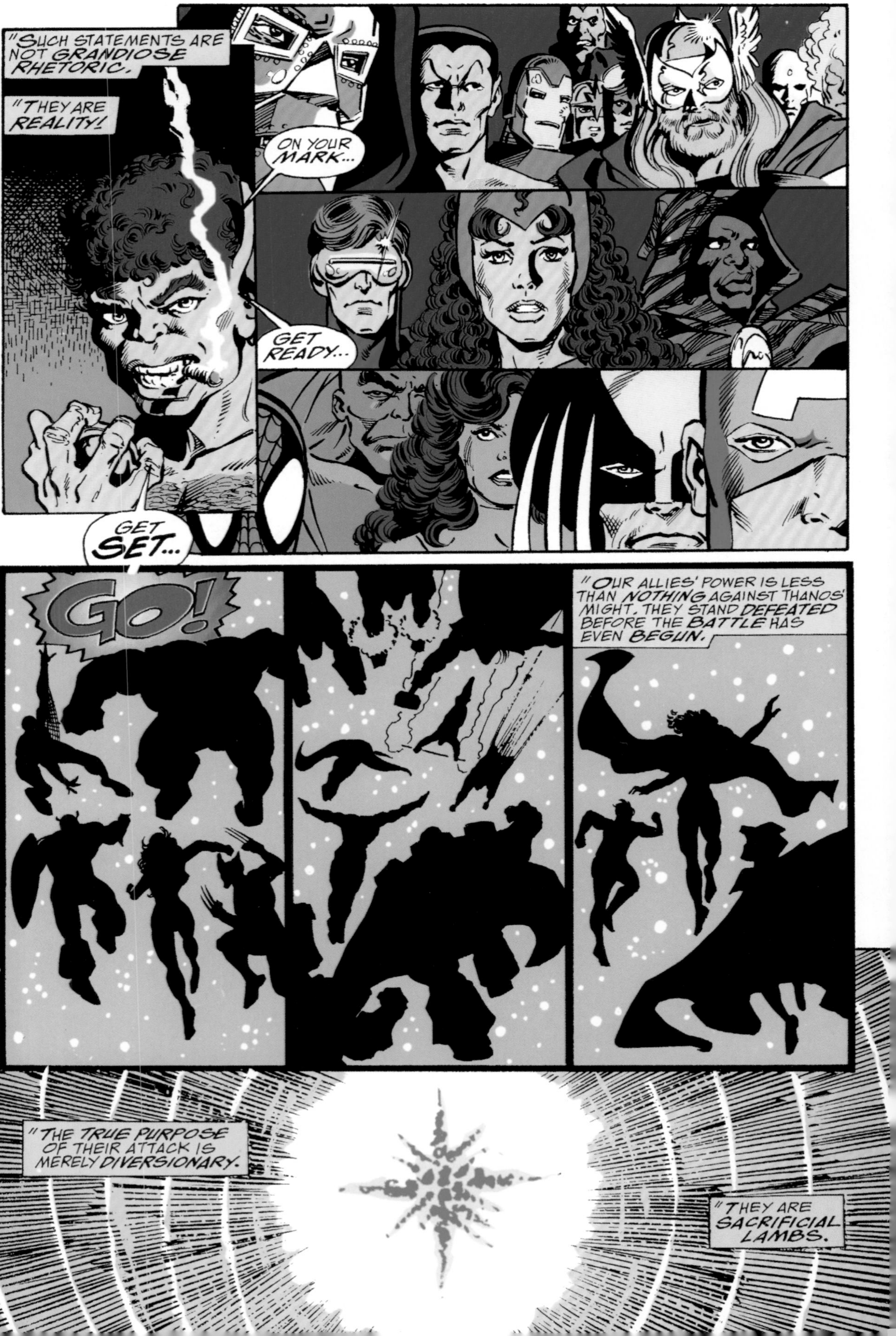
"SUCH STATEMENTS ARE NOT GRANDIOSE RHETORIC.
"THEY ARE REALITY!
ON YOUR MARK...
GET READY...
GET SET...
GO!
"OUR ALLIES' POWER IS LESS THAN NOTHING AGAINST THANOS' MIGHT. THEY STAND DEFEATED BEFORE THE BATTLE HAS EVEN BEGUN.
"THE TRUE PURPOSE OF THEIR ATTACK IS MERELY DIVERSIONARY.
"THEY ARE SACRIFICIAL LAMBS.

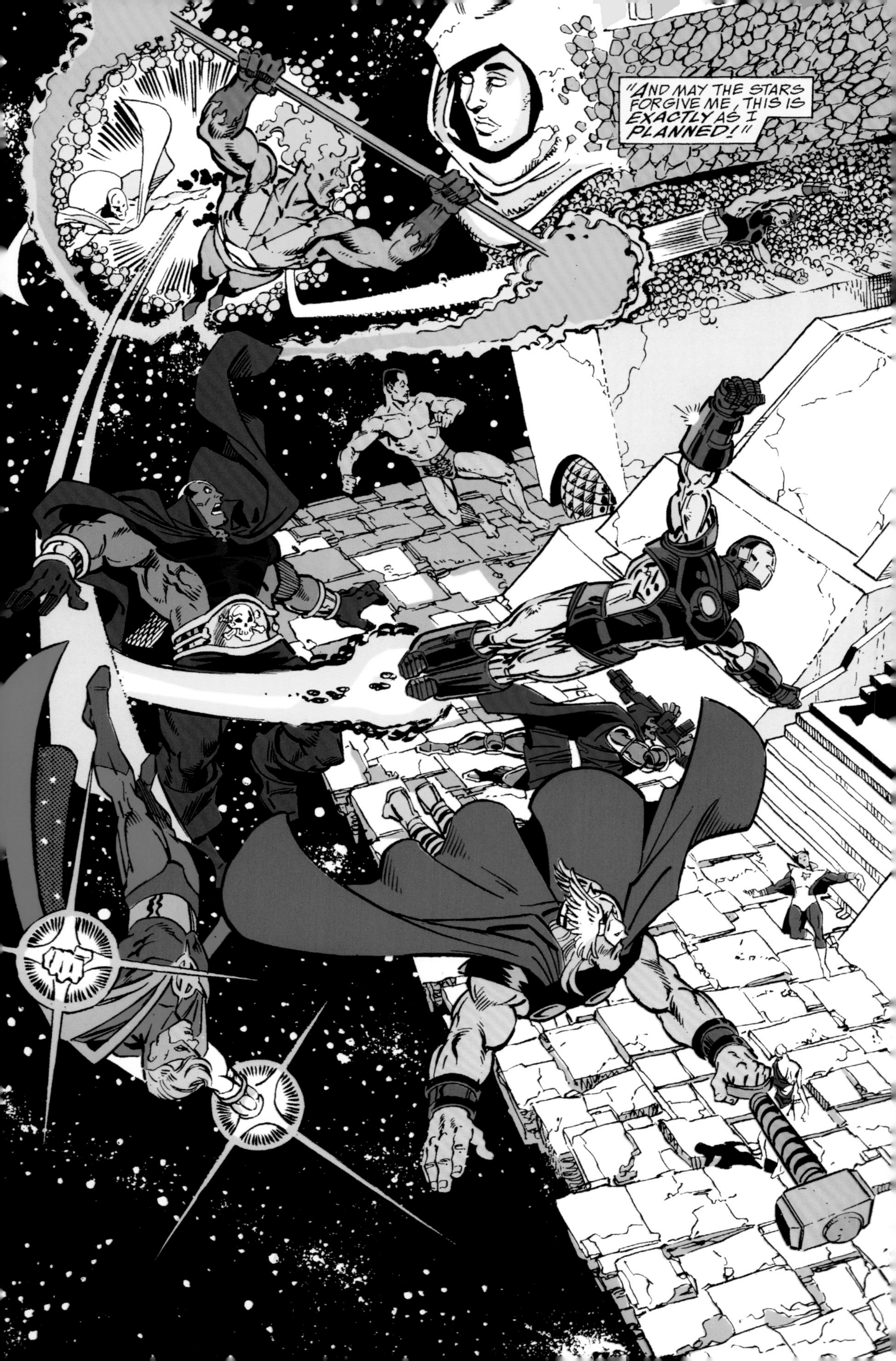
"AND MAY THE STARS FORGIVE ME, THIS IS EXACTLY AS I PLANNED!"

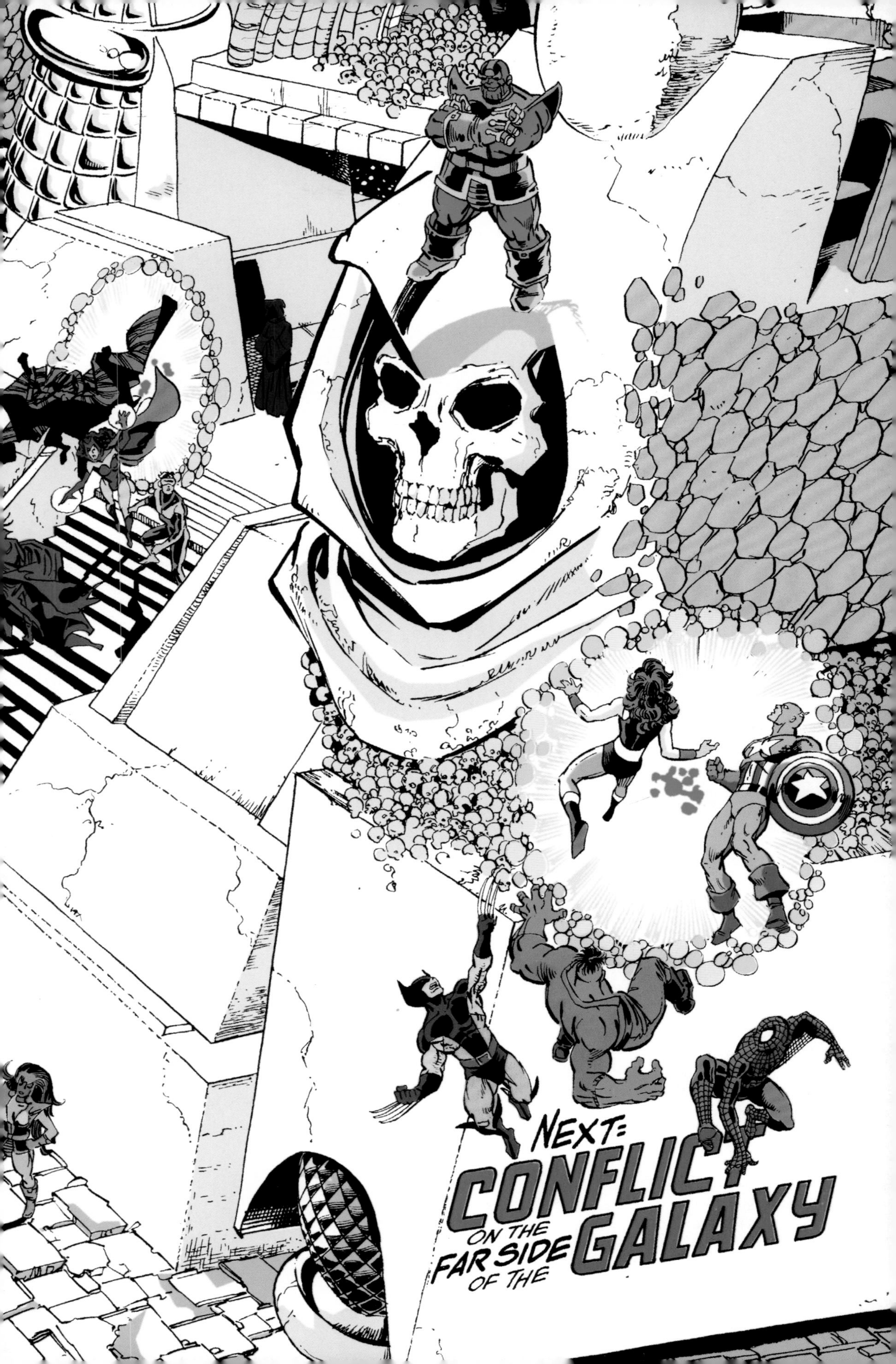
NEXT:
CONFLICT ON THE FAR SIDE OF THE GALAXY

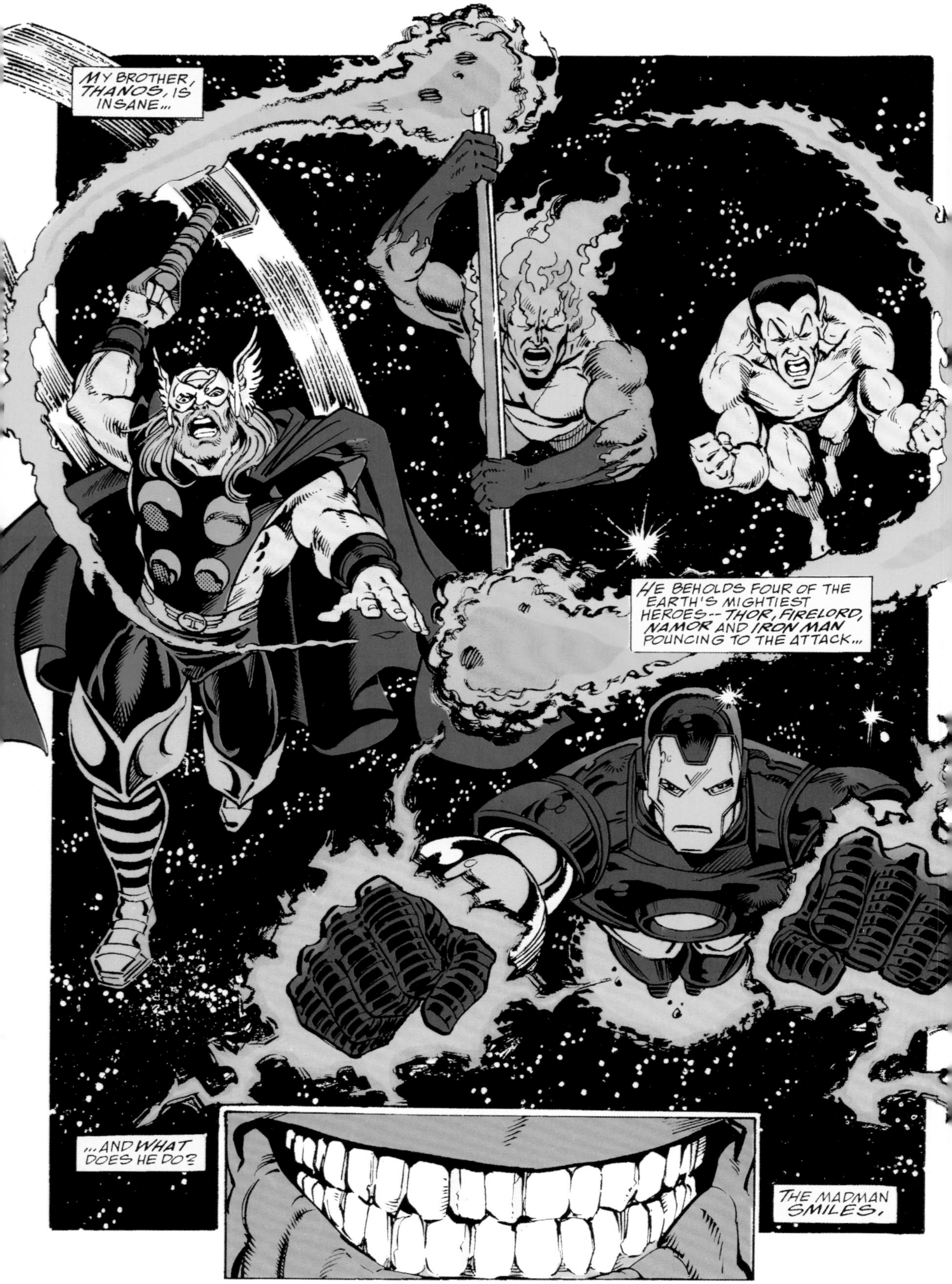
MY BROTHER, THANOS, IS INSANE...
HE BEHOLDS FOUR OF THE EARTH'S MIGHTIEST HEROES-- THOR, FIRELORD, NAMOR AND IRON MAN POUNCING TO THE ATTACK...
...AND WHAT DOES HE DO?
THE MADMAN SMILES.

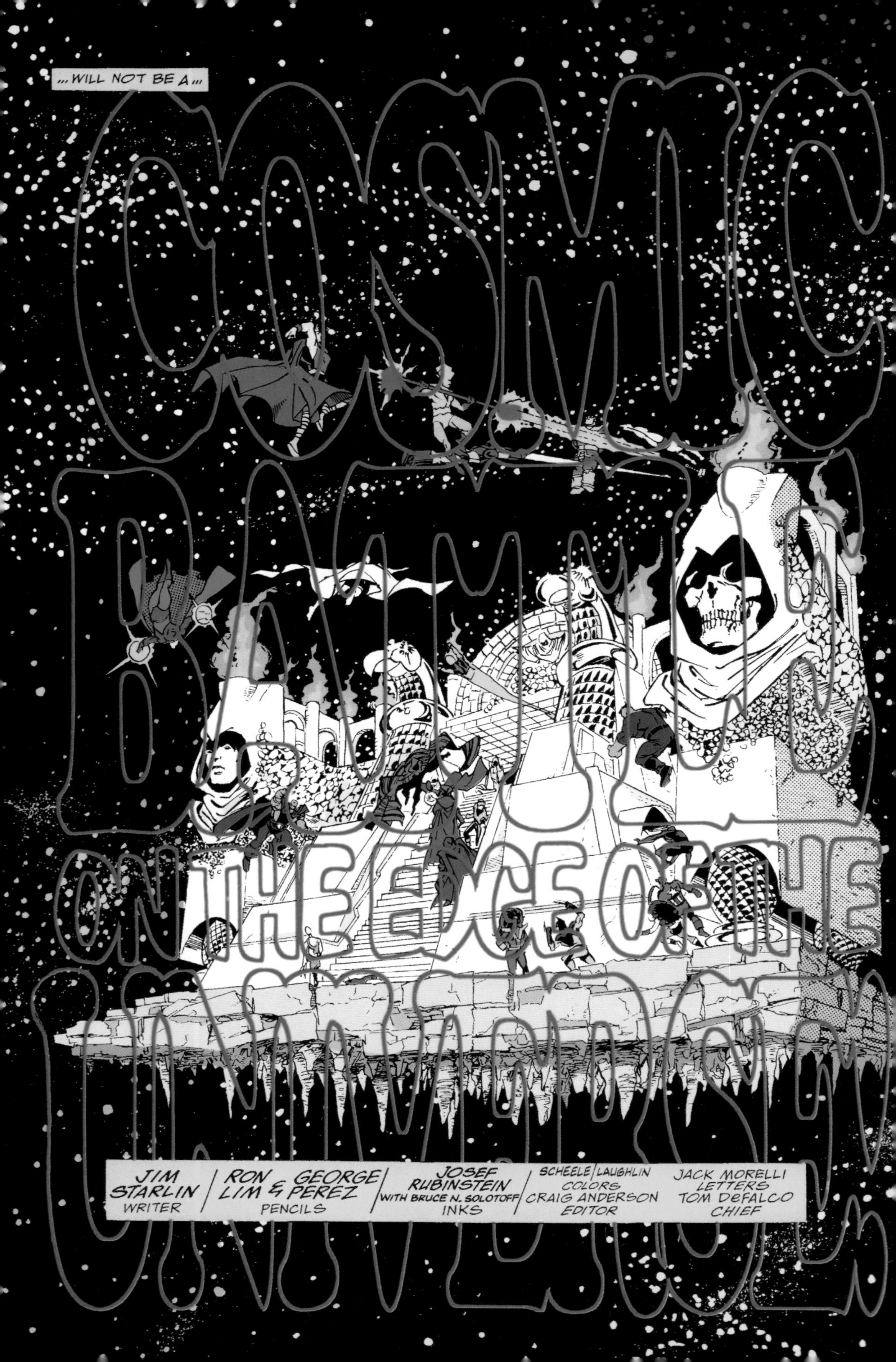
...WILL NOT BE A...
COSMIC BATTLE ON THE EDGE OF THE UNIVERSE!
JIM STARLIN WRITER
RON LIM & GEORGE PEREZ PENCILS
JOSEF RUBINSTEIN WITH BRUCE N. SOLOTOFF INKS
SCHEELE / LAUGHLIN COLORS
CRAIG ANDERSON EDITOR
JACK MORELLI LETTERS
TOM DEFALCO CHIEF

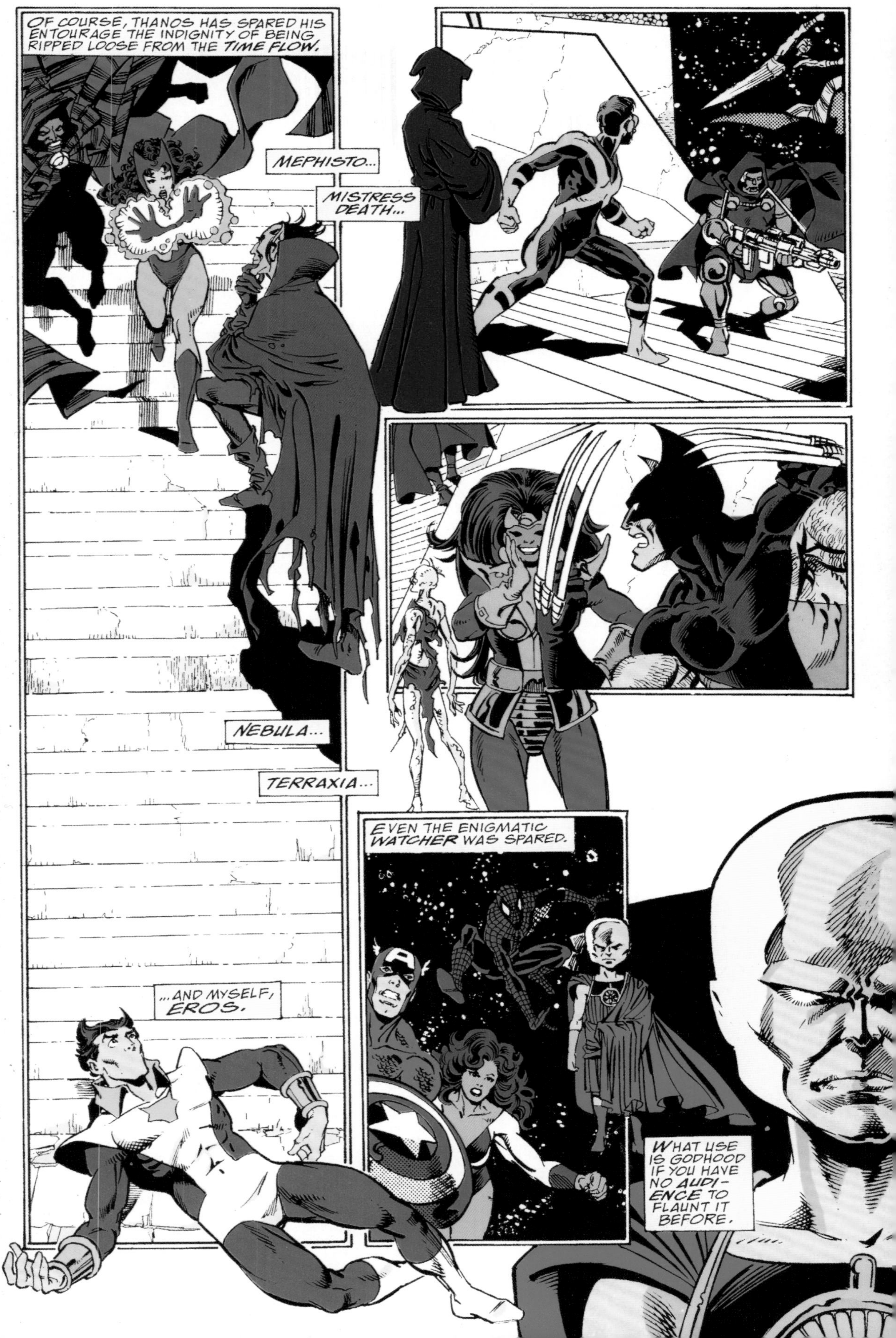
OF COURSE, THANOS HAS SPARED HIS ENTOURAGE THE INDIGNITY OF BEING RIPPED LOOSE FROM THE TIME FLOW.
MEPHISTO...
MISTRESS DEATH...
NEBULA...
TERRAXIA...
...AND MYSELF, EROS.
EVEN THE ENIGMATIC WATCHER WAS SPARED.
WHAT USE IS GODHOOD IF YOU HAVE NO AUDIENCE TO FLAUNT IT BEFORE.

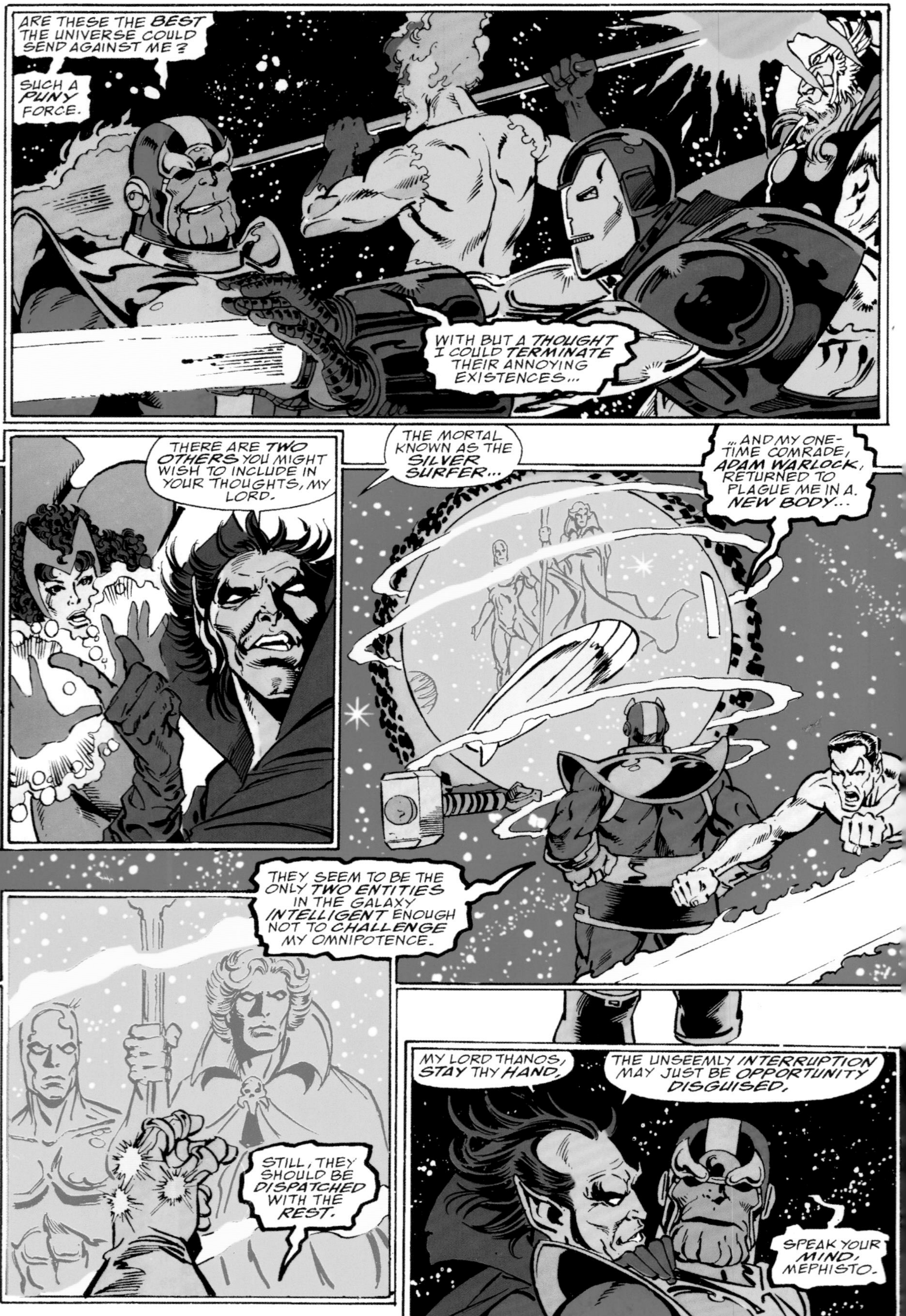
ARE THESE THE BEST THE UNIVERSE COULD SEND AGAINST ME?
SUCH A PUNY FORCE.
WITH BUT A THOUGHT I COULD TERMINATE THEIR ANNOYING EXISTENCES...
THERE ARE TWO OTHERS YOU MIGHT WISH TO INCLUDE IN YOUR THOUGHTS, MY LORD.
THE MORTAL KNOWN AS THE SILVER SURFER...
...AND MY ONE-TIME COMRADE, ADAM WARLOCK, RETURNED TO PLAGUE ME IN A NEW BODY...
THEY SEEM TO BE THE ONLY TWO ENTITIES IN THE GALAXY INTELLIGENT ENOUGH NOT TO CHALLENGE MY OMNIPOTENCE.
STILL, THEY SHOULD BE DISPATCHED WITH THE REST.
MY LORD THANOS, STAY THY HAND,
THE UNSEEMLY INTERRUPTION MAY JUST BE OPPORTUNITY DISGUISED,
SPEAK YOUR MIND, MEPHISTO.

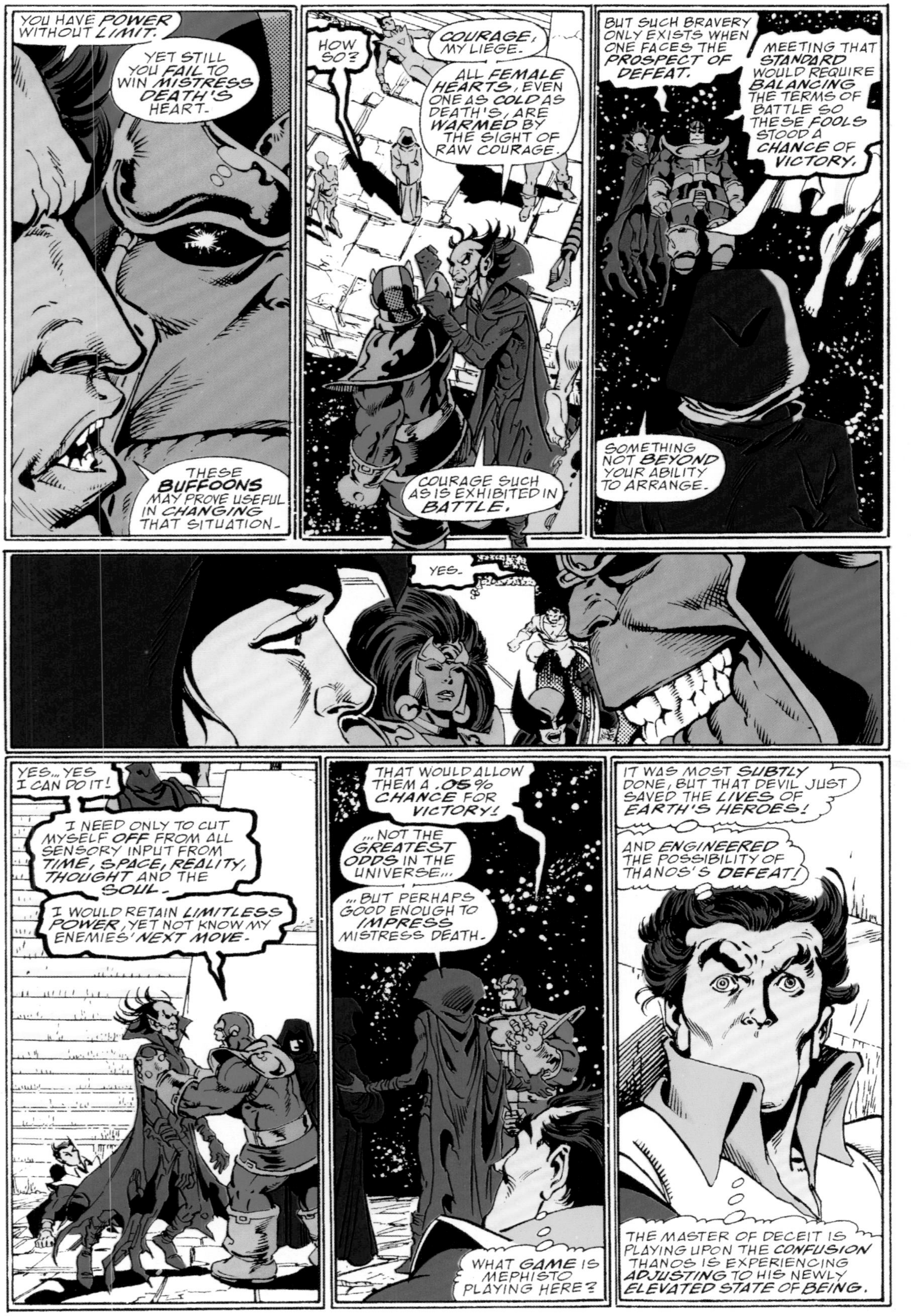

YOU HAVE POWER WITHOUT LIMIT.
YET STILL YOU FAIL TO WIN MISTRESS DEATH'S HEART.
THESE BUFFOONS MAY PROVE USEFUL IN CHANGING THAT SITUATION.
HOW SO?
COURAGE, MY LIEGE.
ALL FEMALE HEARTS, EVEN ONE AS COLD AS DEATH'S, ARE WARMED BY THE SIGHT OF RAW COURAGE.
COURAGE SUCH AS IS EXHIBITED IN BATTLE.
BUT SUCH BRAVERY ONLY EXISTS WHEN ONE FACES THE PROSPECT OF DEFEAT.
MEETING THAT STANDARD WOULD REQUIRE BALANCING THE TERMS OF BATTLE SO THESE FOOLS STOOD A CHANCE OF VICTORY.
SOMETHING NOT BEYOND YOUR ABILITY TO ARRANGE.
YES.
YES... YES I CAN DO IT!
I NEED ONLY TO CUT MYSELF OFF FROM ALL SENSORY INPUT FROM TIME, SPACE, REALITY, THOUGHT AND THE SOUL.
I WOULD RETAIN LIMITLESS POWER, YET NOT KNOW MY ENEMIES' NEXT MOVE.
THAT WOULD ALLOW THEM A .05% CHANCE FOR VICTORY!
...NOT THE GREATEST ODDS IN THE UNIVERSE...
...BUT PERHAPS GOOD ENOUGH TO IMPRESS MISTRESS DEATH.
WHAT GAME IS MEPHISTO PLAYING HERE?
IT WAS MOST SUBTLY DONE, BUT THAT DEVIL JUST SAVED THE LIVES OF EARTH'S HEROES!
AND ENGINEERED THE POSSIBILITY OF THANOS'S DEFEAT!
THE MASTER OF DECEIT IS PLAYING UPON THE CONFUSION THANOS IS EXPERIENCING ADJUSTING TO HIS NEWLY ELEVATED STATE OF BEING.

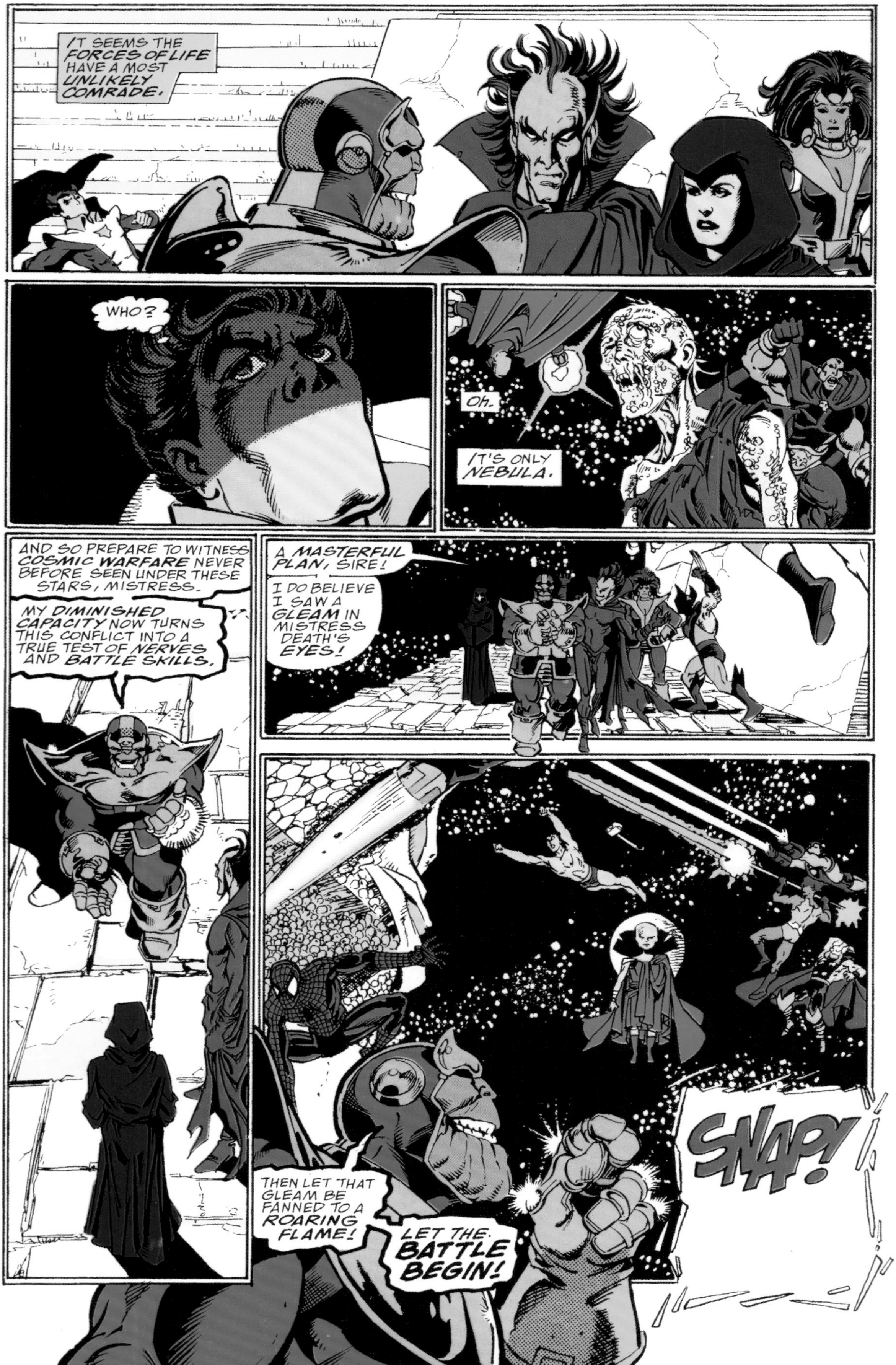

IT SEEMS THE FORCES OF LIFE HAVE A MOST UNLIKELY COMRADE.
WHO?
Oh.
IT'S ONLY NEBULA.
AND SO PREPARE TO WITNESS COSMIC WARFARE NEVER BEFORE SEEN UNDER THESE STARS, MISTRESS.
MY DIMINISHED CAPACITY NOW TURNS THIS CONFLICT INTO A TRUE TEST OF NERVES AND BATTLE SKILLS.
A MASTERFUL PLAN, SIRE!
I DO BELIEVE I SAW A GLEAM IN MISTRESS DEATH'S EYES!
THEN LET THAT GLEAM BE FANNED TO A ROARING FLAME!
LET THE BATTLE BEGIN!
SNAP!

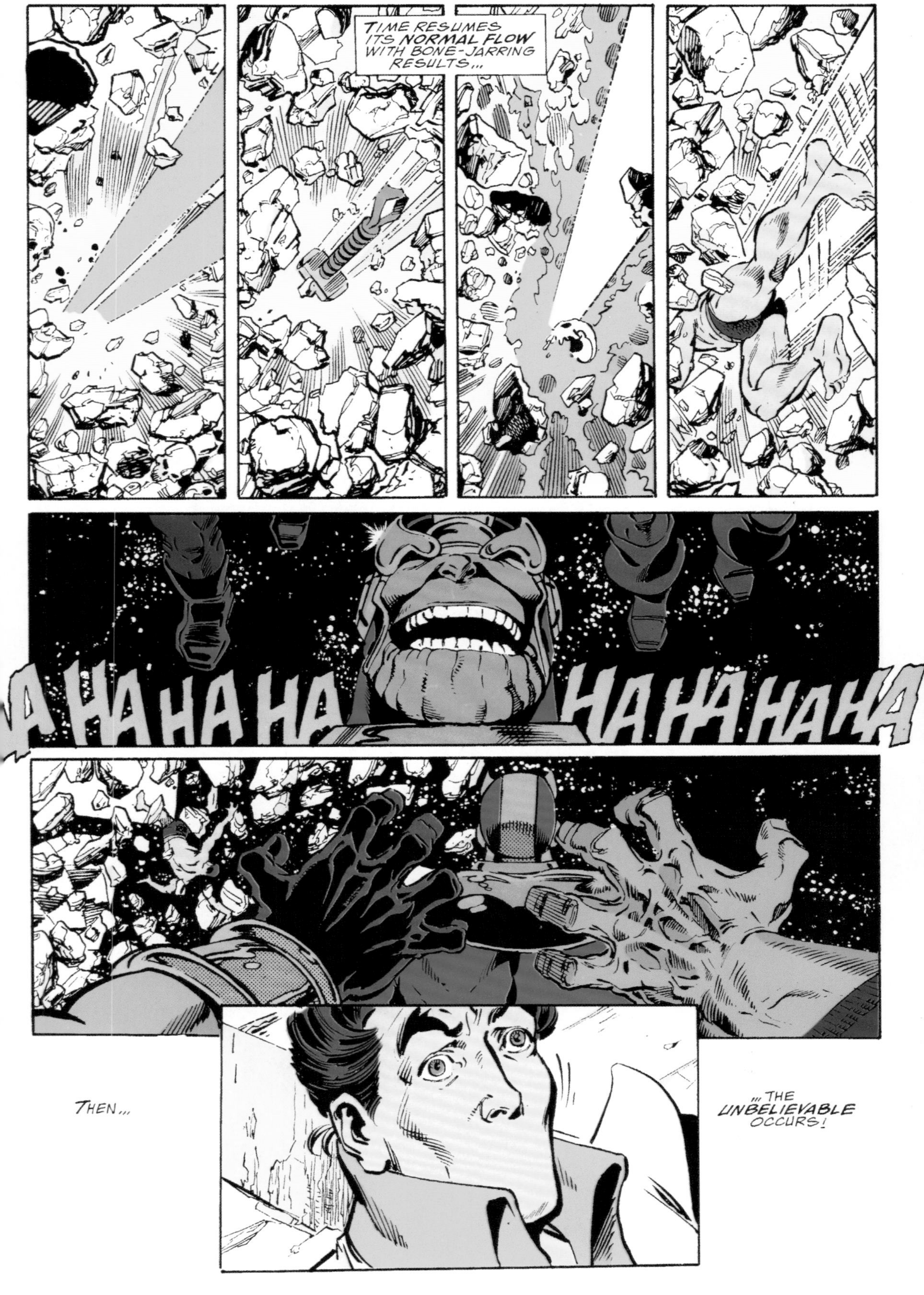

TIME RESUMES ITS NORMAL FLOW WITH BONE-JARRING RESULTS...
HAHAHAHAHA
HAHAHAHAHA
THEN...
...THE UNBELIEVABLE OCCURS!

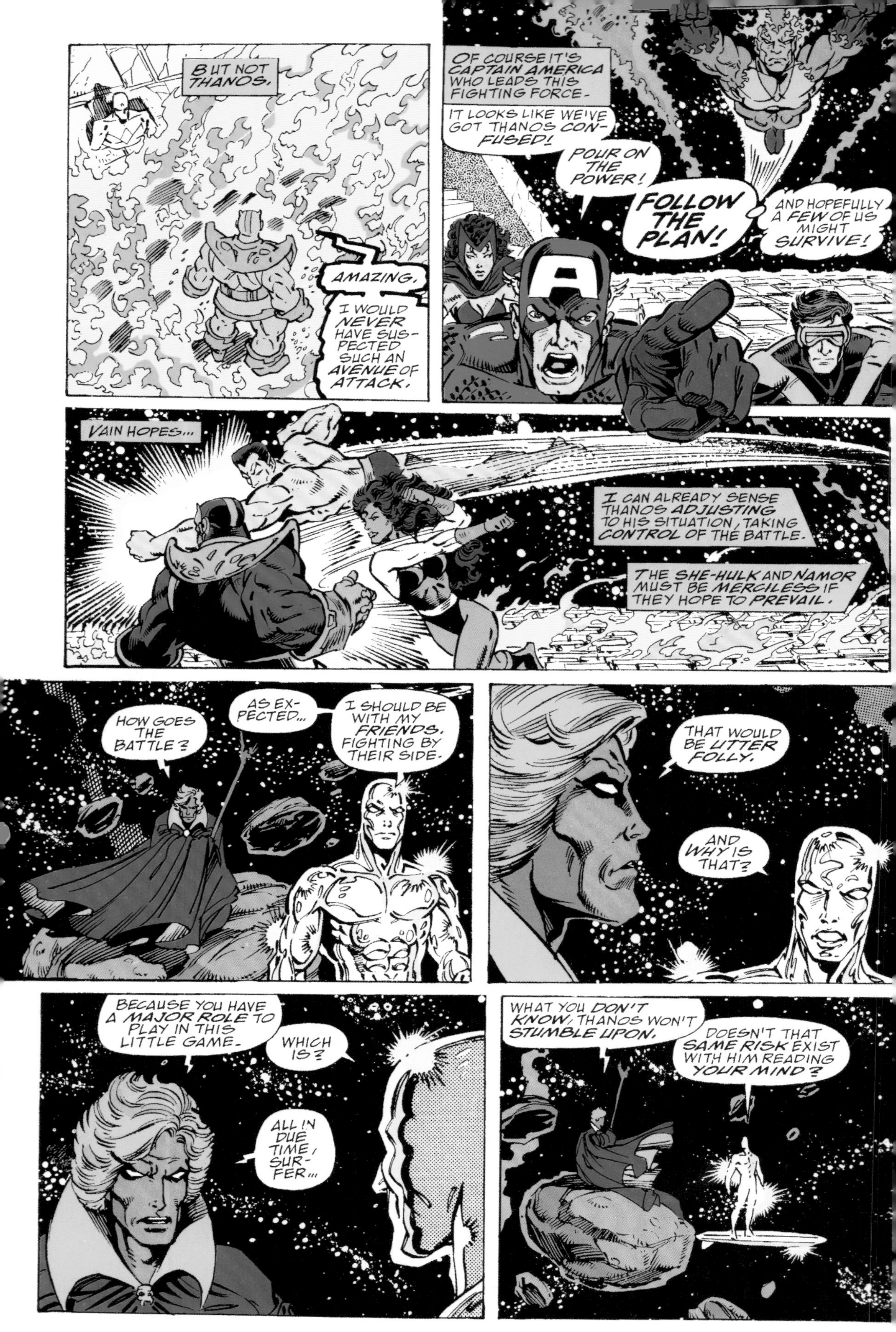
BUT NOT THANOS.
AMAZING.
I WOULD NEVER HAVE SUSPECTED SUCH AN AVENUE OF ATTACK.
OF COURSE IT'S CAPTAIN AMERICA WHO LEADS THIS FIGHTING FORCE.
IT LOOKS LIKE WE'VE GOT THANOS CONFUSED!
POUR ON THE POWER!
FOLLOW THE PLAN!
AND HOPEFULLY A FEW OF US MIGHT SURVIVE!
VAIN HOPES...
I CAN ALREADY SENSE THANOS ADJUSTING TO HIS SITUATION, TAKING CONTROL OF THE BATTLE.
THE SHE-HULK AND NAMOR MUST BE MERCILESS IF THEY HOPE TO PREVAIL.
HOW GOES THE BATTLE?
AS EXPECTED...
I SHOULD BE WITH MY FRIENDS, FIGHTING BY THEIR SIDE.
THAT WOULD BE UTTER FOLLY.
AND WHY IS THAT?
BECAUSE YOU HAVE A MAJOR ROLE TO PLAY IN THIS LITTLE GAME.
WHICH IS?
ALL IN DUE TIME, SURFER...
WHAT YOU DON'T KNOW, THANOS WON'T STUMBLE UPON.
DOESN'T THAT SAME RISK EXIST WITH HIM READING YOUR MIND?

NO.

THANOS KNOWS ME.

HE'LL NOT RISK SUCH A *DISTRACTION* WHILE IN THE MIDST OF BATTLE—

"*THANOS* HAS *NARROWED* THE SCOPE OF HIS *GODHOOD* JUST AS HE WAS BEGINNING TO *ADJUST* TO IT—

"HIS MIND MUST BE *REELING* FROM THE *CHANGES.*

"OF COURSE THAT MAKES HIM NO LESS *DANGEROUS,*"

AWAY FROM ME YOU *CLOWNS!*

NAMOR-- THERE'S SOMETHING *GROWING* WHERE THANOS *TOUCHED US!!*

REMOVE IT, *QUICKLY!*

SORRY, NAMOR, MY BROTHER WOULD NEVER LAY A TRAP SO EASILY *EVADED.*

TO YOUR SORROW, THERE ARE *TRUTHS* THAT CANNOT BE *DENIED.*

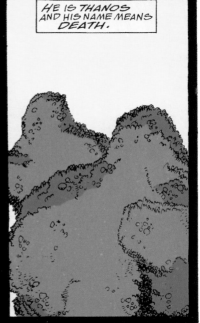

HE IS THANOS AND HIS NAME MEANS *DEATH.*

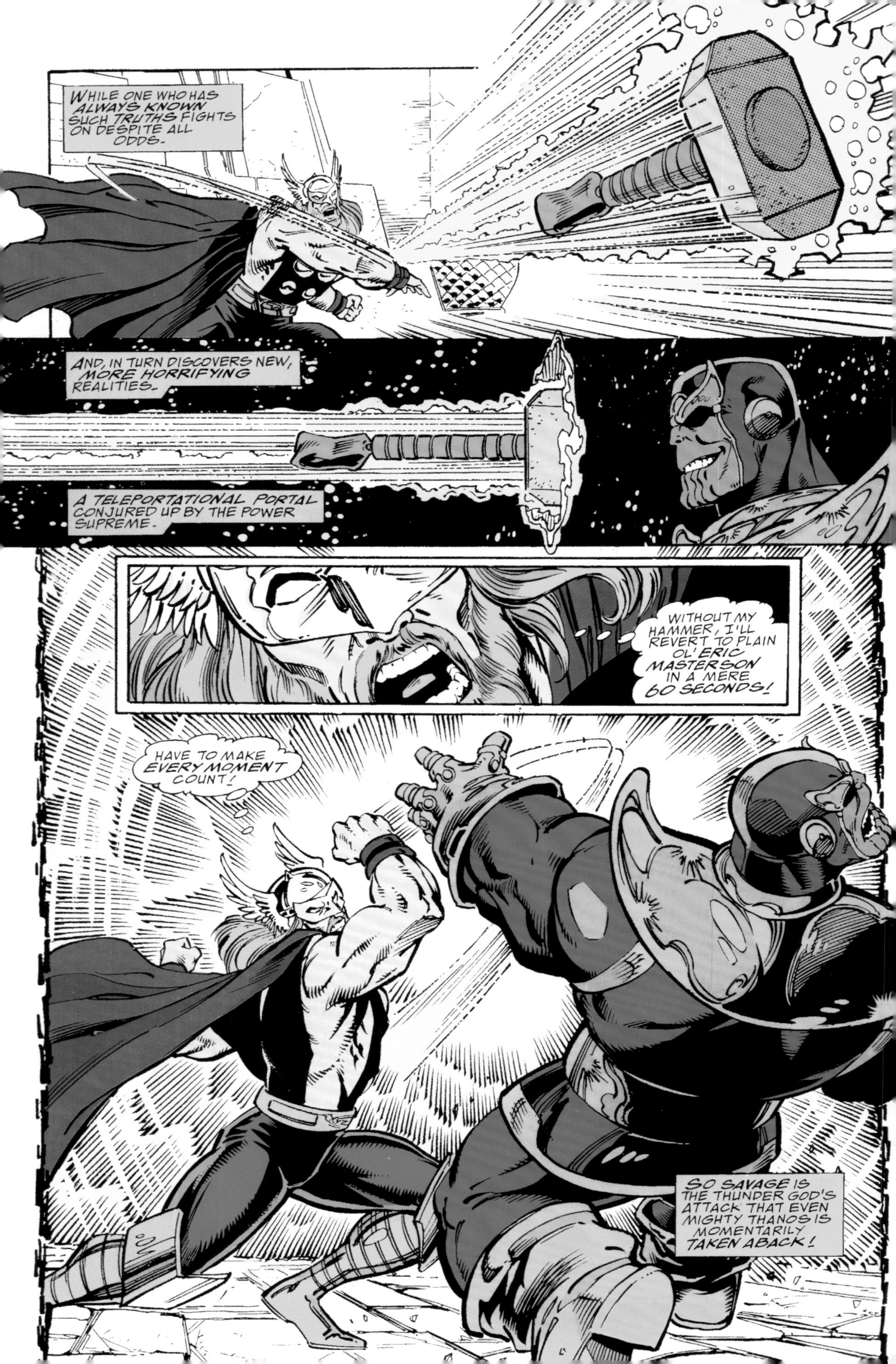
WHILE ONE WHO HAS ALWAYS KNOWN SUCH TRUTHS FIGHTS ON DESPITE ALL ODDS.
AND, IN TURN DISCOVERS NEW, MORE HORRIFYING REALITIES.
A TELEPORTATIONAL PORTAL CONJURED UP BY THE POWER SUPREME.
WITHOUT MY HAMMER, I'LL REVERT TO PLAIN OL' ERIC MASTERSON IN A MERE 60 SECONDS!
HAVE TO MAKE EVERY MOMENT COUNT!
SO SAVAGE IS THE THUNDER GOD'S ATTACK THAT EVEN MIGHTY THANOS IS MOMENTARILY TAKEN ABACK!

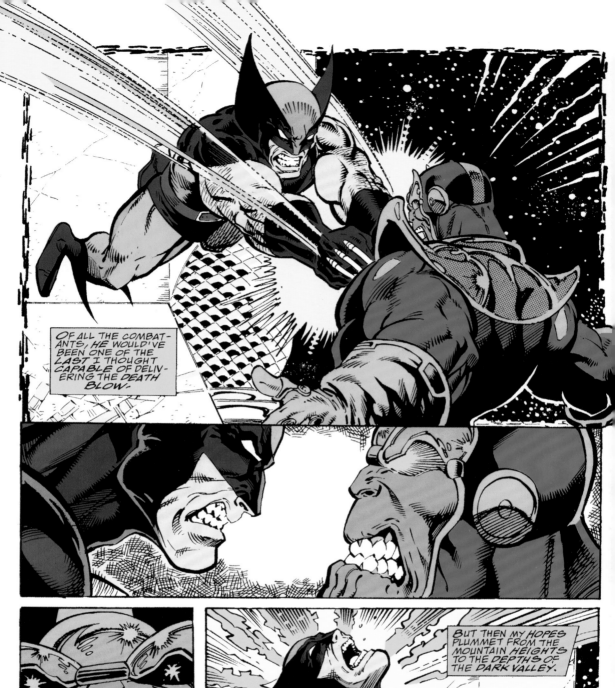

OF ALL THE COMBATANTS, HE WOULD'VE BEEN ONE OF THE LAST I THOUGHT CAPABLE OF DELIVERING THE DEATH BLOW-

BUT THEN MY HOPES PLUMMET FROM THE MOUNTAIN HEIGHTS TO THE DEPTHS OF THE DARK VALLEY.

EEYAARRGH!

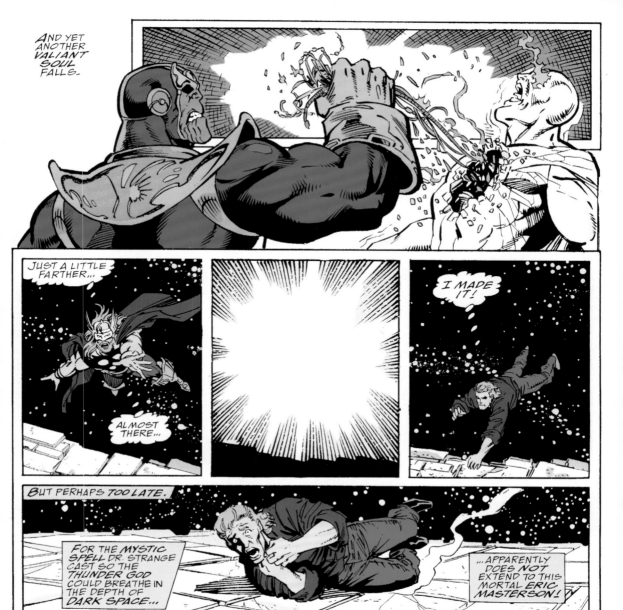

AND YET ANOTHER VALIANT SOUL FALLS.

JUST A LITTLE FARTHER...

ALMOST THERE...

I MADE IT!

BUT PERHAPS *TOO LATE.*

FOR THE MYSTIC SPELL DR. STRANGE CAST SO THE THUNDER GOD COULD BREATHE IN THE DEPTH OF DARK SPACE...

...APPARENTLY DOES *NOT* EXTEND TO THIS MORTAL *ERIC MASTERSON!*

HE'S *DEAD!*

YOU MURDERED HIM, YOU COLD-HEARTED *MONSTER!*

SUCH AN EMOTIONAL OUTBURST--

--NOT AT ALL WHAT I EXPECTED FROM THE LEGENDARY *CAPTAIN AMERICA!*

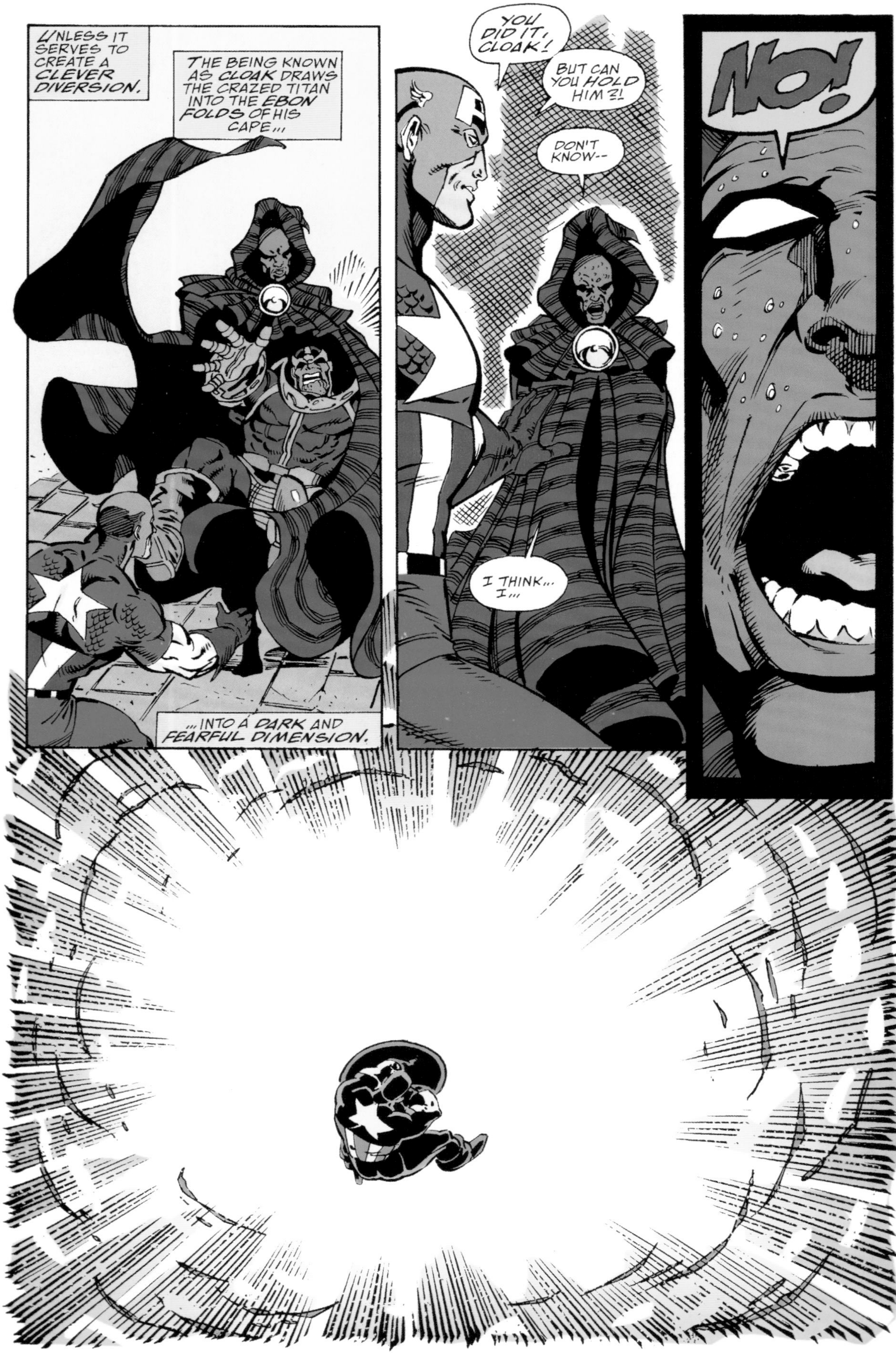

UNLESS IT SERVES TO CREATE A CLEVER DIVERSION.
THE BEING KNOWN AS CLOAK DRAWS THE CRAZED TITAN INTO THE EBON FOLDS OF HIS CAPE...
...INTO A DARK AND FEARFUL DIMENSION.
YOU DID IT, CLOAK!
BUT CAN YOU HOLD HIM?!
DON'T KNOW--
I THINK... I...
NO!

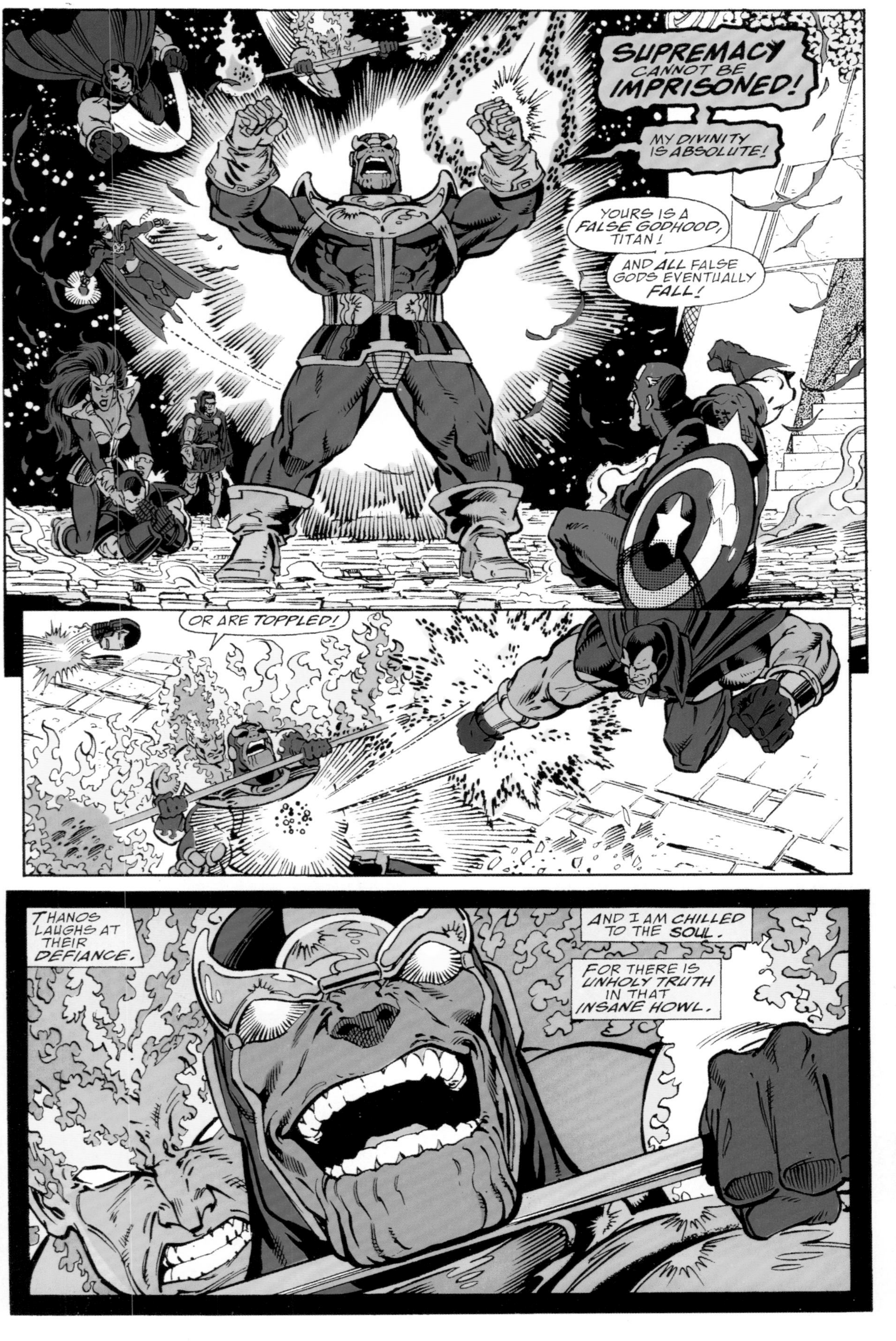

SUPREMACY CANNOT BE IMPRISONED!
MY DIVINITY IS ABSOLUTE!
YOURS IS A FALSE GODHOOD, TITAN!
AND ALL FALSE GODS EVENTUALLY FALL!
OR ARE TOPPLED!
THANOS LAUGHS AT THEIR DEFIANCE.
AND I AM CHILLED TO THE SOUL.
FOR THERE IS UNHOLY TRUTH IN THAT INSANE HOWL.

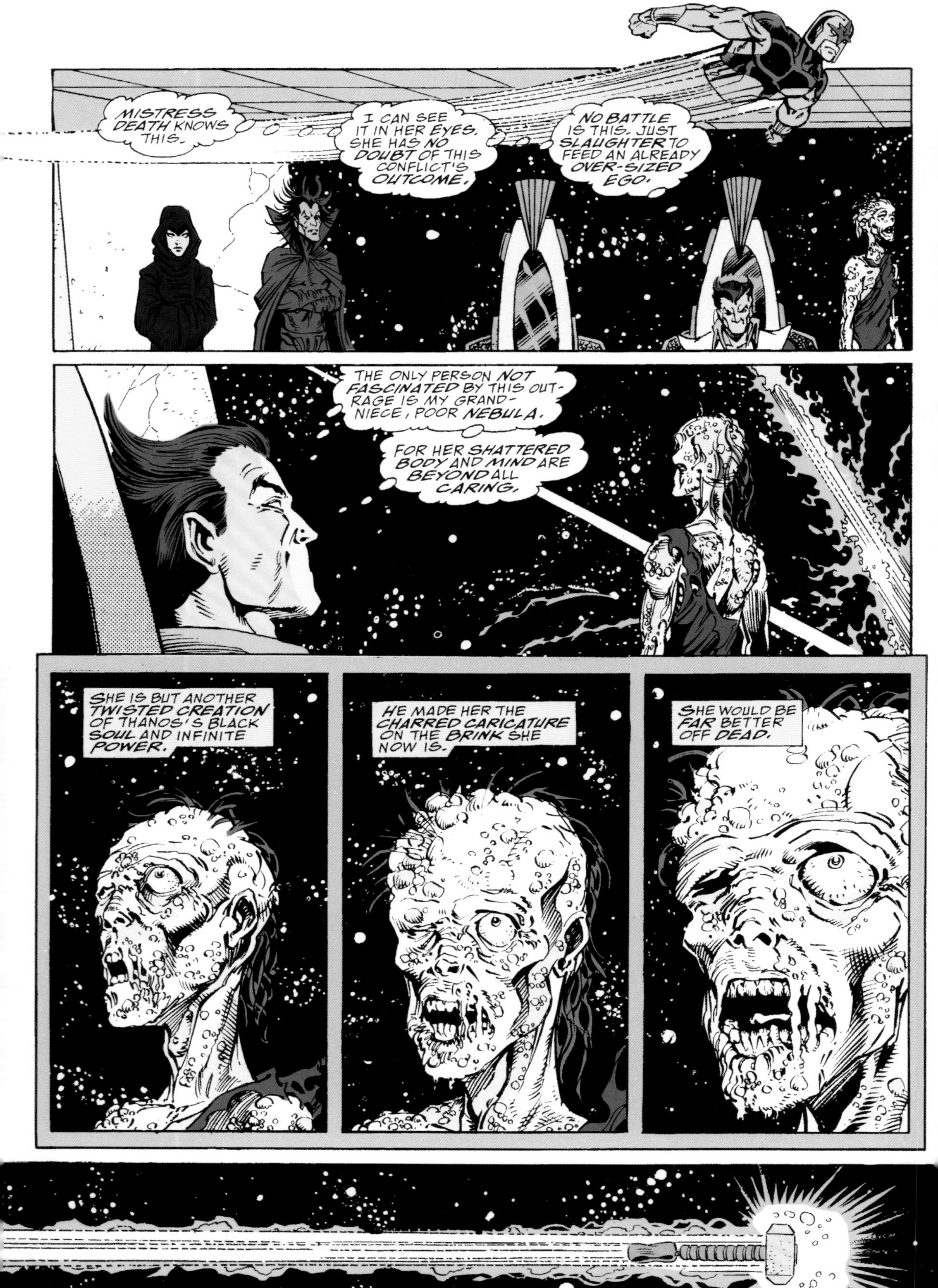
MISTRESS DEATH KNOWS THIS.
I CAN SEE IT IN HER EYES. SHE HAS NO DOUBT OF THIS CONFLICT'S OUTCOME.
NO BATTLE IS THIS. JUST SLAUGHTER TO FEED AN ALREADY OVER-SIZED EGO.
THE ONLY PERSON NOT FASCINATED BY THIS OUTRAGE IS MY GRAND-NIECE, POOR NEBULA.
FOR HER SHATTERED BODY AND MIND ARE BEYOND ALL CARING.
SHE IS BUT ANOTHER TWISTED CREATION OF THANOS'S BLACK SOUL AND INFINITE POWER.
HE MADE HER THE CHARRED CARICATURE ON THE BRINK SHE NOW IS.
SHE WOULD BE FAR BETTER OFF DEAD.
STILL, SOME DREAMS REFUSE TO DIE.

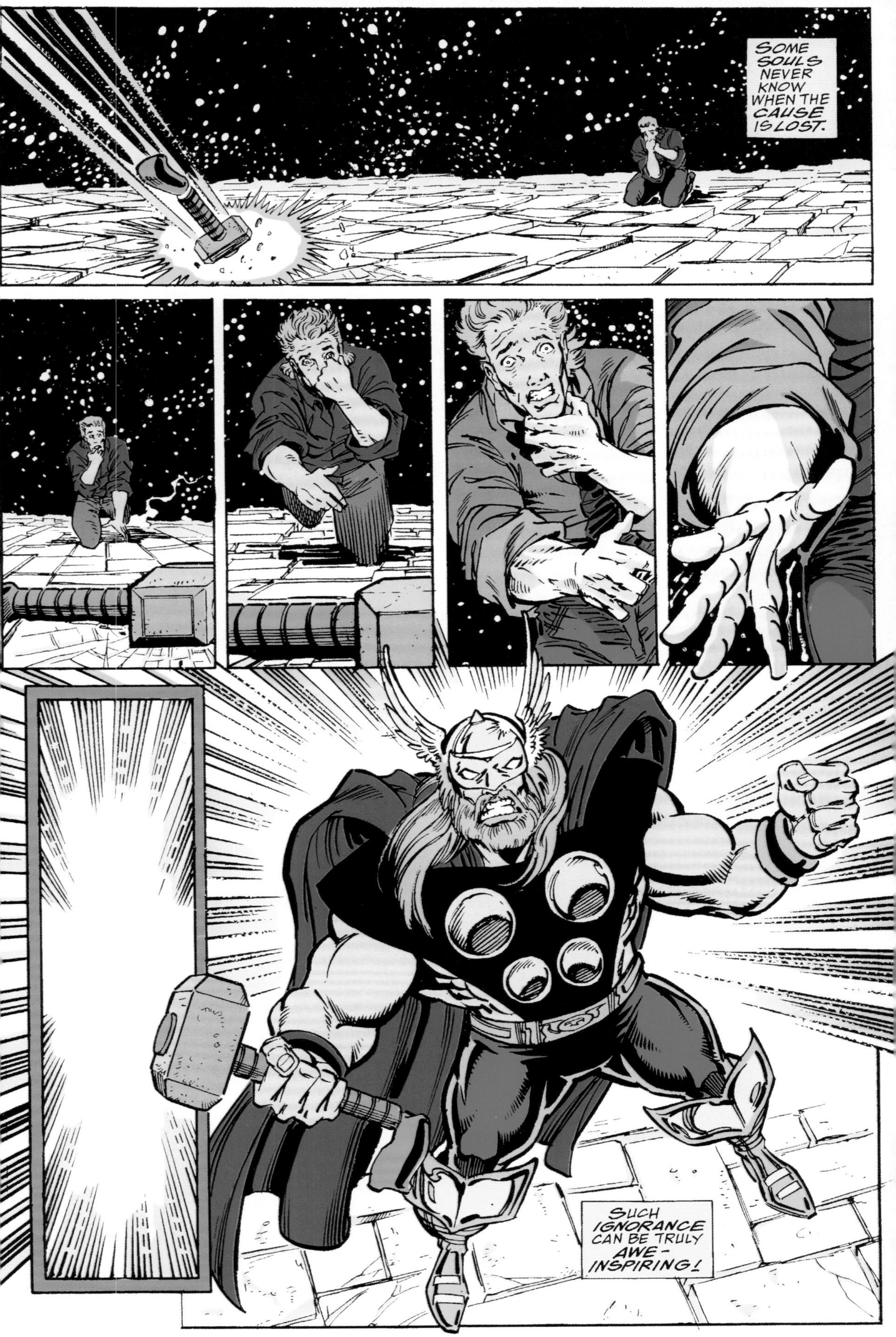
SOME SOULS NEVER KNOW WHEN THE CAUSE IS LOST.
SUCH IGNORANCE CAN BE TRULY AWE-INSPIRING!

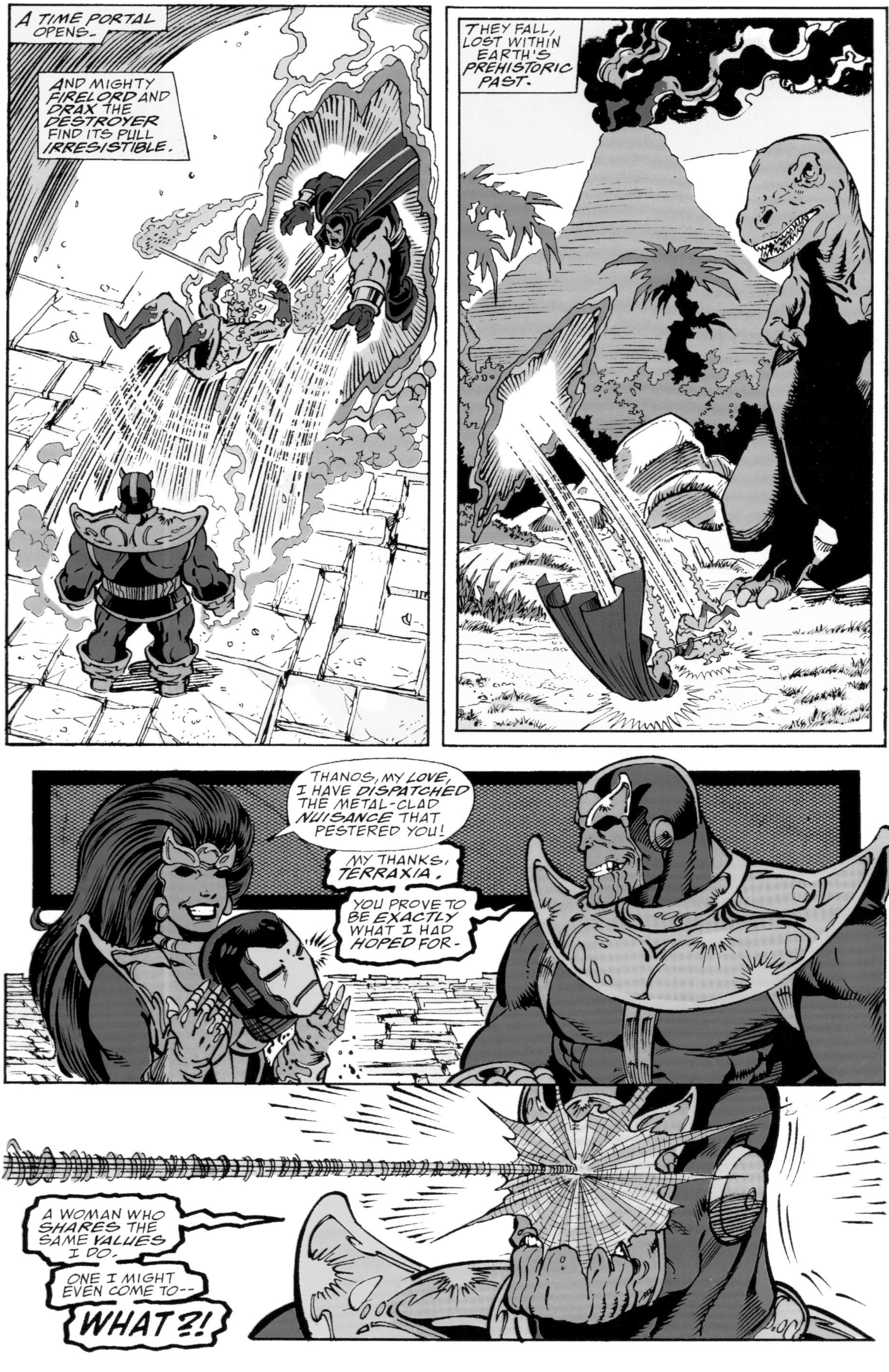

A TIME PORTAL OPENS-
AND MIGHTY FIRELORD AND DRAX THE DESTROYER FIND ITS PULL IRRESISTIBLE.
THEY FALL, LOST WITHIN EARTH'S PREHISTORIC PAST.
THANOS, MY LOVE, I HAVE DISPATCHED THE METAL-CLAD NUISANCE THAT PESTERED YOU!
MY THANKS, TERRAXIA.
YOU PROVE TO BE EXACTLY WHAT I HAD HOPED FOR-
A WOMAN WHO SHARES THE SAME VALUES I DO.
ONE I MIGHT EVEN COME TO--
WHAT?!

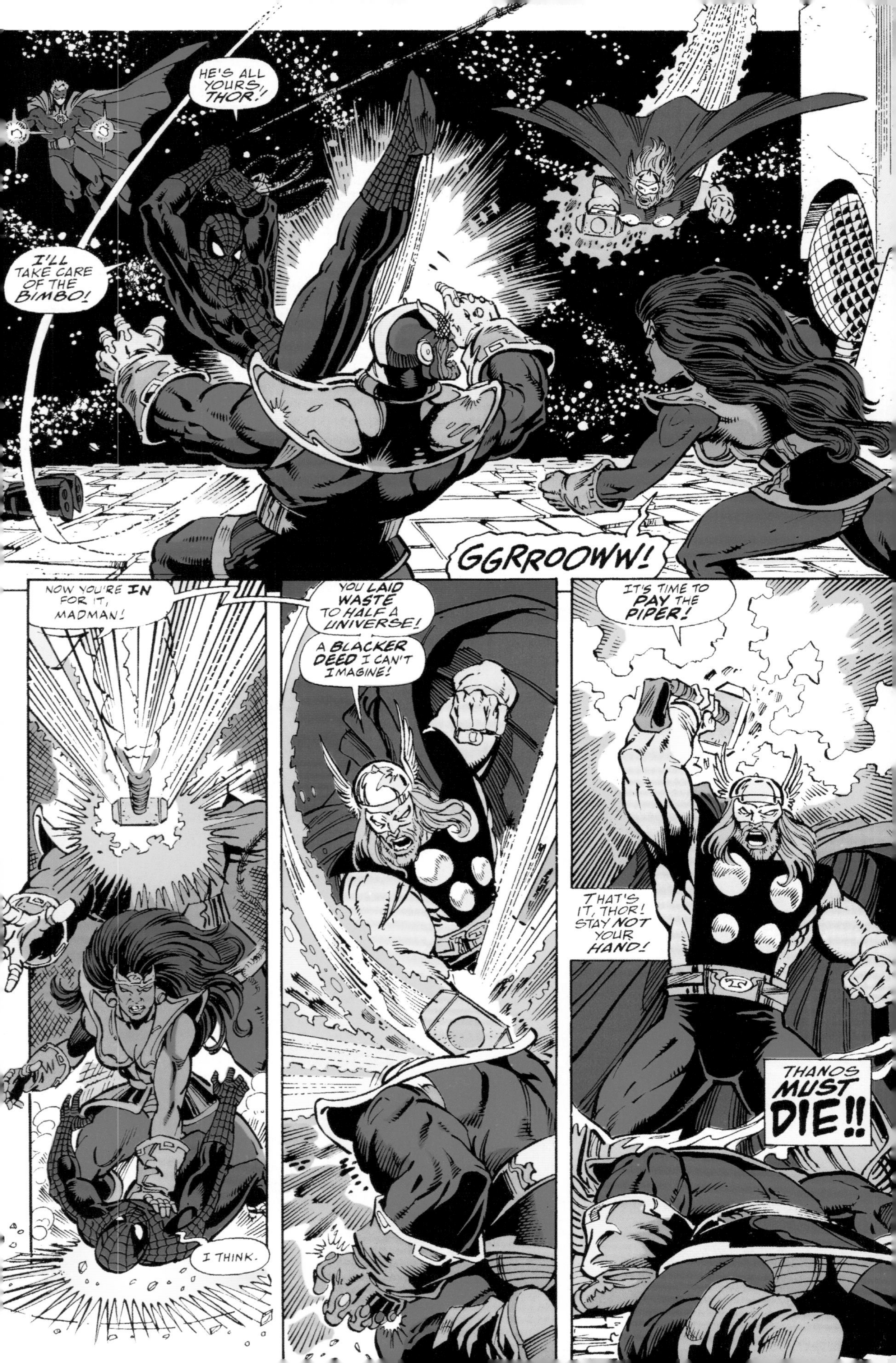
HE'S ALL YOURS, THOR!
I'LL TAKE CARE OF THE BIMBO!
GGRROOWW!
NOW YOU'RE IN FOR IT, MADMAN!
YOU LAID WASTE TO HALF A UNIVERSE!
A BLACKER DEED I CAN'T IMAGINE!
IT'S TIME TO PAY THE PIPER!
THAT'S IT, THOR! STAY NOT YOUR HAND!
THANOS MUST DIE!!
I THINK.

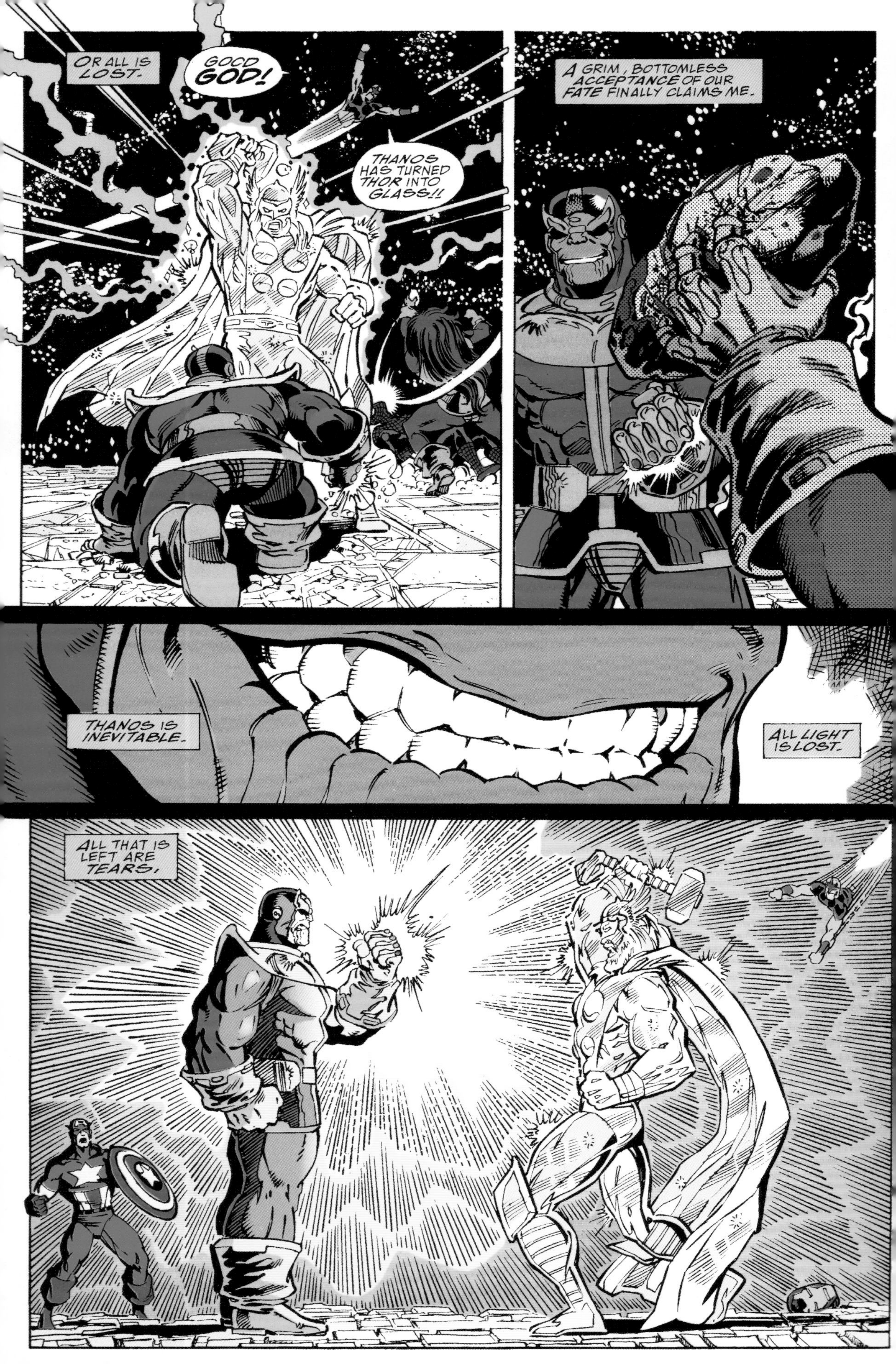
OR ALL IS LOST.
GOOD GOD!
THANOS HAS TURNED THOR INTO GLASS!!
A GRIM, BOTTOMLESS ACCEPTANCE OF OUR FATE FINALLY CLAIMS ME.
THANOS IS INEVITABLE.
ALL LIGHT IS LOST.
ALL THAT IS LEFT ARE TEARS.

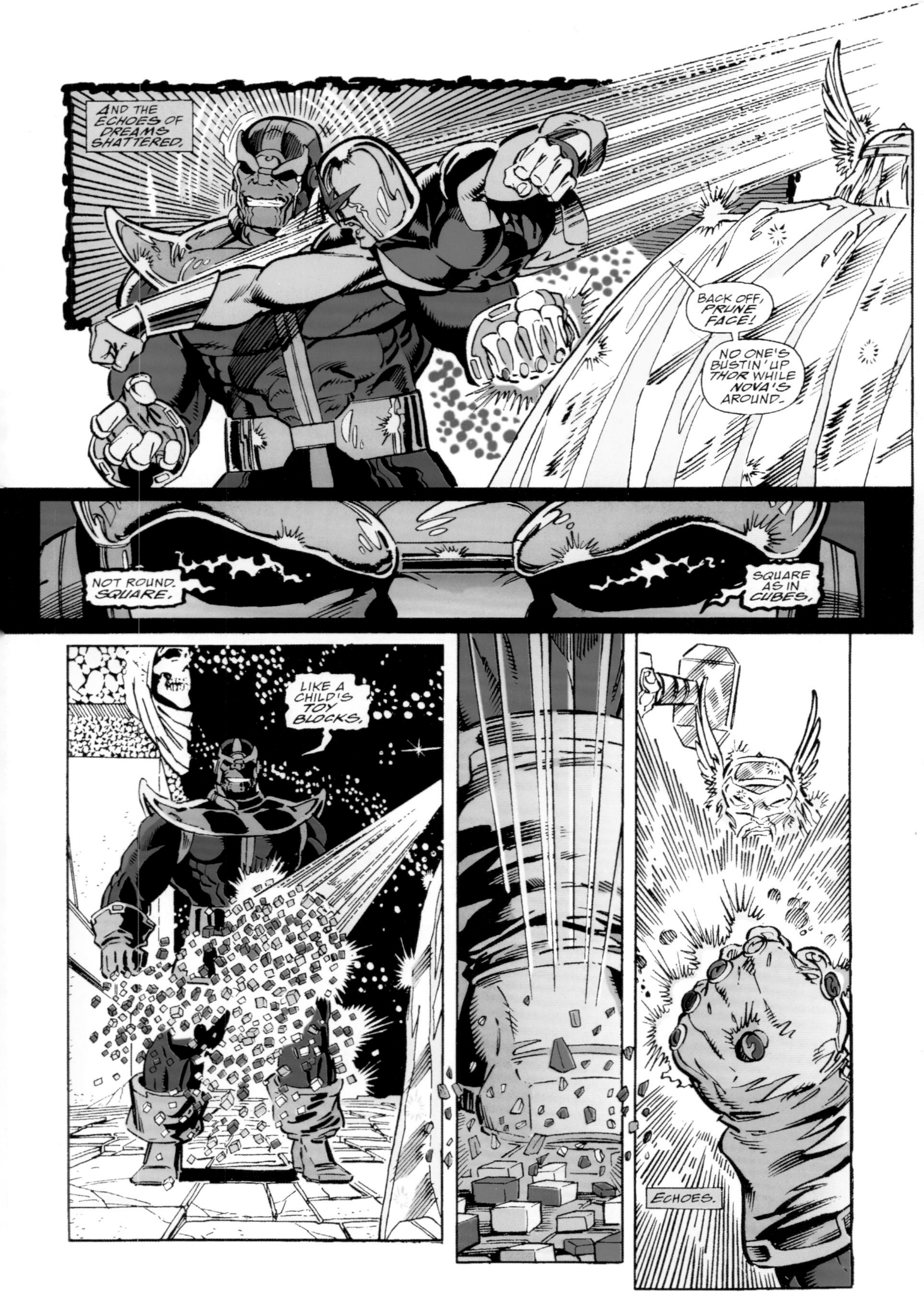
AND THE ECHOES OF DREAMS SHATTERED,
BACK OFF, PRUNE FACE!
NO ONE'S BUSTIN' UP THOR WHILE NOVA'S AROUND.
NOT ROUND. SQUARE.
SQUARE AS IN CUBES,
LIKE A CHILD'S TOY BLOCKS,
ECHOES.

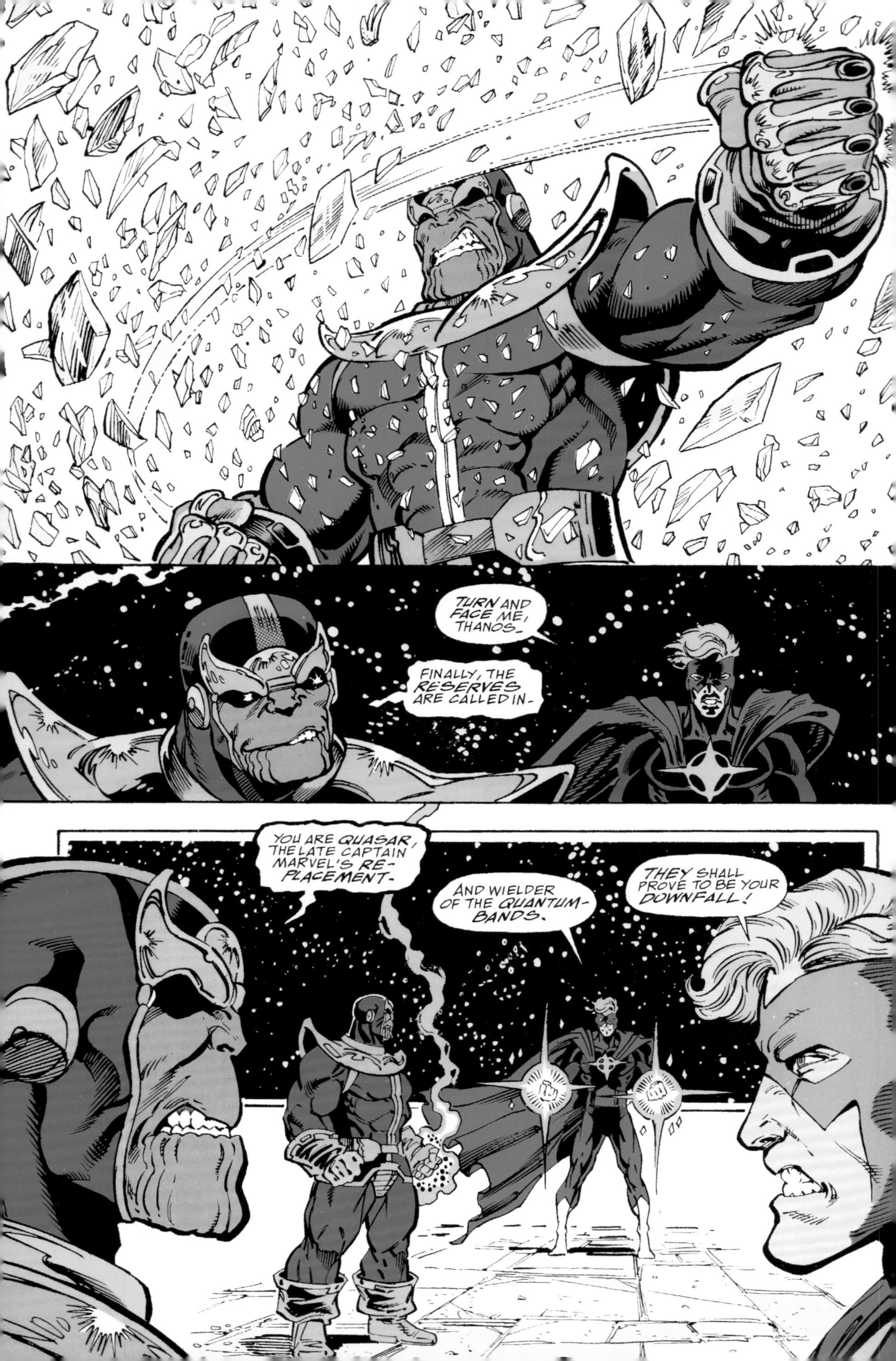
TURN AND FACE ME, THANOS--
FINALLY, THE RESERVES ARE CALLED IN--
YOU ARE QUASAR, THE LATE CAPTAIN MARVEL'S RE-PLACEMENT--
AND WIELDER OF THE QUANTUM-BANDS.
THEY SHALL PROVE TO BE YOUR DOWNFALL!

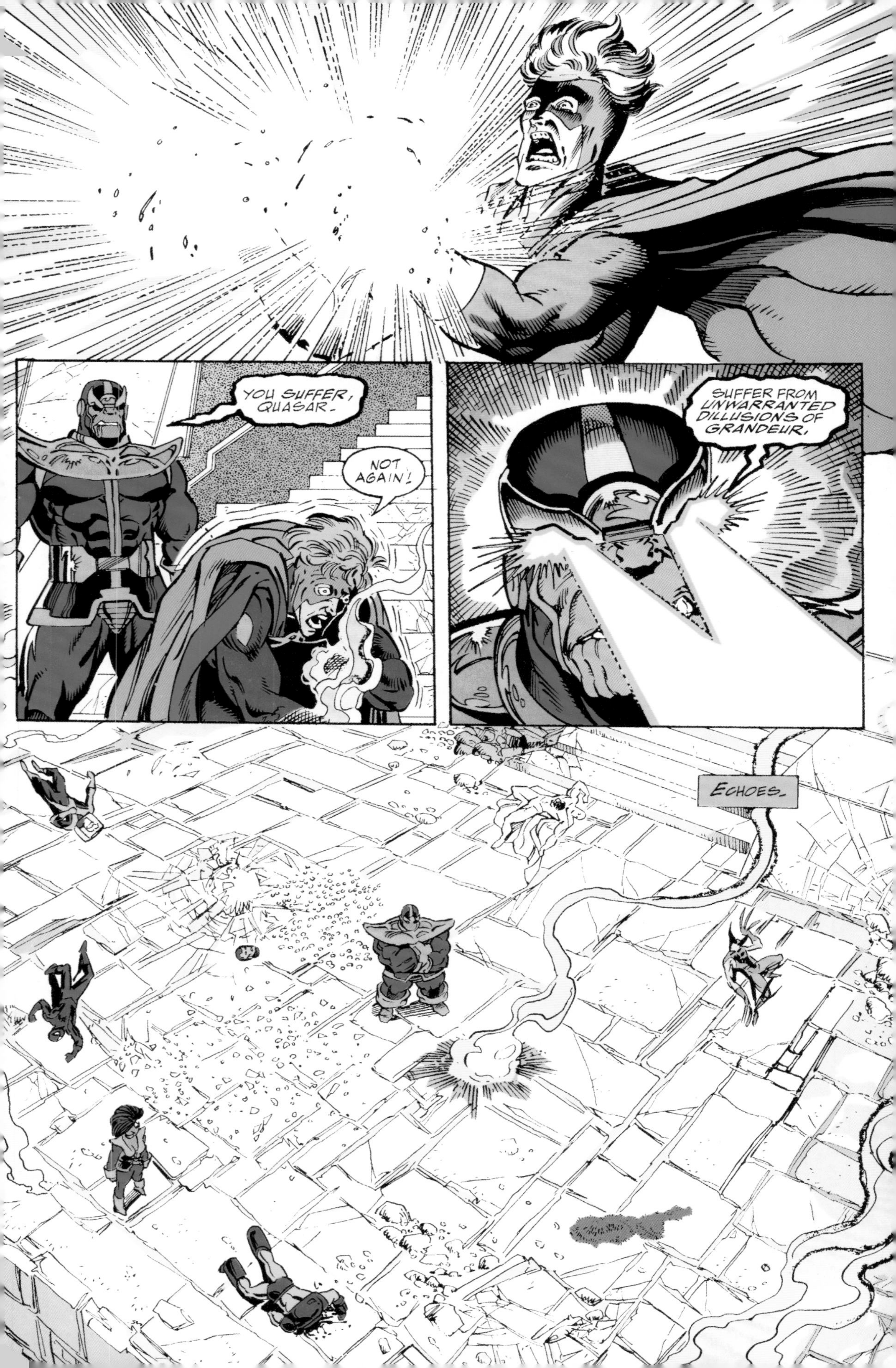
YOU SUFFER, QUASAR-
NOT AGAIN!
SUFFER FROM UNWARRANTED DILLUSIONS OF GRANDEUR,
ECHOES-

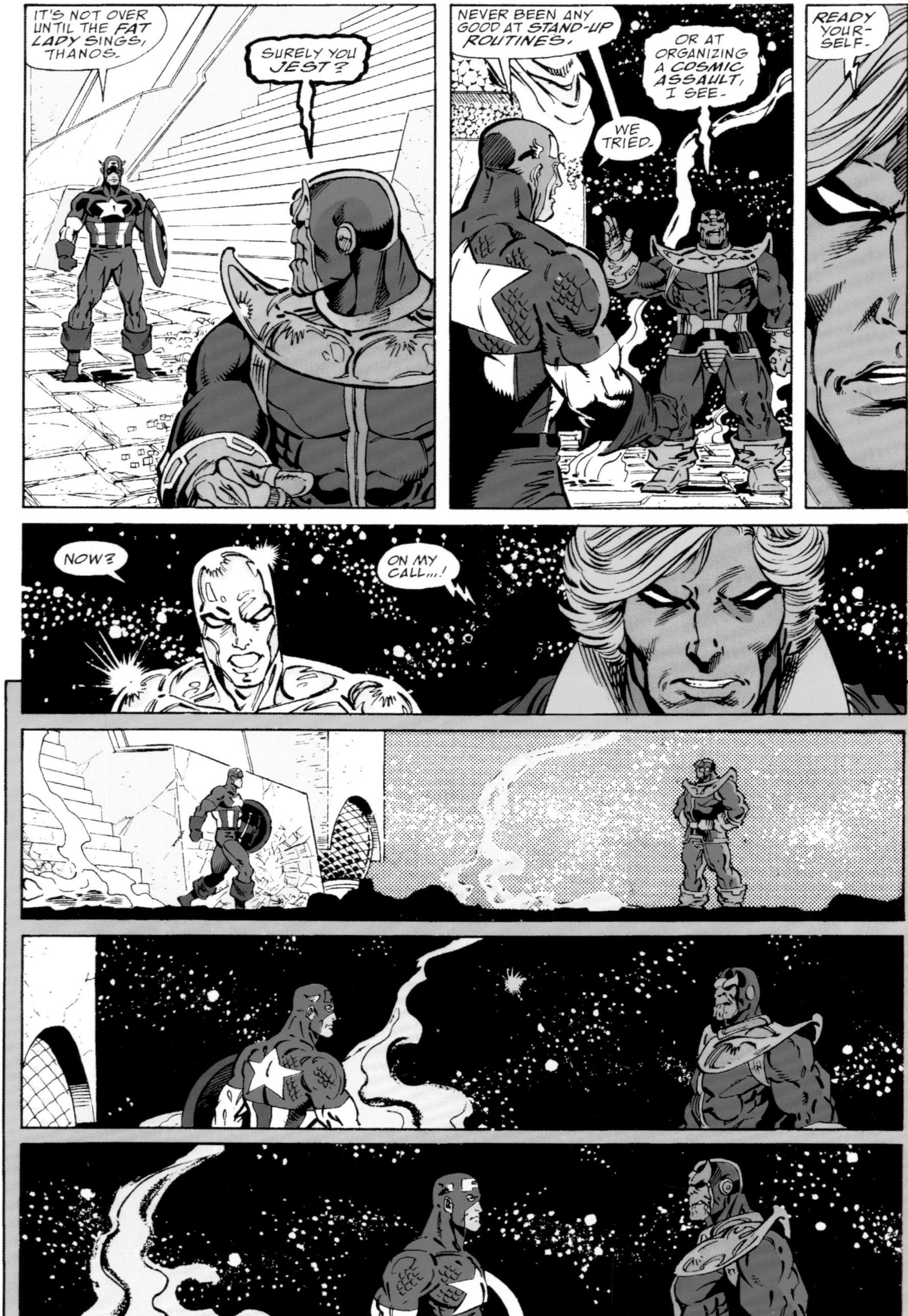

IT'S NOT OVER UNTIL THE FAT LADY SINGS, THANOS.
SURELY YOU JEST?
NEVER BEEN ANY GOOD AT STAND-UP ROUTINES.
OR AT ORGANIZING A COSMIC ASSAULT, I SEE.
WE TRIED.
READY YOUR-SELF.
NOW?
ON MY CALL...!

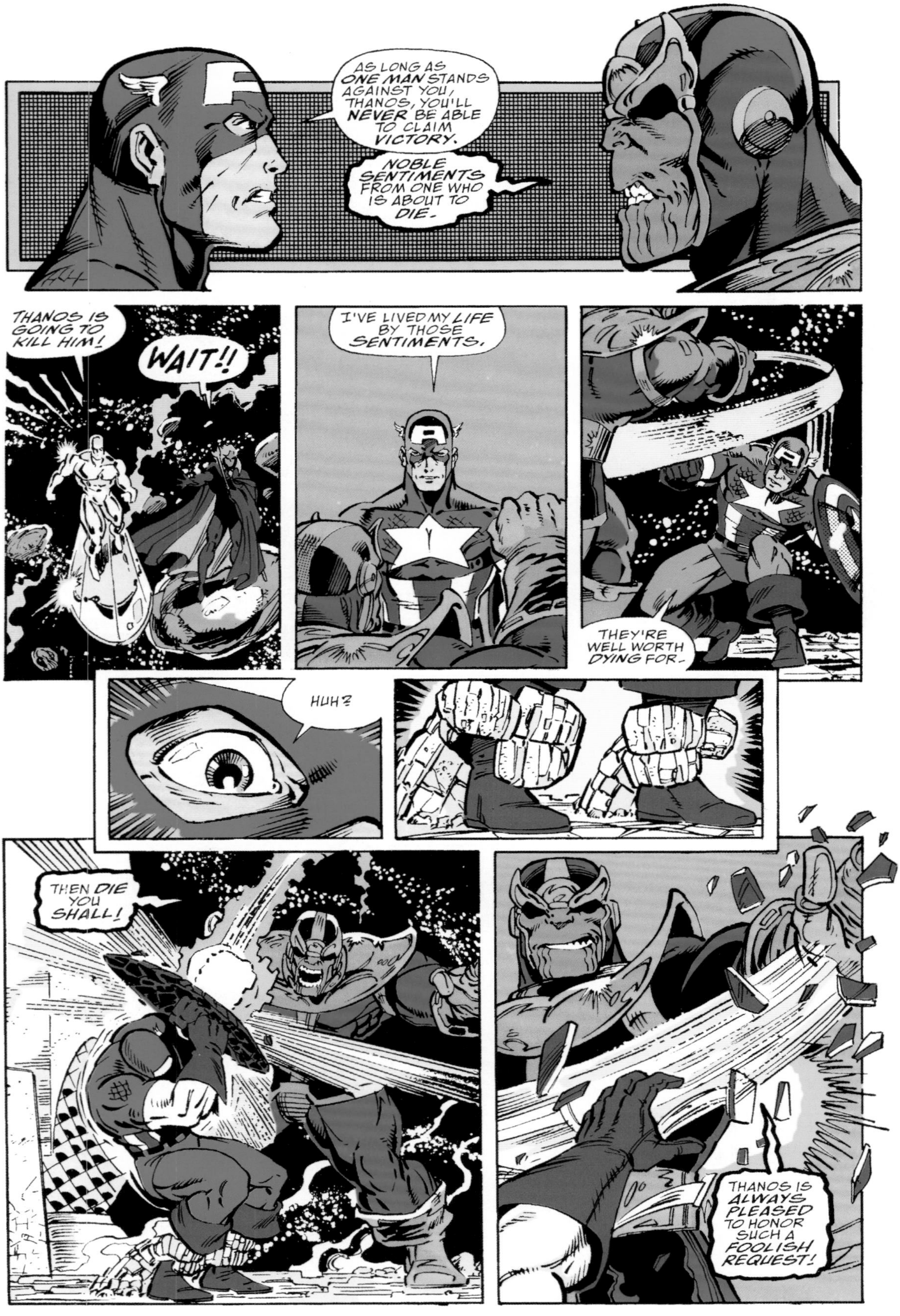
AS LONG AS ONE MAN STANDS AGAINST YOU, THANOS, YOU'LL NEVER BE ABLE TO CLAIM VICTORY.
NOBLE SENTIMENTS FROM ONE WHO IS ABOUT TO DIE.
THANOS IS GOING TO KILL HIM!
WAIT!!
I'VE LIVED MY LIFE BY THOSE SENTIMENTS.
THEY'RE WELL WORTH DYING FOR.
HUH?
THEN DIE YOU SHALL!
THANOS IS ALWAYS PLEASED TO HONOR SUCH A FOOLISH REQUEST!

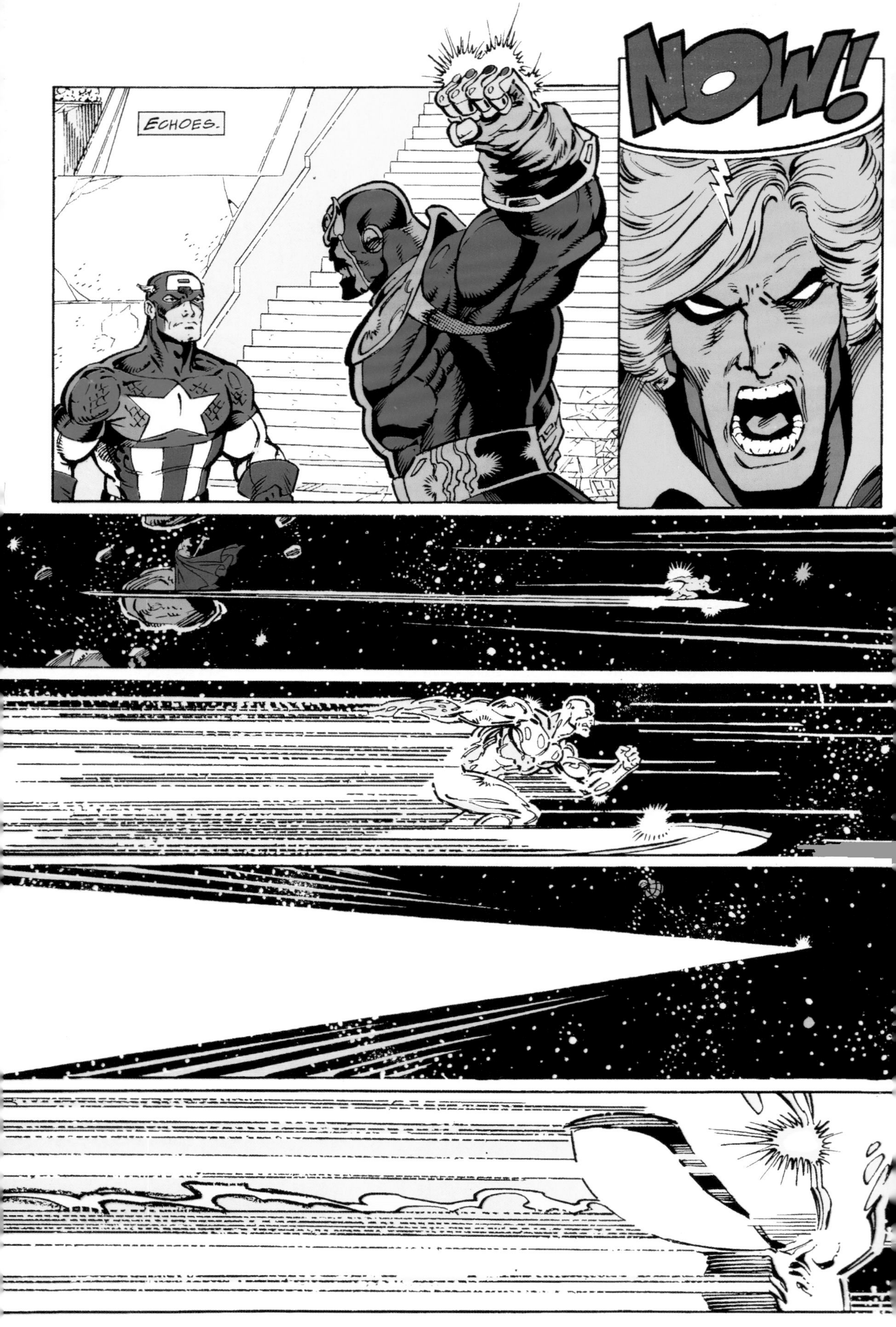
ECHOES.
NOW!

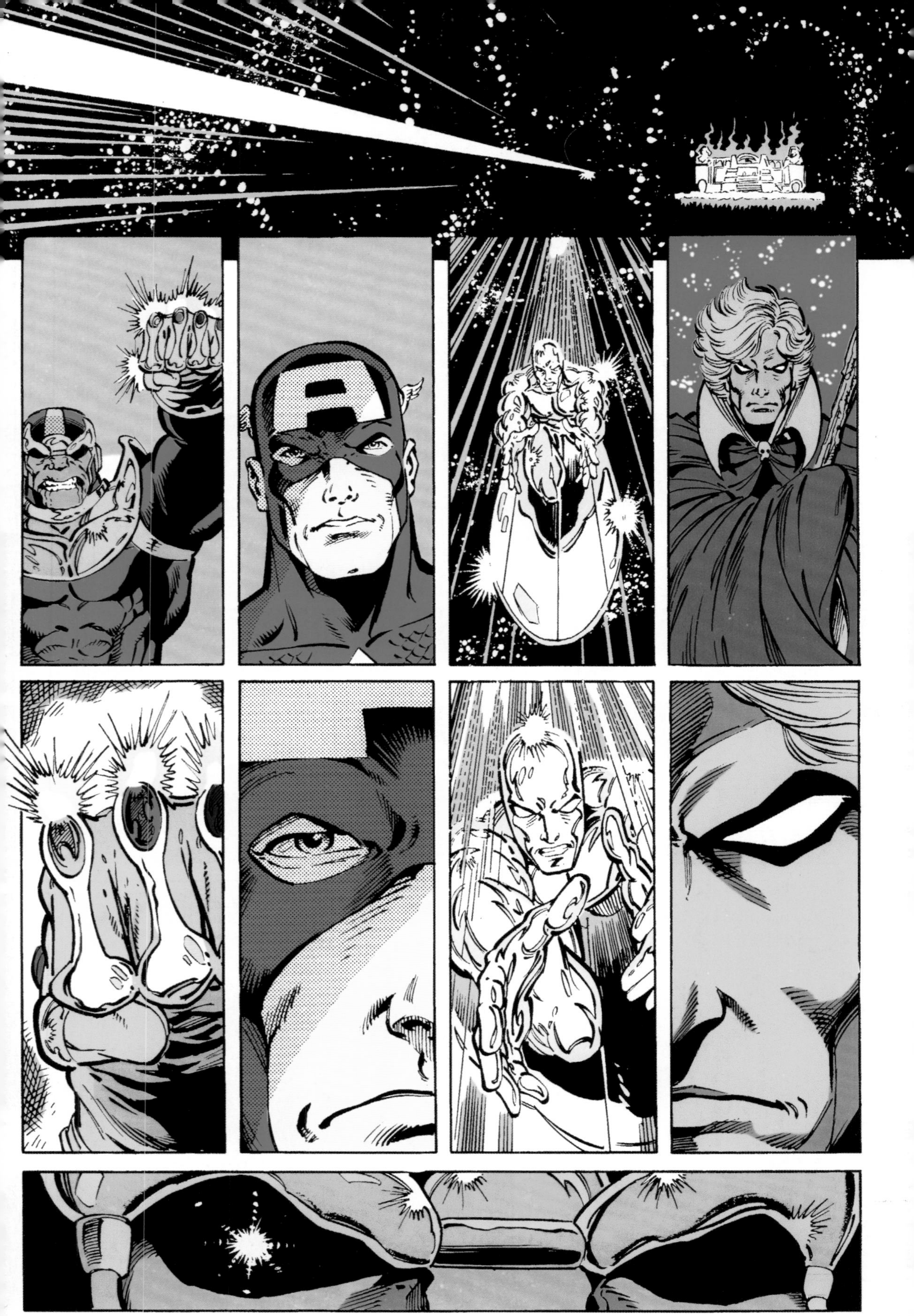

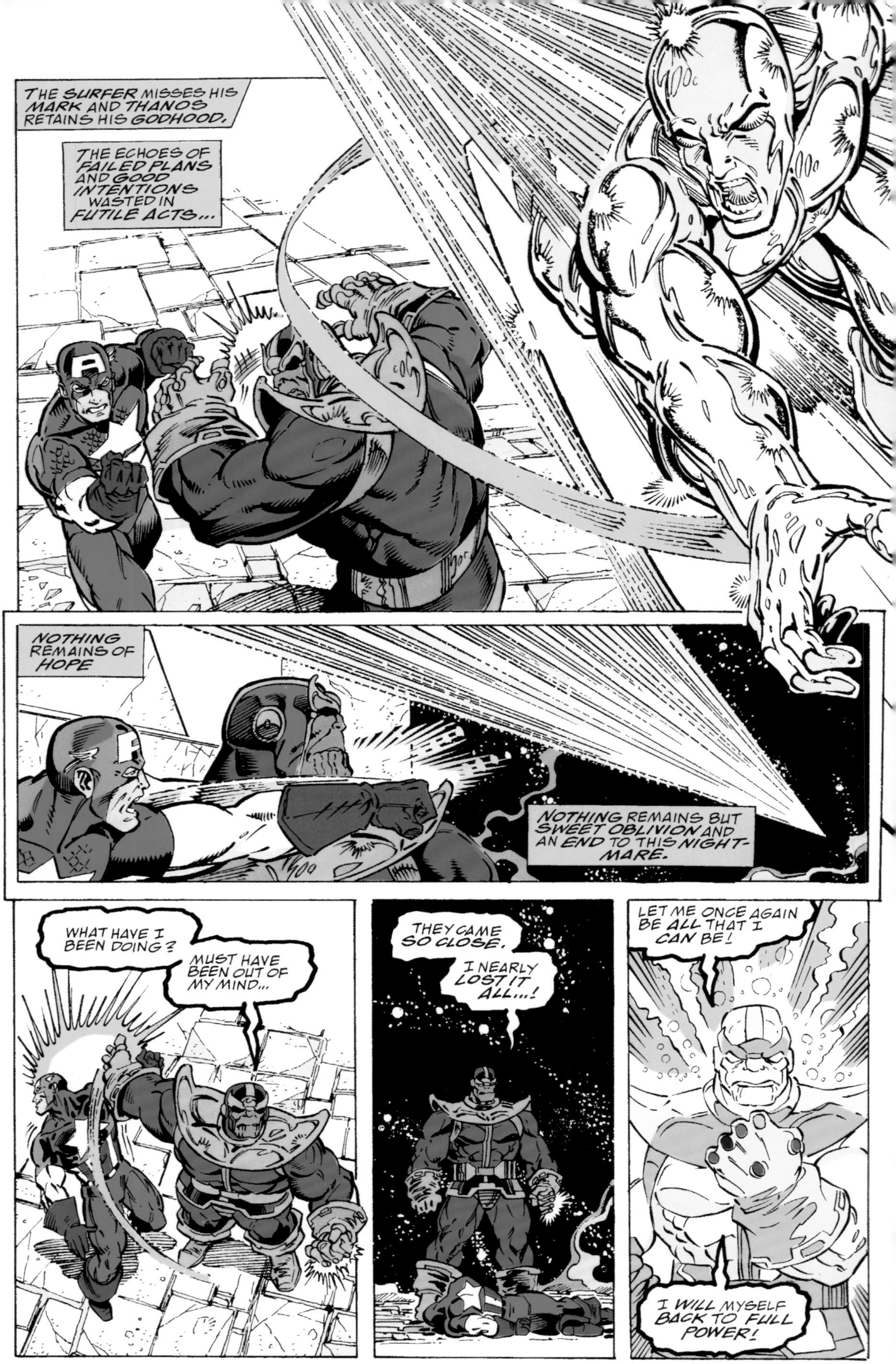
THE SURFER MISSES HIS MARK AND THANOS RETAINS HIS GODHOOD.
THE ECHOES OF FAILED PLANS AND GOOD INTENTIONS WASTED IN FUTILE ACTS...
NOTHING REMAINS OF HOPE
NOTHING REMAINS BUT SWEET OBLIVION AND AN END TO THIS NIGHT-MARE.
WHAT HAVE I BEEN DOING?
MUST HAVE BEEN OUT OF MY MIND...
THEY CAME SO CLOSE.
I NEARLY LOST IT ALL...!
LET ME ONCE AGAIN BE ALL THAT I CAN BE!
I WILL MYSELF BACK TO FULL POWER!

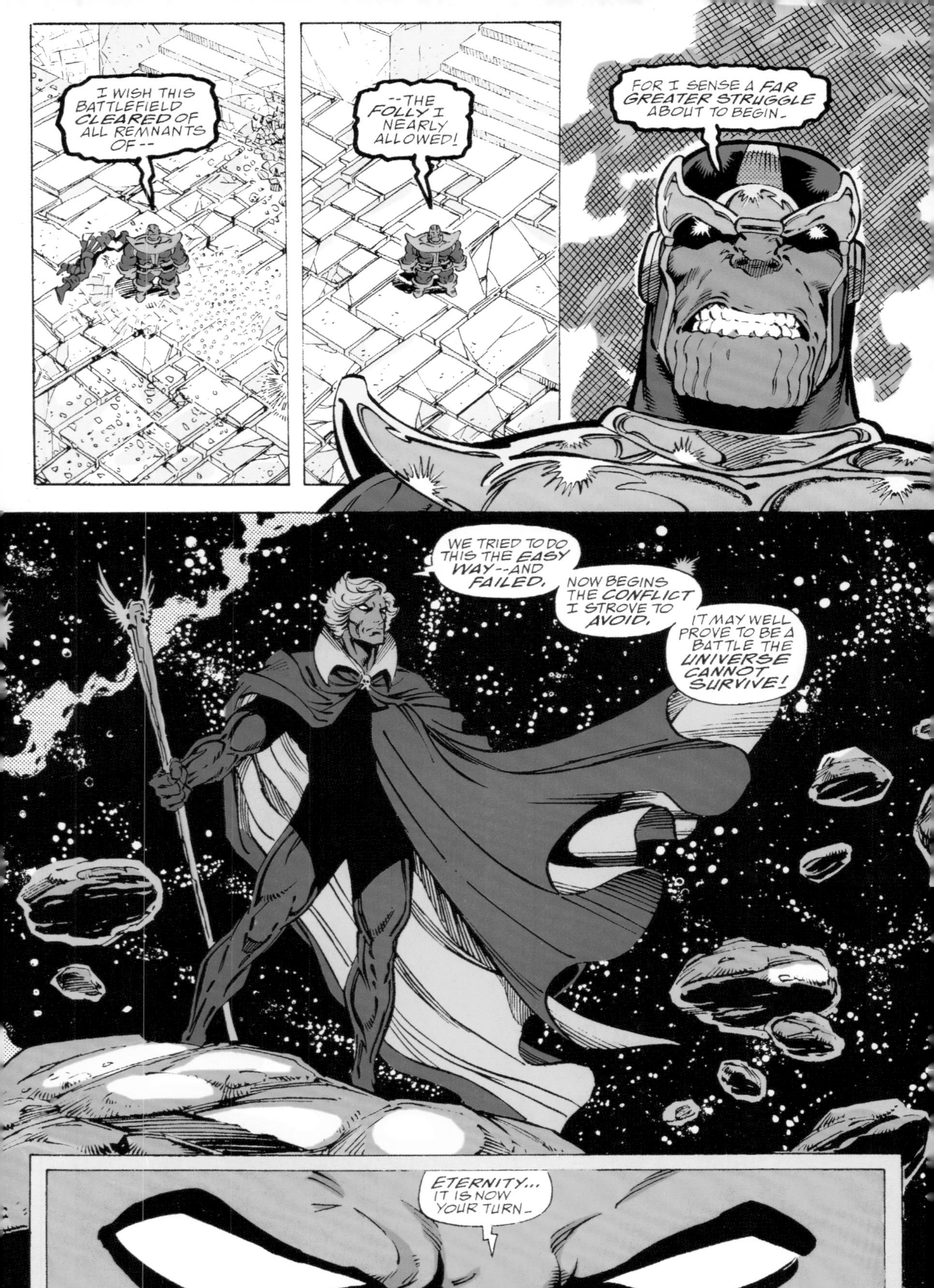
I WISH THIS BATTLEFIELD CLEARED OF ALL REMNANTS OF --
--THE FOLLY I NEARLY ALLOWED!
FOR I SENSE A FAR GREATER STRUGGLE ABOUT TO BEGIN.
WE TRIED TO DO THIS THE EASY WAY--AND FAILED.
NOW BEGINS THE CONFLICT I STROVE TO AVOID.
IT MAY WELL PROVE TO BE A BATTLE THE UNIVERSE CANNOT SURVIVE!
ETERNITY... IT IS NOW YOUR TURN.

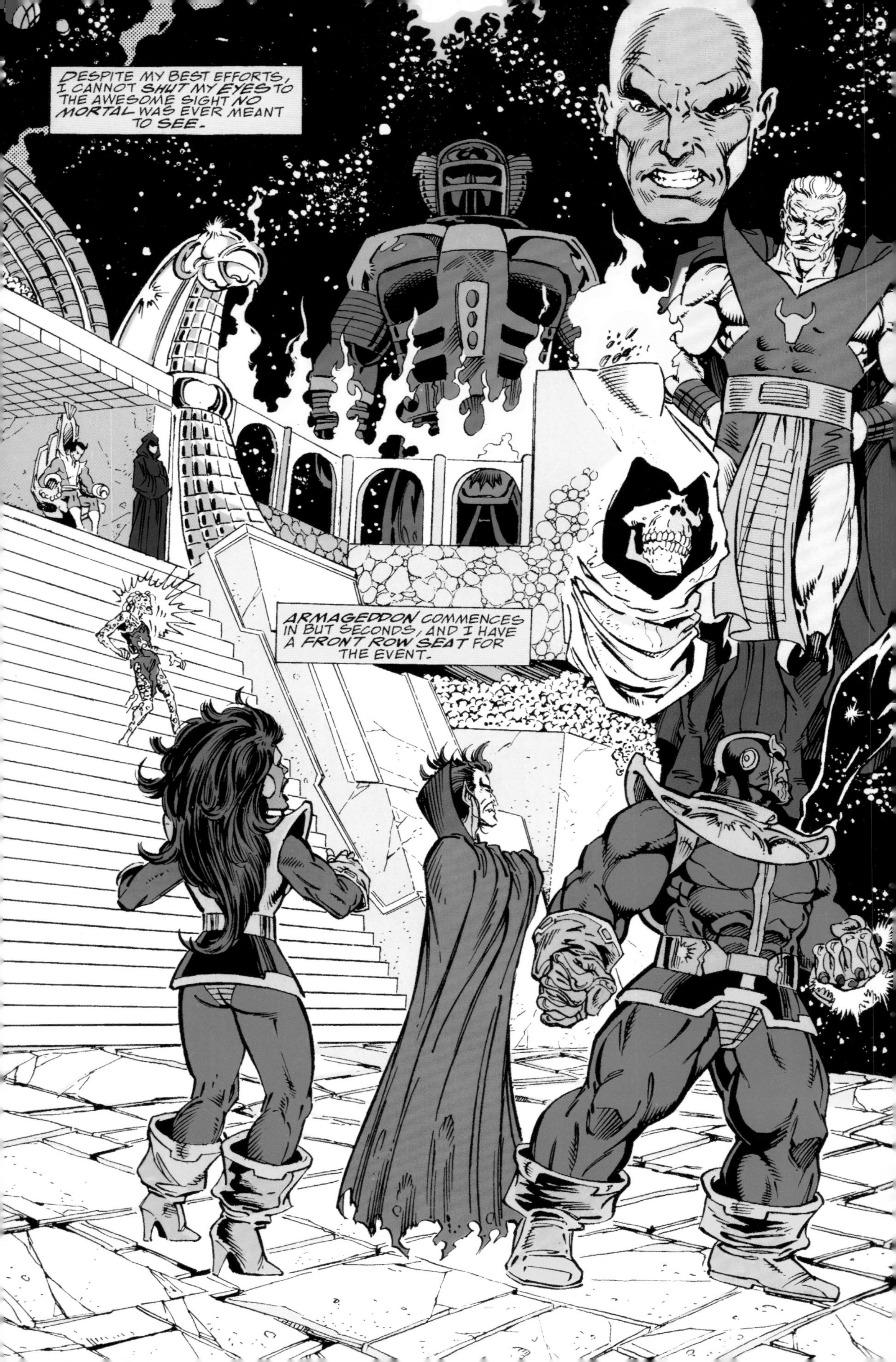
DESPITE MY BEST EFFORTS, I CANNOT SHUT MY EYES TO THE AWESOME SIGHT NO MORTAL WAS EVER MEANT TO SEE.
ARMAGEDDON COMMENCES IN BUT SECONDS, AND I HAVE A FRONT ROW SEAT FOR THE EVENT.

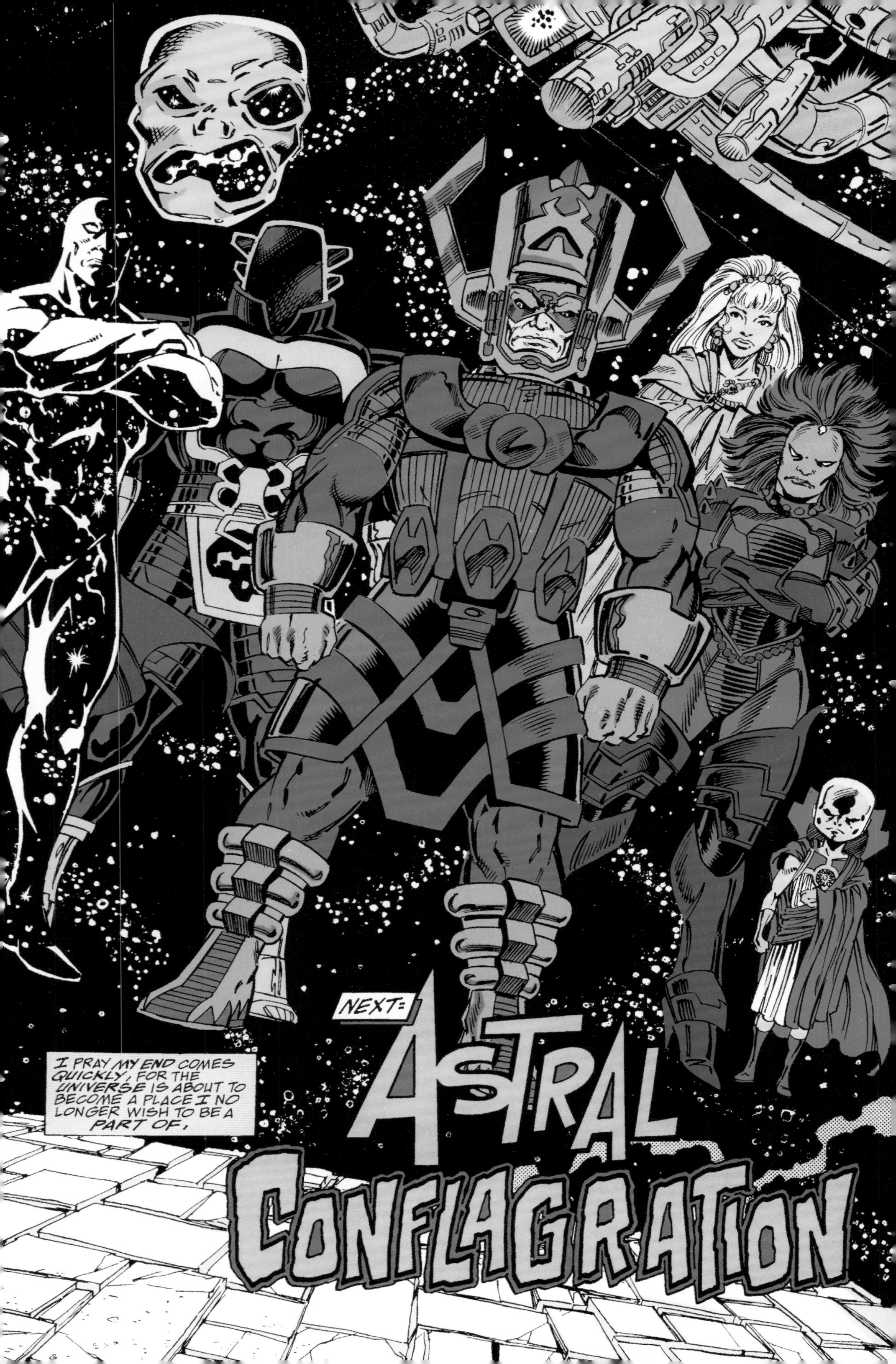
I PRAY MY END COMES QUICKLY, FOR THE UNIVERSE IS ABOUT TO BECOME A PLACE I NO LONGER WISH TO BE A PART OF.
NEXT:
ASTRAL CONFLAGRATION

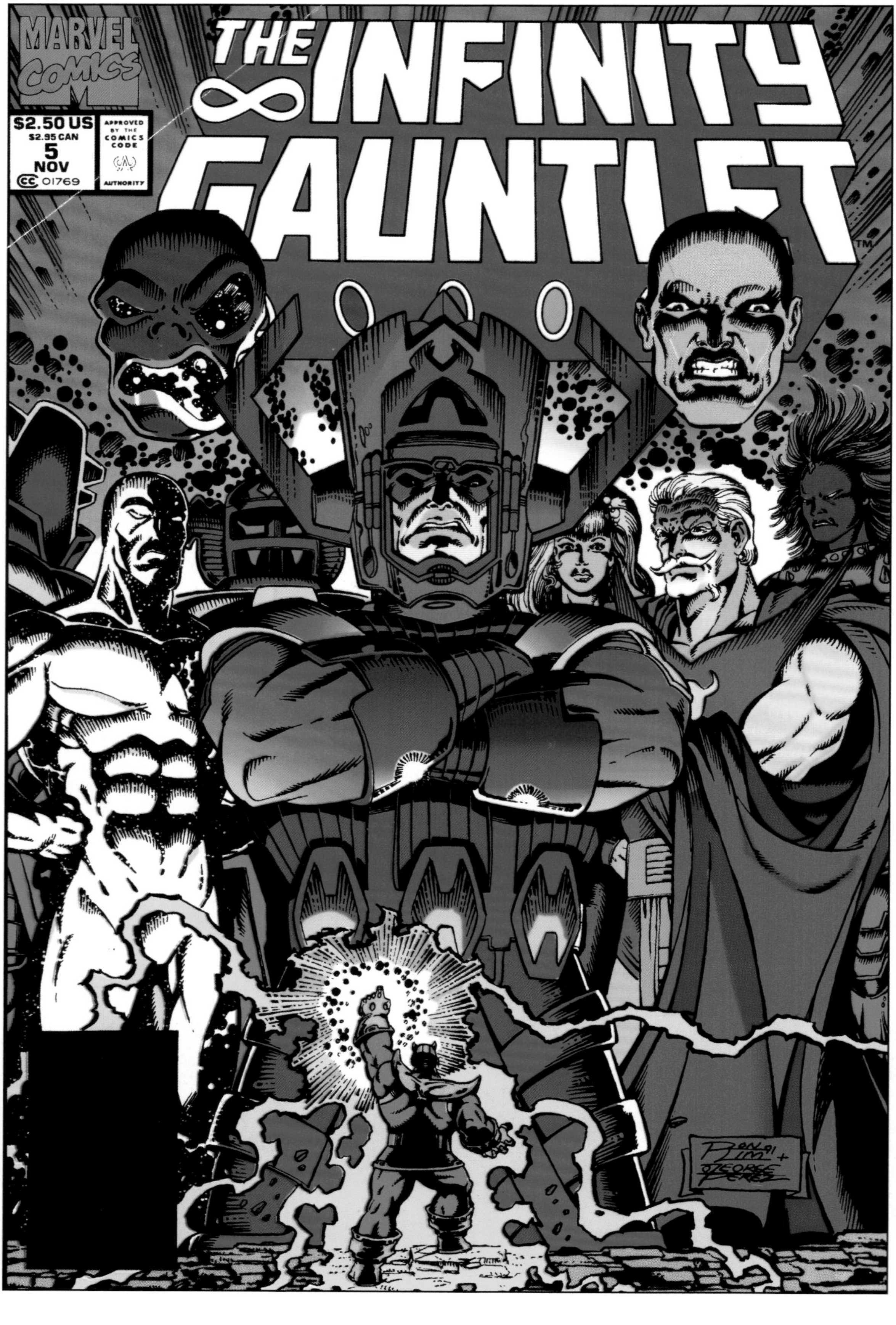
MARVEL COMICS
THE INFINITY GAUNTLET
$2.50 US
$2.95 CAN
5
NOV
APPROVED BY THE COMICS CODE AUTHORITY

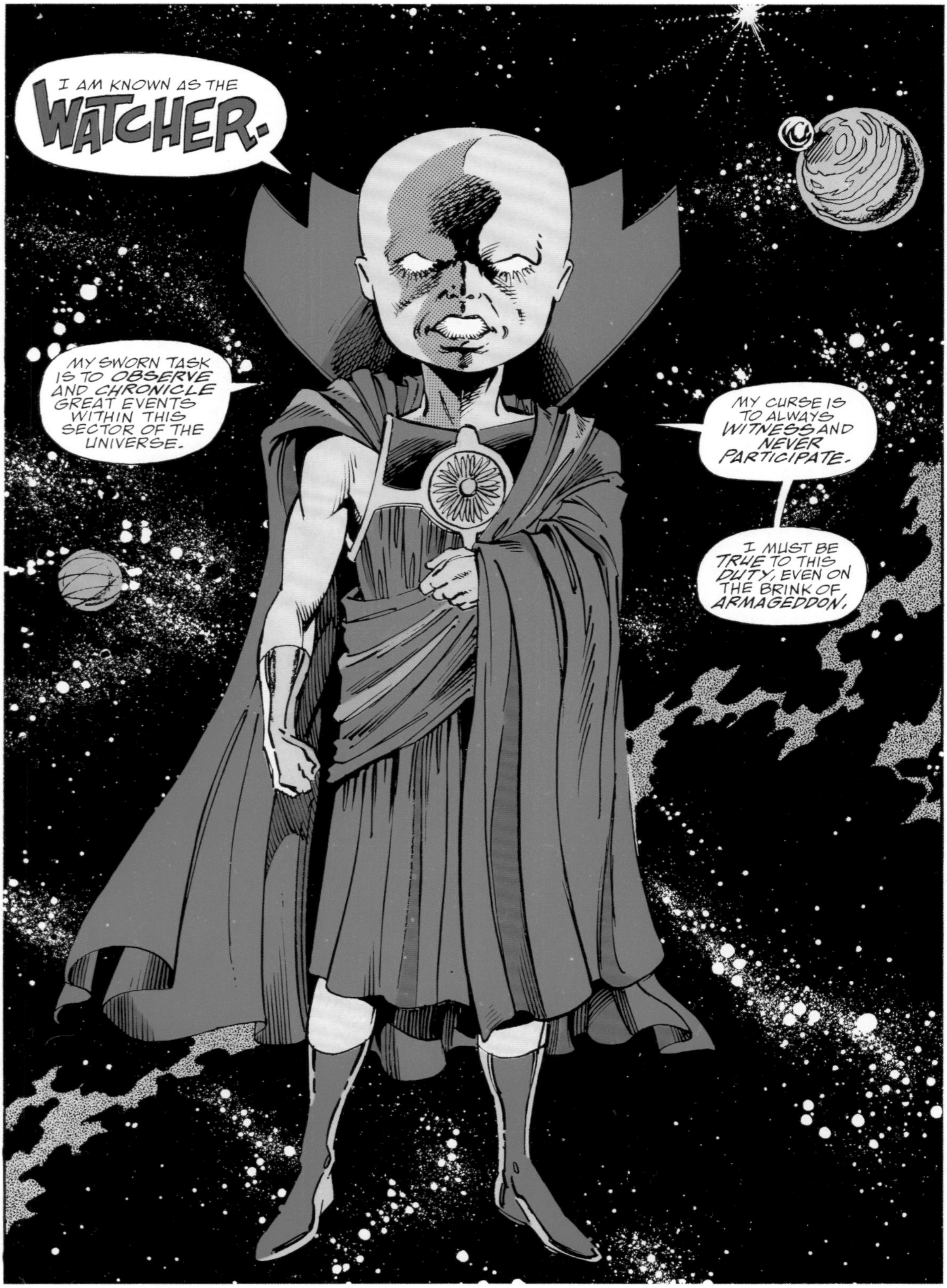
I AM KNOWN AS THE WATCHER.
MY SWORN TASK IS TO OBSERVE AND CHRONICLE GREAT EVENTS WITHIN THIS SECTOR OF THE UNIVERSE.
MY CURSE IS TO ALWAYS WITNESS AND NEVER PARTICIPATE.
I MUST BE TRUE TO THIS DUTY, EVEN ON THE BRINK OF ARMAGEDDON.

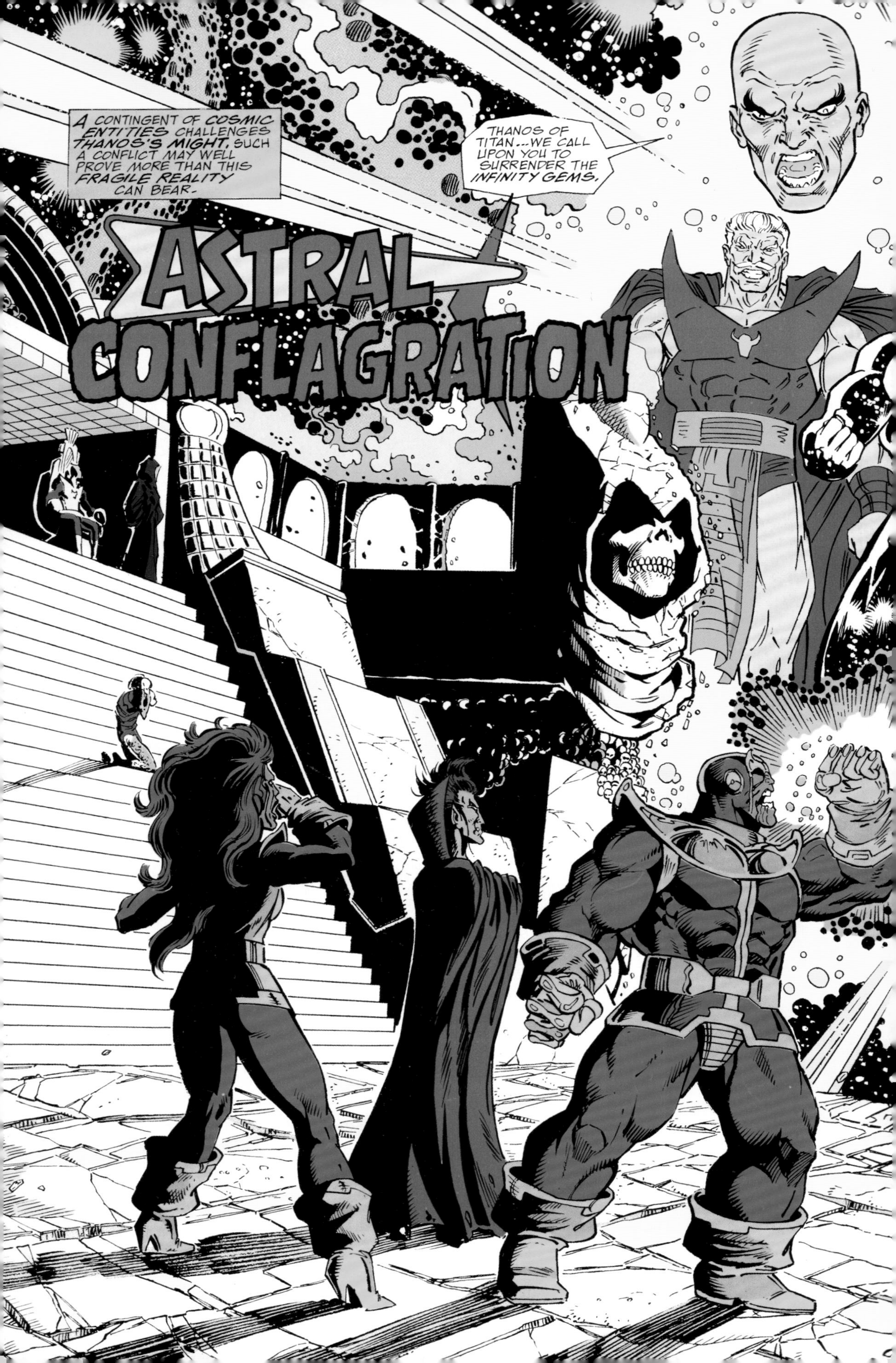
A CONTINGENT OF COSMIC ENTITIES CHALLENGES THANOS'S MIGHT. SUCH A CONFLICT MAY WELL PROVE MORE THAN THIS FRAGILE REALITY CAN BEAR.
THANOS OF TITAN...WE CALL UPON YOU TO SURRENDER THE INFINITY GEMS.
ASTRAL CONFLAGRATION

THAT WHICH YOU CHALLENGE IS *BEYOND* EVEN YOUR *MYSTIC* UNDERSTANDING.

BEGONE, FOOLISH *GODLINGS*, OR SUFFER MY *CELESTIAL* WRATH.

I FANCY YOUR *BROTHER* IS ABOUT TO PUT ON QUITE A *SHOW* FOR US, YOUNG *EROS*!

WITH SUCH GRAND FORCES ALIGNED AGAINST HIM, THANOS WILL UNLEASH THE *FULL FURY* OF HIS *POWER*.

STILL, THE *OUTCOME* OF THIS BATTLE YET REMAINS *UNCERTAIN*.

THERE'LL BE NO *TIME* TO WORRY ABOUT OR *ENERGY* TO BE WASTED ON *NON-ESSENTIAL* PRIORITIES,

SUCH AS THIS *MONUMENT* OR *RELATIVES*.

I DOUBT YOU'LL LAST MORE THAN A FEW *MICRO-SECONDS* INTO THE *CONFLICT*.

BUT IT SHOULD BE A *QUICK DEATH*.

OF COURSE, LORD THANOS HAS THE POWER TO *REBUILD* HIS *LOVE MONU-MENT* AFTER-WARDS.

HE'LL MAKE IT AS *GOOD* AS NEW.

PERHAPS HE'LL DO THE *SAME* FOR *YOU*.

JUST LOOK AT THE *MARVELOUS* JOB HE DID ON *NEBULA*.

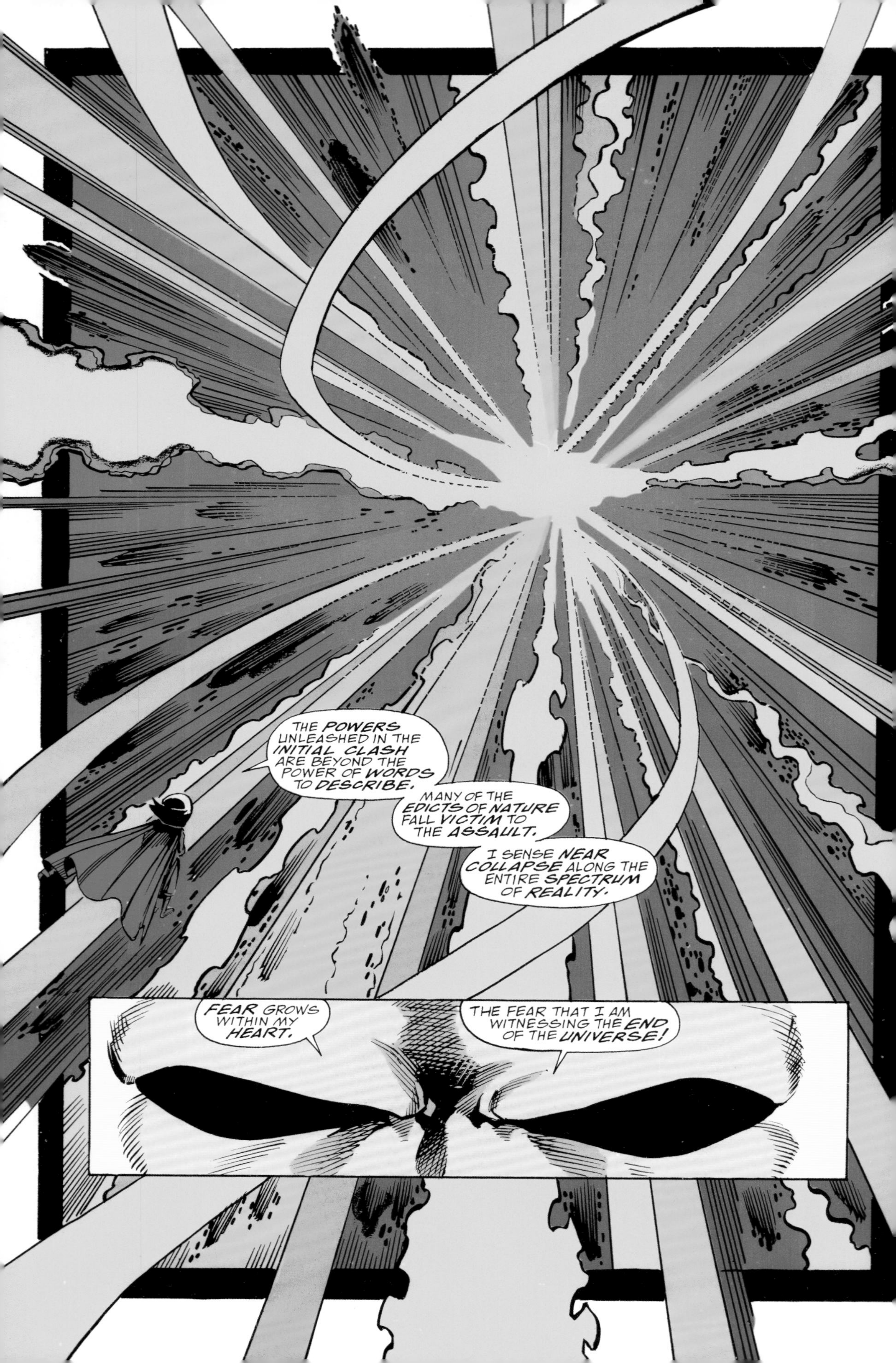
THE POWERS UNLEASHED IN THE INITIAL CLASH ARE BEYOND THE POWER OF WORDS TO DESCRIBE.
MANY OF THE EDICTS OF NATURE FALL VICTIM TO THE ASSAULT.
I SENSE NEAR COLLAPSE ALONG THE ENTIRE SPECTRUM OF REALITY.
FEAR GROWS WITHIN MY HEART.
THE FEAR THAT I AM WITNESSING THE END OF THE UNIVERSE!

ENTIRE *SOLAR SYSTEMS* IN THE IMMEDIATE VICINITY ARE *RAVAGED* BY THE EFFECTS OF THIS *CELESTIAL CLASH.*

CALCULATING THE *BILLIONS* OF LIVES LOST AS A RESULT OF THIS CONFRONTATION WILL HAVE TO *WAIT.*

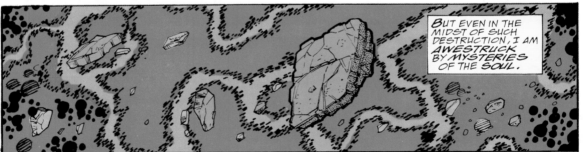

BUT EVEN IN THE MIDST OF SUCH *DESTRUCTION*, I AM *AWESTRUCK* BY MYSTERIES OF THE *SOUL.*

THE TITAN, *EROS,* FELT CERTAIN THAT *DEATH* WAS NEAR TO CLAIMING HIM.

THE ONLY THING *GREATER* THAN HIS *SURPRISE* AT FINDING HIMSELF AMONG THE *LIVING...*

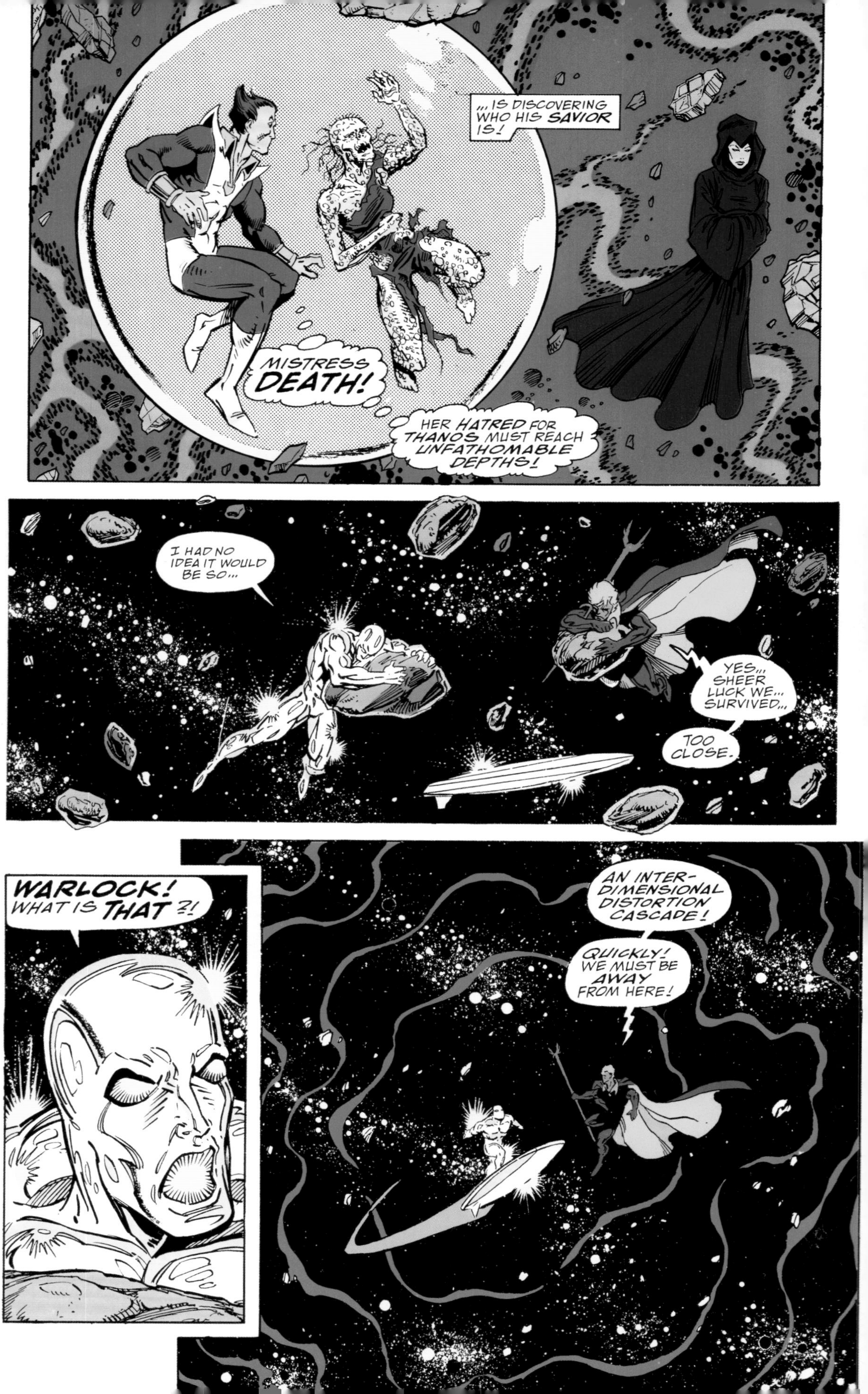

...IS DISCOVERING WHO HIS SAVIOR IS!
MISTRESS DEATH!
HER HATRED FOR THANOS MUST REACH UNFATHOMABLE DEPTHS!
I HAD NO IDEA IT WOULD BE SO...
YES... SHEER LUCK WE... SURVIVED...
TOO CLOSE.
WARLOCK! WHAT IS THAT?!
AN INTER-DIMENSIONAL DISTORTION CASCADE!
QUICKLY! WE MUST BE AWAY FROM HERE!

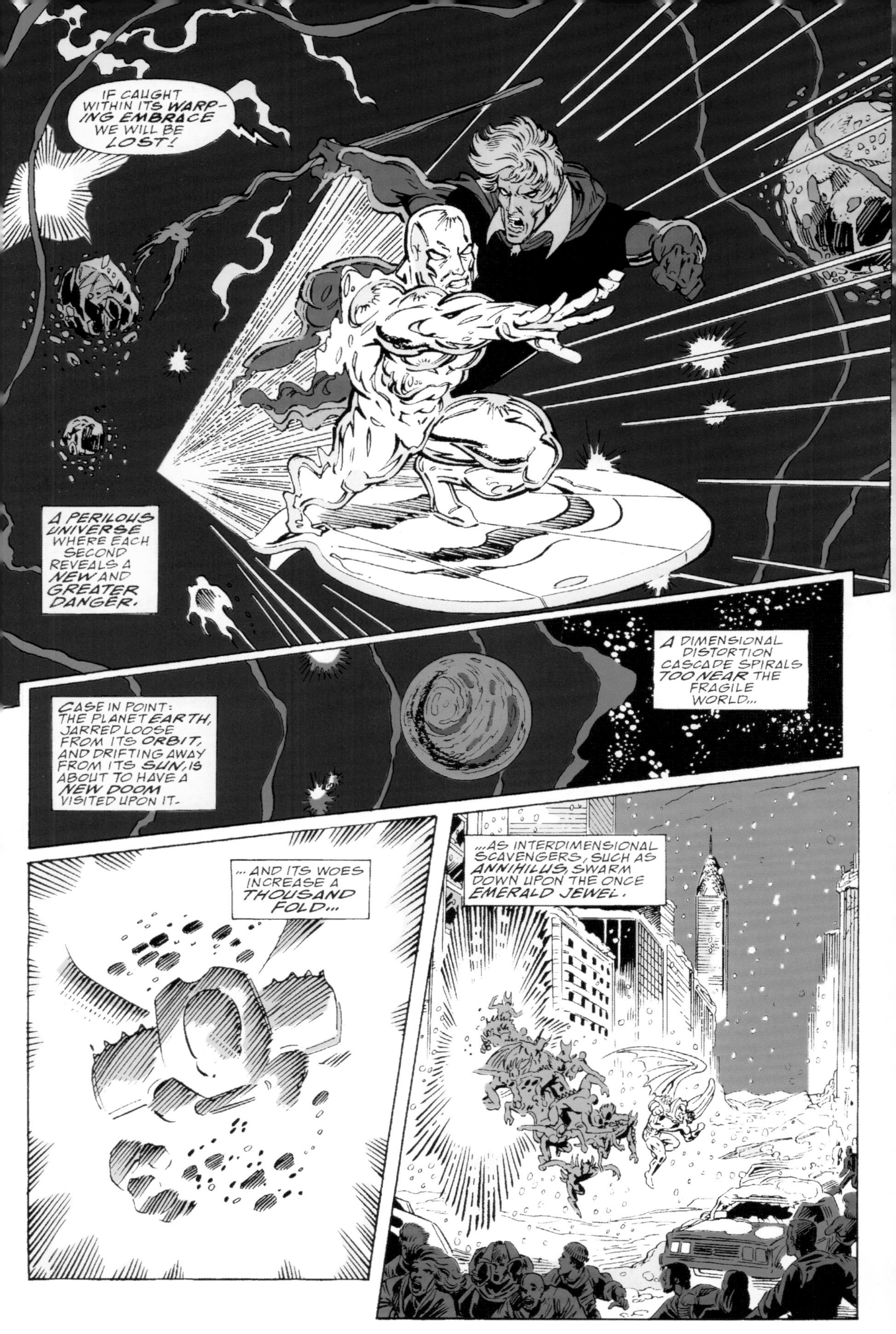
IF CAUGHT WITHIN ITS WARPING EMBRACE WE WILL BE LOST!
A PERILOUS UNIVERSE WHERE EACH SECOND REVEALS A NEW AND GREATER DANGER.
CASE IN POINT: THE PLANET EARTH, JARRED LOOSE FROM ITS ORBIT, AND DRIFTING AWAY FROM ITS SUN, IS ABOUT TO HAVE A NEW DOOM VISITED UPON IT.
A DIMENSIONAL DISTORTION CASCADE SPIRALS TOO NEAR THE FRAGILE WORLD...
...AND ITS WOES INCREASE A THOUSAND FOLD...
...AS INTERDIMENSIONAL SCAVENGERS, SUCH AS ANNIHILUS, SWARM DOWN UPON THE ONCE EMERALD JEWEL.

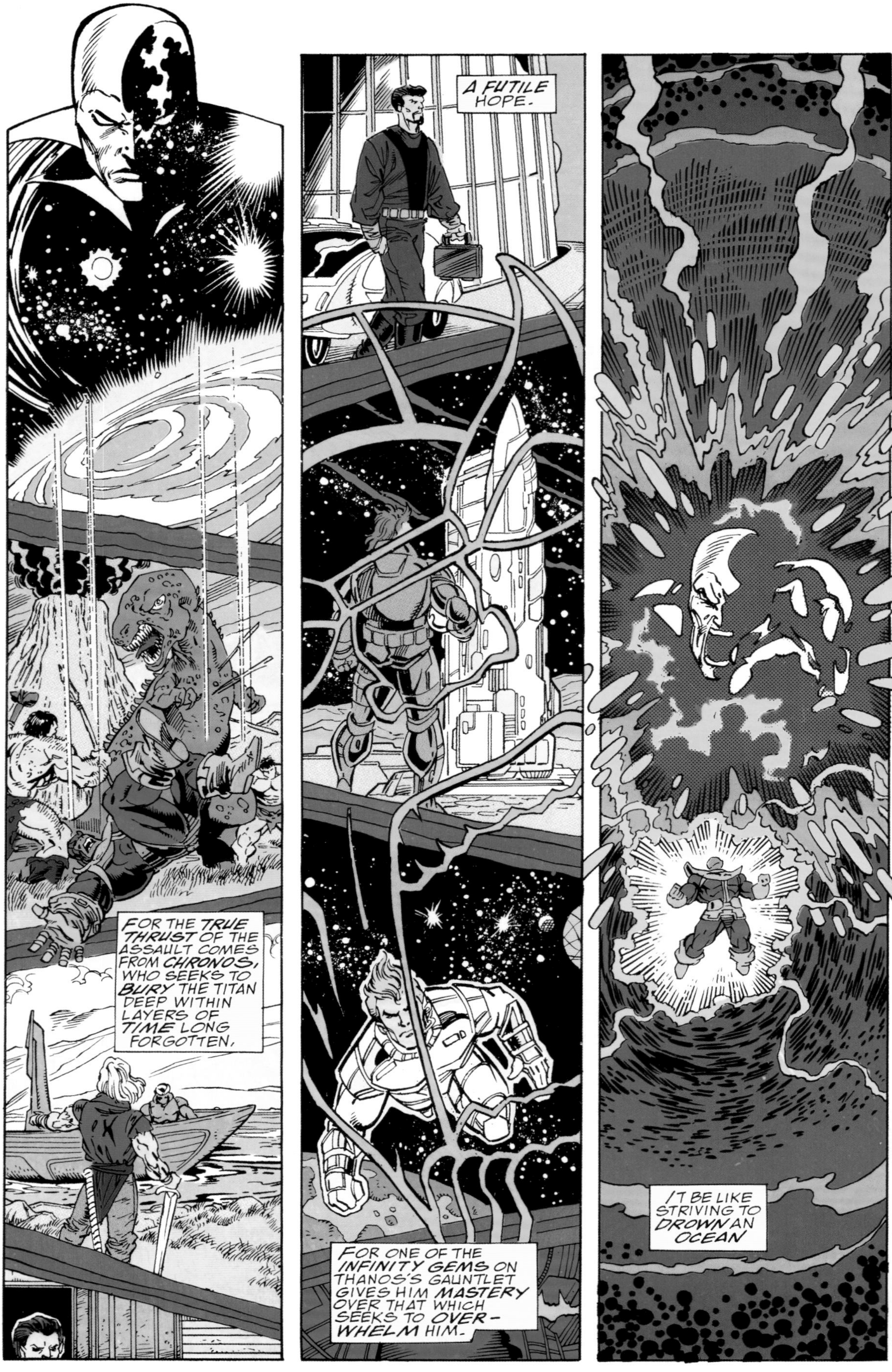

FOR THE TRUE THRUST OF THE ASSAULT COMES FROM CHRONOS, WHO SEEKS TO BURY THE TITAN DEEP WITHIN LAYERS OF TIME LONG FORGOTTEN,
A FUTILE HOPE.
FOR ONE OF THE INFINITY GEMS ON THANOS'S GAUNTLET GIVES HIM MASTERY OVER THAT WHICH SEEKS TO OVER-WHELM HIM.
IT BE LIKE STRIVING TO DROWN AN OCEAN

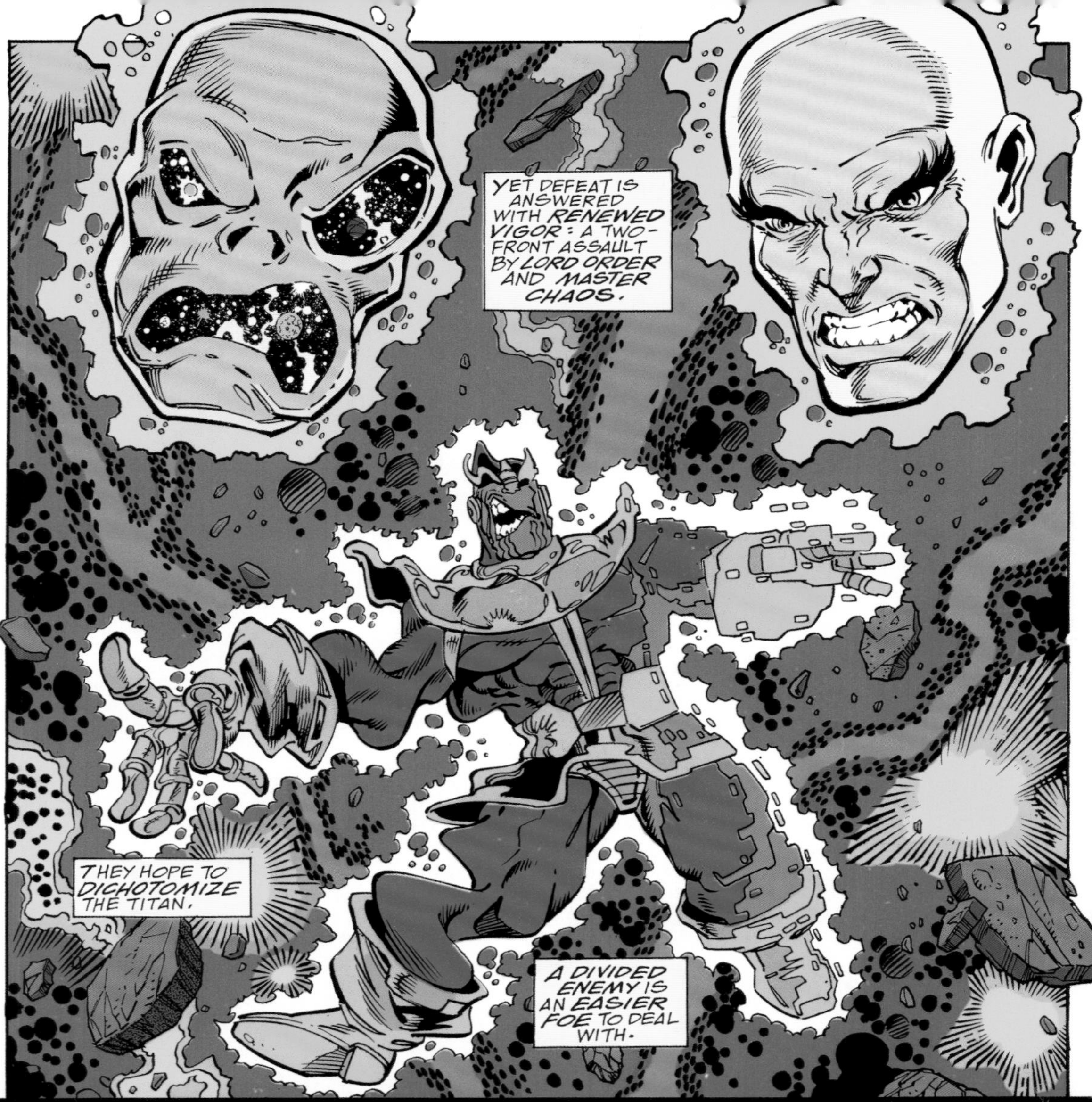
YET DEFEAT IS ANSWERED WITH RENEWED VIGOR: A TWO-FRONT ASSAULT BY LORD ORDER AND MASTER CHAOS.
THEY HOPE TO DICHOTOMIZE THE TITAN.
A DIVIDED ENEMY IS AN EASIER FOE TO DEAL WITH.
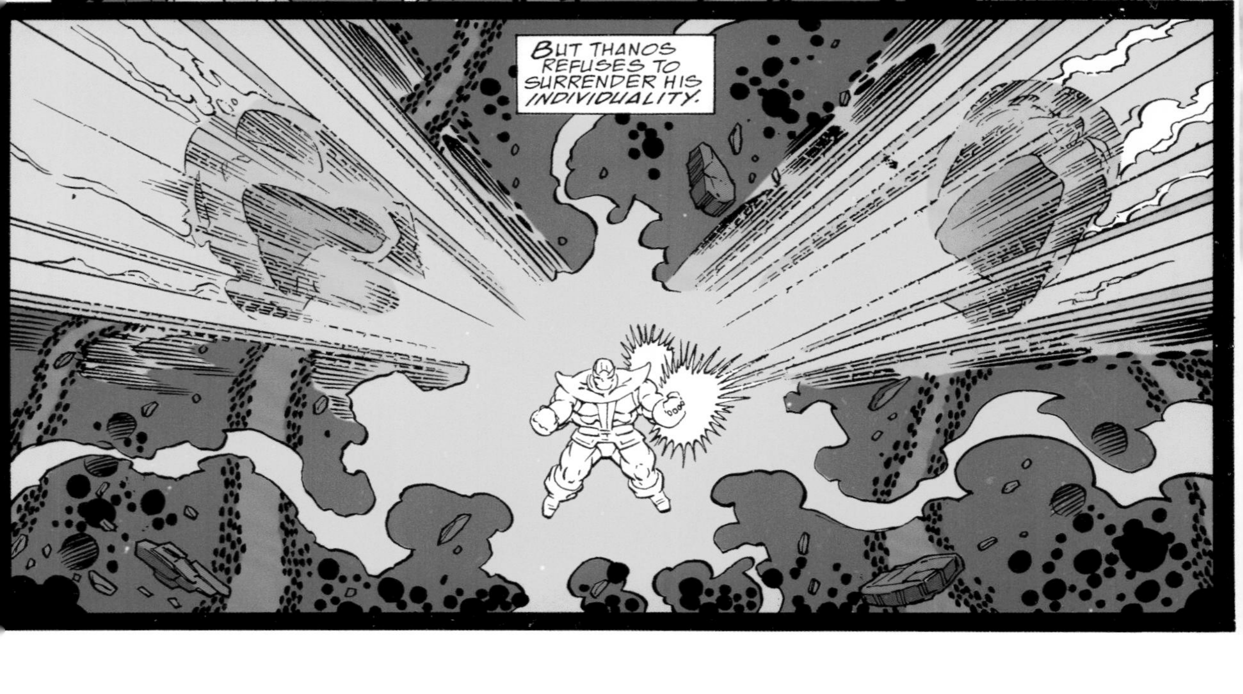
BUT THANOS REFUSES TO SURRENDER HIS INDIVIDUALITY.

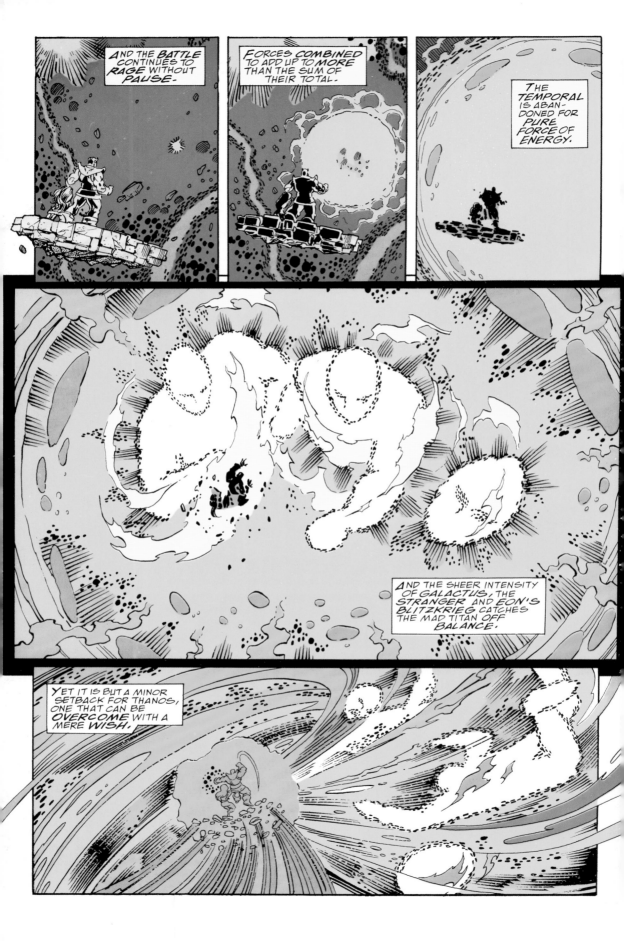

AND THE *BATTLE* CONTINUES TO *RAGE* WITHOUT *PAUSE*.

FORCES COMBINED TO ADD UP TO *MORE* THAN THE SUM OF THEIR TOTAL.

THE *TEMPORAL* IS ABANDONED FOR *PURE* FORCE OF *ENERGY*.

*A*ND THE SHEER INTENSITY OF GALACTUS, THE STRANGER AND EON'S *BLITZKRIEG* CATCHES THE MAD TITAN OFF *BALANCE*.

YET IT IS BUT A MINOR SETBACK FOR THANOS, ONE THAT CAN BE *OVERCOME* WITH A MERE *WISH*.

CONFLICTING EMOTIONS... TEARING ME APART...

THIS CAN ONLY BE THE WORK OF--

-- MISTRESS *LOVE* AND SIRE *HATE*!!

HOW *DARE* YOU *TAMPER* WITH ME SO?!

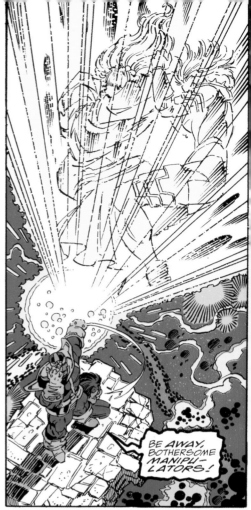

BE *AWAY*, BOTHERSOME MANIPU-LATORS!

BUT ALSO BEWARE *DECEIVERS, TITAN...*

HELL'S FIRE, *WHAT?!*

EXACTLY, MY LIEGE!!

MEPHISTO!

COME TO *RELIEVE* YOU OF YOUR *BURDEN* OF *SUPREMACY!*

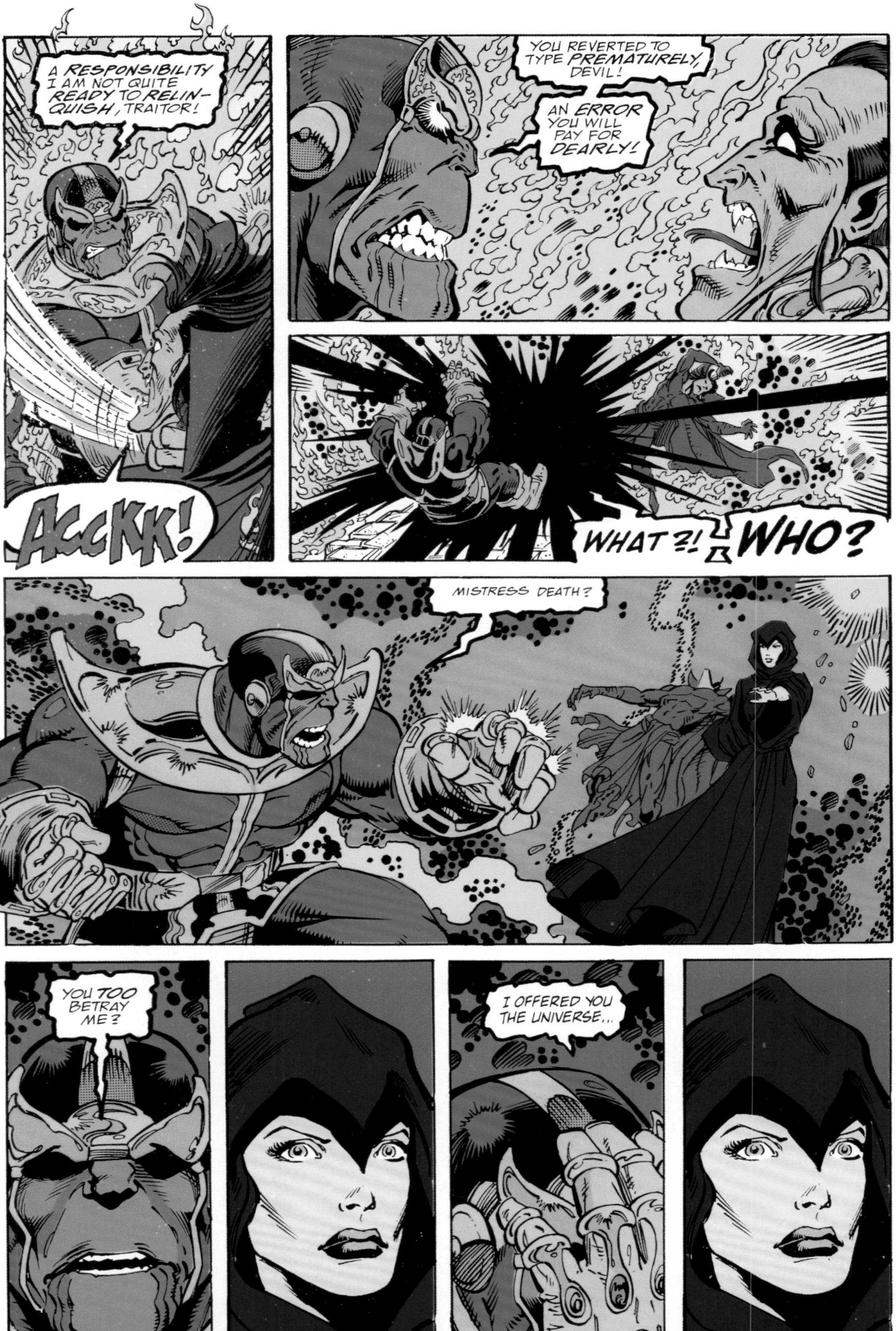
A RESPONSIBILITY I AM NOT QUITE READY TO RELINQUISH, TRAITOR!
ACCKK!
YOU REVERTED TO TYPE PREMATURELY, DEVIL!
AN ERROR YOU WILL PAY FOR DEARLY!
WHAT ?!
WHO?
MISTRESS DEATH?
YOU TOO BETRAY ME?
I OFFERED YOU THE UNIVERSE...

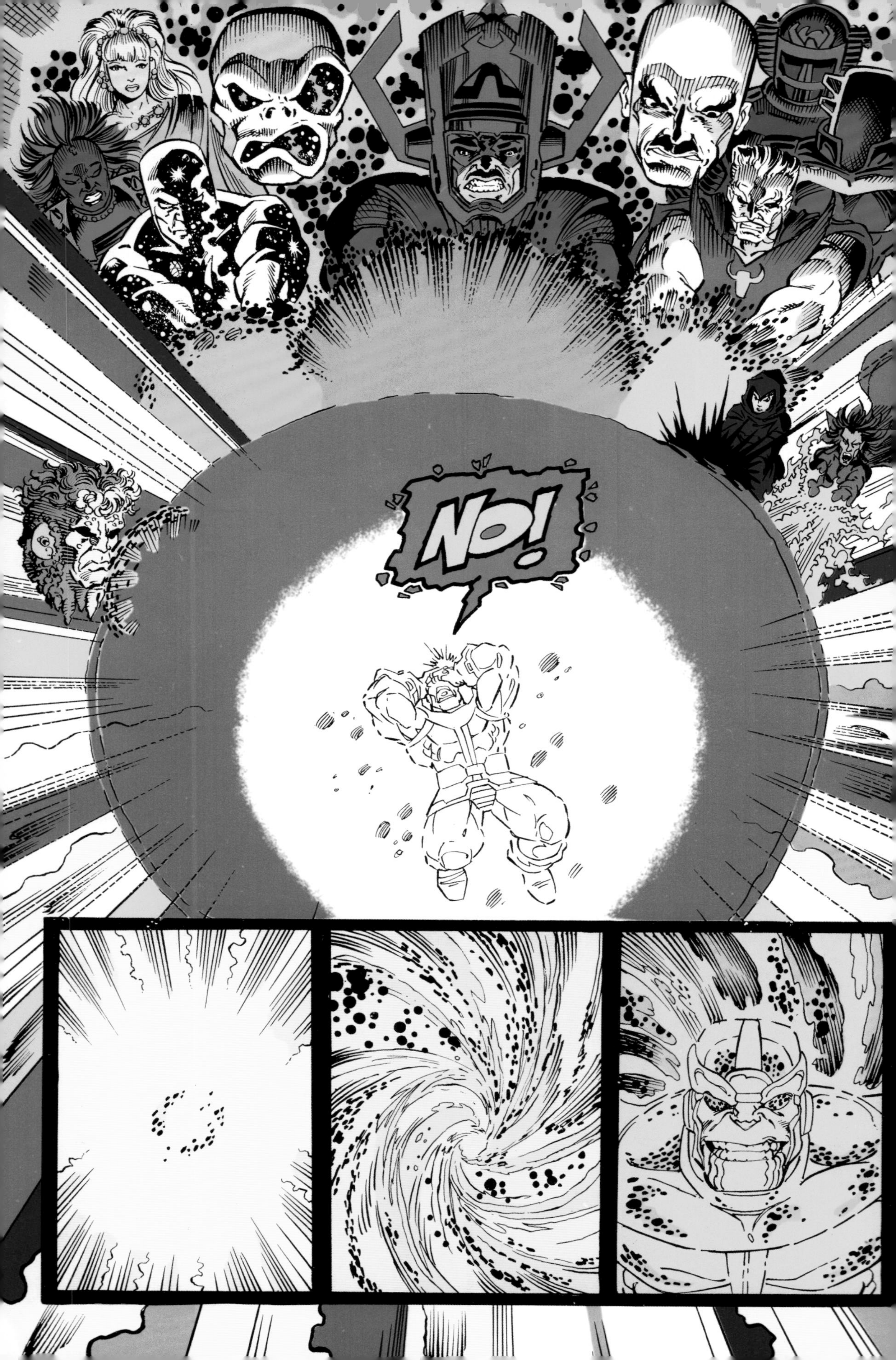
NO!

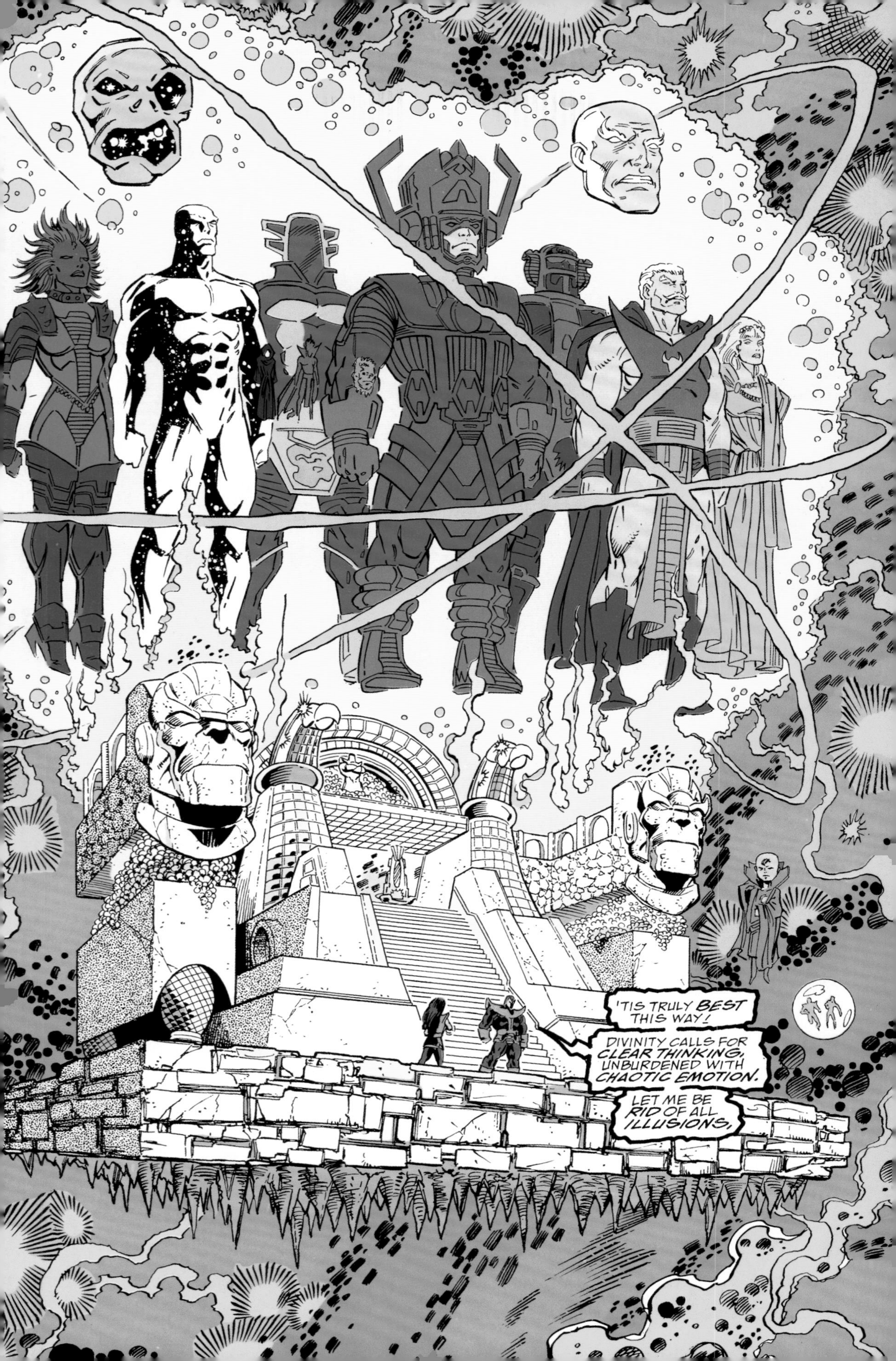

'TIS TRULY BEST THIS WAY!
DIVINITY CALLS FOR CLEAR THINKING, UNBURDENED WITH CHAOTIC EMOTION.
LET ME BE RID OF ALL ILLUSIONS,

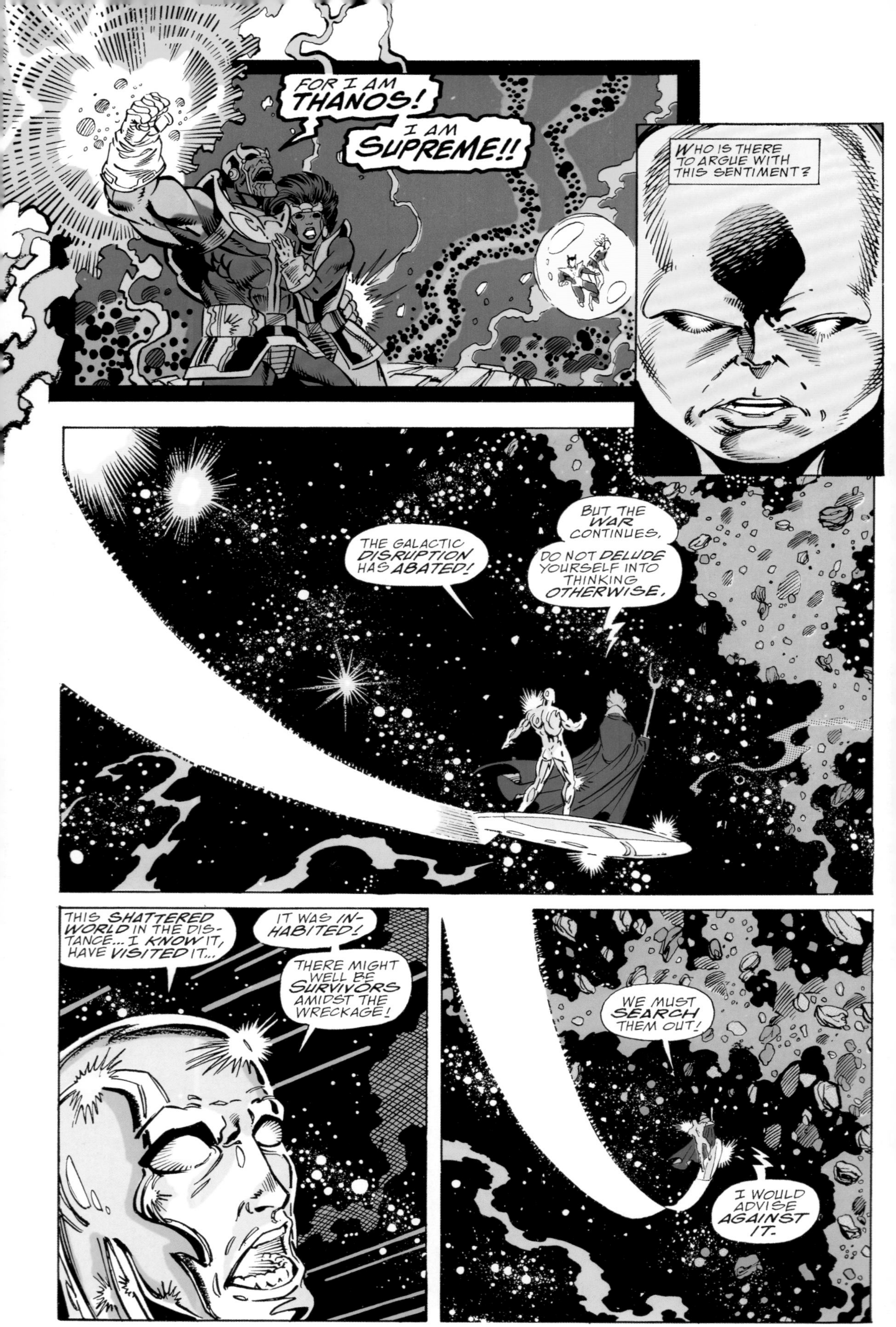

FOR I AM THANOS!
I AM SUPREME!!
WHO IS THERE TO ARGUE WITH THIS SENTIMENT?
THE GALACTIC DISRUPTION HAS ABATED!
BUT THE WAR CONTINUES.
DO NOT DELUDE YOURSELF INTO THINKING OTHERWISE.
THIS SHATTERED WORLD IN THE DISTANCE... I KNOW IT, HAVE VISITED IT...
IT WAS INHABITED!
THERE MIGHT WELL BE SURVIVORS AMIDST THE WRECKAGE!
WE MUST SEARCH THEM OUT!
I WOULD ADVISE AGAINST IT.

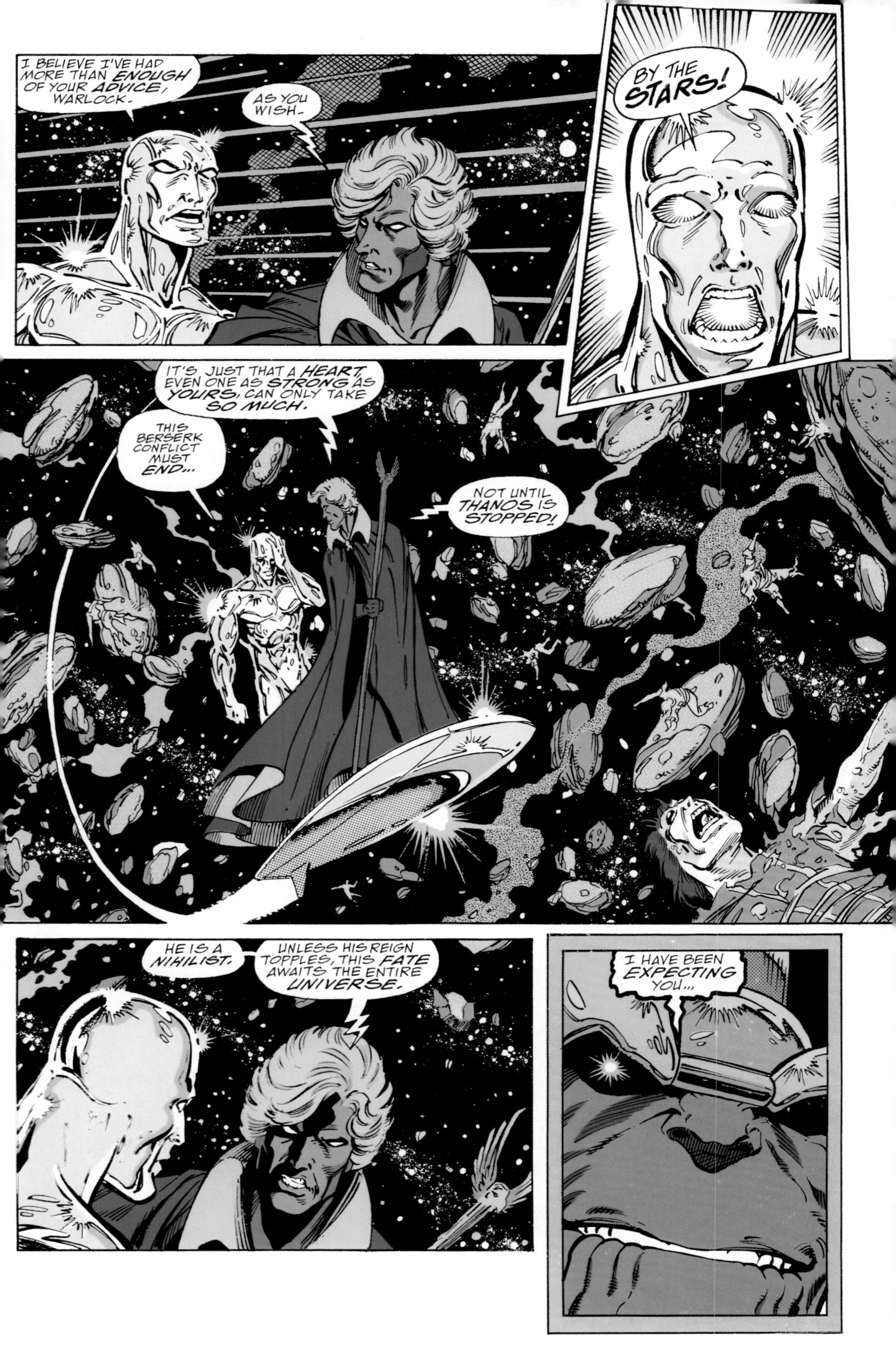
I BELIEVE I'VE HAD MORE THAN ENOUGH OF YOUR ADVICE, WARLOCK.
AS YOU WISH.
BY THE STARS!
IT'S JUST THAT A HEART, EVEN ONE AS STRONG AS YOURS, CAN ONLY TAKE SO MUCH.
THIS BERSERK CONFLICT MUST END...
NOT UNTIL THANOS IS STOPPED!
HE IS A NIHILIST.
UNLESS HIS REIGN TOPPLES, THIS FATE AWAITS THE ENTIRE UNIVERSE.
I HAVE BEEN EXPECTING YOU...

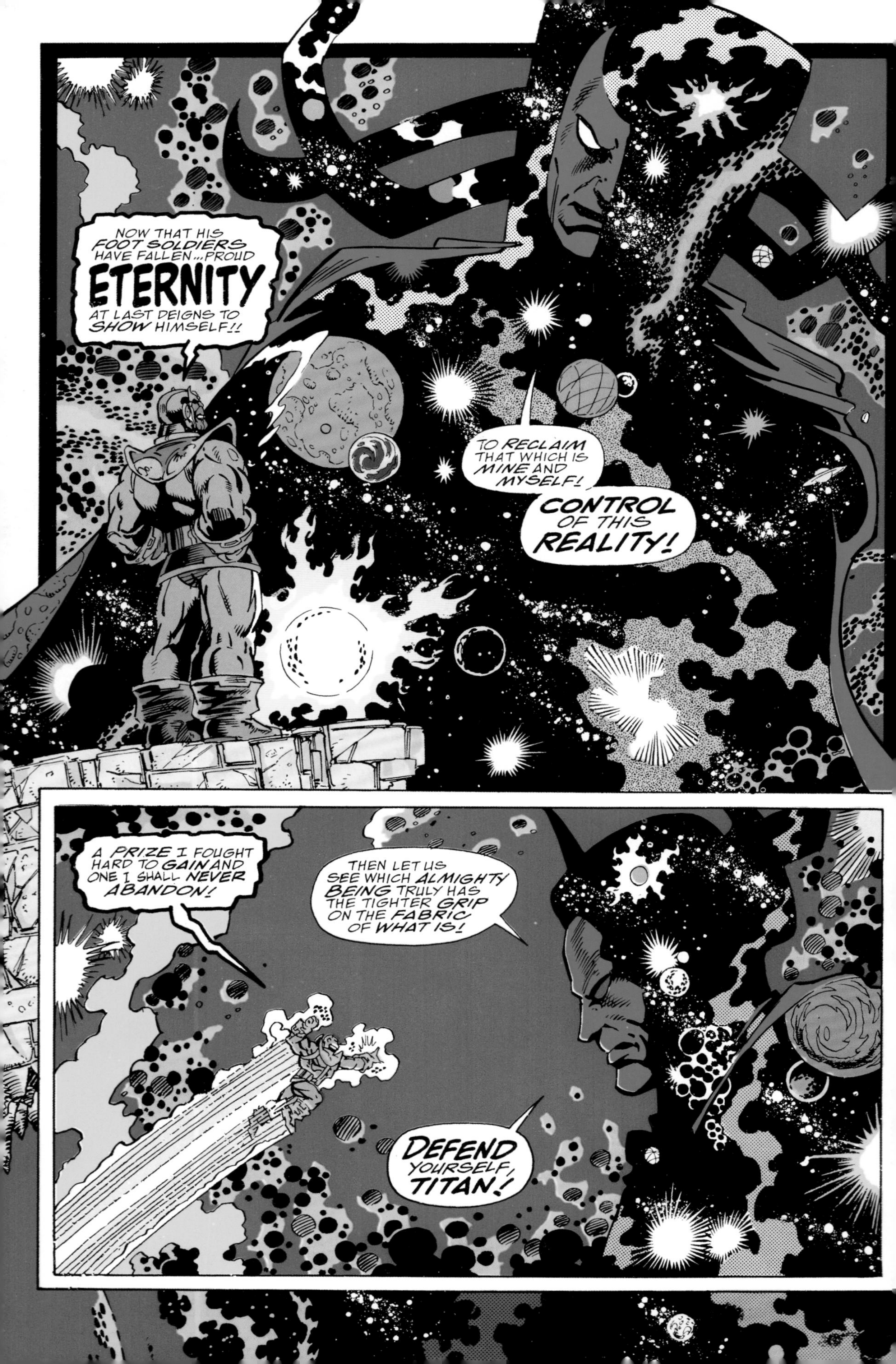

NOW THAT HIS FOOT SOLDIERS HAVE FALLEN... PROUD ETERNITY AT LAST DEIGNS TO SHOW HIMSELF!!
TO RECLAIM THAT WHICH IS MINE AND MYSELF!
CONTROL OF THIS REALITY!
A PRIZE I FOUGHT HARD TO GAIN AND ONE I SHALL NEVER ABANDON!
THEN LET US SEE WHICH ALMIGHTY BEING TRULY HAS THE TIGHTER GRIP ON THE FABRIC OF WHAT IS!
DEFEND YOURSELF, TITAN!

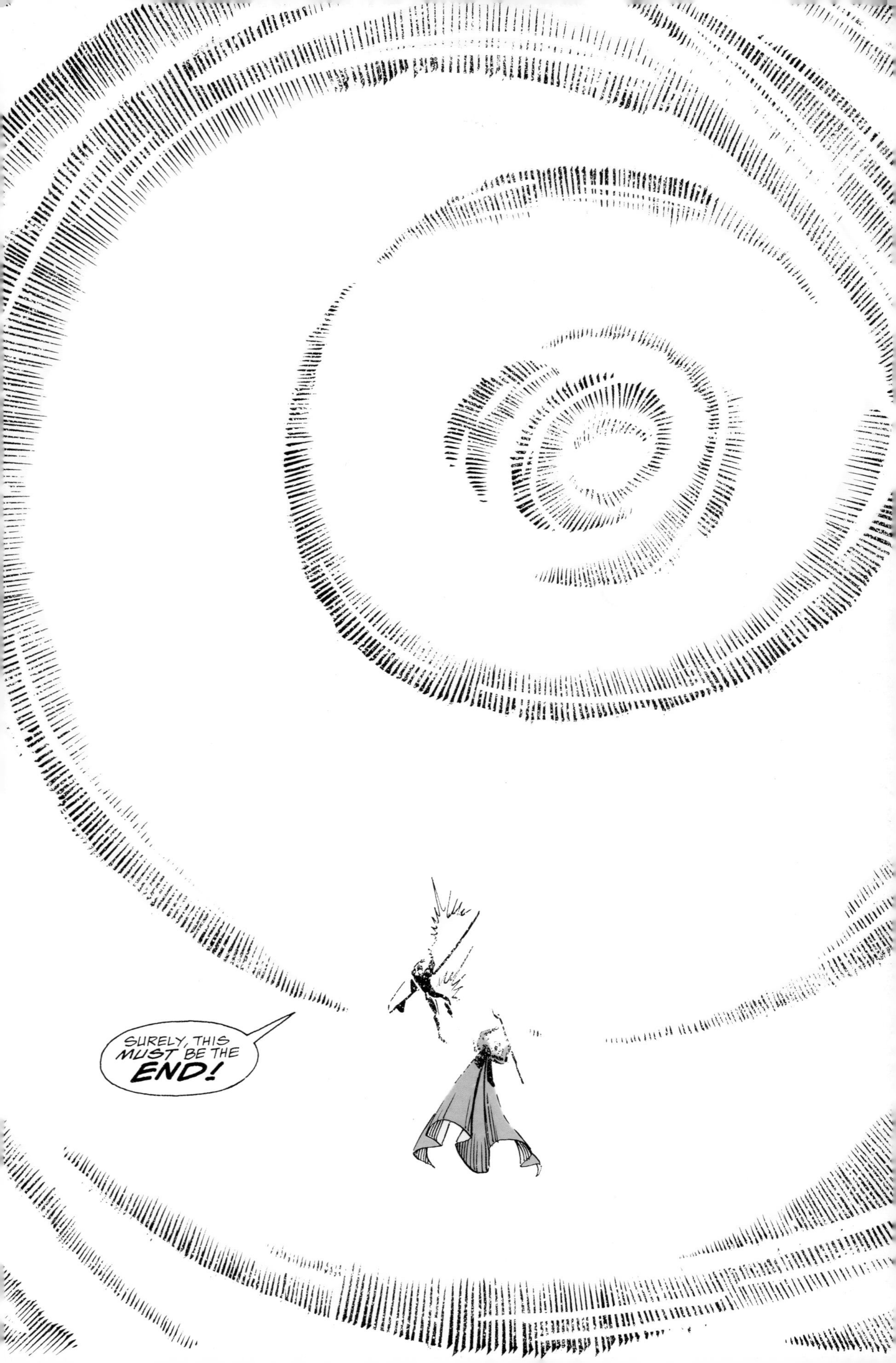
SURELY, THIS MUST BE THE END!

NO, THE *OUTCOME* OF YONDER COSMIC BATTLE IS ALREADY *DECIDED.*

HOW CAN YOU KNOW THIS? I AM *LINKED* TO THE *INFINITY GEMS* IN WAYS EVEN I DO NOT FULLY UNDERSTAND.

THE MASTERY OF ALL *ACTUALITY* IS NOW FIRMLY IN THE GRASP OF *ONE INDIVIDUAL.*

THANOS OR *ETERNITY*?! WHO PREVAILED?

ONE WHO ONLY *LOSES* WHEN HIS *SUBCONCIOUS DESIRES* BETRAY HIM—

YOU MEAN...

I *DO.* AND IN THAT *SLIM HOPE* DOES SURVIVAL LAY—

MORE *RIDDLES,* WARLOCK?? IS SPEAKING *PLAINLY* BEYOND YOUR *ABILITY*?!

PERHAPS.

DR. *STRANGE,* RETRIEVAL IS IN ORDER!

HOW GOES THE STRUGGLE?

POORLY.

HORRENDOUSLY.

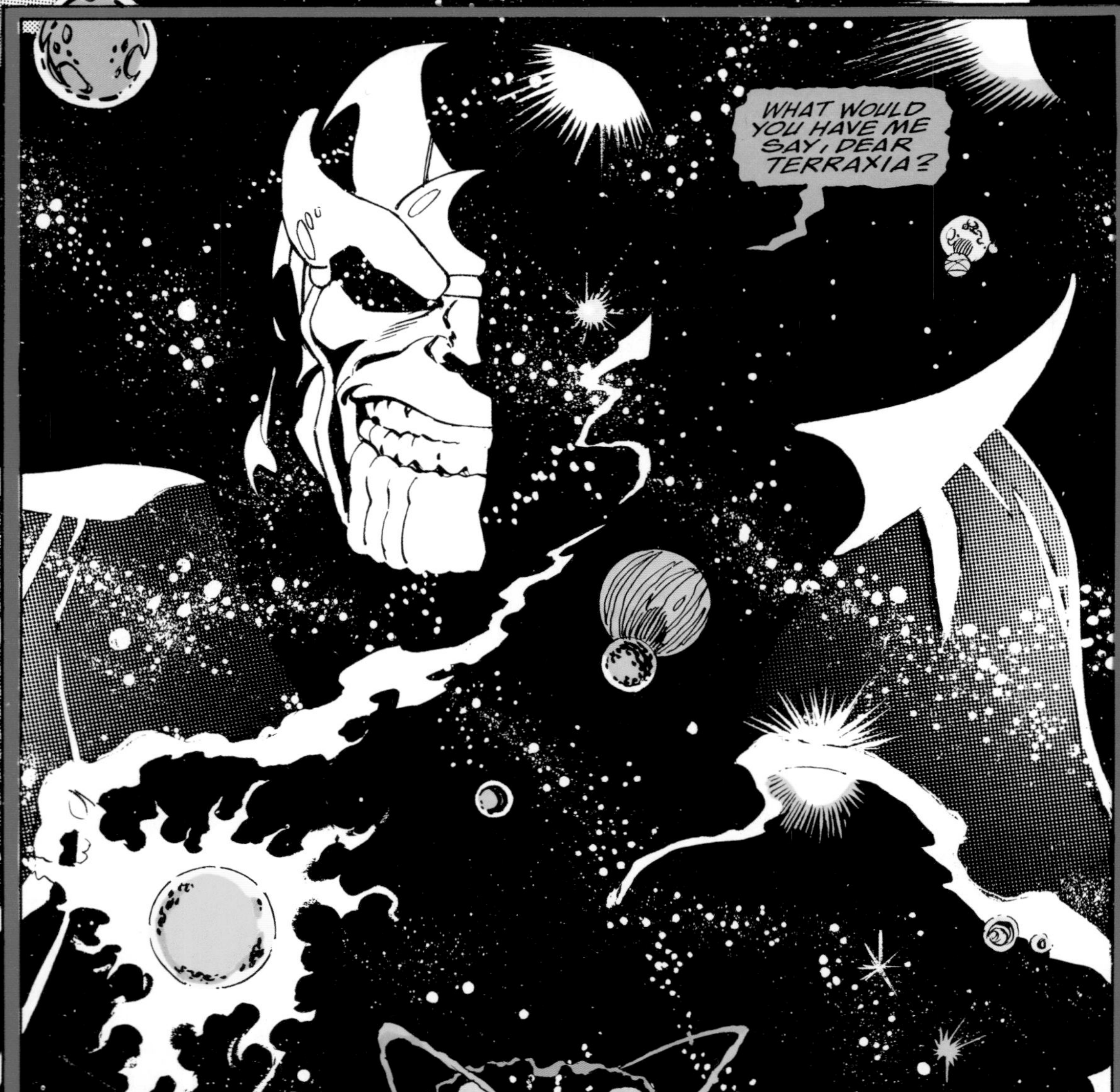
WHAT WOULD YOU HAVE ME SAY, DEAR TERRAXIA?

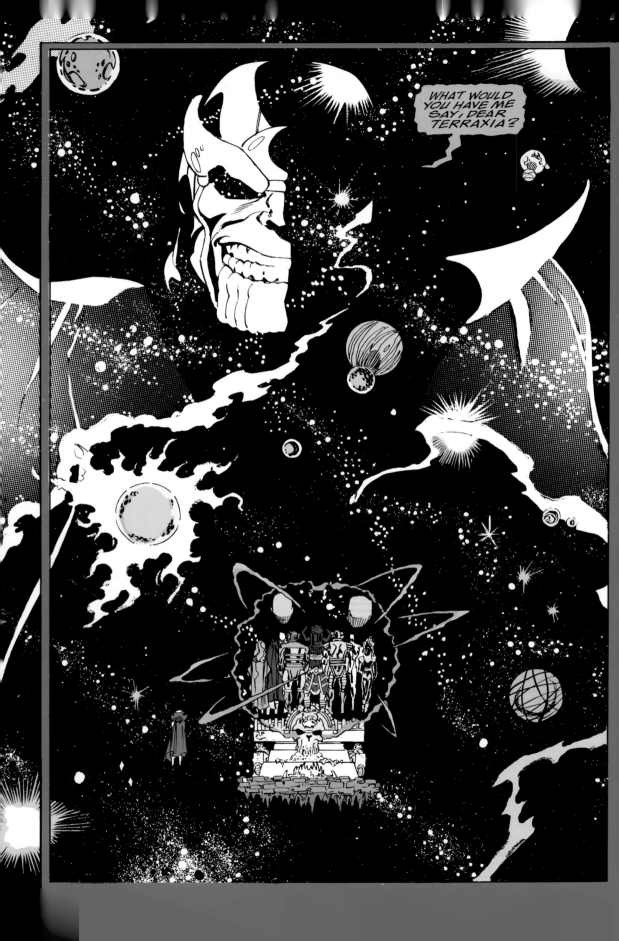

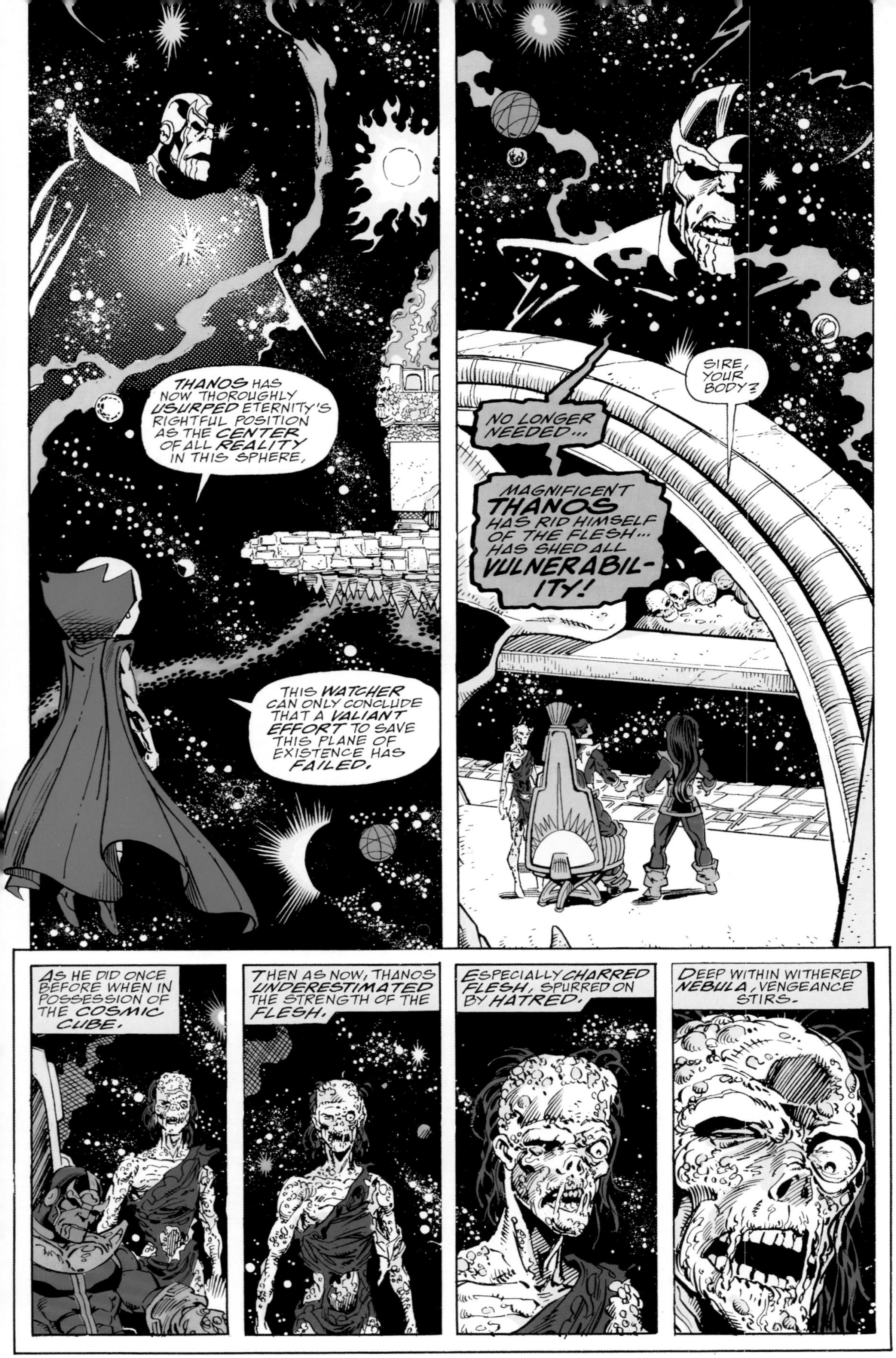
THANOS HAS NOW THOROUGHLY USURPED ETERNITY'S RIGHTFUL POSITION AS THE CENTER OF ALL REALITY IN THIS SPHERE,
THIS WATCHER CAN ONLY CONCLUDE THAT A VALIANT EFFORT TO SAVE THIS PLANE OF EXISTENCE HAS FAILED.
SIRE, YOUR BODY?!
NO LONGER NEEDED...
MAGNIFICENT THANOS HAS RID HIMSELF OF THE FLESH... HAS SHED ALL VULNERABIL-ITY!
AS HE DID ONCE BEFORE WHEN IN POSSESSION OF THE COSMIC CUBE.
THEN AS NOW, THANOS UNDERESTIMATED THE STRENGTH OF THE FLESH.
ESPECIALLY CHARRED FLESH, SPURRED ON BY HATRED.
DEEP WITHIN WITHERED NEBULA, VENGEANCE STIRS.

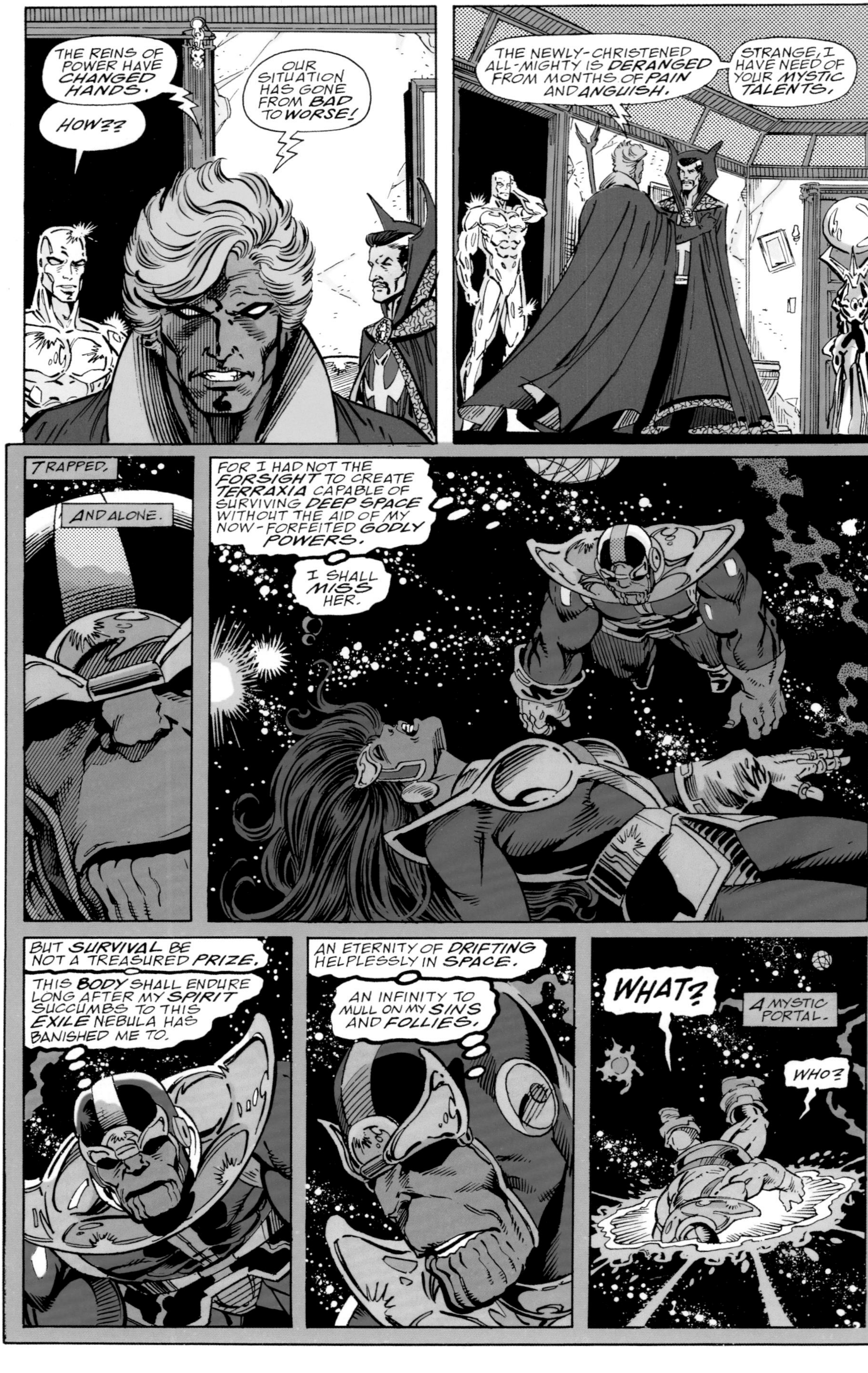
THE REINS OF POWER HAVE CHANGED HANDS.
HOW??
OUR SITUATION HAS GONE FROM BAD TO WORSE!
THE NEWLY-CHRISTENED ALL-MIGHTY IS DERANGED FROM MONTHS OF PAIN AND ANGUISH.
STRANGE, I HAVE NEED OF YOUR MYSTIC TALENTS.
TRAPPED.
AND ALONE.
FOR I HAD NOT THE FORSIGHT TO CREATE TERRAXIA CAPABLE OF SURVIVING DEEP SPACE WITHOUT THE AID OF MY NOW-FORFEITED GODLY POWERS.
I SHALL MISS HER.
BUT SURVIVAL BE NOT A TREASURED PRIZE.
THIS BODY SHALL ENDURE LONG AFTER MY SPIRIT SUCCUMBS TO THIS EXILE NEBULA HAS BANISHED ME TO.
AN ETERNITY OF DRIFTING HELPLESSLY IN SPACE.
AN INFINITY TO MULL ON MY SINS AND FOLLIES.
WHAT?
A MYSTIC PORTAL.
WHO?

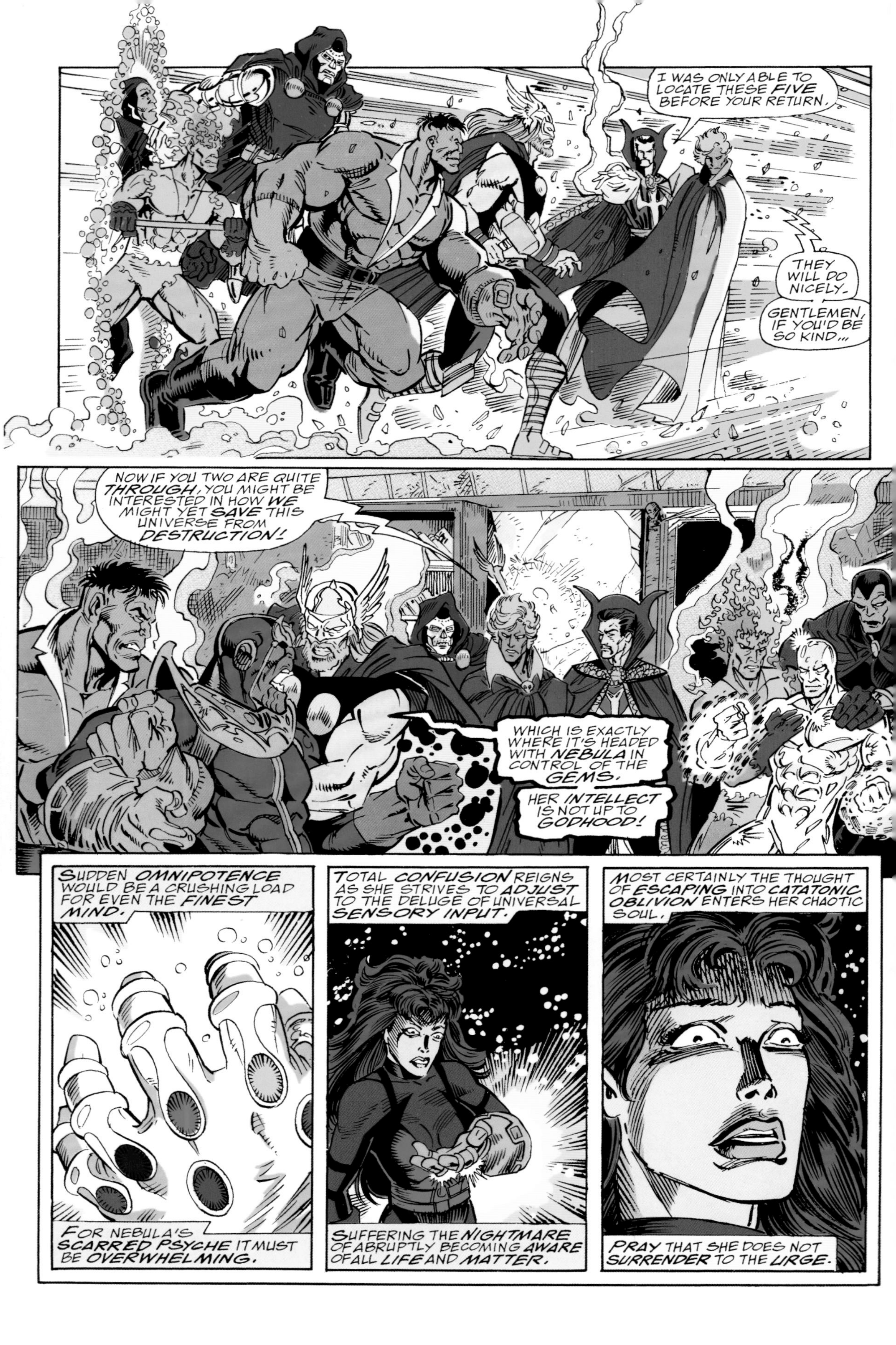

I WAS ONLY ABLE TO LOCATE THESE FIVE BEFORE YOUR RETURN.
THEY WILL DO NICELY.
GENTLEMEN, IF YOU'D BE SO KIND...
NOW IF YOU TWO ARE QUITE THROUGH, YOU MIGHT BE INTERESTED IN HOW WE MIGHT YET SAVE THIS UNIVERSE FROM DESTRUCTION!
WHICH IS EXACTLY WHERE IT'S HEADED WITH NEBULA IN CONTROL OF THE GEMS.
HER INTELLECT IS NOT UP TO GODHOOD!
SUDDEN OMNIPOTENCE WOULD BE A CRUSHING LOAD FOR EVEN THE FINEST MIND.
FOR NEBULA'S SCARRED PSYCHE IT MUST BE OVERWHELMING.
TOTAL CONFUSION REIGNS AS SHE STRIVES TO ADJUST TO THE DELUGE OF UNIVERSAL SENSORY INPUT.
SUFFERING THE NIGHTMARE OF ABRUPTLY BECOMING AWARE OF ALL LIFE AND MATTER.
MOST CERTAINLY THE THOUGHT OF ESCAPING INTO CATATONIC OBLIVION ENTERS HER CHAOTIC SOUL.
PRAY THAT SHE DOES NOT SURRENDER TO THE URGE.

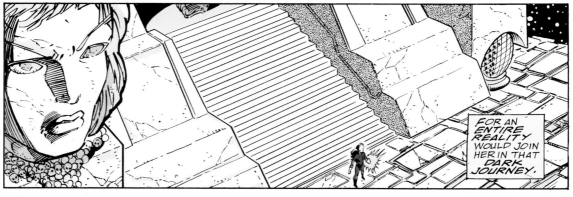

FOR AN *ENTIRE REALITY* WOULD JOIN HER IN THAT *DARK JOURNEY.*

THEN IT IS AGREED, WE GO WITH *MY DESIGN?*

THIS PLAN STINKS OF *RISK.*

BUT I SEE *NO ALTERNATIVE.*

NOR DO I.

IN THAT CASE, A WORD *ALONE* WITH THANOS IS NEEDED *BEFORE* WE CAN PROCEED.

SO THAT YOU CAN *SCHEME UP* SOME NEW *DEVILTRY* AGAINST US?

I TELL YOU THIS WARLOCK IS OBVIOUSLY THANOS'S *SECRET PARTNER!*

TO THE *DOOR,* DOOM...

YOU FOOL, YOU WILL *REGRET* NOT HEEDING MY WARNING! THEY USED TO BE COMRADES!

WELL, COMRADE, WHAT NOW?

STRAIGHT-FOWARD CONVER-SATION.

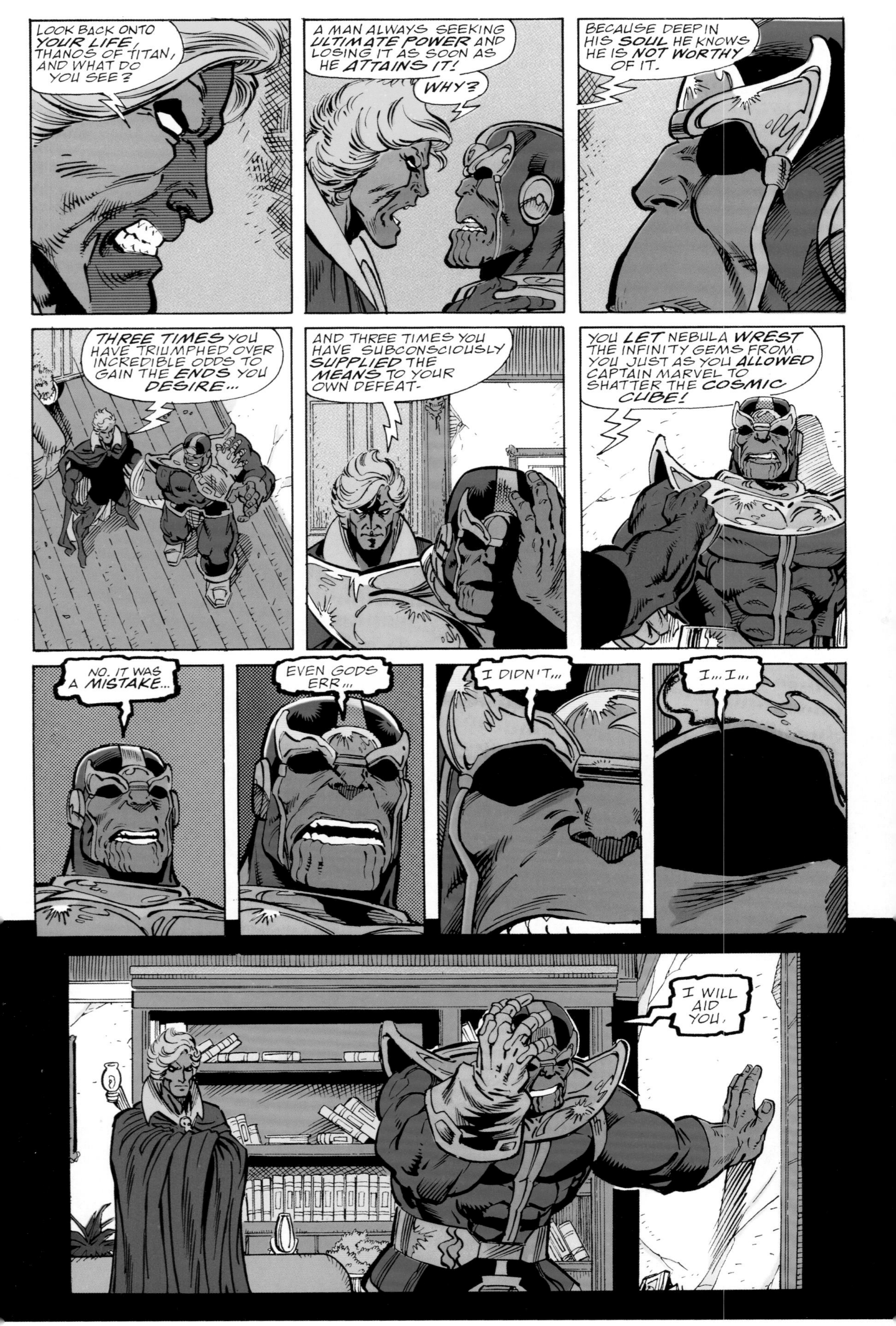
LOOK BACK ONTO YOUR LIFE, THANOS OF TITAN, AND WHAT DO YOU SEE?
A MAN ALWAYS SEEKING ULTIMATE POWER AND LOSING IT AS SOON AS HE ATTAINS IT!
WHY?
BECAUSE DEEP IN HIS SOUL HE KNOWS HE IS NOT WORTHY OF IT.
THREE TIMES YOU HAVE TRIUMPHED OVER INCREDIBLE ODDS TO GAIN THE ENDS YOU DESIRE...
AND THREE TIMES YOU HAVE SUBCONSCIOUSLY SUPPLIED THE MEANS TO YOUR OWN DEFEAT-
YOU LET NEBULA WREST THE INFINITY GEMS FROM YOU JUST AS YOU ALLOWED CAPTAIN MARVEL TO SHATTER THE COSMIC CUBE!
NO. IT WAS A MISTAKE...
EVEN GODS ERR...
I DIDN'T...
I... I...
I WILL AID YOU.

I BEGIN TO UNDERSTAND THANOS'S *HUNGER* FOR THIS *INFINITE MIGHT.*

TOMORROW IS MINE TO *SCULPT* TO MY *FANCY.*

THE *UNIVERSE* IS *CLAY* WAITING TO BE *MOLDED.*

NEVER AGAIN WILL I BE *VICTIMIZED* OR *SURPRISED*; FOR I HAVE SEEN MY EVERY *WAKING MOMENT* STRETCHING OFF INTO *FOREVER!*

IN FACT, A MOST *SATISFYING INSTANT* IS ALMOST UPON US.

ALREADY THE *MIST* BEGINS TO *PART.*

THE *FUTURE* CLEARS FOR ME,

AND SO DOES MY *DESTINY.*

IN EXACTLY *FIVE SECONDS* FROM NOW I WILL BE RECEIVING *VISITORS.*

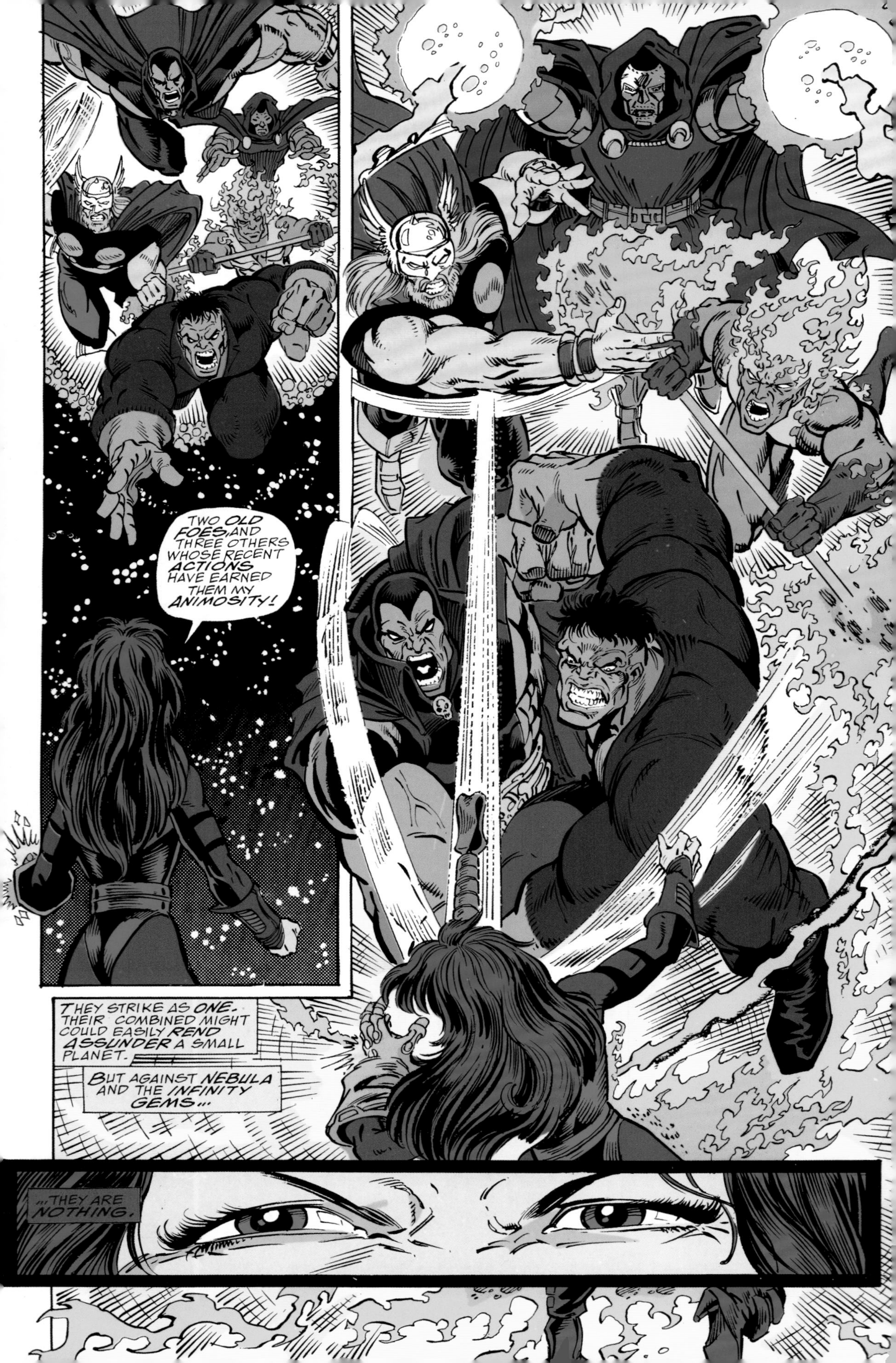
TWO OLD FOES, AND THREE OTHERS WHOSE RECENT ACTIONS HAVE EARNED THEM MY ANIMOSITY!
THEY STRIKE AS ONE. THEIR COMBINED MIGHT COULD EASILY REND ASSUNDER A SMALL PLANET.
BUT AGAINST NEBULA AND THE INFINITY GEMS...
...THEY ARE NOTHING.

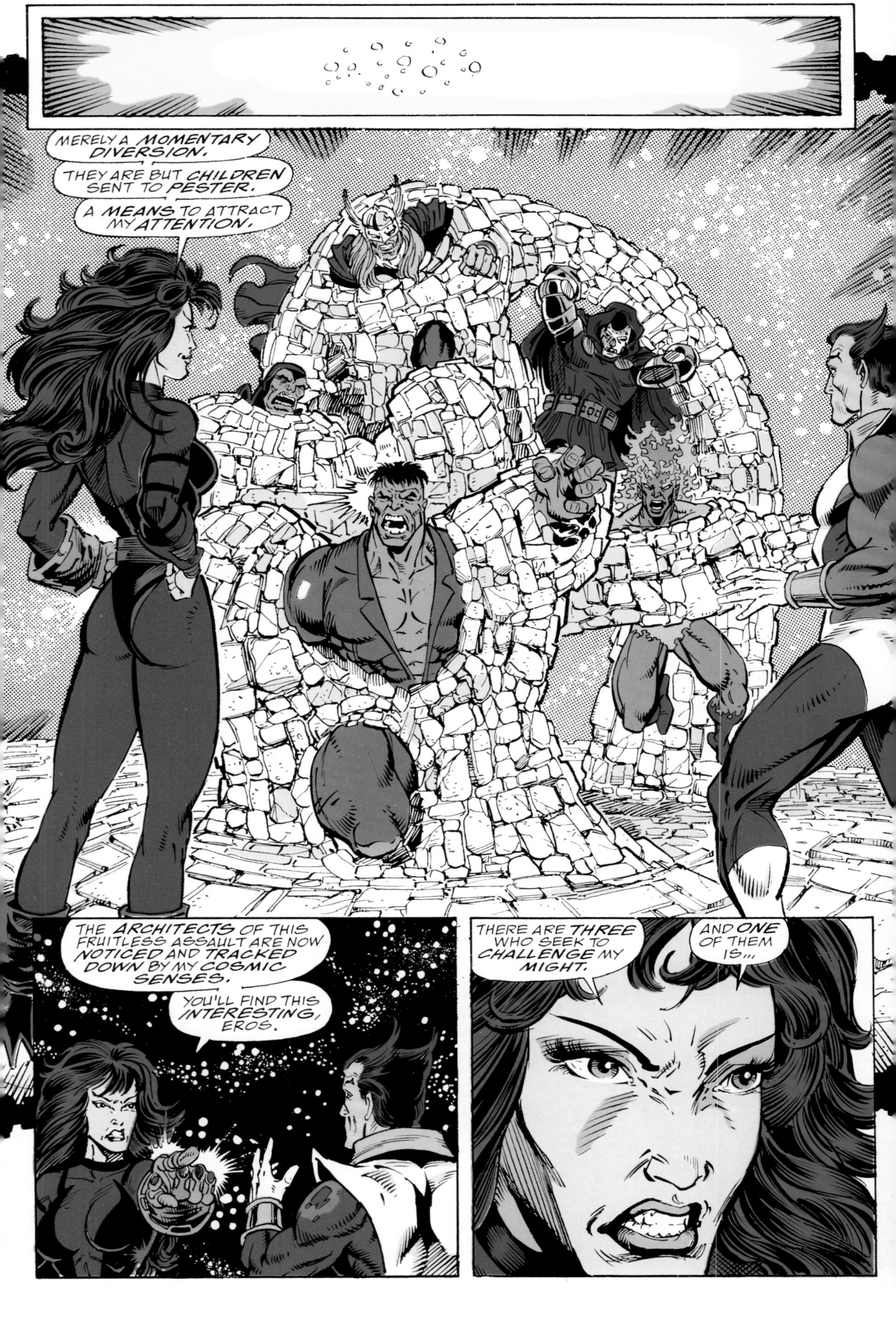
MERELY A MOMENTARY DIVERSION.
THEY ARE BUT CHILDREN SENT TO PESTER.
A MEANS TO ATTRACT MY ATTENTION.
THE ARCHITECTS OF THIS FRUITLESS ASSAULT ARE NOW NOTICED AND TRACKED DOWN BY MY COSMIC SENSES.
YOU'LL FIND THIS INTERESTING, EROS.
THERE ARE THREE WHO SEEK TO CHALLENGE MY MIGHT.
AND ONE OF THEM IS...

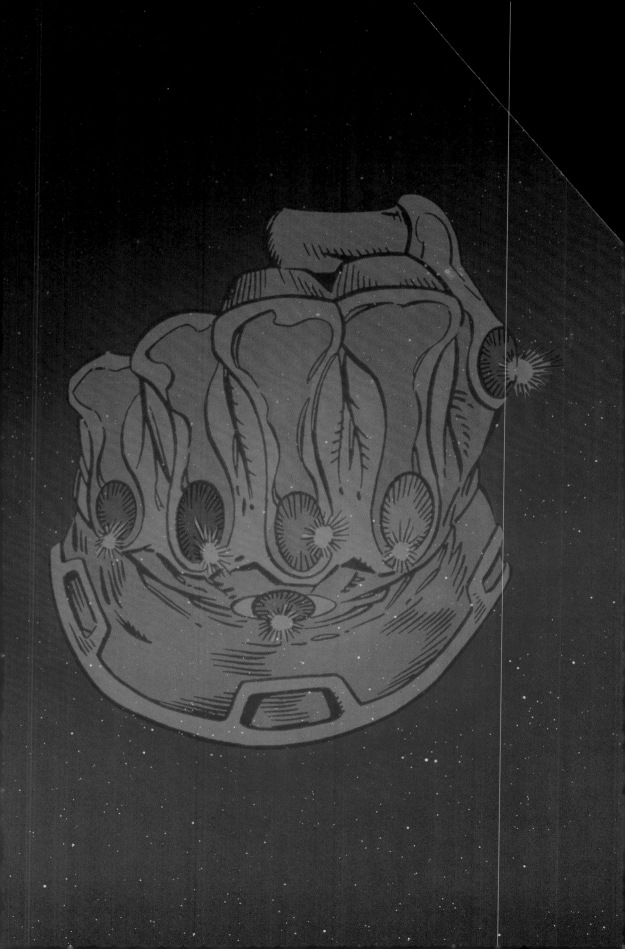

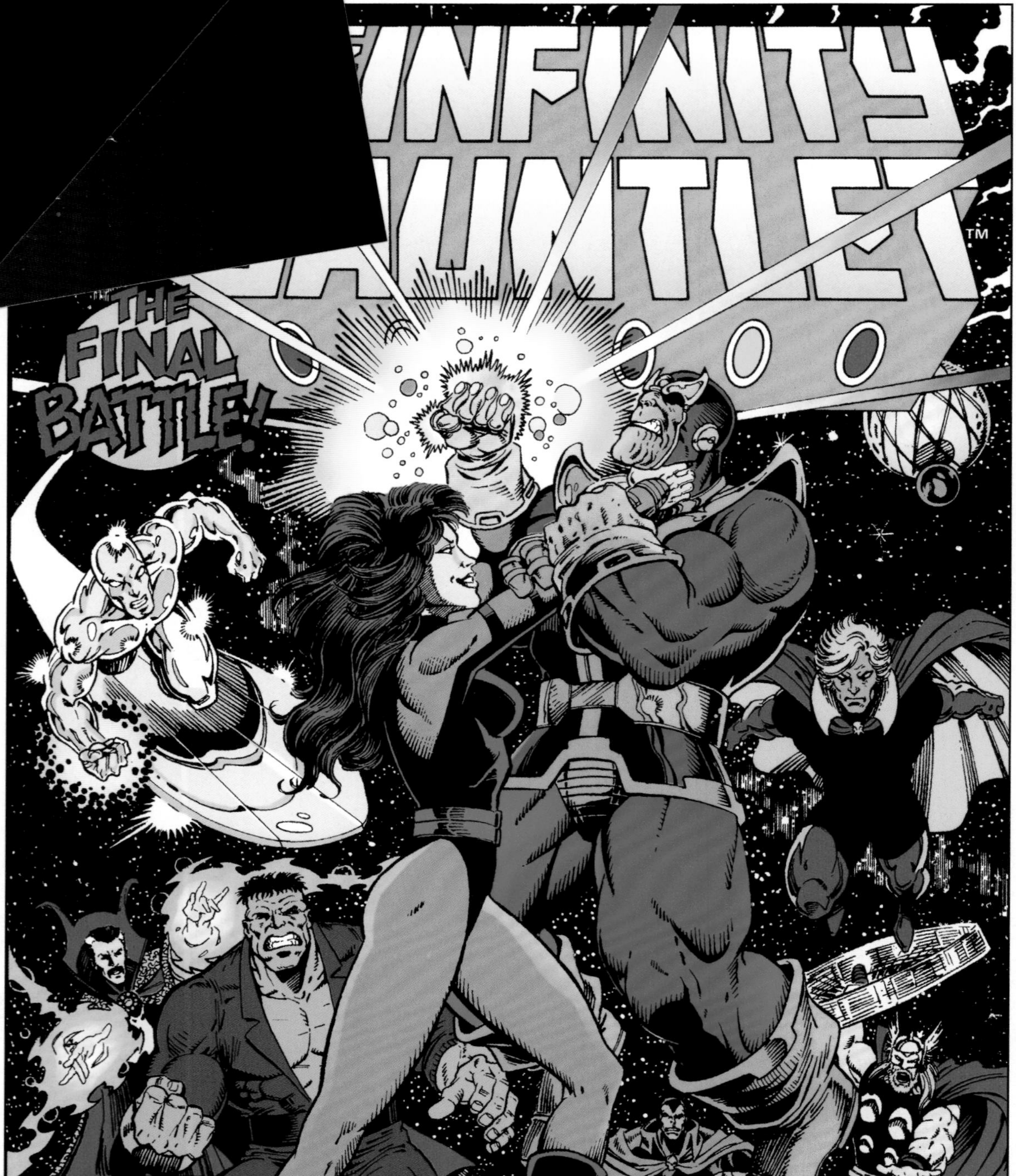
THE FINAL BATTLE!

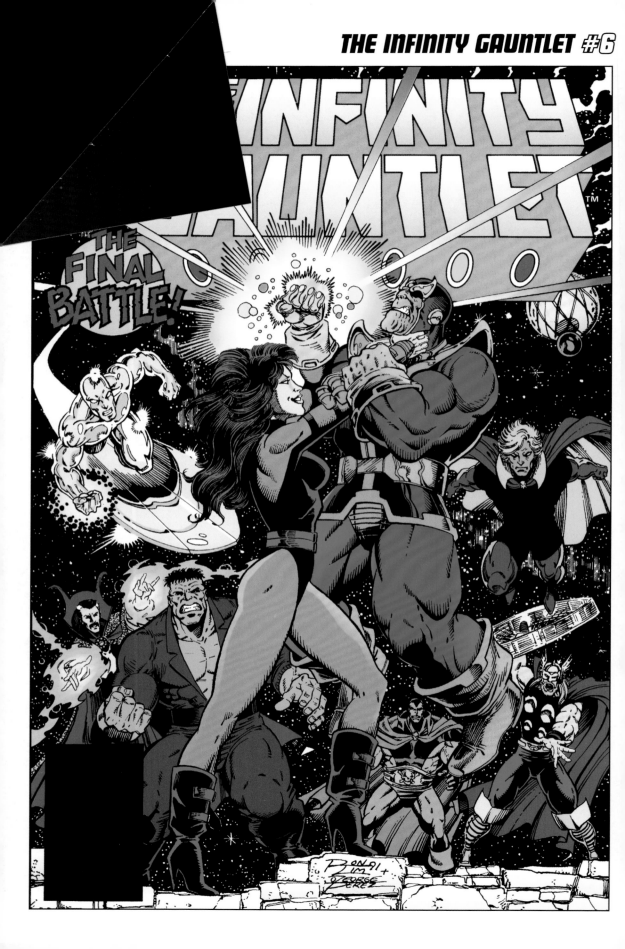

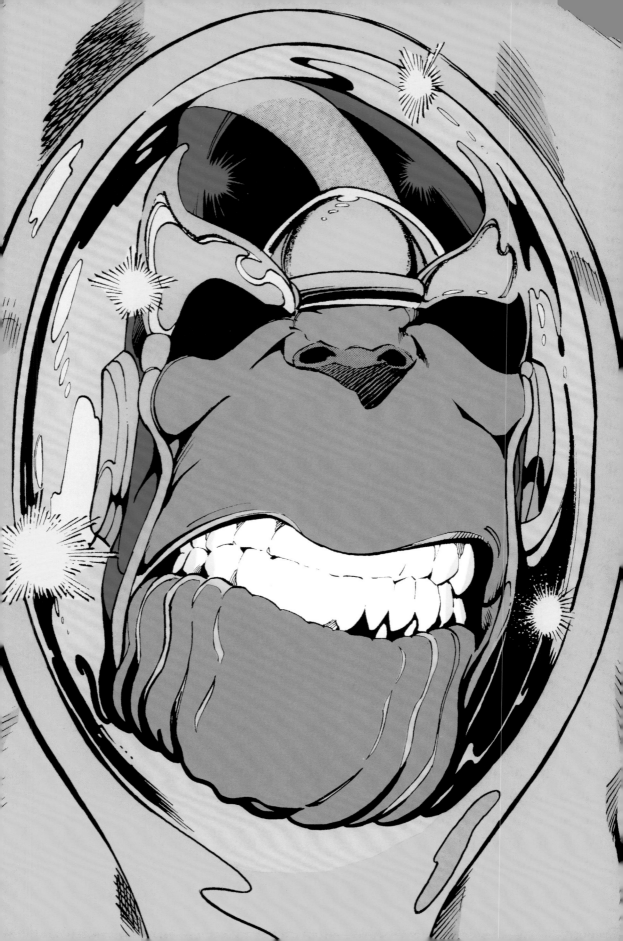

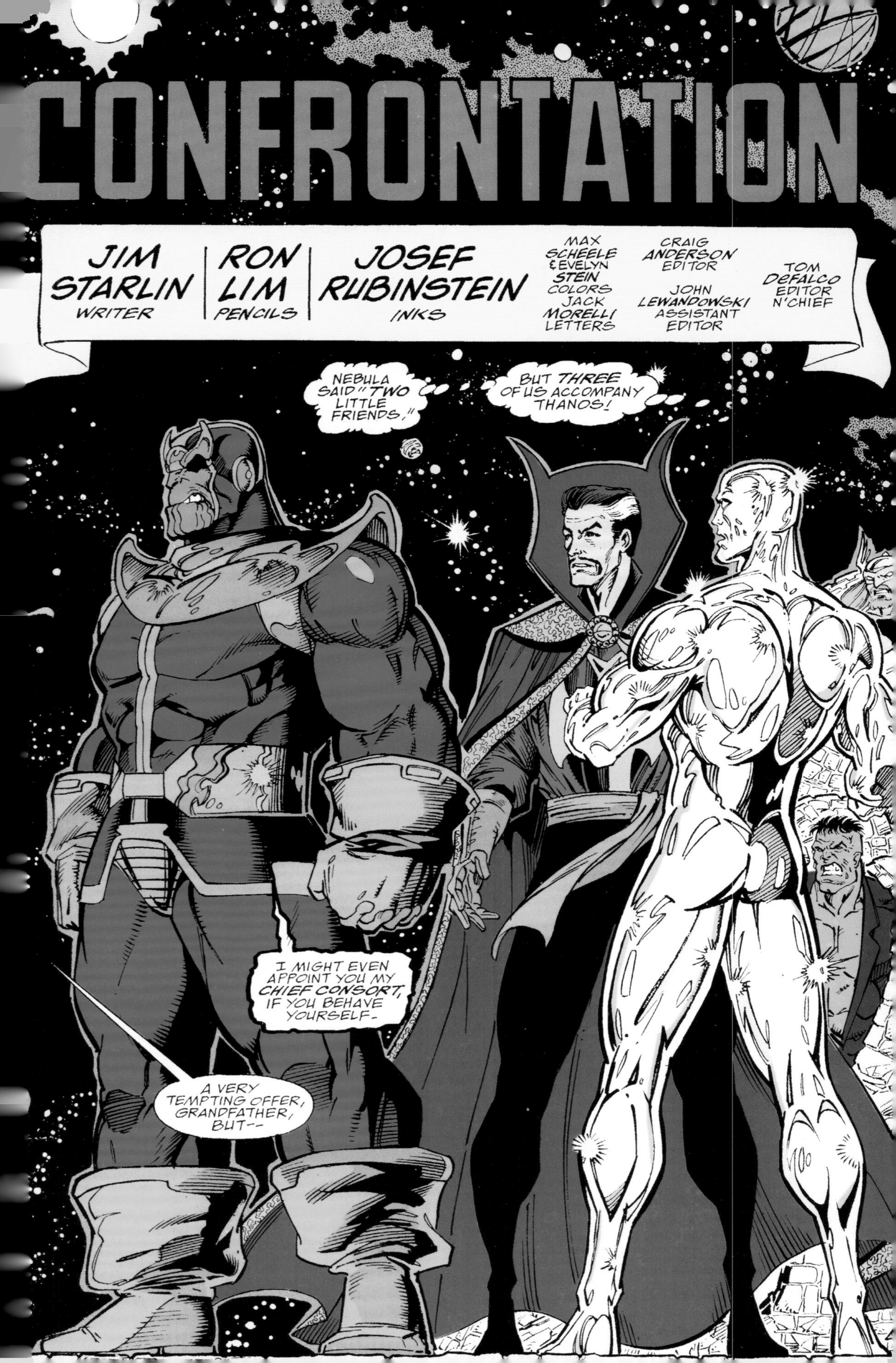

CONFRONTATION
JIM STARLIN WRITER
RON LIM PENCILS
JOSEF RUBINSTEIN INKS
MAX SCHEELE & EVELYN STEIN COLORS
JACK MORELLI LETTERS
CRAIG ANDERSON EDITOR
JOHN LEWANDOWSKI ASSISTANT EDITOR
TOM DEFALCO EDITOR N'CHIEF
NEBULA SAID "TWO LITTLE FRIENDS,"
BUT THREE OF US ACCOMPANY THANOS!
I MIGHT EVEN APPOINT YOU MY CHIEF CONSORT, IF YOU BEHAVE YOURSELF-
A VERY TEMPTING OFFER, GRANDFATHER, BUT--

THINNING THE HERD.

SHEER INSANITY.

A GRANDEUR BEYOND YOUR COMPREHENSION!

SOPHISTRY!

YOUR REIGN AS A SUPREME BEING IS A BLASPHEMY WHICH CANNOT BE ALLOWED TO STAND!

AND BY THE POWER OF THE INFINITY GEMS I SHALL SEE THAT IT DOES NOT!

WITH THE EXCEPTION THAT I RETAIN POSSESSION OF THE INFINITY GAUNTLET, LET EVERYTHING BE AS IT WAS--

--TWENTY FOUR HOURS AGO!

NO!

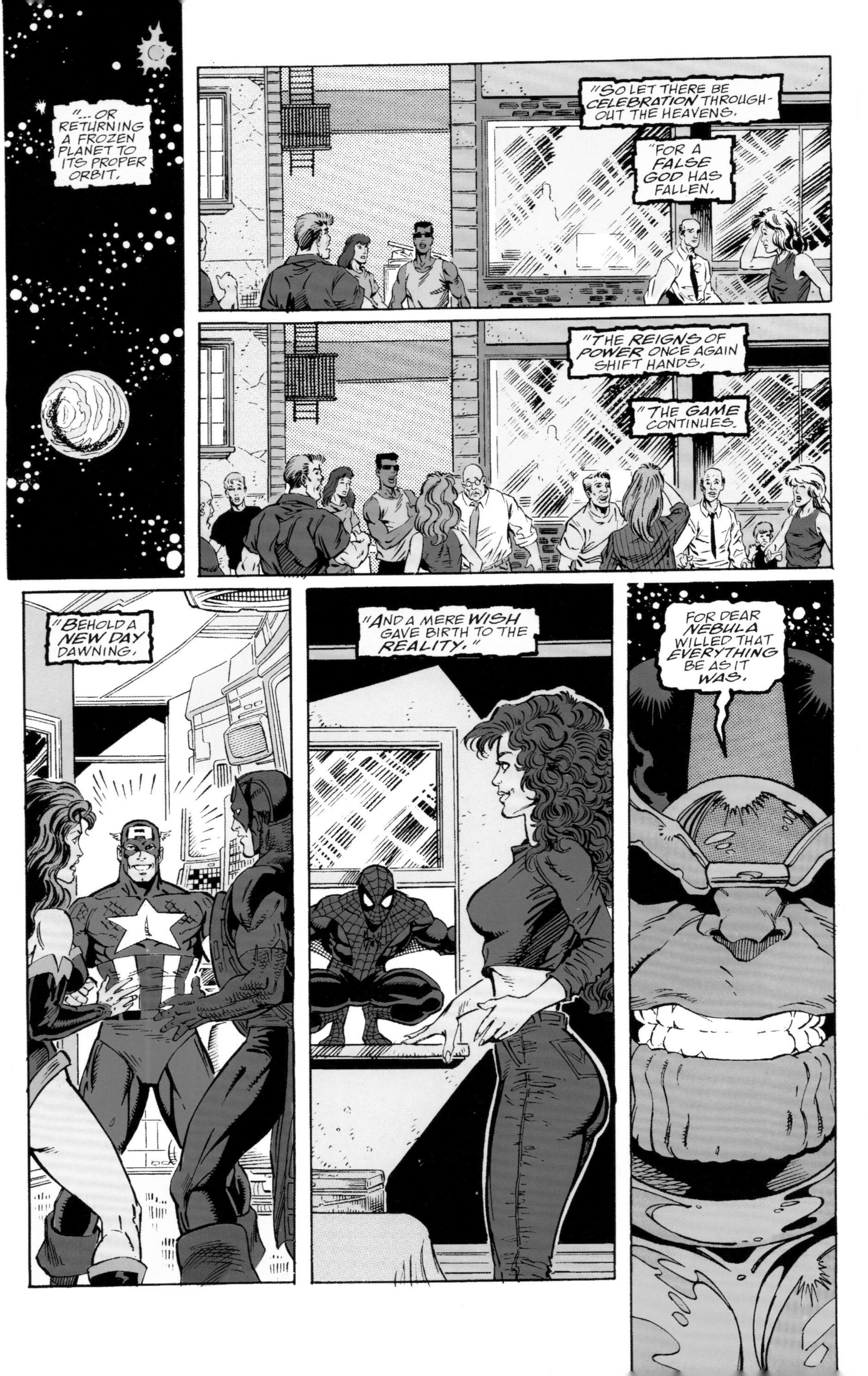
"...OR RETURNING A FROZEN PLANET TO ITS PROPER ORBIT.
"SO LET THERE BE CELEBRATION THROUGH-OUT THE HEAVENS.
"FOR A FALSE GOD HAS FALLEN.
"THE REIGNS OF POWER ONCE AGAIN SHIFT HANDS.
"THE GAME CONTINUES.
"BEHOLD A NEW DAY DAWNING.
"AND A MERE WISH GAVE BIRTH TO THE REALITY."
FOR DEAR NEBULA WILLED THAT EVERYTHING BE AS IT WAS.

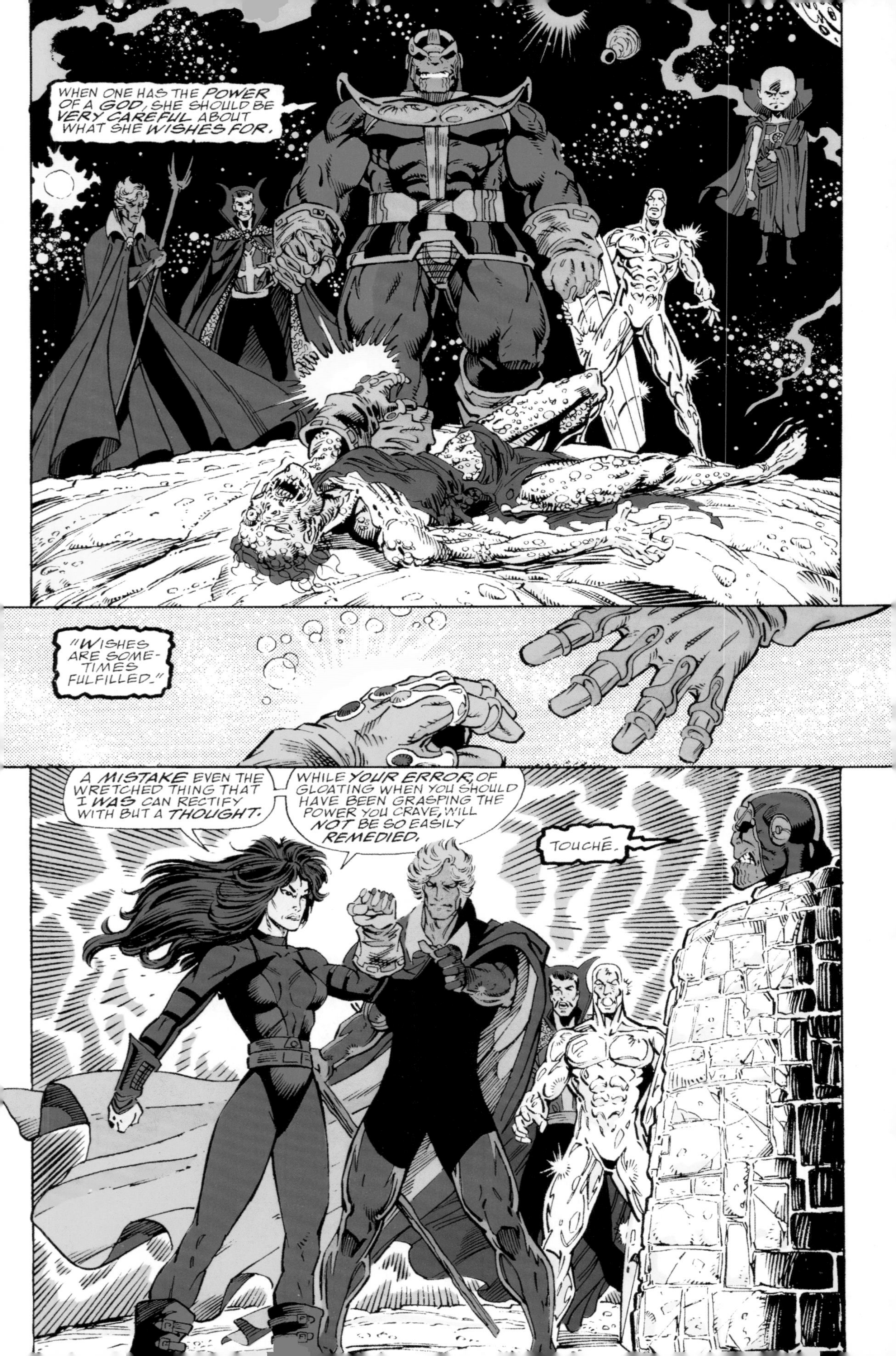
WHEN ONE HAS THE POWER OF A GOD, SHE SHOULD BE VERY CAREFUL ABOUT WHAT SHE WISHES FOR.
"WISHES ARE SOMETIMES FULFILLED..."
A MISTAKE EVEN THE WRETCHED THING THAT I WAS CAN RECTIFY WITH BUT A THOUGHT.
WHILE YOUR ERROR, OF GLOATING WHEN YOU SHOULD HAVE BEEN GRASPING THE POWER YOU CRAVE, WILL NOT BE SO EASILY REMEDIED.
TOUCHÉ.

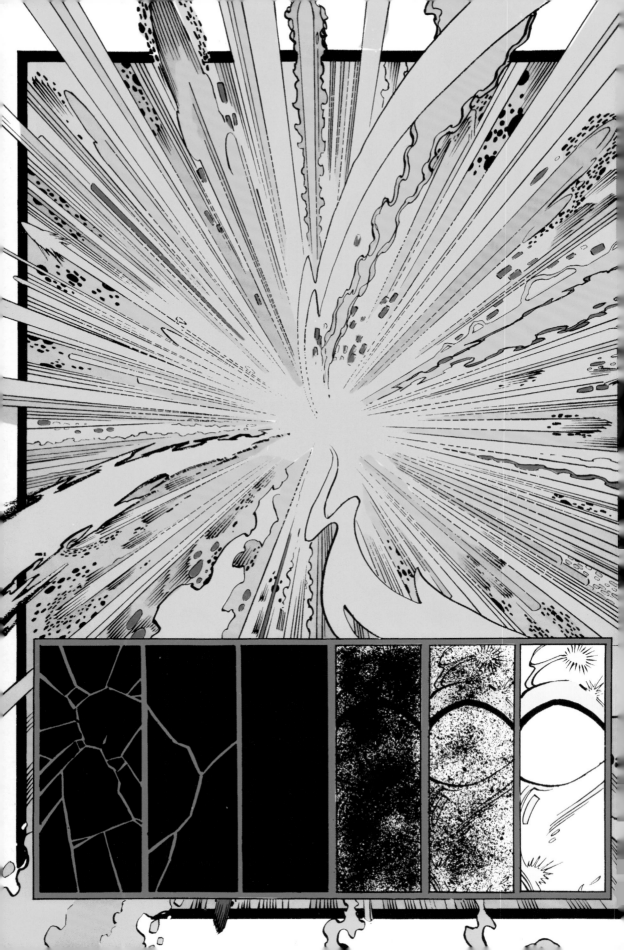

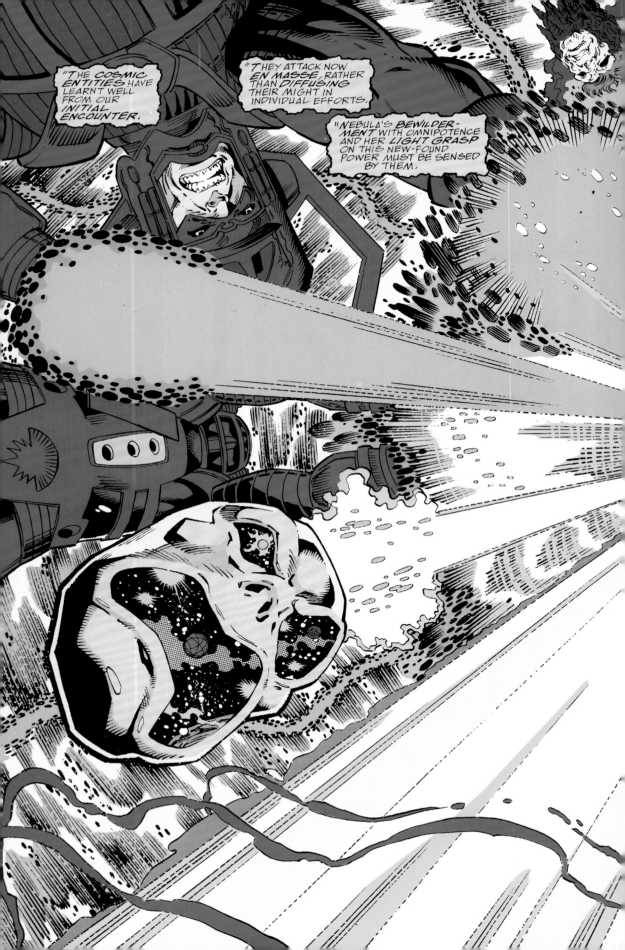

OF COURSE SUCH A TACTIC WOULD HAVE PROVEN *FUTILE* AGAINST *ME*.

THE *SCOPE* AND PARTICULARS OF MY *PLAN* ARE NOW *CLEAR* TO YOU?

YES, BUT *ILLUMINATION* AND *UNDER-STANDING* ARE NOT ONE AND THE SAME—

NOW YOU KNOW *ALL* THAT IS *ADAM WARLOCK*.

I STILL CANNOT FATHOM YOUR *ATTITUDE* TOWARD THIS ENTIRE SITUATION...

...TOWARD *ALL LIFE* IN GENERAL.

AND YOU, *NORRIN RADD*.

SO *DETACHED*.

EMOTIONAL NERVES CAUTERIZED, I SUPPOSE.

SOMEHOW, I MANAGE.

IT IS OF NO *IMPORT* AT THE MOMENT.

ONCE AGAIN, THE *UNIVERSE* NEEDS *SAVING!*

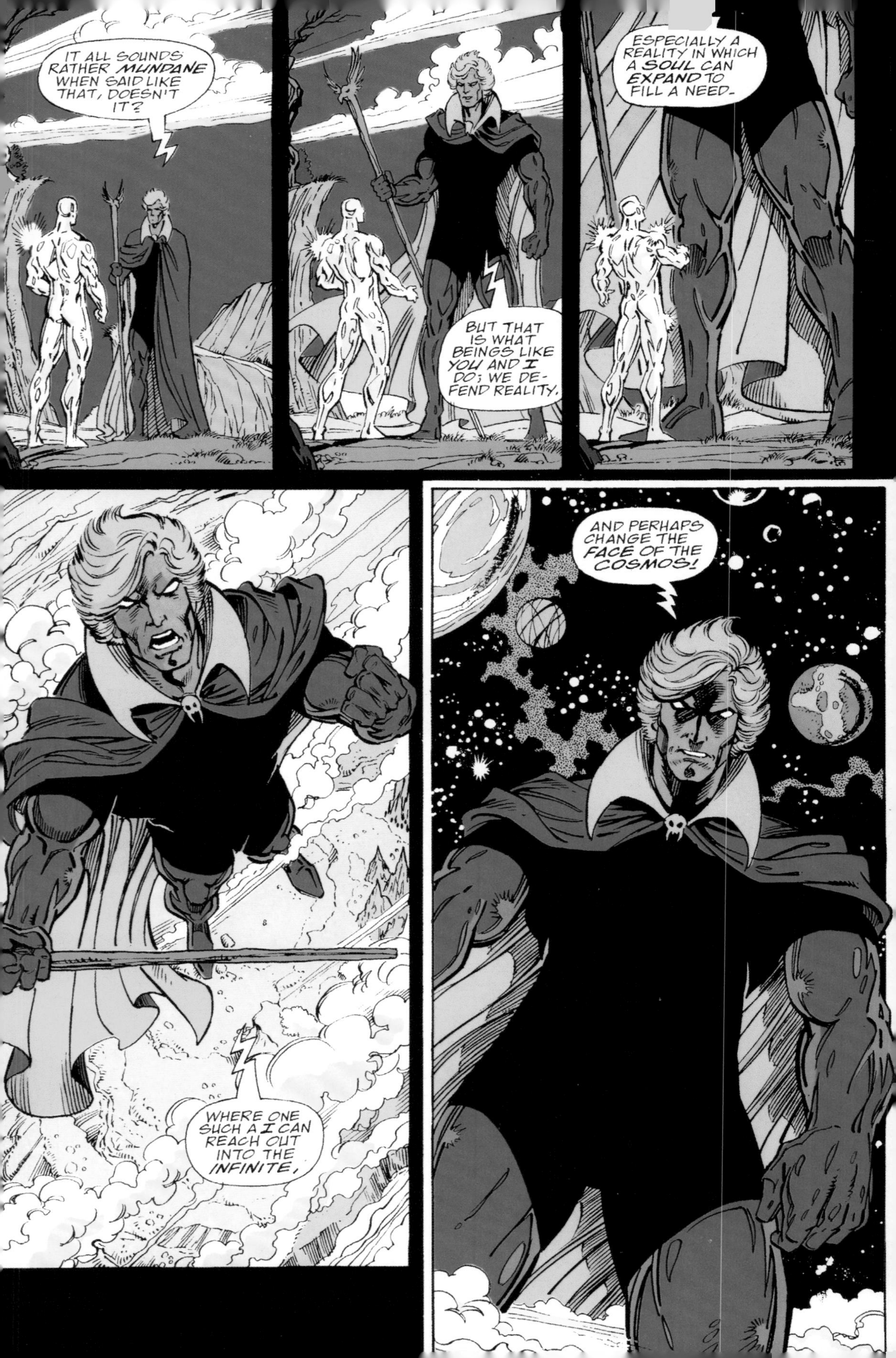
IT ALL SOUNDS RATHER MUNDANE WHEN SAID LIKE THAT, DOESN'T IT?
BUT THAT IS WHAT BEINGS LIKE YOU AND I DO; WE DEFEND REALITY.
ESPECIALLY A REALITY IN WHICH A SOUL CAN EXPAND TO FILL A NEED.
WHERE ONE SUCH AS I CAN REACH OUT INTO THE INFINITE,
AND PERHAPS CHANGE THE FACE OF THE COSMOS!

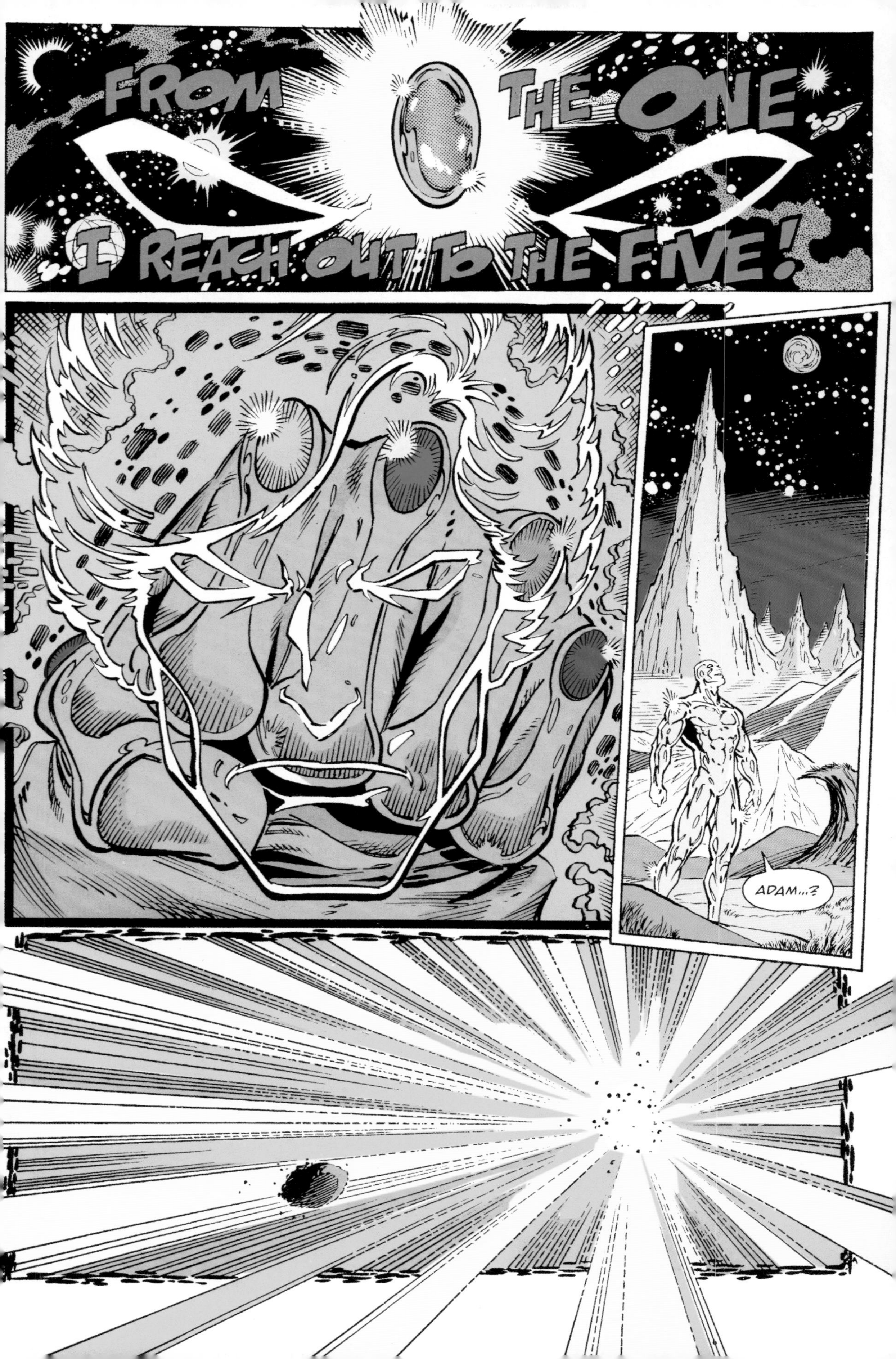
FROM THE ONE
I REACH OUT TO THE FIVE!
ADAM...?

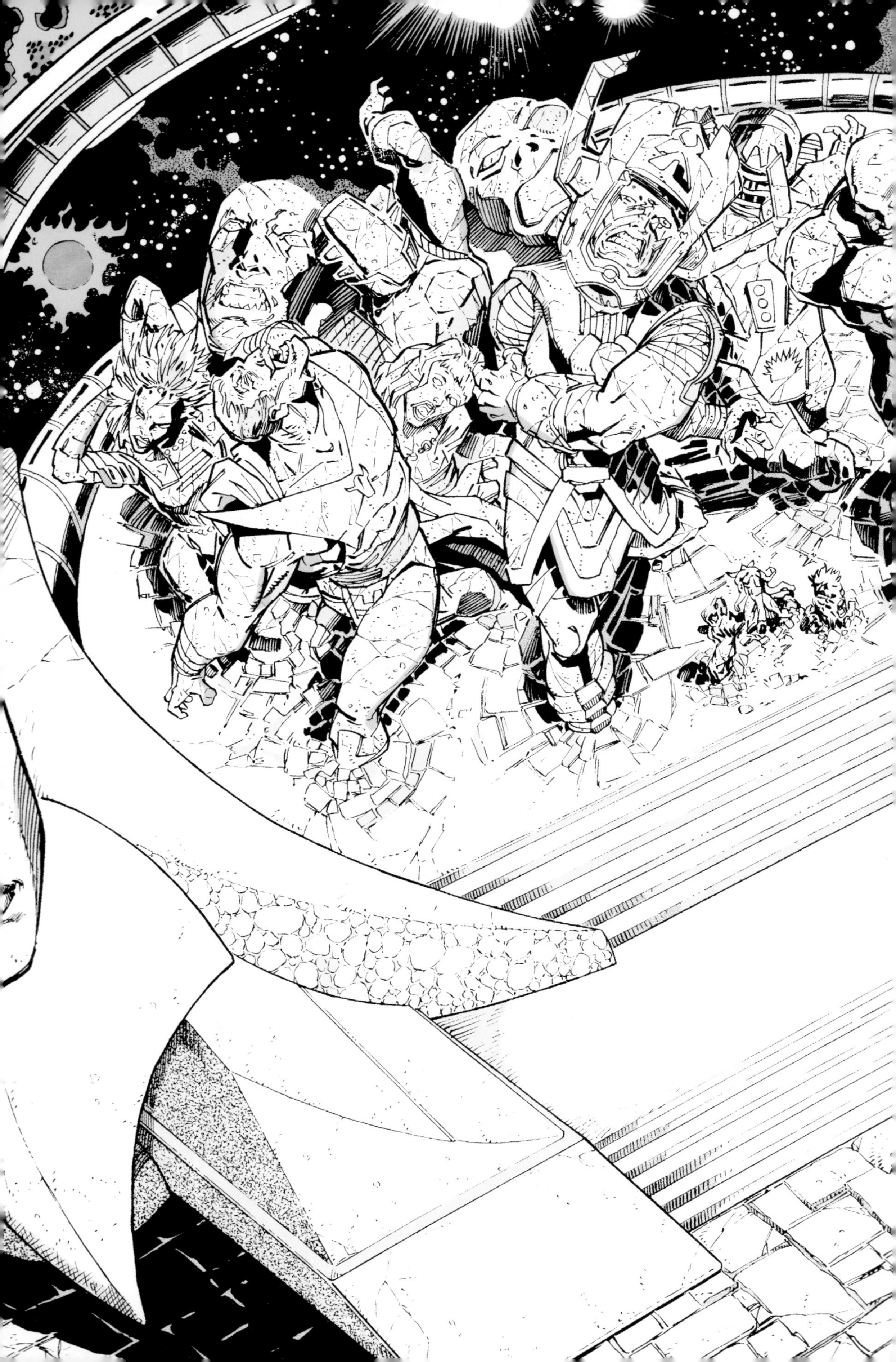

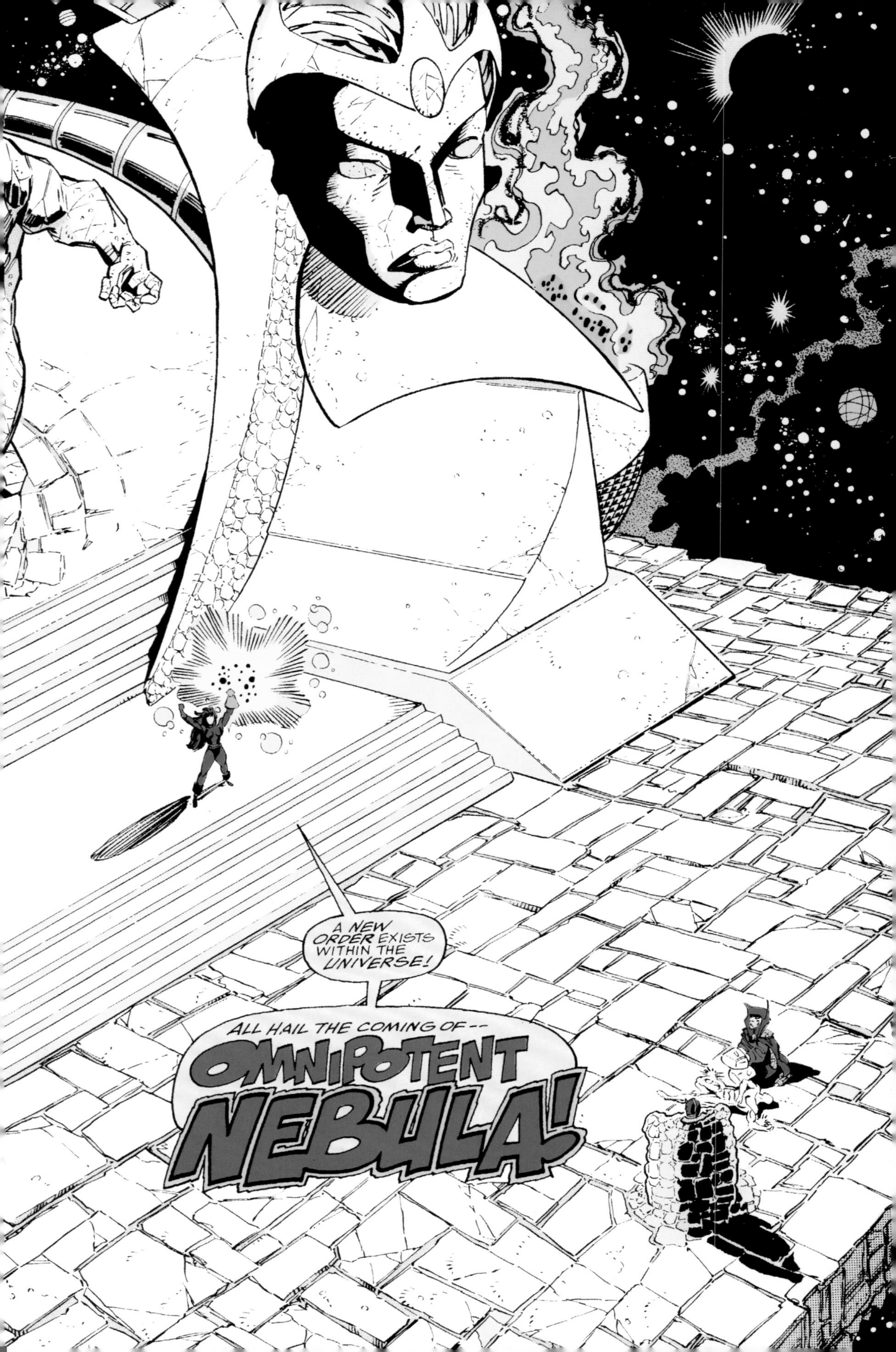
A NEW ORDER EXISTS WITHIN THE UNIVERSE!
ALL HAIL THE COMING OF--
OMNIPOTENT NEBULA!

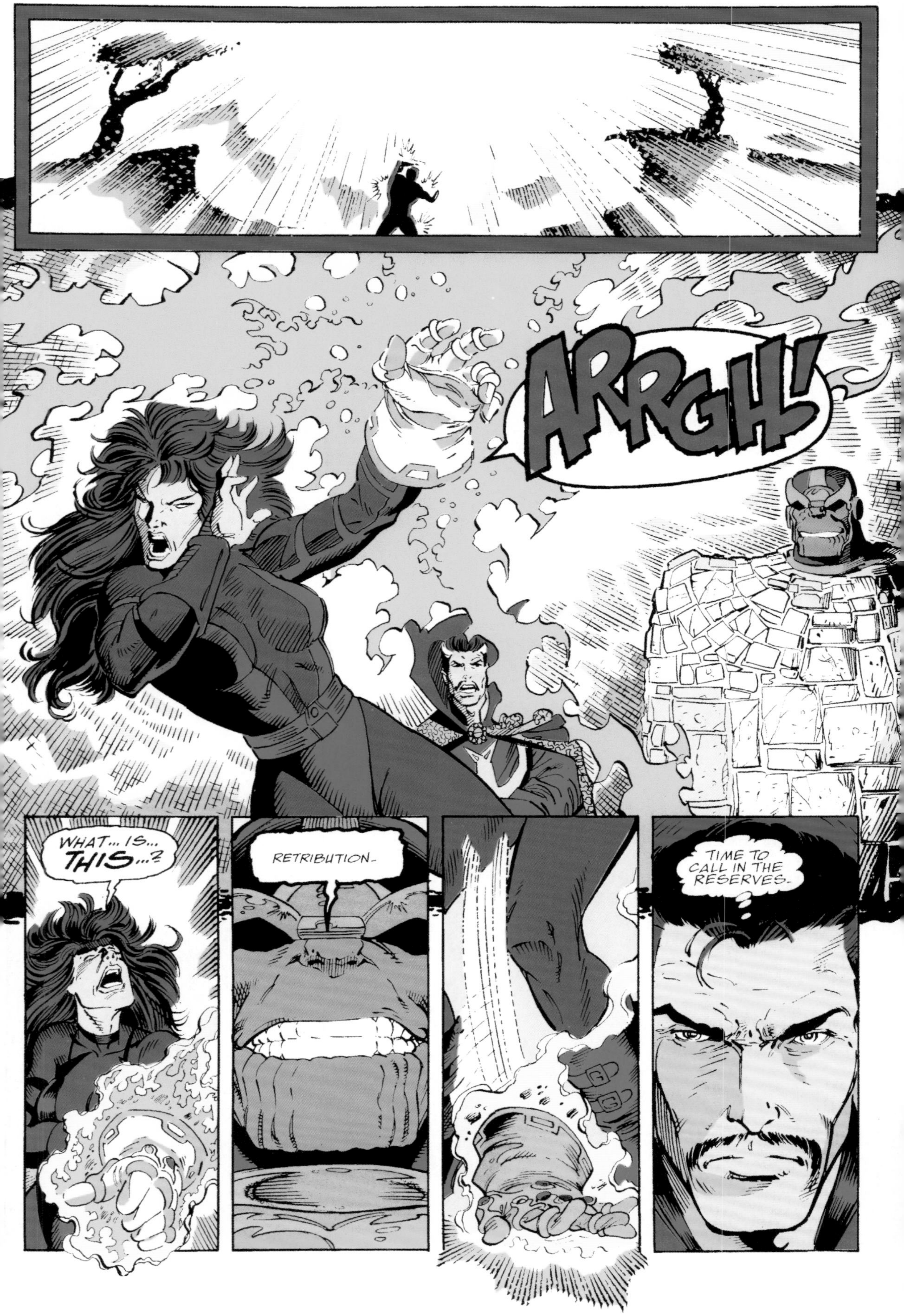
ARRGH!
WHAT... IS... THIS...?
RETRIBUTION.
TIME TO CALL IN THE RESERVES.

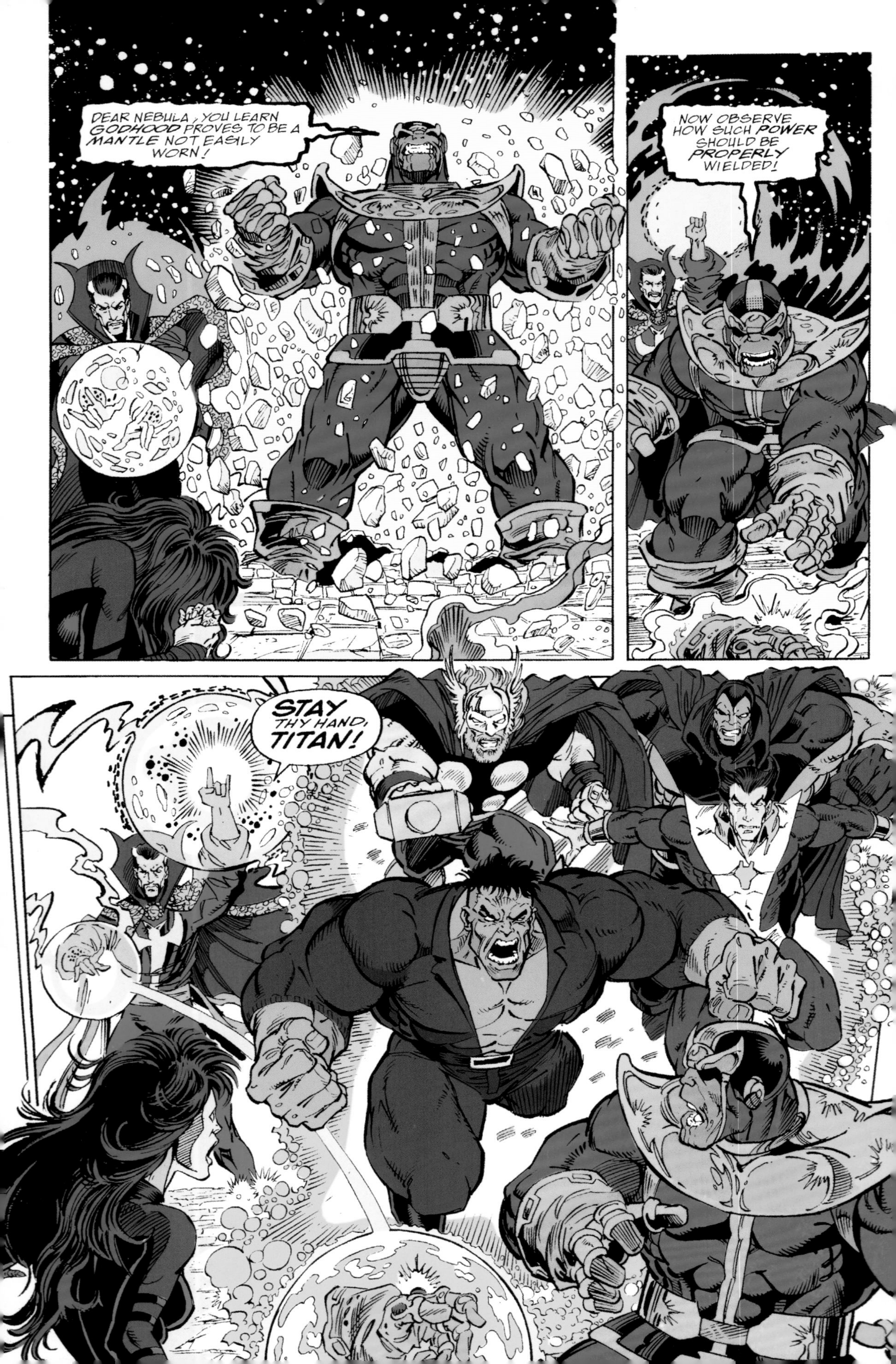
DEAR NEBULA, YOU LEARN GODHOOD PROVES TO BE A MANTLE NOT EASILY WORN!
NOW OBSERVE HOW SUCH POWER SHOULD BE PROPERLY WIELDED!
STAY THY HAND, TITAN!

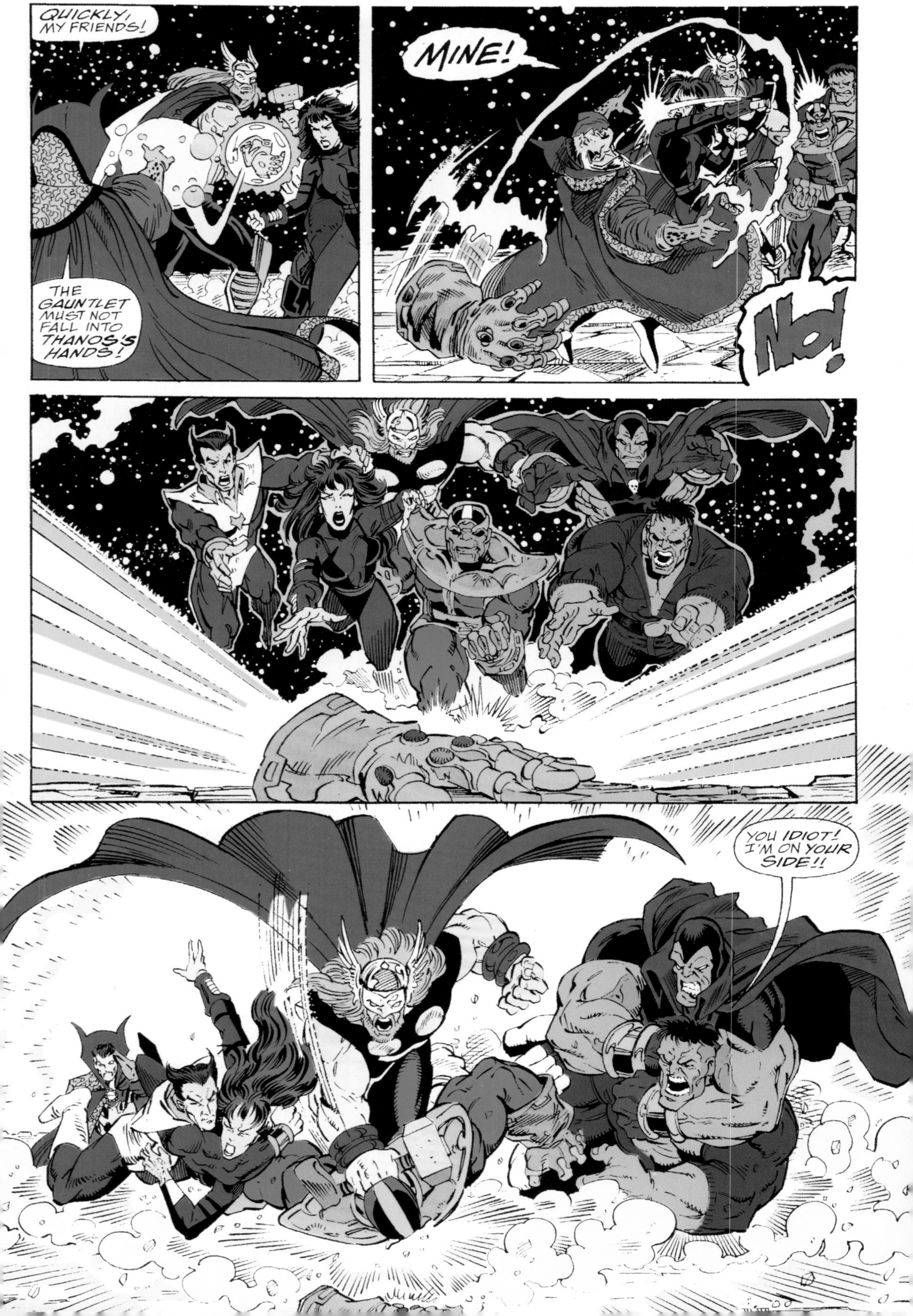
QUICKLY, MY FRIENDS!
THE GAUNTLET MUST NOT FALL INTO THANOS'S HANDS!
MINE!
NO!
YOU IDIOT! I'M ON YOUR SIDE!!

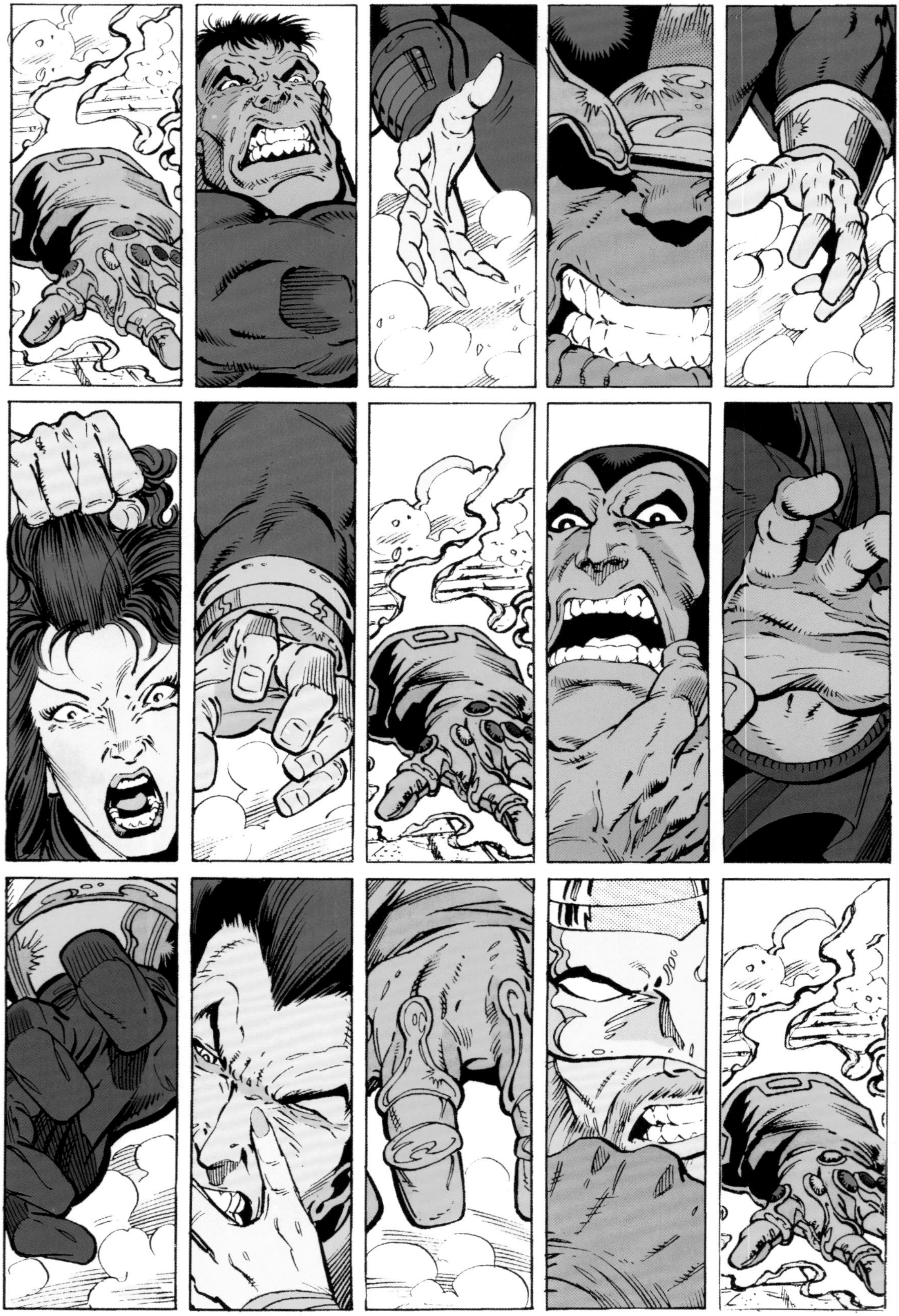

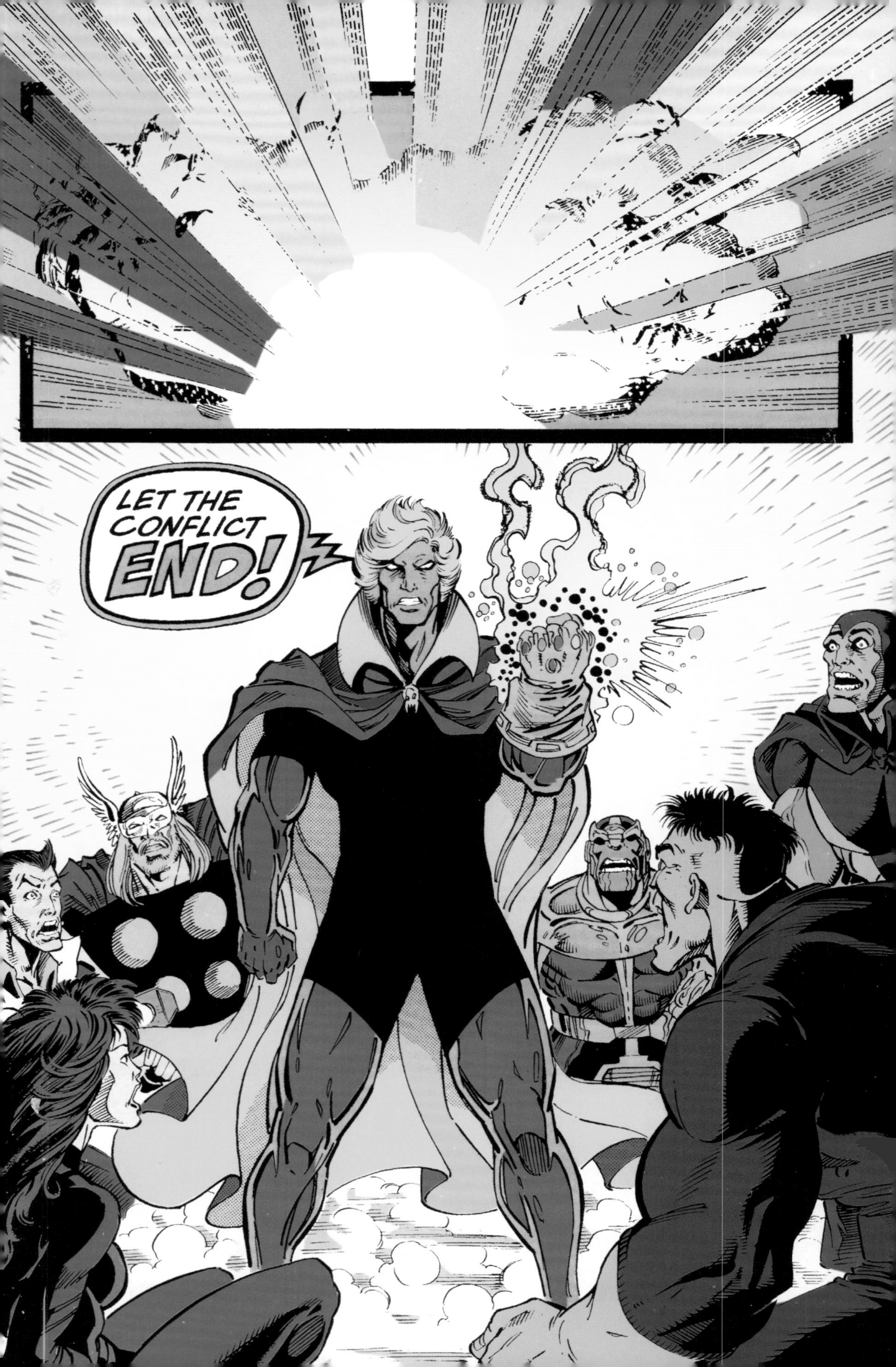
LET THE CONFLICT END!

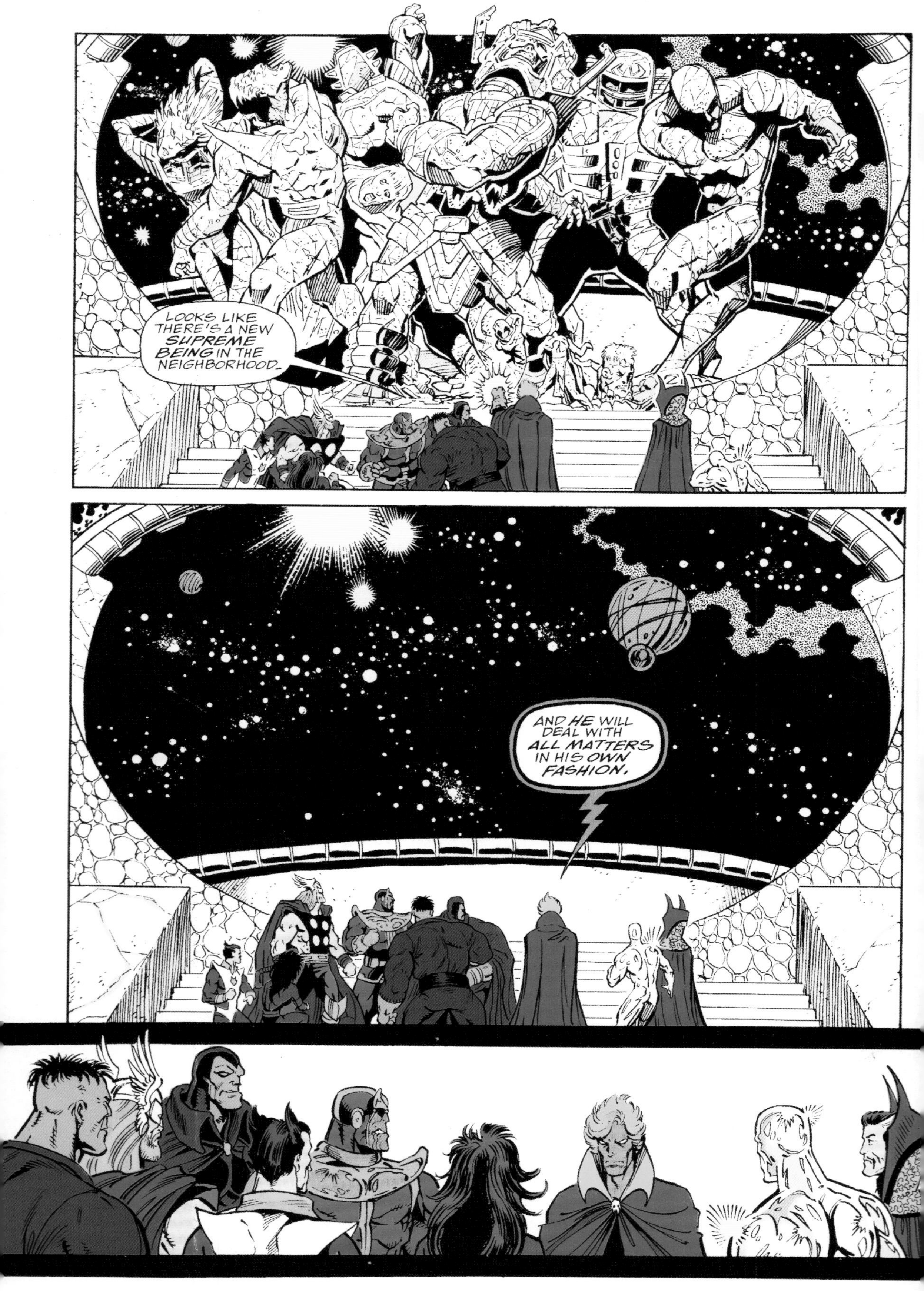
LOOKS LIKE THERE'S A NEW SUPREME BEING IN THE NEIGHBORHOOD--
AND HE WILL DEAL WITH ALL MATTERS IN HIS OWN FASHION.

YET **WE** REMAIN- WHY?

BECAUSE EACH OF YOU HAVE GAZED INTO THE DEPTHS OF MY HEART.

BEFORE YOU BECAME POWER INCARNATE,

IT MAKES NO DIFFER-ENCE. MY SOUL IS KNOWN TO YOU-

GO FORTH AND TELL THE MASSES THAT ADAM WARLOCK IS A GOD WHO CAN BE TRUST-ED.

I'M NOT SO SURE WE CAN TRUTH-FULLY DO THAT-

THAT POWER CORRUPTS IS A TRUISM THAT CANNOT BE IGNORED!

YOU FEAR A COSMIC DESPOT?

SURELY YOU MUST REALIZE THAT EVEN BEFORE THANOS YOU LIVED UNDER SUCH TYRANNY.

BUT IT WAS A BENIGN REIGN, RANDOM AND UNFOCUS-ED.

AND NOW THAT IT IS CALCULATING YOU FIND THIS UNSETTLING?

AFRAID REPLACING YOUR USUAL CHAOS WITH ORDER MIGHT PROVE UNPALATABLE?

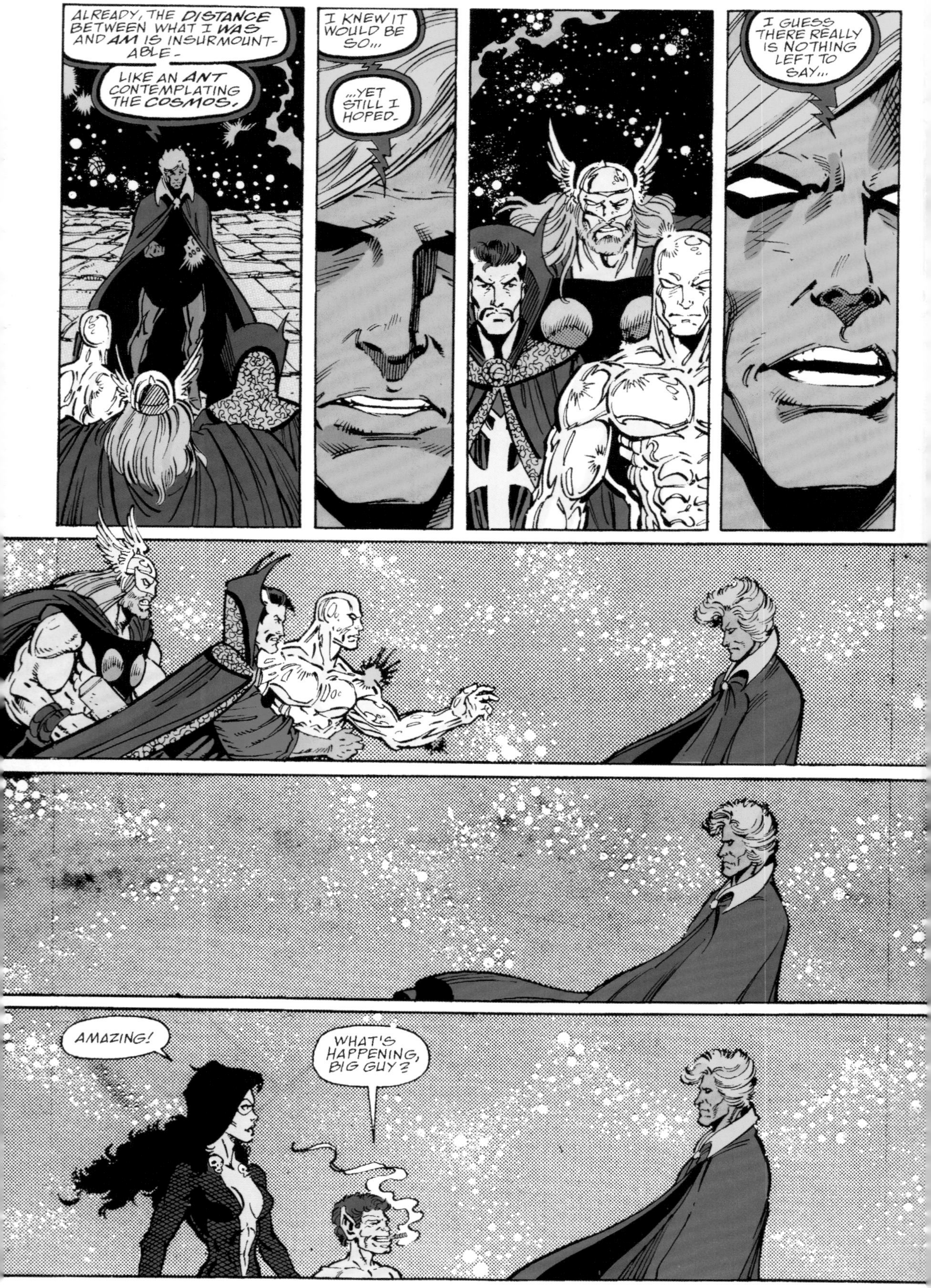
ALREADY, THE DISTANCE BETWEEN WHAT I WAS AND AM IS INSURMOUNT-ABLE-
LIKE AN ANT CONTEMPLATING THE COSMOS.
I KNEW IT WOULD BE SO...
...YET STILL I HOPED.
I GUESS THERE REALLY IS NOTHING LEFT TO SAY...
AMAZING!
WHAT'S HAPPENING, BIG GUY?

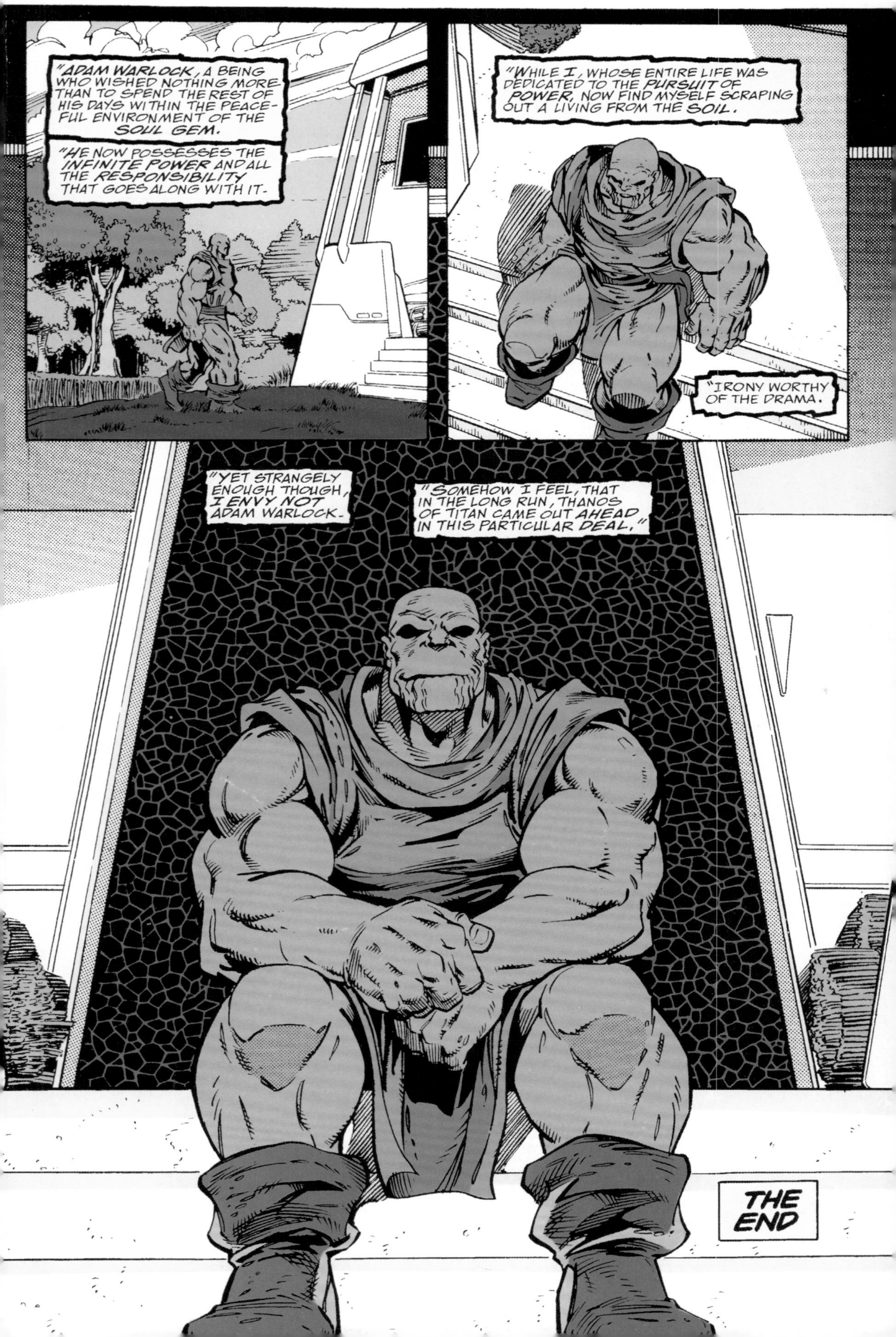
"ADAM WARLOCK, A BEING WHO WISHED NOTHING MORE THAN TO SPEND THE REST OF HIS DAYS WITHIN THE PEACE-FUL ENVIRONMENT OF THE SOUL GEM.
"HE NOW POSSESSES THE INFINITE POWER AND ALL THE RESPONSIBILITY THAT GOES ALONG WITH IT.
"WHILE I, WHOSE ENTIRE LIFE WAS DEDICATED TO THE PURSUIT OF POWER, NOW FIND MYSELF SCRAPING OUT A LIVING FROM THE SOIL.
"IRONY WORTHY OF THE DRAMA.
"YET STRANGELY ENOUGH THOUGH, I ENVY NOT ADAM WARLOCK.
"SOMEHOW I FEEL, THAT IN THE LONG RUN, THANOS OF TITAN CAME OUT AHEAD IN THIS PARTICULAR DEAL."
THE END

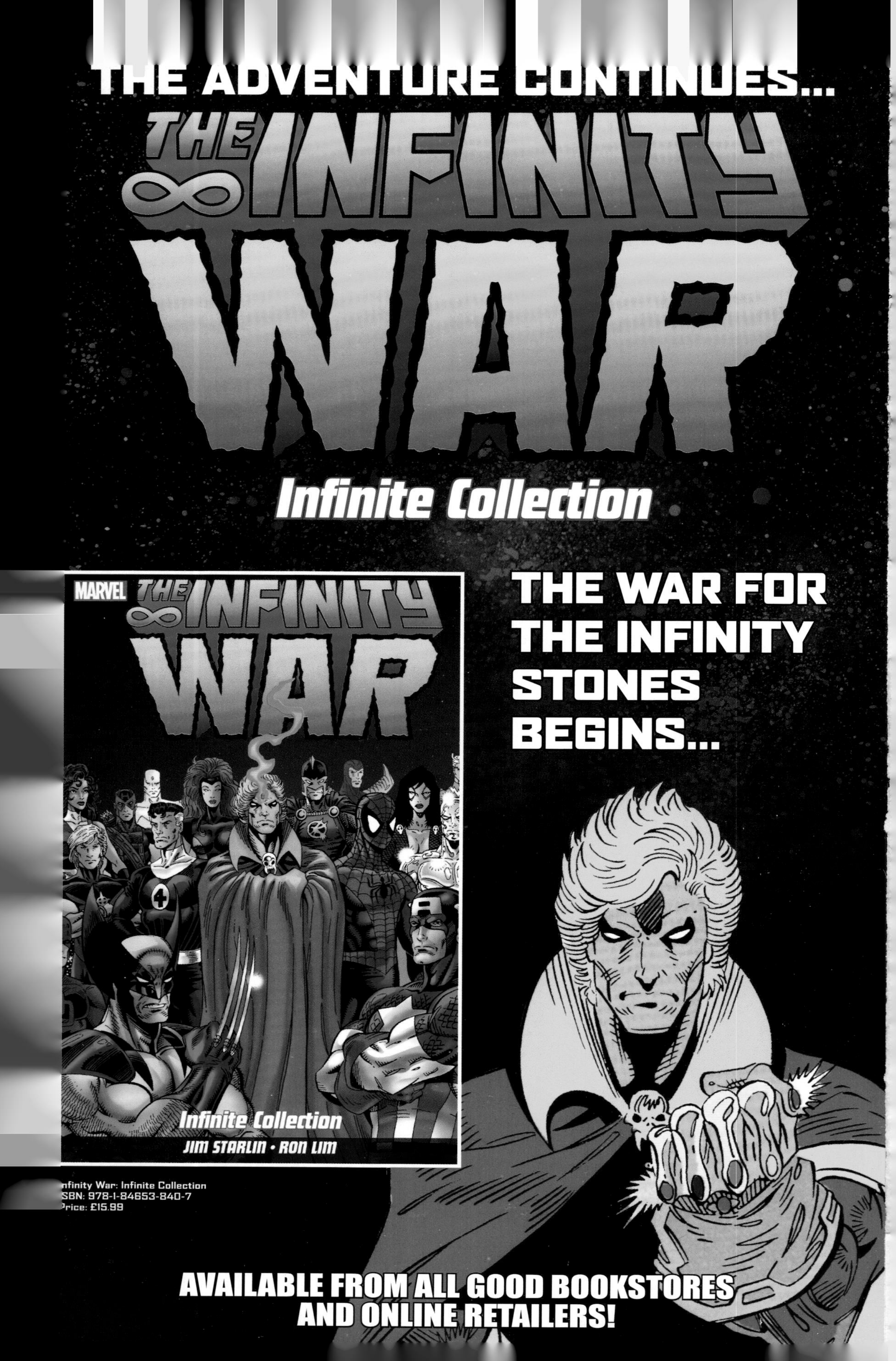
THE ADVENTURE CONTINUES...
THE INFINITY WAR
Infinite Collection
MARVEL
THE INFINITY WAR
Infinite Collection
JIM STARLIN • RON LIM
nfinity War: Infinite Collection
SBN: 978-1-84653-840-7
rice: £15.99
THE WAR FOR THE INFINITY STONES BEGINS...
AVAILABLE FROM ALL GOOD BOOKSTORES AND ONLINE RETAILERS!